VIOLENCE/NON-VIOLENCE

Some Hindu Perspectives

VIOLENCE/NON-VIOLENCE

Some Hindu Perspectives

Edited by

DENIS VIDAL, GILLES TARABOUT
ERIC MEYER

MANOHAR

CENTRE DE SCIENCES HUMAINES
2026

First published in French, 1994, Paris, EHESS

English translation by Chandrasekhar and Nissim Marshall (except for the Introduction translated by Christopher J. Fuller, and Chapter 12, already in English in the original).
The translation has been funded by the French Embassy in India and by the Institute for Research in Development (IRD), Paris

First published in English 2003
Reprinted 2021, 2022, 2023, 2026

ISBN 978-81-7304-471-7

Published by
Ajay Kumar Jain for
Manohar Publishers & Distributors
4753/23 Ansari Road, Daryaganj
New Delhi 110 002

Printed at
Replika Press Pvt. Ltd

Contents

Contributors

All contributors other than R.S. Bajwa and Veena Das are members of the Centre for Indian and South Asian Studies (CEIAS), Paris. This Centre is the only French research institute in social sciences dealing with the main countries of the Indian subcontinent (India, Bangladesh, Pakistan, Sri Lanka, Nepal). It is attached to the School for Higher Studies in Social Sciences (EHESS), and associated with the National Centre for Scientific Research (CNRS).

The academic background of its scholars covers a wide range of specialities including social anthropology, demography, geography, economic, social and intellectual history, ancient and modern languages and literature, linguistics, philosophy and history of science, political science, religion, sociology. The Centre has built up a library with the largest holdings in France of books and periodicals on modern South Asia, and a union catalogue of publications on the subject available in the main French libraries. When the Centre was created in the mid-1950's by Louis Dumont, its aim was to renovate the study of India by bringing together the methods and findings of the social sciences with those of classical indology. L. Dumont, L. Bernot, J.L. Chambard (social anthropology), D. Thorner (economic history), R. Lingat (law), M. Biardeau (religion) were among its founding members. Under the direction of Madeleine Biardeau and her successors, research has continued on an interdisciplinary basis, both individually and jointly in seminars and workshops where specialists with different intellectual approaches exchange their views on common themes.

Since 1975, the Centre has published under the title of Purusartha a series of collective volumes presenting the findings of French and foreign scholars. This series reflects the main research trends and scientific issues debated in the Centre.

R.S. BAJWA has collaborated with Professor Veena Das on a joint research project about Punjab at the Centre for the Study of Developing Societies (CSDS).

MADELEINE BIARDEAU, Philosopher, Sanskritist, is Hon. Professor at the Ecole Pratique des Hautes Etudes, Paris (Religious Sciences), and has published extensively on Puranas, *Ramayana* and *Mahabharata*.

VÉRONIQUE BOUILLIER, Anthropologist, Senior fellow (CNRS); her main studies concern the Saiva ascetic castes in Nepal (Jangam, Dasnami Sannyasi, Kulse-Kapali, Kanphata Yogi) and, more recently, in Rajasthan.

JEAN-LUC CHAMBARD, Ethnologist, Hon. Professor at the National Institute of Oriental Languages and Civilizations, has made prolonged field study of a village in Madhya Pradesh. Since 1977, his research bears on women's songs, and on the yearly cycle of Hindu festivals.

CATHERINE CLÉMENTIN-OJHA, Historian of religions, Director of Studies, EHESS (Paris), has worked on Hindu female ascetics, on the relationship between Vishnuite sects and Jaipur state in the nineteenth century, and more generally on the history and organization of monastic orders in north India.

VEENA DAS, Anthropologist, Professor of Sociology, University of Delhi, is currently Professor in the Department of Anthropology at Johns Hopkins University. She has worked intensively on questions of violence, social suffering, and subjectivity, and is presently studying disease and heatlh-seeking behaviour among the urban poor in Delhi.

MARIE FOURCADE, Research Assistant at the EHESS, is editorial secretary of the 'Purusartha' series published by the Centre for Indian and South Asian Studies, Paris. She has academic training in history and anthropology. She has studied the 19th British concept of 'Criminal castes and tribes' in India, and French Orientalism through the writings of Theophile and Judith Gautier.

GÉRARD HEUZE, Sociologist, Research fellow (CNRS), has studied contemporary Indian labour and the relationship betwen unemployment and Hindu religious fundamentalism, in north Bihar, Chhotanagpur, Chhattisgarh, Mumbai.

CHRISTOPHE JAFFRELOT, Research fellow (CNRS), Director of the Centre for the Study in International Relationships. His main research has been on nineteenth century socio-religious reform movements and the twentieth century Hindu nationalist movement. He has now turned to the evolution of democracy in India.

CHARLES MALAMOUD, Linguist, Sanskritist, is Hon. Professor at the Ecole Pratique des Hautes Etudes, Paris (Religious Sciences), and has studied the structures of civilization and the systems of thought revealed in Sanskrit texts and more specifically in the Vedas.

ÉRIC MEYER, Historian, Professor at the National Institute of Oriental Languages and Civilizations, has specialized on the interaction between colonial capitalism and rural society in Sri Lanka, and on the origins of the present political crisis in this country.

BORIS OGUIBÉNINE, Sanskritist, Professor at Strasbourg University, studies Vedic religion in a descriptive as well as historical perspective, Vedic philology and linguistics, the links between Vedic religion and the ancient Indo-European religions.

GILLES TARABOUT, Anthropologist, Senior fellow (CNRS), has studied Kerala's society and popular religious practices.

DENIS VIDAL, Anthropologist, Research fellow (Institute for Research in Development), has published studies on Himachal Pradesh, Rajasthan and Delhi. He is currently working and teaching about the visual anthropology of South Asia

On the Concepts of Violence and Non-Violence in Hinduism and Indian Society

DENIS VIDAL, GILLES TARABOUT AND ÉRIC MEYER

How do we understand those Indian ascetics who have developed an extremely elaborate martial tradition and yet have always taken strict vows of non-violence, especially when, for some ascetics today, that tradition has been put at the service of the most extreme forms of Hindu militancy? And how is it that tough union leaders can, with conviction, share the same ideas as Gandhi, or that Brahmins scarcely hesitate before using the stick, even though they loudly and insistently advertise their faith in non-violence? These ways of acting may in fact allow to reconsider the understanding of the concepts of violence and non-violence in Hinduism, for there are many aspects of Indian society and culture which effectively contradict ideas, often taken for granted since Gandhi, about the role of violence in it.

In fact, Gandhi did not always succeed in persuading his compatriots to practise non-violence, as the often dramatic history of the Indian nationalist movement shows. But he was able to give the impression, most especially in the West, that non-violence really is, above all else, the cardinal value of Indian civilization, of its culture and society. This claim can be put forward enthusiastically or, as is more common, sceptically, but in either case, in the West, the concept of non-violence is generally understood not only as an ideal, but also as an expression of idealism or as the antithesis of realism. Thus non-violence is considered to be a frame of mind which may be desirable in the abstract, but which might retain no more than a distant relationship with reality. Such a viewpoint also fits perfectly with the stereotypes, widely expounded about India and Hinduism, which have long stressed the 'idealist' character of the civilization and its people. The result of such stereotypes is that news about violence in India are often received with surprise.

It should be underlined that Gandhi's own point of view was much more nuanced. As Bhikhu Parekh observes: 'Gandhi contended that, contrary to the general impression, there was a deep streak of violence in Indian culture.' Gandhi chided his friend C.F. Andrews for insisting that non-violence was the central theme of the major Indian texts: 'I see no sign of it in the *Mahabharata* and the *Ramayana*, not even in my favourite Tulsidas'.[1] In reality, how the concepts of 'violence' and 'non-violence' are defined cannot be understood if they are dissociated from each other. Rather, as the articles in this volume show, violence very frequently legitimates itself in the name of non-violence as well.

Problems of Method

The problem of violence can be approached in many different ways. For example, the forms that violence takes may be studied in the hope of understanding its causes and implications better, in order to find a cure for it and to denounce its use. Another approach is to ask, in a more general way, about the role played by violence in society, about the place it comes to have in the establishment, perpetuation, transgression or subversion of social ties. As all research devoted to the anthropology of violence shows, however, such approaches become far more complicated once one tries to analyse how violence is conceived in different contexts, taking into account the fact that its definition varies between different cultures but is also crucially at stake in the very heart of each society.

The scope of the present volume is more restricted. We do not claim to have revealed or denounced the forms of violence existing in Indian society,[3] nor to contribute, except very indirectly, to any general anthropology of violence. Our perspective was different. What we rather sought is a better understanding of the terms in which the question of violence has been *discussed* within Indian culture, and more specifically in Hinduism. Given such a limited aim, we could evade various pitfalls inherent in all research devoted to violence, but we have come across others instead, which are more directly connected with the present state of research on Hinduism and Indian society.

The anthropological and historical studies in India have rapidly developed, since the 1950s, by questioning many of their own assumptions. The anthropologists, in particular, began to attack the tendency to see the Indian society as no more than a mixture of heterogeneous cultures and communities, a tendency that gave insufficient attention to the social and cultural factors which would allow India's unity and homogeneity to be explained. Then some studies which stressed the homogenity of Indian culture came under renewed criticism. These were the works of Dumont, Pocock, Marriott and others who made use of the body of knowledge provided by the orientalist tradition. They were criticized for attending too exclusively to the realities which seemed to testify to the most specific and characteristic values of Hinduism, at the risk of perpetuating a particular conception of Indian civilization which appeared to other authors as essentialist, monolithic and ahistorical. In particular, it has now been shown that some institutions and values supposedly belonging to the very foundations of India's cultural and social traditions were far more profoundly redefined and altered by the colonial presence and ideology than had previously been supposed.

During the last two decades, in history first of all but also in anthropology a marked inclination to scrutinize the premises on which the majority of analyses of Indian society were based has therefore emerged. Alongside such a critical re-evaluation, far more attention has also been paid to categories of population, forms of discourse, modes of behaviour or systems of values, that were previously completely marginalized or hardly studied at all; in particular, we have in mind the works of the Subaltern Studies school.

As a result, research devoted to Indian society and culture has reached a decisive stage in its development. The accumulated knowledge is now greater and more diverse than it used to be, and today there is a real dialogue among different disciplines. Yet, new questions have also emerged. For instance, nobody can seriously doubt the central importance of the set of traditions and beliefs which are regarded as characteristic of Hinduism if one wants to understand Indian society and its values properly. However, equally if not more so, nobody would claim to establish with complete confidence the precise influence of those traditions on the society as a whole, nor to trace the history of the traditions and their transmission over the '*longue durée*'.

Furthermore, we could also be at risk of returning to a conception of history and society that is, once again too fragmented, a conception actually closer than might be thought to the colonial ideology, in which any unity or coherence in the Indian society and culture was flatly denied. It is one thing to show, as Romila Thapar rightly does, that the very notion of Hinduism is indissolubly linked to the distinctive ideology of the colonial period, however, it is quite another to deny, in the same breath, that there was any content to that label by reducing every belief to what is now conveniently called 'invented tradition'. Similarly, attention should be paid to all social and cultural forms that do not necessarily correspond to the dominant culture at any given period in the society's history, and yet it is just as crucial that the importance of the dominant ideology is not lost sight of because it is indeed the dominant one.

If the most original research in recent years has been one which allows to 'deconstruct' a large number of the concepts on which knowledge of Indian society and culture had been hitherto based, the very success of those studies means that new requirements are going to be imposed not before long. Thus, it will plainly be necessary to ask not only about the factors that give Indian civilization its diversity, richness and multiplicity, but also about those that contribute to this society's global identity as a unity. The latter problem has to be grasped by asking, in concrete terms, the manner in which the transmission of Indian culture's most central traditions and values has been played out, and that question arises the moment one ceases to consider their existence as a simple matter of fact.

It is from such a perspective, above all, that the articles in this volume have been brought together. In choosing to study the texts and modes of behaviour which raise the problem of concepts of violence and non-violence in Hinduism, we claim no exhaustive treatment of them. Furthermore, there is no pretence to trace the history of those concepts nor to specify their overall influence on Indian society. The goal of this volume will be achieved if it allows its readers to gain a better feel for the important and specific features pertaining to violence found in Hindu traditions, without appealing to implicit and untestable assumptions about the purported essence of the Indian society and civilization.

The Elements Constituting Hindu Representations of Violence and Non-Violence

DISTINGUISHING, SACRALIZING AND EUPHEMIZING VIOLENCE

An essential part of the Brahminical tradition has been its endeavour to lay out the conditions for the exercise of meaningful violence, by definition opposed to violence 'without religion or law', which is a symptom of disorder. In the Vedic period, which is the oldest known to us through the texts, sacrifice served as the great ordering principle and as the foundation of the universe itself, including the 'natural' world. In that period, by virtue of their being inscribed in ritual, various forms of violence, such as, abduction or conquest during contests with other potential sacrificers, or the killing of animals were exalted. Indeed, it is in relation to this sacralized violence, a second type already split off from anomic violence, that the first speculations about *ahimsa*, the 'non-desire-to-cause-any-harm', appear to have been built. One is reminded of this by Oguibénine's study of how the Hindu ideal of non-violence gradually evolved from Vedic violence to Brahminical sacrificial practice, which sought to attenuate and even obliterate any trace of violence. The term '*ahimsa*' has benefited from an unexpected posterity because later discussions about 'non-violence' have been focused on it, although the vocabulary of 'violence'—coercion, aggression, murder—is far more diversified. In its origins, the term *ahimsa* displays a twofold characteristic: on the one hand, its field of reference is narrow because it refers above all to ritual, and on the other, it is a secondary elaboration because it is defined both within the context of and in relation to the violence of sacrifice, already constructed as another type.

In this respect, Vedism is far from proposing a uniform point of view. From the most ancient hymns to the later texts, it is possible to trace an evolution, as well as contrasting positions. Initially, what seems to be at stake is less a preoccupation with ethical order than a concern to avoid the vengeance that the victim could inflict in the other world. Thus, the victim must be 'appeased' so that it 'consents'. The act of putting to death is rhetorically denied: in sacrifice 'killing is not killing'. For instance, to reduce the inauspicious fallout of violence, although not its nature, plants are substituted for animals. That sacrificial violence is euphemized shows that it does not lose all its menacing characteristics, despite its sacralization. As Oguibénine suggests, the highly distinctive details of the Vedic sacrifice, just as much as the countless interpretations of it which have been given, unceasingly aim at minimizing the violence committed in sacrifice. This would scarcely make sense if the sacrifice had the effect of neutralizing all violence. Moreover, rather than analysing sacrifice as a ritual which abolishes violence, it is necessary to understand it as a complex operation, in which rite and rhetoric complement each other. It aspires to give to violence a consistently more reduced and abstract form, provided the supreme effect that issues from the ideal offering, wherein the sacrificer is himself the victim, is not lost.

Making the violence in sacrifice sacred and making it euphemistic have, therefore, been in constant tension with each other since ancient times. This tension is also found in the later Brahminical texts studied by Biardeau, principally the *Laws of Manu* and the *Mahabharata*. In these texts, the question of vegetarianism, for example, is sometimes the subject of contradictory rules. For instance, some passages permit the consumption of meat whenever it derives from sacrifices, whereas others accord a superior value to abstention. The same tension can be found later, from the sixteenth century onwards, among the theistic movements, when Vaishnavite and Shakta sects oppose each other over the practice of animal sacrifice, as is shown by Clémentin-Ojha's study of a north Indian Vaishnavite text from the early eighteenth century. In a different context and without any specific connection to Vedism, the tension can finally be seen in the modern period as well, as among the hill populations of Himachal Pradesh described by Vidal, whose article mainly discusses the tradition and practice of feuds among Rajput clans. In the hills, everyone, even the Brahmins, eat meat but only if it is of the animals offered in sacrifice. Furthermore, some of the murders committed because of the traditional rivalry between warrior clans were also interpreted from a sacrificial viewpoint, and they did not, at least until Independence, lead to any serious guilt or impurity for the perpetrators. Even in cases of this kind, however, the violence inherent in the acts was not eliminated, for it crystallized on the ghost of the victim, which became dangerous to its own clan, rather than on the murderer, until the destructive effect was redirected onto the enemy clan.

INTERNALIZING VIOLENCE

Little is known about the actual historical conditions which gave birth to the high evaluation of vegetarianism in the ancient period. This evaluation led to the displacement and extension of 'non-violence' from the domain of ritual action to that of the rules governing personal life. It could have appeared among the 'renouncers' (see Oguibénine and Biardeau) who, in their quest for personal salvation, cut themselves off from mundane social ties, or it could have even come from a dynamic process already present in the Vedic sacrifice.[4] In any case, from very early on, asceticism served as a model for enlarged conceptions of non-violence, which linked together two characteristics.

The first characteristic, as Oguibénine emphasizes, is the product of an internalization of sacrifice, of a channelling of sacrificial violence onto the ascetic himself. His fasts and privations, and the fact that he thus becomes his own oblation, mean that the ascetic accumulates inside himself a formidable magical power, which makes him into an enemy or an ally of the kings. The ascetic then becomes simultaneously representative of both 'non-violence' and limitless power, and a central and recurrent figure in all representations pertaining to violence and non-violence, as the majority of contributions in this volume show. The second characteristic is that the renouncer's non-violence appears as linked to his disinterest in worldly goods, which is sometimes highly theoretical in nature, as Bouillier's study of north Indian fighting ascetics shows. Such disinterest can be curiously reinterpreted within the context of political action by kings or those who play their role, and it allows for the legitimation of all kinds of coercion, even the most brutal.

GUARANTEEING ORDER

At no time during the ancient period did the question of *ahimsa* arise for the king in exercising his own function, as is underlined by the work of Biardeau and Malamoud. The king's role is to guarantee the maintenance of a global order, the *dharma*, and to that end practically all means are acceptable.

Thus Malamoud, in his remarks on dissuasion in ancient India, begins with the classical treatise on the art of government, the *Arthasastra*, and reveals the fundamental pragmatism that should guide the king's actions. Peace is not considered as superior in value to war, but instead as one possible form of relationship with other kingdoms. Moreover, the 'good' king is, above all, a victorious king, a conqueror. The terror that he inspires externally, like the threat of punishment (which is supposed to be deployed with discrimination) within his kingdom, constitute means of deterrence to maintain order, as well as an inducement to his subjects to practise *ahimsa* in their own lives. Hence, the peace of the kingdom becomes a sign of the quality of his rule. The ideal of non-violence does not imply that all violence is totally excluded; not only is violence legitimate when it is a matter of safeguarding order as a whole, but a refusal to engage in it would actually be considered a serious lapse.[5]

In the *Mahabharata* epic, as studied by Biardeau, this 'pragmatism' is located within a renewed perspective that connects royal power and individual salvation. Thus, styles of reflection developed among the renouncers are introduced into the epic and are expressed in the form of praise for renunciation of the fruits of action. The king must act, and this includes killing human beings, but he does so in the name of *dharma*. Pushing this radical perspective further, the epic affirms that any attempt to escape from violence, understood as an attack on any form of life whatsoever, is doomed to failure. From this point of view, the ascetic is simply wasting his time. What counts is not abstention from violent action, but the rigour with which the actor detaches himself from any personal investment in his action. Each and everyone is violent, but each and everyone can also remain non-violent in his innermost being. If the legitimation of royal violence is not in itself peculiar to India, it undoubtedly is a specifically Indian characteristic to try to situate the personal salvation of the king within his dispassionate exercise of unavoidable destruction.

THREE DYNAMIC ELEMENTS

Sacrificial violence, internalized violence and punitive violence are the three dynamic elements which, in practice, constantly interact and combine with each other, so as to generate a variety of configurations at the heart of the 'classical' tradition. Moreover, as that tradition is reinvented, it explicitly refers to these three elements, as the article by Jaffrelot on the 'construction' of a tradition of violent nationalism among Chitpavan Brahmins amply shows. A few other brief examples will illustrate this.

In opposition to Shakta sects revering the Goddess, the Vaishnavite tradition has progressively rejected the idea that the killing of an animal can be justified within the framework of sacrifice. A hagiographic tale from the eighteenth century, studied by Clémentin-Ojha, shows that this Vaishnavite conception of 'non-violence' finally triumphs because a double compulsion is at work. There is the coercion which comes from the magical power of an ascetic, notably when he submits himself to the internalized violence of a fast, and there is also the coercion which comes from the Goddess herself who, once she has been 'converted' to the superiority of *ahimsa* by the human saint, does not hesitate to use her weapons to punish those who do not yield to this view of *dharma*.

The fighting ascetics, studied by Bouillier, justified their initial recruitment, in particular from warrior castes, in terms of a 'disinterested' need to protect the non-combatant renouncers of their order. At issue was the defence of the *dharma*, a legitimation of armed activity which then allowed some ascetics to become mercenaries or to discharge the princely function at the local level. Feared too for their magical power, derived from their asceticism, such men took a vow of *ahimsa* which thus corresponded in practice to vegetarianism.

In general, for Brahmins as a caste, more so than for others, 'non-violence' is a vocation. In the central Indian village in which Chambard lived, the Brahmins are economically and politically 'dominant', and they ensure respect for the local social order. As Chambard's discussion of their recourse to violence shows, this order is conflated with the Brahmins' defence of their own position. Hence the Brahmins themselves do not hesitate to resort to strong-arm methods as soon as they perceive a threat to their position, whether it comes from a modification of the relations of power with the service castes, attacks on their purity, or doubts about the ethnographer. On each occasion, breaches by others create a crisis which the Brahmins are quick to resolve by any means and with right entirely on their side.

Plainly, knowing how to evaluate the extent to which the use of violence conforms to the ideal of 'detachment' is problematic. Thus, as Heuzé demonstrates in relation to a contemporary coalfield at Dhanbad in Bihar, such an ideology of detachment is the one to which recourse is made, even today, by people who are pursuing their own vested interests, as well as those who are not. Hence everyone proceeds to legitimate his own violence with a very similar rhetoric, which proves that in this case one is dealing with a set of shared values. And if violence is justified as soon as it is deployed in the name of both a global order and of the people who will enjoy the resulting peace, how can one analyse the situation of those who are identified as the causes of disorder, but will often only be the victims of the order that is then established? This problem, moreover, is comparable to the one raised by Biardeau, when she emphasizes the absence of a concept of the 'rights of man' *qua* man in the Brahminical tradition. Violence is not so much thought of in universal, 'moral' terms in relation to its victims, but rather in the context of a problematic directed towards limiting its inauspicious consequences *for the perpetrators.*

To conclude this section, let us note that there are other representations of violence which are equally traditional, but do not spring from Brahminism, or at least are not made explicit in Brahminical texts, even if there may be some recourse to classical references (for example, from the epics). Three brief illustrations follow.

First, there are the 'chains of vengeance' or vendettas which are known throughout India, and are discussed here for Himachal Pradesh by Vidal and among the Sikhs by Das and Bajwa, whose article describes two opposite forms of violence—martyrdom and feud—as modes of defining 'community' in the contemporary Punjab. In these vendettas, the murders are integrated into well-defined patterns of social exchange and rivalry.

Secondly, there is the figure of the martyr, who concentrates within himself the violence of others and not, like the ascetic, his own. The martyr transforms the violence to which he submits, and ideally accepts willingly, into a weapon against his oppressors (see Das and Bajwa). This is a conception of violence which, paradoxically, is not always so far removed from Gandhi's conception of non-violence; it is also found in the action of some dissident Marxist trade-unionists linked to the 'tribal' and Dalit movements (see Heuzé).

Thirdly, there is the protection offered to one's own victim. This is a tried and tested device that consists of protecting those who have been made to taste aggressive force, and it is as much at work in the coalfield studied by Heuzé, as it is in the constructs of witchcraft in Kerala described by Tarabout. Fourcade's article discusses the so-called 'Criminal Tribes' of colonial India, and her analysis of the relationship between thieving and guarding in south India shows that there it depends on a complex system for the collective, non-localized regulation of violence, in which ideas of honour are just as much involved as an unfeeling calculation of damages. Such a system could only come into conflict with the British desire to guarantee the maintenance of centralized order, as well as with a view of society that tends to distinguish sharply between policemen and thieves.

Constructing Meaning

The dynamic elements outlined above, whether or not they arise from the Brahminical tradition, have a single *raison d'être*: to render violence meaningful. The studies in this volume show that this elaboration of meaning is oriented by two principal axes, which cut across each other: one defined in relation to the act of killing and the other in relation to 'non-violence', however that expression may be understood.

The Semantics of Murder

The denial of murder in the sacrificial context—'to kill is not to kill'—which is a strictly rhetorical modification of the semantics of murder (see Oguibénine), has already been noted. There are, however, other aspects as well.

Whether sacrificial offering or punishment is involved, the nature of the victim is not unimportant (see Oguibénine and Biardeau). The series of possible surrogates in sacrifice—from humans to animals, from animals to plants—implies a continuity of beings, as well as a gradation not of the violence done to them, but of its risks for the sacrificer and thus of the 'meaning' conveyed in the violence. In the same way, before the enactment of laws during the colonial period, human lives were not equivalent in the face of death. Even when killing was executed in the name of *dharma*, their value depended on the caste of the person who carried out the act, as well as that of the victim. Killing a Brahmin is not the same as killing an 'Untouchable'; the two acts do not signify the same thing. The meaning of the act of killing, whether it is legitimate or not, is not given once and for all in any absolute sense, since it is inscribed in the ideological and social relations of power.

Moreover, to legitimate a killing—in a sacrifice, in a vendetta or for the protection of *dharma*—is also to exonerate the killer from the consequences of his action. Legitimation confers a positive value on the act and in fact eliminates violence as such from it.[6] Other forms of violence, however, never are or could be eliminated from social life. Acts of violence by others, which lack the legitimacy that can be granted to one's own violence, as well as random, futile violence, are all devoid of ethical value. From the killer's point of view, the distinction between 'meaningful' and 'meaningless' violence frequently works by calling on a rhetorical language of desire and necessity in which a higher mediating category intervenes, such as the gods, *dharma* or 'non-violence', but also loyalty to kith and kin, socialism or progress. Then too, the evaluation of the 'necessity' in question is inscribed in the relations of power. After all, as the *Arthasastra* (the treatise analysed by Malamoud) emphasized long ago, the good of the kingdom is identical with the king's struggle to retain power, and this kind of argument, without sounding too discordant, can be adopted by the mafia-like trade-unionists of the coalfield (see Heuzé).

THE RELATIONSHIP WITH NON-VIOLENCE

As we have seen, for different spokesmen and in different historical periods or contexts, 'non-violence' can take on very different meanings, such as vegetarianism, refusal to sacrifice animals, detachment from the fruits of action, and (since Gandhi) a style of political activity. Moreover, this polysemy is undoubtedly essential in order that non-violence in itself can nowadays be represented as a *single* value that is widely shared throughout India. Such unanimity rests on a misunderstanding that covers up all the variations and levels of meaning which the expression can assume. Whatever meaning is accorded to it, however, the very fact of marking out non-violence, and usually granting it a positive evaluation, cannot but modify considerably the meaning that can be assumed by violence, even though it does not expunge it or prevent its appearance.

First of all, simple realism generally dictates that non-violence is only possible if it is defended and protected by violence. What is then valued is the non-violence that violence allows. This outlook is described in practically all the articles in this volume, and is perhaps most strikingly in evidence in the studies by Clémentin-Ojha and Bouillier. These two authors open up a new perspective on asceticism by showing, as a matter of fact, that the ascetic's individual vocation, oriented towards non-violence, requires this ideal to be propagated within society and, if necessary, to be defended by force of arms. The quest for non-violence on the part of individuals thus appears as a choice of lifestyle and as a moral category that would be incapable of realization outside the network of social ties, including those to which the ascetics are subject. Such a quest therefore has to take place within a form of society that makes it feasible.

Furthermore, non-violence is one of the essential elements in legitimating the recourse to violence. As Heuzé notes, non-violence then transforms senseless violence into meaningful violence. Together with the deterrent use of terror (well discussed by Malamoud), non-violence thereby becomes an element of power and of the consensus that forms around it. Thus a leader, if he wants to be charismatic, must devote himself to avoiding all direct contact with the degrading events which he can nevertheless be instigating.

Hence the construction of meaning around violence or non-violence is always effected by the ideological and social relations of power to whose determination it is contributing. At the same time, such a construction is open both to a relativity of points of view and to a certain measure of specialization within society.

Let us first consider the relativity of points of view. If violence is done by others, counter-violence does not have the same meaning and is not truly violence anyway, because it is a question of legitimate defence. Such a logic emerges strongly from the reactions of the Brahmins in the village studied by Chambard, and it is also at the root of the discourse on witchcraft discussed by Tarabout. This kind of argument is also found among latter-day rioters. Inverting the relationship between aggressor and victim, rioters justify the massacres in which they engage by the need to 'defend' themselves and to 'teach a lesson' to their victims.[7] The latter, as one may appreciate, are not only unable to share the aggressors' point of view, but suffer a violence that is all the greater because they cannot make any sense of it.[8] The relativity of points of view is, in addition, connected to the fact that in India there is no unanimity on the value to be granted to non-violence. Instead of being considered as a weapon to turn against oppressors, it can also be denounced as a sign of weakness (see Jaffrelot, and Das and Bajwa), two attitudes expressed through contrasting ideologies, social roles, and political strategies.

To turn now to specialization within society: although the violent defence of non-violence can be carried out by those with an interest in the latter (as among the ascetics studied by Bouillier and the Brahmins described by Chambard), in India it is more usual to delegate the task. As the logic of caste testifies, no other society, perhaps, has so clearly drawn distinctions between the roles and statuses of its members, in such a way that their behaviour can be regarded as perfectly legitimate and desirable, without a like judgement being applied to society as a whole. Thus, many divergent understandings and evaluations of violence, or non-violence, find expression alongside each other by being differentially articulated in social groups and relationships. The classical archetype of these relationships being the protection of 'non-violent' Brahmins by princes and warriors who value fighting (passionlessly, of course). The social polarization of violence which emerges from this, together with all the restrictions that flow from the different levels of meaning ascribed to 'violence' or 'non-violence', is therefore one of the elements defining the identity of social groups.

CONSTRUCTING IDENTITIES

Violence, therefore, is a criterion by which groups place themselves in mutual opposition or are opposed from the outside by others. Thus, the coalfield studied by Heuzé is seen as a violent place by people living in the surrounding villages. The phenomenon is even more true for castes, as one may see in the discourse on witchcraft in Kerala, in which the Brahmins as a group seem radiantly non-violent, whereas the low castes, in contrast, are charged with the worst kinds of occult violence (see Tarabout). It is crucial to note too that the dietary prohibitions specific to each caste are also directly connected with representations of violence (as inflicted on animals in particular), and that these representations—although obviously not only them—are therefore central to the definition of castes and inter-caste relationships. In traditional society, however, the complexity of these representations turns them into an essentially flexible tool for defining identities, which is open to diverse points of view. In some cases, though, group identity has been externally reified, notably by British rule and the western values of which it was a vehicle. Castes in which fighting was highly valued were classified as 'martial', though only if they were of middle or higher status, or 'criminal', if they were of low status. Fourcade's study reveals the stage at which certain castes were simultaneously frozen into a unique role and criminalized, in order to comply at one and the same time with the idea of a uniform ethical code for all, the 'scientific' vision derived from a kind of social biologism vigorous in the period, and the demands imposed by the centralized maintenance of order.

Moreover, in its concrete deployment, violence can serve either to constitute or dissolve social ties, and thus contribute to the fashioning of the social morphology. Two of the studies explicitly place emphasis on this point, although in the majority of the others, this aspect of violence is also apparent just below the surface. Vidal demonstrates how the vendettas which oppose the clans in Himachal Pradesh to each other put into play a common ritual and social language, how they depend on rivalries but also on reciprocal obligations between the clans, and how they can be resolved through heroic tales that link together ancient adversaries. Simultaneously, therefore, both fission and fusion are in evidence in these 'chains of vengeance'. The same point is equally stressed in Das and Bajwa's article; as they show, among the Sikhs, these deadly exchanges are distinctive of the Jats, who are characterized by these particular rifts. Furthermore, the Sikhs as a whole re-cognize their own unified, collective identity through the martyr, who is another, though inverted, figure of violence.

CONCLUSION: 'TRADITION' AND 'MODERNITY'

It should now be clear that in India the delimitation of meaningless violence, and the valuation or devaluation of non-violence, do not proceed without tensions or contradictions. These exist because of the inevitable disparity of viewpoints among the protagonists, the ideological inscription of violence in power relations, and the diversity of elements within representations of violence. According to the historical period and the context, interpretations and reinterpretations come into play on different levels of discourse, and in varying traditional and institutional frameworks. Thus Das and Bajwa, as well as Fourcade, show how traditional forms of violence (vengeance, banditry) take on a new twist within the judicial system established by the British. Thus, too, Vidal reveals the tensions which can exist, within the same tradition, between interpretations deriving from local versions of the *Mahabharata*, conceptions purporting to be more 'orthodox' and referring to classical treatises, and modern reinterpretations of the latter.

The ostensible unity that seems to have been effected by the Brahminical tradition—the key reference point for a major part of the population throughout the centuries—often actually consists of a relativization and hierarchical gradation of distinct perspectives, and not of their effacement. More so than ritual or social practices in the strict sense of the term, it is common rhetorical forms which are thereby imposed. In the Brahminical tradition, the high valuation of 'non-violence'—postulated as superior to violence but not exclusive of it—could not have been the object of any consensus unless it was founded on the diversity of interpretations sanctioned by the polysemy of 'violence' and 'non-violence'. The continuity of the tradition is only made possible by means of these constant reinterpretations; they merge into the tradition and render it increasingly complex, and they also become so much freer because the tradition allows for the retention of contrasting points of view.

A significant reformulation is offered by the seemingly opposed tendencies represented by Gandhian ideas and radical Hindu militancy. Jaffrelot indeed emphasizes that the two opposed strategies take up their positions facing a common perception of 'Hindu vulnerability' attributed to social divisions. The one, following Gandhi, strives to transform 'non-violence' into a political weapon. The other, on which Jaffrelot's contribution is focused, seeks to promote a sense of strength through a martial ethos, in which political non-violence is seen as an 'emasculation of the Hindu community'. The two opposed viewpoints are engaged in recreating thoroughly the 'tradition' while claiming it for themselves. Gandhi's conception of non-violence is premised on his personal reading of the *Bhagavad Gita*,[9] the very same text which legitimated Gandhi's assassination in his murderer's eyes.

In all this, one sees a striking fact about the contemporary epoch. By extending the field of non-violence to social action as a whole, within a context in which western values were making progress, Gandhi paradoxically contributed to the development of two poles which tend to be seen in a mutually exclusive and no longer complementary way— it is violence *or* it is non-violence. This dichotomy adds up to an extra step in the reinvention of tradition and represents the current stage in a process which has undoubtedly never stopped.

NOTES

This text has benefited from the comments of Jackie Assayag and Catherine Clémentin-Ojha, who are hereby thanked. It is a slightly adapted version of an English translation of the French original, published separately in *South Asia Research*, vol. 14, no. 2, Autumn 1994, and prepared by C.J. Fuller whom we would like to thank heartily.

1. B. Parekh, *Gandhi's Political Philosophy: A Critical Examination* (London: Macmillan, 1989), p. 48.
2. See, for example, *Études Rurales*, 95–96: *La violence* (July–December 1984), and D. Riches (ed.), *The Anthropology of Violence* (Oxford: Blackwell, 1986).
3. See Veena Das (ed.), *Mirrors of Violence: Communities, Riots and Survivors in South Asia* (Delhi: Oxford University Press, 1990).
4. A point of view defended by J.C. Heesterman, 'Non-violence and sacrifice', *Indologica Taurinensia*, 12, 1984, pp. 119–27.
5. In this respect, the Buddhist conception of the king has to cope with still more formidable contradictions, for Buddhism rejects any legitimation of royal violence by a specialization of social functions.
6. In contrast, in Buddhism, the sovereign's violence is not effaced, and remorse consequently plays an important role.
7. A fact that is well illustrated by J. Spencer, 'Problems in the analysis of communal violence', *Contributions to Indian Sociology*, n.s., 26: 2, 1992, pp. 261–79.
8. On this subject, see the remarkable article by Veena Das on the riots in Delhi in 1984, 'Our work to cry: your work to listen', in Das (ed.), *Mirrors of Violence*, pp. 345–98.
9. Several times over, Gandhi felt the need to justify his vision of the *Gita*, for example in the face of critics who reproached him for taking a 'Christian' approach. Cf. the compilation of his articles in M.K. Gandhi, *Hindu Dharma* (Ahmedabad: Navajivan Publishing House, 1950).

The Violence of the Non-Violent, or Ascetics in Combat

VÉRONIQUE BOUILLIER

> The origin of the fakirs goes back, as I said, to Ravana who lost his Empire to Rama and who was so deeply displeased by the loss that he resolved to wander around the world as a vagabond, poor and shorn of all possessions, even his very clothes. Several people flocked to follow Ravana, for it was a life that gave them complete freedom. Since they were revered as saints, they had every conceivable chance to commit the sins they desired.
>
> JEAN-BAPTISTE TAVERNIER
> *Les six voyages . . . en Turquie, en Perse et aux Indes*

Renunciation, detachment from passion and the ascetic life are the values that appear to be indissolubly linked in India to the idea of 'non-violence', of respect for life in all its forms, of tolerance. According to the Dharmashastras, the Sannyasi 'should move about avoiding all troubles or injury to creatures, should make all creature safe with him, should bear with indifference all disrespect, should entertain no anger towards him who is furious with him'.[1] *Ahimsa* is the first of the five great vows, five important commitments required to be made by any person seeking *sannyasa.* These five vows (which are no different from those made by Jain or Buddhist monks, who make *ahimsa* the Supreme Value) are the five *yamas*, the five abstinences which constitute the first of the eight stages leading to the ultimate detachment described in Patanjali's *Yogasutras.*[2]

The Sannyasi's commitment to refrain from inflicting harm on any creature is solemnized during the rite of entry into the state of *sannyasa.* The *Vasishtha Dharmasutra* (*Vas.*10.1) enjoins upon the renouncer 'to depart from his house after giving the gift of safety (*abhayadakshina, abhayadana*) to all creatures'.[3]

'The gift of safety,' writes Olivelle (1984: 116), 'is the ritual expression of non-injury (*ahimsa*).' *The Baudhayana Dharmasutra* (*Proto-Bau* 2.11.23, in Olivelle 1984: 121) extends this with the metaphor of the *danda*, or stick, 'A renouncer shall not injure any creature with the three rods (*danda*), viz. words, thoughts and deeds.'

The notion of *ahimsa*, or the 'non-desire to kill', a negative form of a positive idea, seems to have first appeared in Vedic rituals, specifically, in the context of sacrifice (cf. Schmidt 1968; and Oguibenine's paper in this volume). There, it is a matter of metaphors, reparations and substitutes, so that the act of killing sacrificial victims is shorn of any idea of violence, thereby avoiding its far-reaching consequences. If there is ignorance of the proper ritualistic manner of making reparations, it is better to avoid offering victims in sacrifice; as Schmidt writes, 'The [Vedic] student who did not yet sacrifice and did not yet know how to eliminate by magical means the evil consequences of injuring animate beings had to practise *ahimsa*' (1968: 649). Clearly, this is non-violence centered on sacrifice, on magical-religious methods of self-preservation, and not non-violence as an ethical reflection on violence itself.

The pertinence of this generalization appears in the case of the renouncer. Knowing that deeds are impermanent, his sacrifices are so to speak within himself, as he forces himself to attain perfect detachment, complete autonomy. He is free of all desire, particularly of the 'desire to kill'. *Ahimsa*, then, becomes predominant. Among Brahmins, it even goes beyond ritual sacrifice. Apastamba even writes, 'A Brahmana shall not take a weapon, not even if he only wants to inspect it' (*Ap*. 1. 10, 29.6, cited by Schmidt 1968: 633).

However, hand in hand with this all-encompassing apologia for *ahimsa*, due allowance is made for other sorts of behaviour: the king, the Kshatriya kill; they hunt and eat meat, and 'the need for a meat-based diet is highlighted as therapy for strength and virility' (Zimmermann 1982: 204). War, like hunting, is then looked upon as an act of ritual sacrifice. Thus 'the Kshatriya feels justified in even his most violent acts' (Biardeau and Malamoud 1976: 134). The emphasis shifts from non-acting to non-desire: *himsa* becomes condemnable when it stems from a 'desire to kill' and the consumption of meat can only be considered violent 'by virtue of the passion' that accompanies it (Zimmermann, citing Chakrapanidatta 1982: 210). This logic finds its culmination in the moral teachings dispensed by the *Bhagavad Gita*, where only the disinterested act matters, that act which is executed within the bounds of *dharma* (of personal *dharma*, as much that of the Brahmin as that of the Kshatriya or of the butcher, each of whom will see his particular kind of violence thus absolved), and in an inner attitude of renunciation (cf. Biardeau and Malamoud 1976: 119–38). 'If,' as Biardeau points out, 'every disinterested act amounted to ritual sacrifice, there would be no more violence and the problem would no longer exist' (ibid.: 130).

Another justification for violence appears in the theory pertaining to the *avataras* of Vishnu. The action to safeguard *dharma* is encouraged rather than acts free from desire. Violence is legitimate when used against the enemies of *dharma*, as it is when deployed against enemies of the king, who is entrusted with the protection of *dharma*.

By definition, ascetic sages, who occupy the very summit of Brahminical purity, are as distant as possible from the need for action: *ahimsa* is their province, par excellence. Yet, even the Dharmashastras are not free of some ambiguity in this regard. Although renouncers must not inflict harm on any living creature (and abstinence from the consumption of meat follows logically therefrom), the texts also prescribe the use of animal hides by these ascetics. Thus, the *Vasishtha Dharmasutra*, for instance, instructs ascetics to drape their bodies with a piece of cloth or in a deer skin (10.9–11, in Kane 1968, II: 2, 933). A tiger skin is draped over the throne of the supreme ascetic, Shiva.

Even if one allows that the ascetics may merely use the skin of animals slain by someone else, as they may sometimes be authorized to consume the meat of animals in whose death they have no direct hand,[4] violence—sometimes death-dealing violence—on another living creature stands in contradiction with the ascetics' vows of renunciation. However, Indian history and legends abound with proofs of such violence. The fear that ascetics induced and continue to induce demonstrates that the power attributed to them is not felt to be only benevolent.

Is this violence the object of justification? What forms does such violence take? Does it seek legitimation in Vishnu's violent *avataras*, meant to nullify threats to world order and restore order? Does the ascetic have the right to take recourse to every means necessary to restore *dharma*? Who are the enemies of the *dharma*? What are the stakes involved? So many such questions, each still relevant, will confront one when one observes that many renouncers have reconciled the vow of *ahimsa* with armed struggle.

Magical Violence

Even before considering history, one realizes that these questions arise in the context of hagiographic legends, in which glorification of the ascetic arises from a demonstration of his pre-eminence and power.

Supernatural as the ascetic's exploits may be, that does not make them any less violent.

Such violence is used against ascetics belonging to rival sects and against Muslims in exactly the same modalities. Elsewhere in this book, Catherine Clémentin-Ojha offers an example of Keshava Kashmiri's heroic exploits against the Tantrika Kashmiris. In other writings (1990: 340), she speaks of how Keshava's 'spiritual power' enabled him in a peaceful manner to overwhelm the Muslims of Mathura and convert them to Vaishnavism.

The major characteristic of combat involving ascetics is already discernible in these magical conflicts: the sheer violence of inter-sectarian conflicts. For instance, in his biography of Shankara, Madhava relates the philosopher's troubles with the terrifying *sadhu*, Kapalika Krakaca, who killed a thousand of Shankara's disciples, all defenceless Brahmins. When the survivors sought their guru's intervention, he used his yogic powers to reduce his enemies to ashes (cited by Lorenzen 1978: 65). A much later illustration, from the time of Prithvi Raj of Amber, is offered by the ritual combat between Yogi Taranath, the Raja's guru and head of the Galta monastery, and Bairagi Krishnadas Payahari. Taranath is overpowered and his men are pursued actively by the Bairagis (Orr 1940: 86).

The stakes involved are clear: pride of place by the side of the sovereign and a monopolistic hold on the use of magic in the service of the king. Such a mutually beneficial cooperation between king and ascetic is at the core of several legends in which violence through magical intervention figures prominently. Thus, for example, Prince Sajanvinod of Mewar receives a charm from Yogi Jallundarnath which will enable him to control the course of the river. This enables the king to consign the army of his enemies to a watery death (Gupta 1960: 60).

These narratives take us to the very heart of the paradox: to wit, the unrestricted and unflinching use of violence by one who has solemnly sworn never to inflict harm on a living creature, and the fact that such violence can be used for the benefit of kings, and serve their conquests, by those who have sworn to retire from the world. While *sadhus'* violence may initially have been sporadic and unorganized, an extension of the magical powers attributed to them, it is probable that for a long time armed *sadhus* have swept northern India, in the service of sundry sovereigns. As early as in the *Harshacharita*, we are offered proof thereof, in the description of the *sadhus* surrounding the ascetic Bhairavacharya, who later become the personal bodyguard of King Pushpabhuti (Ghurye 1953: 112; Kane 1968, III: 46-50).[5]

Nevertheless, one is not dealing yet, as one will later, with organized groups, and in any case one can merely offer hypotheses in the absence of reliable documents pertaining to the period preceding the fifteenth–sixteenth centuries. The first historical accounts about armed *sadhus*, going back to the sixteenth century, are indicative of a practised habit, where there are no improvizations and no impromptu innovations. However, during the first Muslim raids of the tenth-eleventh centuries, and the great destruction wreaked by Mahmud of Ghazni, the *sadhus* do not take to arms to defend the temples.

Rivalry with Muslims and Organization of the *Sannyasis*—the Pretext

Dasnami Sannyasi tradition, as retailed by Farquhar (1925: 483), holds that the ascetics were forced to organize themselves and create an armed wing in order to cope with Muslim, especially *faqir*, harrassment and persecution. This would indicate that armed Muslim renouncers were organized in groups even before the Hindus, although this is more a matter of allusion than reliable proof. Thus, in his report on Shahabad district, Francis Buchanan speaks of a holy martyr who accompanied Mahmud of Ghazni on his raids and about whom, according to Buchanan, 'it is alleged that this prince, so zealous for the propagation of the Faith, had in his army a number of saints, who led on the batallions' (1934: 88). No further details are offered. There were, to be sure, holy warriors such as Ghazi Miya, though that case was rather different. They were not ascetics organized in groups but warriors who were 'canonized' during the course of their careers.

However, there is an account of a Sufi band accompanying a holy warrior in Bengal, the Turkestan-born Sheikh Jalal, whose *jihad* campaign brought him to Sylhet at the beginning of the fourteenth century. Sayyid Ahmad Yasawi offered him seven hundred of his best disciples as an escort, 'Their expedition was not an ascetic or peaceful one. The booty gained from their warring enabled them to live luxuriously. Sheikh Jalal would leave various saints along the way to propagate Islam in the newly acquired territories.' After thus installing his disciples, and still a bachelor, he founded a *khanqah* (Rizvi 1978: 314).

Hindu *sadhus* would thus have borne the brunt of persecution by these groups. 'In the sixteenth century, according to Farquhar, there were in north India thousands of Muslim *faqirs* who went about armed, took part in the wars of the time, and, when there was no regular war, fought for their own hand. One of their practices, as good Muslims, was to attack and kill *sannyasis* as representatives of Hinduism' (1925a: 483). These Sannyasis, adds Farquhar, 'were prevented from taking violent measures against their enemies by their vow of *ahimsa*' (op. cit.): a fine justification which only serves to underscore the paradoxical nature of militant *sadhu* groups! Their own tradition gives the following account of their creation: in 1565, the well known scholar on Vedanta, Madhusudana Sarasvati, a Dasnami Sannyasi of Varanasi, sought an audience with the emperor Akbar to obtain protection for those belonging to his order. Raja Birbal, who was present, suggested a solution to Madhusudana, which was, 'to initiate large number of non-Brahmans into the Sannyasi order and arm them for the protection of Brahman Sannyasis. . . . Madhusudana, then, initiated large numbers of Kshatriyas and Vaisyas into seven of the sub-orders' (Farquhar, ibid.).[6] However, since such initiation marks entry into *sannyasa*, and therefore a commitment to *ahimsa*, the contradiction remains.

In fact, it is strengthened by another. The militant ascetics are known as Nagas, or the 'Naked Ones'. As P. Olivelle has shown, the term 'Naga' is reserved for the *Panchamashramaviddhi*, or the rite of initiation to the fifth *ashrama*, the highest spiritual state. This state concerns those who have forsaken even the symbols of renunciation, that is, the water pot, the staff and the loin cloth. Olivelle believes no date can be assigned to this particular rite, which derives from the Advaita tradition and is meant exclusively for *paramahamsas*.[7] When he forsakes clothing, the Naga renouncer becomes as he was when he was born, 'He is naked both externally (without clothing) and internally (without possessions and desires). Henceforth he is expected to live alone totally dedicated to the contemplation of the Self' (Olivelle 1980: 137).

This idea is also taken up by Wilkins, albeit with some corrections, 'All the great Hindu sects have a division of Nagas, i.e. those who carry their religious earnestness to an extreme length. These men discard all clothing; and though regarded as saints by the community, are known to be a most dissolute set of men' (Wilkins 1887: 332).

What links exist between these militant ascetics and Nagas believed to have attained the ultimate state of detachment? Why are militant ascetics known by the fact of being nude, and why are they nude in the first place? It may be possible to imagine that these warrior Naga *sadhus* have attained a spiritual level that enables them to fight for the defence of *dharma* with the detachment enjoined by the *Bhagavad Gita*. However, both the legend surrounding their foundation and the subsequent development of their branches would scarcely argue such extreme spiritual elevation for the Naga *sadhus*. As one has seen, armed ascetics and violent conflicts existed well before the dispute that necessitated Akbar's intervention. Some monastic orders claim, albeit without proof, even earlier origins. One knows for a fact that the Nagas as an organized body is only spoken of around that time.

Thus, it was the Dasnami Sannyasis, the 'Ten Names' ascetic sect founded by Shankaracharya, who first created a militant wing in their ranks. Novices are initiated under the overall laws applicable to the Dasnamis and then affiliated to one or the other of the seven orders which are open to non-Brahmins.[8] After a twelve-year apprenticeship, they are initiated as Naga *sadhus* and attached to an *akhara*. This term, regarding the Naga *sadhus* whether Shaivite or Vaishnavite, designates the Naga monastery as well as a level of organization and as a kind of regiment mobilized mainly at *Kumbha Melas*. The Dasnami Naga Sannyasis are divided into six major *akharas* (Juna, Avahana, Niranjani, Ananda, Mahanirvani, Atal), but often they constitute themselves into small mobile groups, called *jhundi*.[9]

The Naga *sadhus*, thus armed, ensure the protection of the unarmed ascetic groups. In exchange, each monastery where they halt is expected to pay them a remuneration; sometimes, this is paid with great reservations or only owing to the threat of armed aggression on the part of the ascetics.

The Naga *sadhus* did intervene to protect Hindu interests and sacred places from the Muslims. For example, according to the chronicles of the Nirvani Akhara, they took on Aurangzeb's army in Varanasi, in 1664,

> Raman Giri [and others] did heroic deeds. Ghanashyam Puri planted the banner, Dharam Puri . . . played the naubat music, Bishwambar Bharati held the sword, Lalit Bhagwan Puri held the peacock fan. Jogindra received honour. Narayan Ban's family was holding the mace. . . . From sunrise to sunset, the battle raged and the Dasnamis proved themselves heroes; they preserved the honour of Vishvanath's seat. (Sarkar 1959: 87)

The 'honour' was to take a battering, however, when the temple was destroyed in August 1669.

The Yogis would also appear to have given battle to the emperor Aurangzeb, or at least his generals, at Devi Patan, near the Nepal border. Victorious they massacred their enemies and buried the rival commander-in-chief: since then, the tomb was ritually contaminated each year with the sacrifice of a pig!

Such skirmishes, however, seem to have been few and far between, at least in the light of the number of places of worship supposed to have been destroyed by the Mughals, and by Aurangzeb in particular. The Naga *sadhus*, at least by the accounts one has, do not seem to have been engaged *en masse* in the defence of the endangered temples.

INTER-SECT RIVALRIES

The Nagas' warlike activity is not limited to the defence of a Hindu faith threatened by Islamic activism. On the contrary, in fact, most accounts reveal how rival Hindu sects confronted each other in heated dispute. Was it a matter of converting disciples from another *sampradaya* to one's own? Yet the sheer violence involved when various branches of the same sect settle scores would indicate that other interests were at play.

Most of these conflicts occur at pilgrimage sites, notably at the *Kumbha Melas*. Here is how the Nirvani Akhara took pride in its victory over the Bairagis in one of the innumerable conflicts at a *Kumbha Mela*, 'At Hardwar, [the *sannyasis*] blew conches and planted their flags and standards. They destroyed the army of Ram. . . . The Nirvani Akhara gained the credit of heroic valour' (Sarkar 1959: 86).

Officially, the dispute was about the order of precedence, or which sect would be allowed the privilege of the first dip at the exact auspicious moment, thus deriving the greatest spiritual benefit. Behind this conflict which pitched thousands of *sadhus* against each other in merciless combat, each armed with (at least) tridents and fire-tongs, there laid an economic and far more worldly preoccupation: how to attract large amounts in donation from pilgrims and how to attract the benevolent attention of the mighty. Being the first sect to take the holy dip or the first to lead solemn processions was a sign of the power and reputation of a sect. Apart from attracting a great number of devotees (and their alms), it would ensure that the sect was well placed to take advantage of the various commercial activities involved in a *mela*.

Such rivalries existed not only between sects but also between branches of the same sect. Thus, there is a well known account of how, in 1567, at Thaneswar,[10] two Dasnami orders, the Giris and the Puris, were locked in conflict under the eyes of the emperor Akbar on the issue of collecting alms from the devout. The head of the Puris complained to Akbar that the Giris had usurped the Puris' regular place. Both leaders sought to settle the issue by armed conflict. When he realized that the Puris would have the worst of it, Akbar ensured that some of his own soldiers, disguised as Sannyasis, fought on the Puris' side. The Giris fled; many were pursued and slayed by Akbar's soldiers.[11]

THE BAIRAGIS AND THEIR ORGANIZATION

With the rising importance of these sectarian conflicts, the Vaishnavite Bairagis found themselves in a difficult position, especially after the Shaivites organized themselves and created the militant Naga wings. Ramanandi legend has it, in fact, that two Giri Nagas swore, not to uphold *ahimsa*, but to kill at least one Ramanandi a day (Van Der Veer 1988: 136). The Bairagis, too, felt the need to create militant wings, which in fact they proceeded to do at the beginning of the eighteenth century.

Their relative inferiority in military terms is clear from a contemporaneous account from Ayodhya. There a crowd had assembled to celebrate the birth of Ram:

> There was an unlimited (number of) strong warriors in sannyasi garb, carrying weapons, with matted hair and ashes smeared on every limb, an unlimited army of soldiers taking pleasure in battle. Fighting with the Bairagis broke out. This fight was of no avail (to the Bairagis), owing to lack of strategy. . . . They made a mistake by going there towards them; the Bairagi garb became a source of misery. All people dressed in Bairagi garb fled. . . . Wherever they could they took shelter in a secret place and hid themselves. They changed their dress and hid their sectarian markings. (Van Der Veer 1988: 145)

Vaishnavite Nagas trace their origins to a conference held in Brindavan in 1713, which was presided over by that extraordinary character, Balananda, head of the Jaipur Ramanandis.[12] Thiel-Horstmann's research reveals that these Nagas had been in existence long before they were officially recognized. Jai Singh, the Raja of Jaipur, had in fact sought to rein them in; the first conferences, such as the one at Brindavan, were hostile towards the Nagas. Thiel-Horstmann cites texts in which the Ramanandis vow to refuse admission in their ranks to any armed ascetic.[13] After Jai Singh's death in 1743, his successors were not in a position to oppose the Nagas. At the Galta conference in 1756, they came officially into existence. The Bairagi Nagas were constituted into a single group that transcended sectarian division. Bairagis drawn from all the *Chatuh Sampradayas* (the four

Vaishnavite sects) came together to form a single corps of Nagas. Sectarian division manifested itself at a lower level of the organization, the level of the *akharas*.

The overall organization, indeed their very existence, is most visible during the *Kumbha Melas*, when the Bairagi Nagas congregate in three different armies, or *ani* (literally, 'spear heads'), whose distinctive signs are borne on the ascetics' bodies or on the emblems they carry. The three armies parade in a precise order: the Nirvanis lead the way from the camp to the bathing spot, followed by the Digambaras and finally the Nirmohis. The order is reversed on the return path, though this does not alter the position of the Digambaras. Their median position enables the Digambaras to be considered superior.[14]

The *Kumbha Mela* is the fount of another division, according to the place of initiation of the ascetics to the Naga order. The Hardwaris comprise those initiated at Hardwar, the Ujjainiyas those who took their vows at Ujjain, the Sagariyas those who entered the order at Gangasagar, and the Basantiyas those who were initiated at any place other than the first three.

The three *anis* are divided into *akharas*, which have sectarian loyalties. The Nirmohis have nine *akharas*, the Nirvanis seven and the Digambaras two. Seven of the eighteen *akharas* owe allegiance to the Ramanandis, the remaining eleven to the Krishnaites. The monasteries come under the authority of the *akharas*. Itinerant groups, *jamats* (*jhundis*, *khalsas*) are affiliated to the monasteries.

As in the case of the Shaivites, to enter the state of a Naga entails a preliminary novitiate of twelve years, divided into four *shrinis* (each corresponding to a particular kind of activity), and devoted to the study and practice of '*shastra-shaastra*' (weaponry and scriptures).[15] A Naga's duties are defined as follows, 'get the puja done by the person entrusted with it, raise the vocal tone of the *panktis* (assembled sadhus), cry out "*jaya*", sound the trumpet, roll the drums, scrupulously obey the Panchayat, let the *jamats* circulate, take care of the *sampradaya's* temples and monasteries, organise authentic bathing facilities at Kumbha Melas, preach the Vaishnavite *dharma*' (R. Sastri 2039 VS: 101–2). Though they were so rigorously organized, the Bairagis still could not thwart the rout at the hands of the Naga Sannyasis during the 1760 *Kumbha Mela*. One thousand and eight hundred were killed; the Bairagis were banned from the *mela* until the British came along and settled an agreement. However, the Sannyasis continued to keep their pre-eminence.[16]

The rivalry encompassed all sects. Though conflicts between the Dasnamis and the Bairagis were the most frequent, there were also clashes between Bairagis and Shaktas. Catherine Clémentin-Ojha gives examples of the latter in this volume. One could also cite the example of Assam, where, between the fifteenth and the eighteenth centuries, Shakta Brahmins prompted by the Ahom dynasty and reformist Vaishnavites backed by the Mayamariyas were pitted in battle. After enduring repeated waves of persecution, the latter swore, 'We will kill and be killed, thus repaying our debt to our slain Guru.' Then the Shakta influence began to wane, only for that of Shaivites to rise. Rivalries remained strong between the Mayamariyas and the Gosains, who became advisers to the kings (Neog 1978).

Links between War and Commerce

The violence that accompanied clashes between sects and the very modalities of these clashes lead one to believe that the stakes were not merely spiritual, that the defence of *dharma* was a camouflage for other activities. The links with the king on the one hand and with money on the other reveal the extent to which political, military and commercial power co-mingled.

As early as at the end of the fifteenth century, the saint-reformer, Kabir railed against the *sadhus*' depravity[17] who allied money and arms to conquer territories that could scarcely be described as spiritual,

> Never have I seen such Yogis, brother.
> They wander mindless and negligent
> Proclaiming the way of Mahadev.
> For this they are called great mahants.
> To markets and bazars, they bring their meditation
> False Siddhas, lovers of Maya.
> When did Dattatreya attack a fort?
> When did Sukadeva join with gunners?
> When did Narada fire a musket?
> When did Vyasadeva sound a battle cry?
> These make war, slow-witted.
> Are they ascetics or archers?
> Become unattached, greed is their mind's resolve.
> Wearing gold they shame their profession.
> Collecting stallions and mares and
> Acquiring villages they go about as tax collectors!
>
> (*Kabira-bijaka*, *Ramaini* 69, cited in Lorenzen 1978: 61)

The Nagas could justify themselves with the pretext of defending and protecting their ascetic brethren, of ensuring that the life of wandering and solitude did not make one vulnerable to attacks. But the protection offered by their military organization also served the purposes of monasteries plentifully endowed in wealth and land.

On the one hand, these rich monasteries could use armed ascetics to protect their properties and also to collect funds, such as land revenue and taxes. The royal house of Nepal conferred on some ascetics the power to levy a tax of one rupee per household on certain sections of the populace—who were often loath to pay. The monasteries also employed the *sadhus* to make sure there was no squatting on their lands. Naga *sadhus* were engaged by monasteries in Bengal to protect their properties from other passing ascetics.

On the other hand, during the seventeenth and eighteenth centuries in particular, the monasteries themselves had become financial and commercial powers of some consequence.One sees then the parallel development of Naga militarization and of the economic role of those whom the British referred to as Gosains (the Dasnamis). Commercial itineraries grew alongside pilgrim itineraries. Naga *jamats* ensured the protection of these ascetics-pilgrims-traders when the *jamats* were not themselves moving around. These itineraries went roughly from the Himalayas to Bengal or the Deccan, passing briefly through the Dasnamis' central warehouses at Mirzapur and Jhansi, to collect the merchandise that would be transferred by north Indian Gosains to their south Indian counterparts. From the north, they brought silk, gold dust, musk, copper. Trade was usually for cash, or, occasionally, spices and cloth. Jhansi fort, controlled by the Giris, was an important store house as early as 1750, and had become one of India's richest commercial centres by 1835 (Kolff 1971: 216).

The Nagas worked of course also for their own benefit. For over three hundred years, the Naga-controlled Pujari math at Bhaktapur, the largest in the Kathmandu valley, carried on trade with Tibet. Even after their eviction in 1763, a memory of this trade link must have remained for Tibet continued to send gold, silk and money to the monastery (S. Amatya 1988: 3). As B. Cohn observes (1964: 180), 'The disturbed political and military condition of the eighteenth century India disrupted regular channels of trade and enabled the Gosains to take over some of the long-distance trading.' I would add for my part that if they could do so it was owing to the protective presence of their Naga armies.

How the Nagas Fought

The prime distinguishing characteristic of the Nagas is their nudity. Nowadays, it is only at the *Kumbha Melas* that they are completely nude. This was not the case earlier, if one goes by indignant Muslim accounts of the Battle of Panipat where totally naked Naga mercenaries preceded the Muslims into battle.[18] Ashes are smeared over the Naga *sadhus*' bodies. Both Shaivites and Vaishnavites bear marks of their sectarian loyalty on their foreheads. Their weapons, obviously, kept pace with the times. Broadly, these comprise a bow and arrows, a shield and a spear, a short sword or a dagger. Later, they carried firearms, notably matchlocks. On some occasions, they even had cannons, transported by bullocks or camels, with rockets, 'a kind of glorified jumping cracker composed of a strong metal cylinder to which knives were attached' (Orr 1940: 94), and umbrellas, 'consisting of a circle of iron balls suspended from a central rod' (loc. cit.). Even today, at the *Kumbha Melas*, it is possible to see Nagas completely nude except for a gun strung on a shoulder strap.

A *mahant* (or head of a monastery) would lead a campaign, usually mounted atop an elephant and preceded by standard-bearers from each *akhara* and drummers (*nagaras*). Leading a campaign or being preceded with such paraphernalia was part of the privileges granted to those who headed Naga mercenary groups. All Nagas, regardless of their sectarian affiliations, made widespread use of intoxicants. This, according to Orr, explains why they seemed to move as though they were in a trance, 'when going into action, their progress was less of a march than a kind of whirling dance during which they became wrought up to a pitch of uncontrollable excitement' (ibid). The English officials charged with the pursuit of the Nagas in Bengal concurred in highlighting and deploring this extraordinary speed.

The Nagas would hurl themselves at their adversaries with 'ear-piercing yells', seeking body contact, 'In addition to being excellent swordsmen, the Nagas were also skilled wrestlers, always eager to get to hand-to-hand grips with their antagonists' (ibid). Their employers derived great satisfaction from the Nagas' courage in battle, their disdain for death, symbolic in a way of their ascetic detachment from worldly ties. Moreover, their undying loyalty to their leaders, in keeping with the ascetic tradition of respect for one's guru, made them particularly precious during the decline of the Mughal empire, at a time of shifting alliances and internecine rivalries. In a word, the Nagas were formidable warriors and 'their frightsome appearance and the superstitious terror with which they were regarded contributed no little to the success of their arms' (ibid).

As ascetics, they also enjoyed the advantage that their adversaries frequently hesitated to attack them. Ghosh mentions how sepoys refused to obey an order to attack the Sannyasis with bayonets. Likewise, when the British asked the king of Nepal to evict Sannyasis and *faqirs* from their bases in Morang, in the Nepalese *terai*, he replied that he was willing to expel them from Nepal but that, 'his religion would not allow him to put a faqir to death' (Ghosh 1930, Chap. XII). Anup Giri (Himmat Bahadur), one of the most celebrated Naga warriors, was accused of using black magic to attack Mahadji Scindia. Anup Giri took refuge with Ali Bahadur Peshwa, who promptly handed him over to Mahadji Scindia. The Naga *sadhu* warned that he and his three hundred followers would take their own lives. The Scindia king, contemplating this prospect (the suicide of a renouncer-expert in black magic, followed by his curse duly multiplied three hundred times), immediately capitulated and went to pay homage to Anup Giri, 'presenting him with a robe of honour, a horse and elephants' (Sarkar 1959: 252).

A perusal of the chronicles of the *akharas* leaves little room for doubt about their martial vocation and the values in which they took pride. In the genealogy of Atal Akhara, which like some other monasteries kept records of ascetic prowess, of the knowledge and generosity of each *mahant* or *sadhu*, it is noted, 'Mahesh Giri and Manohar Giri released Shaikh Singh from captivity. Rajendra Giri was a hero. Pratap Giri in the country of Narwar [*sic*], took Ramraj Singh prisoner. Rameshwar Puri beat the war-drum. Umrao Giri gained victory in the battle and forced Maur Bundela, Ram Singh and Jawahir Singh to turn their backs. Sanja Bharati took Shova Singh Bundela prisoner. Jandhari Puri and Dip Ban took the life of Bhola Singh Bundela' (Sarkar 1959: 84).

Mercenary Warfare

These names introduce one to mercenary warfare, the next phase in Naga activity which reached its apogee between 1750 and 1800, under Anup Giri. Around 1750, it would appear that the Nagas would move around in sizeable armed and autonomous groups led by a *mahant*. Kings sought to recruit these groups temporarily for monetary considerations. The contacts were usually established at pilgrim centres such as Hardwar or Varanasi. A few examples of such recruitments are given below.

In 1768, the Newar kings of the Kathmandu valley, besieged by Prithvi Narayan Shah, called upon five hundred Nagas whom they recruited at Varanasi.[19] Prithvi Narayan Shah noted later in his autobiography that he denied them entry by massacring them at a pass giving access to the valley, but the fact is that the Nagas had been victorious before being killed.

Mohan Singh, a usurper, was thrown out of Kumaon by the raja of Garhwal in 1779. He went to Allahabad, where he recruited Naga *sadhus*, four *mahants* and sixteen thousand men, offering them the sacking and pillaging of Almora in exchange. However, they were defeated and lost seven hundred men (Atkinson 1980, II: 602).

Vaishnavite and Shaivite Nagas alike took part in almost all conflicts that broke out in Rajasthan during this time. After 1780, the Jaipur royal line officially employed Bairagi Nagas, notably the Dadupanthis, and continued to do so until 1938. The Bairagis confronted the Sannyasis who, under the leadership of Anup Giri, sought to extort tributes to the emperor from the raja. In Jodhpur, however, Sannyasis and Vishnuswamis joined hands to form regiments within the regular army, from 1779 uptil 1875. Similarly, Sannyasis and Yogis are to be found in great numbers in Udaipur.[20]

Rajendra and Anup Giri

The eventful career of these two Dasnami Nagas clearly illustrates Naga militancy and the contradictions in which it operates.

Rajendra Giri

His story begins in the Jhansi fort, an important storehouse on the commercial routes between the Deccan and northern India. The fort came theoretically under the rule of the raja of Orccha. It was governed by the *mahant* Rajendra Giri who was also known as Raja Indragir Gosain. This speaks volumes of the power wielded by the Sannyasis. Although he was protected by a Naga garrison in the fort, Rajendra Giri was driven out of Jhansi by the Marathas in 1749-50. He sought refuge in Allahabad, then under the control of the nawab of Awadh. He began military campaigns alongside Nawab Safdar Jung, on the grounds that the Hindu faith had to be defended from the Afghan troops led by Ahmad Khan Bangash who had surrounded Allahabad in 1751. Inflamed by the sight of the Afghan atrocities, Rajendra Giri threw his 'death-defying monks' into battle where they were, 'delighted to bask in the sun under enemy fusillade' (Sarkar 1959: 127), thus making the Afghans beat a hasty retreat. Thus, Rajendra entered the service of the nawab, a Muslim. His services were only used when Nawab Safdar Jung was in conflict with other Muslims, such as the Afghans, or the Mughal emperor or other rivals. Rajendra Giri died in battle in Delhi in 1753, 'When the general died, Safdar Jung's cause in the war was lost' (Barnett 1980: 56).

Apart from being a military chief, Rajendra also held high administrative responsibilities. As a *faujdar* in a zone where Afghan nobles and Sayyids had refused to pay taxes, he managed however to collect eight times the regular taxes. Safdar Jung allowed him the privilege of not having to bow before him and to have the drums played when he set out on horseback; such honours were customarily reserved only for the highest dignitaries.

ANUP GIRI

Anup Giri, later known as Himmat Bahadur, and his elder brother, Umrao Bahadur, were both disciples of Rajendra Giri. Umrao took over as head of the Nagas upon the death of Rajendra. The brothers were active during the civil war. When Safdar Jung died, they entered the service of his successor, Shuja, with the title of Commander-in-Chief and the right to recruit men without seeking reference to the nawab. Their wages were substantial and, as Barnett points out (1980: 81), the expenses they incurred on their troops were minimal inasmuch as the soldiers were ascetics with minimal needs in clothing! By allowing Shuja every indulgence at the start of his reign, they managed gradually to establish their influence against that of their rival, Ismael Khan Kabuli, who was the prime minister until 1755. Flouting all notions of Hindu loyalty, they organized the kidnapping of a Kshatriya girl of Faizabad whose charms had captivated Shuja. This led to a great clamour.

Their loyalty to the nawab in the face of their theoretical status as defenders of Hindu faith was to be tested once again, and in an even more radical manner, in 1755, when Shuja declared war on Raja Balwant Singh of Varanasi, who had rebelled after the destruction of the Vishveshwar Mahadev temple. Far from supporting the raja, the Giris fought against him before setting themselves up as intermediaries. Likewise, the 1759 war against the Marathas would once again prove the Nagas' unquestioning loyalty to the nawab. In fact, in a secret operation, the Nagas entered the enemy ranks and massacred two to three hundred men. The culmination was to come at the Battle of Panipat in 1761. The nawab's twelve thousand-strong army was led into battle by the Naga army whose nudity shocked Durrani Shah! However, even when he fought victoriously for Muslims against Hindus, Anup Giri personally ensured that the Maratha generals were cremated with complete funereal rites!

As the supremacy of Awadh declined, the mercenary role of the Nagas and their chiefs became clearer. When the nawab was unseated by the British, after the Battles of Panchpahari and Buxar (where no fewer than five to six thousand Nagas had fought), the Nagas deserted Awadh and went to fight on the side of anyone willing to pay them. Anup Giri's political and economic ambition led him to act purely for himself—changing tack frequently, indulging in intrigues, switching camps often and making a considerable fortune in the totally anarchic conditions prevailing in northern India during that time, around the end of the eighteenth century. He seems, however, to have retained the loyalties of the Nagas under his command. The unshakeable link between guru and *chela* became crucial.

After a brief interlude with the Jats, the Giri brothers remained in Shuja's service until the nawab's death in 1774. Anup at that time had virtually half of Lucknow's troops under his command and controlled about a third of the state's revenue (Barnett 1980: 106).[21] Following Shuja's death, Anup Giri served Mirza Najaf Khan, the regent at Delhi. There are several instances of the role Naga mercenaries played during these decades, and in many battles they were pitted against one another: Naga Sannyasis, led by Anup Giri, fought on the side of the Mughals and in alliance with the Rohilas against Bairagi Nagas led by Balananda, who were in the pay of the Jats (led by Nawal Singh and then later, after Nawal Singh's death in 1775, by Pratap Singh, king of Jaipur).

A war of succession broke out between his lieutenants when Mirza Najaf Khan died in 1782. Anup Giri's love of intrigue came into full play. Supporting Mahadji Scindia (whom he had fought earlier), he threatened from time to time 'to renounce the world' and to lead the life of a mendicant. His power reached its apogee in 1784, as the principal adviser to Mahadji, when he was granted large *jagirs*. However, Mahadji remained wary of Anup Giri. When he was driven away from the court in 1785, he declared bravely, 'I am a faqir and the begging bowl is enough for me; whenever the Maharaja desires, I shall, of my own accord send away horses, elephants and valuables, and retire to the forest, with a rag tied round my waist and a piece of cloth on my head' (Sarkar 1959: 231–2). In another conflict, in 1787, some two thousand Nagas employed by the Scindias and led by Anup Giri's disciple, Moti Giri, took on five thousand Bairagis fighting on the side of the Rajputs, then being advised by Anup Giri. Finally, Anup Giri set about fighting exclusively to protect his own interests, more precisely his fiefdom in Bundelkhand. In 1791, he personally killed the raja of Banda and the raja of Charkhari.

Towards the final stages of his career, he was an ally of the British, 'Enemity to the advancement of British interest was the keynote of the Gosain's career, but for the maintenance of his own position and jagir, he now practically sold himself to them' (Sarkar 1959: 258). As a token of British gratitude, the Shahpur treaty of 1803 conferred upon him a *jagir* worth twenty-two lakh rupees. When he died in 1804, he was master of a territory that was considerable in size, which lay under British protection. When war broke out against the raja of Bundelkhand, the Nagas and British fought together in a single contingent, under the joint command of Colonel Powell and Kumar Kanchan Giri, a disciple of Anup Giri.

'Sannyasi Rebellion'

During the last third of the eighteen century, from around 1765 to 1800, when the British were beginning to consolidate their position in Bengal, the Nagas became the major protagonists in what has mistakenly been referred to as the 'Sannyasi rebellion' (duly idealized by Bankimchandra Chatterjee in his novel, *Ananda Math*), where British supremacy was challenged. The context bears no resemblance to that in which mercenary warfare flourished. The ascetics participated in the movement purely on their own account, in keeping with their status as wandering mendicants. The sheer succession of events may lead to the conclusion that there was an organized 'rebellion' when in fact there were only sporadic movements. The unfolding of these events is known only through the accounts of W.W. Hunter and J.M. Ghosh (copied in a pro-Indian version by A.N. Chandra and analysed by D.N. Lorenzen).

Several factors must be borne in mind in order to understand the context in which the ascetics' violence found expression.

Foremost is the importance of pilgrim routes. These were also routes for trade and corresponded to a precise temporal and spatial cycle. Groups of wandering ascetics, notably the Naga *jamats*, moved from one place to another in accordance with an itinerary fixed in accordance with festivals and *melas*. In Bengal, for example, *sadhus* in groups (sometimes of two or three thousand) would come from Allahabad, passing through the northern parts of Awadh, through the Terai, going into Nepal for the Ram Navami and Ram Vivaha festivals, and then descending through Bengal to visit shrines along the Brahmaputra at the time of the 'bathing festival', before converging on Sagar Island at the mouth of the Ganga in the month of May. Then they would proceed to Puri for the Jagannath festival or reach through Bihar the upper valley of the Ganga at the time of the monsoon. The *sadhus* used to receive donations in cash. It is unlikely that a fine line could be drawn between alms willingly granted, legally defined contributions and sheer extortion, when confronted with bellicose and heavily armed troops.

Nor were these Bairagis and Sannyasis alone. Bengal also saw the passage of Faqir Madaris, who closely resembled the Nagas in appearance and lifestyle.[22] The Madaris' itinerary took them from their founder's grave at Makanpur to various parts of Bengal, notably Mymensingh.

A second element at play was the fact that the East India Company was granted *diwani*, or the right to collect taxes and dispense civil justice, in 1765. The Company raised large taxes which put the *zamindars* in difficulty. They in turn mounted pressure on the peasants even as they protested against the sums exacted by the wandering mendicant groups. Further, the Company imposed a tax on pilgrimages. Matters came to a head after the famine of 1770. Reduced to misery, the peasants began to join the wandering ascetic groups, especially since many of them also owed money to the Sannyasi monasteries. Rich Sannyasis were wont to lend money at high interest not only to the peasants but also to *zamindars*.

Thus the protagonists were drawn as follows: (1) the rapacious East India Company with its regiments (who were often unable to cope); (2) the *zamindars* living off peasant exploitation, but caught in the web of the growing demands of the Company, of the claims made by armed groups of wandering ascetics, and of the usurious rates from Sannyasi moneylenders using their brothers-in-dharma, the Nagas, for recovering their loans forcibly; (3) Sannyasi monasteries that lived like *zamindars* and functioned as a rear base for the Nagas; (4) the peasants, frequently obliged to flee in the face of violence and famine; (5) and finally the Hindu ascetics and Madari Faqirs, sometimes at war with one another, sometimes allied in a joint conflict against their common enemy, the Company. Alliances would fluctuate during these thirty years of conflict. Only the enmity between the Sannyasis and Faqirs on the one side and the British on the other would be constant. Clashes broke out around 1760 when 'groups of Faqirs, outlaws, began to infest the territory'. 'Their stay strikes terror into the country people and greatly hurts the collections in that part.' (Chandra 1977: 35). As a matter of fact, they began to attack factories, extorting alms as they did elsewhere, but the British owners refused to oblige. Conflicts and massacres followed, with British military intervention in 1765.

During their *diwani*, the British frequently deployed their regiments only to face bloody defeats. In 1768, for instance, one Myrtle was killed by a group of Sannyasis when he was looking for wood in Morang district. Captain Mackenzie pursued the Sannyasis, who fled. The following year, lieutenant Keith was sent with a detachment to subdue the Sannyasis, but he was defeated and killed in December that year. The Nagas' rapidity, like their somewhat rudimentary apparel, disconcerted the British. Only when the British deployed horsemen in hot pursuit of the *sadhus* (i.e. after Warren Hastings in 1773), was the advantage of speedy retreat into the jungles nullified. The *sadhus* also had the advantage, at least initially, of collaboration from the peasants who were willing to hide them, especially after the ranks of Sannyasis and Faqirs were swelled by those running away from barren lands.

The situation was further compounded by intrigues and wars of succession in Cooch–Behar, where Sannyasis took part as advisers and mercenaries on both sides (Ghosh 1930, Chap. IX)! The civil war began with the assassination of the maharaja in 1765, at the instigation of Ramananda Gosain, the guru of the Prime Minister Dewan Deo. From 1765 to 1787, the kingdom knew a complicated succession of conflicts, assassinations and alliances, involving among others the Raja of Bhutan and the British. The main protagonists were the Commander–in–Chief Nazir Deo and the Prime Minister Dewan Deo, each seeking to instal a king of his choice. Both sides engaged Naga Sannyasi mercenaries (essentially drawn from deserters from the Maratha ranks). Here, too, the Sannyasis did not hesitate to indulge in the most ignoble violence, flouting all *dharma*. Ganesh Giri was recruited to kill the rajguru, the royal priest, Sarbananda Gosain, and to kidnap the maharani and the maharaja, a minor. Accounts exist of their atrocities and of how Bhimsen Giri struck the maharani to force her to sign. Finally, in 1787, Nazir Deo and his Giri hordes were subdued by the Dewan in alliance with the British. Ganesh Giri, taken prisoner, died during prosecution. The disbanded mercenaries would add to the growing number of 'brigands' who cut a swathe through Bengal, prompting during subsequent years strenuous efforts on the part of the British to cut off their points of entry into Bengal.

Mostly peaceful, the relations between Sannyasis and Faqirs deteriorated into pitched battle in 1777, near Champapur, probably because of a dispute about order of precedence. The Bogra District Gazetteer recounts that, 'the swords of the Nagas are described as lopping off the heads of the Faqirs with as much ease as if they were cutting the stalk of plantain trees' (cited by Chandra 1977: 90). However, by and large, the two groups worked in close cooperation especially during the last period. For example, in 1790, the collector of Mymensingh, M. Wroughton, wrote that Cherag Ali Shah and Moni Giri and their troops had arrived at Jaffarshaly and begun their raids, laying the countryside to waste and pillaging the government of its revenue, filling the peasantry with terror and forcing people to leave their homes. They numbered at least two thousand, he wrote, with about five hundred of them bearing firearms, swords and *talwars*.

The raids would be initiated in Nepal. Ghosh (1930, Chap. XI) mentions a certain number of letters that showed how Musa Shah, who led the Madaris after the death of Majnu, established a large camp in the jungles at Morang. The British sought the intervention of the king of Nepal. As one has seen, the Nepalese king confessed that while he would be willing to oblige, he could not put ascetics to death. As a matter of fact, Musa Shah owned *jagirs* in Morang, which had only recently become part of Nepal and where he could do pretty much as he pleased. The Morang *suba* even had a spy at the court of the Collector of Purnea, who would warn the Faqirs of any impending hot pursuit. Karim Shah, a leader of the group and a disciple of Majnu, was said to have four hundred Faqirs, one hundred Sannyasis and twenty Bairagis under his command. For twelve years, between 1786 and 1798, the British exchanged letters with the raja of Nepal. In each of his letters, the king would undertake to chase away the ascetic groups or would even claim that he had driven them away. Only in 1802, when the Faqirs–Sannyasis began to mount raids within Nepal itself did he make a move against them, quickly making them flee.

It has already been seen how important Sannyasi moneylenders had become. Many sedentary Sannyasis had also become bodyguards and strong men (*burkandaze*) for *zamindars*. In either case, the use of violence was commonplace. The *burkandazes*, in fact, were authorized to use violence even against members of their own sect if they attempted to extort money from the *zamindars*. Moneylending Sannyasis, whether acting in their individual capacity or as heads of a temple, would use violence against defaulting borrowers, whether *zamindars* or peasants. They would seek the support of passing Naga groups. One has accounts of how some two hundred Sannyasis, pitching their spears in the soil, would surround the house of a debtor. It was not uncommon to kidnap a member of the borrower's family and letting that person die or to kidnap the borrower's children and torture them. Certain Sannyasi fiefdoms had become virtual fortresses, for instance, Dombar Giri had two hundred armed Sannyasis and Rup Giri, in the jungles of Madhapur, even had a *zenana*, ladies' quarters. However, their activities diminished gradually following the onset of armed British intervention and the development of money lending at rates far lower than those extorted by the Sannyasi *mahajans*.

Ideological Posterity

In Bengal, as in the rest of northern India, Pax Britannica brought about a radical transformation in the lifestyle of the various units of militant ascetics. The huge *jamats* of earlier times were disbanded during the nineteenth century. A number of Nagas took to a sedentary lifestyle, establishing families and ensconcing themselves on the lands granted to them by diverse protectors at the height of their military glory. Yet, the last had not been seen of the 'Sannyasi rebellion', that explosive cocktail of spiritual asceticism and physical violence idealised by Bankimchandra Chatterjee in his novel, *Ananda Math* (*The Monastery of Felicity*), which appeared in 1882, and which transposed the unorganized violence of the Sannyasis into a liberating utopia, resisting all occupants, whether Muslim or British.[23] The synthesis between spiritual strength, symbolized here by devotion to the Goddess, who is none other than the Indian Mother-Earth, and the virile power of the ascetics who took to arms, would inspire a number of early twentieth century revolutionaries, notably Aurobindo Ghose, who, in *Bhawani Mandir*, would make a mystic extension of the Shakti/India identification. Subsequently, he would clearly justify the use of violence in his volume, *The Doctrine of Passive Resistance*, 'Under certain circumstances, a civil struggle becomes in reality a battle and the morality of war is different from the morality of peace. To shrink from bloodshed and violence under such circumstances is a weakness deserving as severe a rebuke as Sri Krishna addressed to Arjuna when he shrank from the colossal civil slaughter on the field of Kurukshetra' (cited by Gordon 1974: 119). It may be noted that at this time Aurobindo was in contact with a Naga Sannyasi guru, 'Sri Aurobindo had some connection with a member of the governing body of the Naga sannyasis who gave him a mantra of Kali . . . but all this was for political success in his mission and not for Yoga' (cited ibid.: 111). This is yet another example of ascetics in search of power enlisting the support of magical forces (Bouillier 1989).

Following the lead of Aurobindo, Tilak and others, the Hindu revivalists would attempt to justify the use of violence with a view to thwart Gandhi. Thus, Lajpat Rai would declare in 1925, 'Non-violence would result in "laziness", "fake contentment", "cowardice", "lack of spirit" and a "slave mentality" among Hindus' (Andersen and Damle 1987: 29). It was a matter of rejecting the Brahmin model for that of a perfect Kshatriya, 'The Kshatriya model, combining elements of militancy, vigour and domination, was called upon to overcome the perceived cowardice of Hindus' (ibid). Such a virile and courageous Hindu could only be moulded by an ascetic institution, the *akhara*.[24]

It is significant that contemporary militancy should reclaim what used to be a prerogative of the Naga order. The tradition of Naga *akharas* certainly remains alive, and one may cite the example of Hanuman Garhi in Ayodhya, which has been studied by Van Der Veer (1987; 1988: 148–59). Founded in the eighteenth century, during the reign of the nawabs of Awadh, this Ramanandi Naga monastery still brings together several hundred ascetics vowing to practise *shastra-shaastra*. However, 'what was new was that between 1890 and 1910, English-educated students began to attend *akharas*, especially in Maharashtra and Bengal' (McLane 1977: 340). These *akharas* became for them gymnasiums where the quest for physical perfection—'body building' (cf. Parry 1989)—ended in the practice of different forms of wrestling. The *akharas* are still often controlled by ascetics or temples and dedicated to the worship of Hanuman, 'Youths at such gymnasiums were taught that the exercises performed were a form of worship to the God Maruti (or Hanuman). Maruti is among the most demanding gods in the Hindu pantheon, requiring physical strength, subordination and a strict ascetic commitment from his devotees' (Andersen and Damle 1987: 35). Hanuman, the ascetic and celibate deity, exalted for his strength and the abnegation with which he defended *dharma* and fought against the demons, has always been looked upon as a model and worshipped by the Nagas, irrespective of whether they were Vaishnavites or Shaivites.

The marriage of physical, even martial, training and spiritual commitment is an ideal pursued by the Rashtriya Swayamsevak Sangh (RSS). Even as the movement was founded, around 1920, Hedgewar sought recruits in the *akharas* and instructed his followers to go regularly to these gymnasiums.

There is a larger context within which the RSS and other contemporary Hindu extremist movements have re-appropriated militant ascetic institutions (cf. Jaffrelot 1992). It primarily includes a legitimating ideology for the defence of Hinduism, whereby, like the Nagas when their order was first founded, the RSS and its allied movements could proclaim themselves as defenders of Hinduism, as modern *avatars* taking to arms to vanquish enemies of *dharma*, successively identified as the British, the secular State, the Christians and the Muslims. Second, it involves the re-appropriation, by the RSS in particular, of the ascetic, more particularly the Naga symbols, such as the trident, saffron clothes, Hanuman worship, solemn vows, reverence towards the guru (although the saffron flag is the sole guru, the organization is founded on a notion of personal loyalty that owes a great deal to the traditional idea of transmission of knowledge from the master to disciple), emphasis of virtues such as celibacy and frugality, the exclusion of women (at least at the beginning) and equality between members.[25] Moreover, it thrives on the emergence of a collective concern, of an ethic of community work whereby disinterested service for the benefit of others is equated with renunciation. Last, it includes the quest for approval, for support from the spiritual heads of various sects, leading to the founding of the Vishwa Hindu Parishad in 1964.

The Activism of the *Sadhus*

Although huge *jamats* regrouping two or three thousand Nagas disappeared during the nineteenth century, the sects did not give up their Naga identity nor their legitimizing function of defending Hinduism. Once again, the example of Ayodhya would suffice, where, already in

1855, there was a pitched battle between the Ramanandi Nagas of the Hanuman Garhi Akhara and the Muslims, when the latter wanted to reclaim some land on the pretext—which would have its echoes later—that the Nagas had destroyed a mosque in order to establish their monastery.

At the end of the nineteenth century, the Nagas, and ascetics in general, also played an important part in what is referred to as the *Gaurakshini* or 'cow protection' movement, directed against the Muslims and the British government. Meetings were held all over India, apparently at the instance of itinerant ascetics, and the 'government reports suggest that cow protection riots often followed visits by sadhus or sannyasis, many of whom travelled in large bands of "a hundred or more"' (McLane 1977: 300). For example, in 1893, when trouble would break out after every cattle fair in Bihar, or yet when riots occurred from Azamgarh to Bombay, 'hordes of wandering sadhus' were detected in each case (ibid. 317). Several trouble-makers sought to mobilize crowds with a discourse that was as anti-Muslim as it was anti-British: one Sannyasi, Brahmananda Sarasvati, would illustrate his 'objective' discourse on the economic benefits brought by the cow with the picture of a Muslim with the head of a pig slaughtering a cow whose head was composed of images of Hindu divinities (McLane, loc. cit.).

Not even the highest sectarian authorities stand afar from these nationalist and pro-Hindu movements. In 1906, the Shankaracharya of Puri presided over an assemblage of orthodox groups (the Sanatana Dharma, as opposed to the Arya Samaji), the 'Sanatana Dharma Mahasabha'. His successor, Bharati Krishna Tirtha, was involved with the Hindu Mahasabha, as was the Shankaracharya of Karvirpith, Dr Kurtakoti, who was violently opposed to Gandhian ideas and in 1922 declared, '*ahimsa* undermines Hindu self-respect and encourages Muslims to dominate the Hindus', adding that 'passive and non-resisting sufferance is a Christian and not an Aryan principle' (cited by Andersen and Damle 1987: 20). A later Shankaracharya of Puri, Niranjan Dev Tirtha, in alliance with the Shankaracharya of Dwarka, would lead a very active resistance against the Government of India in 1966, mobilizing two hundred thousand people for an assault on Parliament House in Delhi, 'to protest against the Central Government's failure to ban cow slaughter all over India' (Lutt 1978: 418). Eight people were killed and five hundred *sadhus* were arrested. As a pivotal point of the most narrow brahmanic orthodoxy, the Shankaracharya also fought against the ban on child marriage, against birth control and in defence of untouchability.

Although Niranjan Dev Tirtha seemed to be fighting a rearguard action, despite the support he received from the million or more people which he dragged behind him to the *Kumbha Mela* in Hardwar, the same cannot be said of the *sadhus* and spiritual chiefs, *dharmacharyas*, recruited by the RSS in order to form the Vishwa Hindu Parishad and its various other outcrops, such as the Hindu Sansad. The *sadhus* were then entrusted with the responsibility of forging a new Hinduism, of eliminating all sectarian conflict to evolve a 'Hindu *Dharma*'. Successive 'World Hindu Conferences' were occasions for enthusiastic speeches. Swami Satyamitrananda Giri proclaimed,

> It used to be said that it is impossible to weigh frogs or bring Dharmacharyas together. Maybe the frogs could not have been weighed, but Vishwa Hindu Parishad has brought the Dharmacharyas together on one platform. I would like to request them to direct their followers selflessly for re-awakening of Hindu Dharma. They should also ask their followers and devotees to worship Hindu Dharma instead of individual gurus and to hoist the flag of Hindu Dharma.[26]

According to the minutes of the 1979 Conference, 'The Sadhus, with one voice, declared that, "We all are one, we belong to the same stock, we have no differences whatsoever. . . ." This Sadhu Sammelan proved that no differences exist among Hindus. Keeping in view the diversity in various Sampradayas and Panthas, it is often said that Hindus cannot be united. Notwithstanding, Ṣadhu Sammelan has proved it wrong' (cf. note 25; 1979: 73).

The Ayodhya dispute provides the battleground for this new found unity and *Dharmic* activism on the part of the *sadhus.*[27] While the head of the Gorakhpur Nathpanthi monastery presided over the 'Committee for the Liberation of Ram's Birthplace', *sadhus* also played a decisive role not only in the various demonstrations and processions at Ayodhya, but also as *kar sevaks* and in the collection of consecrated bricks, all of which were meant to seal Hindu unity behind the symbol of a fight against Islam. Violence, in word as much as in deed, was normalized. One *mahant* went so far as to proclaim that, 'for each dead "sevak", they would kill a thousand and proclaimed blood for blood' (Datta 1991: 2518), while a little booklet of mythologized history circulated in Ayodhya concludes with the account of the victory of, 'a 10,000-strong army of sadhus trained in martial knowledge, join[ing] the Hindu princes to liberate the *janmabhoomi*' (loc. cit.). That the *sadhus* were ready was proclaimed by Mahant Ram Chandra Paramahamsa, 'We are all saints and do not know the intricacies of politics. We are ready to wait for two months for the so-called removal of hurdles. Then, we, along with the Ram devotees, will demolish the building [i.e. the mosque]' (Awasthi and Aiyar 1991: 17).[28]

Conclusion

In this new situation, i.e. this propagation of a Hinduism that is at once unified and ecclesiastical (Thapar 1985; 1989) founded not any more on Brahminical values but on a Kshatriya ethic of apologia for action, collective service, violence and equality, it would appear that all the *sadhus* involved had become akin to the Nagas! One may say that these ascetics had all gathered under the banners of Ram and Hanuman in response to the cry of 'Hinduism in danger', of 'Hindus (being) a dying race', and that this obsession of a besieged majority had prevented them from turning their weapons against one another. Vaishnavites and Shaivites alike were united in the worship of a militarized Ram, transformed into a warrior god, and of a Shiva whose only violent and destructive aspect was highlighted, 'If Shiva expresses the new militant, aggressive spirit of Hindutva, Rama is projected as the symbol of Hindu unity' (N. Bhattacharya, in S. Gopal, ed., 1991: 129).

The vow of *ahimsa* and the contradictions that should have resulted from this situation did not seem unduly to preoccupy those involved.[29] Consider the Ananda Marg, founded in 1955, numbering some two thousand Sannyasis who pursue socio-political activism even as they practise allegedly criminal ritual activities, exemplified it would appear in their *tandav* dance, 'brandishing skulls, daggers and burning torches, the priests and nuns are required to dance disrobed on every midnight' (Hamid 1983:26). Their discourse on violence typifies the inconsistencies in the various levels at which *ahimsa* is apprehended. Thus, in an extremely normative fashion, the secretary general of the movement declared, 'We don't approve of violence. Every Margi must follow "*yama*" and "*niyama*". "*Yama*" includes *ahimsa*, so how can we approve of violence' (interview in *Sunday*, 1982, cited by Hamid 1983: 26)? Yet, Sarkar, the founder of the movement, 'has openly advocated the use of violence to achieve Margi objectives."Violence," he has been reported to stress recently, "is the essence of life. Lack of violence means death"' (Hamid 1983: 23).

In the uncertainties reflected in these declarations, one may discern three attitudes that are not necessarily mutually exclusive. The first attitude is of an erudite rationalization which re-situates *ahimsa* in the context of sacrifice, where it first appeared, thus exempting renouncers, who are outside the logic of sacrifice, from making any compromise with violence. Second, it is a militant articulation of demands, as evidenced in recent examples, whereby violence is legitimized when it is directed against those who threaten *dharma* (whatever one might mean by that term which, at some points of time, does not seem to apply to anything more than practices specific to a guru and a handful of his disciples), with a re-interpretation of the *Bhagavad Gita* in this perspective becoming the point of reference or the absolute truth. Last, it is an *a minima* reinterpretation of *ahimsa* as, quite simply, abstinence from eating meat. In a way, this is a semiological loop: *ahimsa*, which began as a refusal of sacrificial violence, grew to embrace the refusal to take any form of life, spread through traditional Brahminical society as vegetarianism and returned to the fold of militant ascetics in that very form. In their *akharas*, the Nagas emphasize the fact that they are vegetarians, even as they underscore the military exploits of their predecessors. To refrain from consuming meat is then looked upon as the only way to uphold a vow of *ahimsa*.[30] Thus, Swami Narayan, founder of a sect virulently opposed to animal sacrifice and meat eating, who might have been expected to be an ardent propagator of *ahimsa*, did not shy away from military trappings. A surprised Bishop Heber noted in 1825, 'He came in a somewhat different style from all which I had expected, having with him near two hundred horsemen, mostly well armed with matchlocks and swords, and several of them with coat of mails and spears' (Pocock 1973: 133; Mallison 1974: 449).

In our times, even *ahimsa* reduced to simple vegetarianism gives rise to polemics for meat has always been looked upon as the diet of Kshatriyas, with associations of virile courage, strength and weaponry (which the beef-eating British stoutly encouraged). And many voices have also been raised to exhort the new Hindu to repudiate even this form of non-violence.[31]

NOTES

The French version of this article was written in 1991. Many events happened and many studies were published since. Notable among others is the work of William R. Pinch.

1. Kane 1968, II: 2, 923; cf. Manu VI: 40, 47–8.
2. The term 'sannyasi', in this paper, is used in its all-encompassing sense, to denote those who have adopted the path of renunciation. However, a distinction must be drawn between:

   - Sannyasis *stricto sensu* with Shaivite affiliations, members of the 'Ten-name' or Dasnami sect (referred to as Gosains in some English-language texts), founded by Sankara in the ninth century, which developed a militant wing, the Naga Sannyasis (cf. passim);
   - Shaivite Kanphata Yogis, followers of Gorakhnath;
   - The Vaishnavite Bairagis, who are sub-divided into four major sects: Ramanandis, Nimbarkis, Vishnuvamis and Madhvas. These sects form the Catuh Sampradaya, they established among themselves a unified branch of militant Naga Bairagis.

   Founded by Dadu in the sixteenth century, the Dadupanthis are a Vaishnavite sect.

   In this paper, I shall not, however, speak of individual ascetics who adopt *vamachara tantric* practices for inversion of values and become extremist in their behaviour, such as the *Kapalikas* or members of certain *Shakta* cults, who are credited with the most violent acts, including human sacrifice.
3. Olivelle 1984: 116. According to the other Dharmashastras, this commitment comes at the conclusion of the rites, after the would-be Sannyasi solemnly pronounces the *praisa mantra*, or his vow to renounce (cf. Kane 1968, II, 2: 955, 960).
4. 'The Jain monk is to accept only food which has been prepared, i.e. killed, by others, including water which must be boiled. Only this way is he safeguarded against any complicity in depriving an animate being of its life' (Schmidt 1968: 624–5).
5. Bhairavacharya, an ascetic belonging to Thaneswar, is surrounded by three disciples who, clearly, are 'intrepid fighters' (Ghurye 1953: 112). He needs the king's military might to enable him to overpower a supernatural being who stands between him and his pursuit of *siddhi*. The king prevails and the *siddha* takes leave of the world, 'two of his ascetic disciples preferred to follow Pushpabhuti, the king, and take employment as his personal guards to be in attendance with drawn swords' (ibid.).

6. A contemporaneous account, from the Nagas of Varanasi, is related by Sinha and Saraswati (1978: 94). This combines several aspects of Naga tradition: their ancient origins, the ferocity of the *faqirs*, Akbar's impartiality, and Rajput support.

   'From ancient times, the Naga ascetics were peregrinating in the country in groups called Jhundi. During the reign of Akbar, the Moslem Malanga Faqirs were troubling the Hindu villagers . . . This exploded into an open clash between the Nagas and the Malangas. The Malangas were already equipped with swords, they killed the Naga ascetics mercilessly. When the Hindus approached Akbar for justice, the latter said: two cows are fighting, which indicated his helplessness or non-interference in this religious matter. On this, the princes of Rajputana sent them some soldiers in the guise of ascetics to defend the Hindu sannyasis and villagers from the ravages of the Malanga Faqirs. It was on this occasion that for the first time the Naga ascetics were supplied with arms by the Hindu kings. These ascetics gradually trained themselves in fighting, and subsequently fought many battles and took part in many a skirmish' (Sinha and Saraswati, loc. cit.)

7. The term '*paramahamsa*' applies to those ascetics who have attained such a high degree of spirituality that they can consider themselves above ordinary rules and observances. According to Ghurye (1953: 81), 'they not only are prepared to act as teachers and leaders of the Nagas or the naked sub-section of the Dasnamis, but also dine in the same row with them. They are generally preachers and teachers . . . great scholars, well versed in Sanskrit learning.'
8. There exist ten branches amongst the Dasnamis. Till that day in 1565 when admission to other varnas were opened in seven of these, only Brahmins were admitted. The three remaining orders—Tirtha, Ashrama, Sarasvati—which are reserved for Brahmins are most widespread in the south.
9. Each *akhara* has its own centre and possesses branches in different parts of northern India. The various *maths* and *akharas* of the Dasnamis fall into twelve *mandals*, supervised by a *mandalesvara*. The *akharas* come under the authority of the Panchayatam Akhara System, with each *akhara* being administered by an elected group known as *Shri Panch*. The *akharas* are sub-divided into *dawas*, each under the supervision of a *mahant*, who is assisted by a *senapati*, or military adviser (Gross 1992). Each *jhundi mahant* is responsible for his mobile group or *jhundi*, while a *thanapati* is entrusted with economic administration. Each *akhara* was founded independent of the others, each has its own history and its own presiding deity: the Juna Akhara, apparently founded in Prayag in 1146, appears to be the oldest. Bhairav, who was the first presiding deity, has now made way for Dattatreya.

10. See Ghurye's account (1979: 114–15) citing Farquhar who in turn based his work on Vincent Smith and Muslim historians such as Abu-l-Fazl, Al-Badaoni and Nizam-u'd-din Ahmad Bakshi (*Tabaqat-i-Akbari*).
11. See *Ain-i-Akbari*, II, 423. According to Al-Badaoni, the conflict was between Yogis and *Sannyasis* (Ghurye 1979: 115).
12. Van Der Veer (1988: 137) is repeating the oral tradition which attributes to Balananda the leadership of a group of armed *sadhus* engaged in the trading of horses and camels, much before he assumed his role as organizer of the Ramanandi Nagas.
13. 'On behalf of all akharas, the Ramanandis had to abjure arms. They had to assert that they would not admit an armed vairagi into their pankti and confirmed that wearing arms would lead to excommunication from the "seven sampradayas" of Shri Sita Ramji. In another document, Ramanandis confirm that keeping arms would be considered a violation of the rules of the chatuhsampradaya and a crime against God, Guru and King' (M. Thiel-Horstmann, 'Warrior Ascetics . . .', p. 9 of the manuscript).
14. The 'centrality' is noticeable too in the manner in which the various distinctive signs are borne. The locks of the *laturi*, or top knot, of the Nirmohis fall to their right, those of the Nirvanis to the left, whilst the Digambaras allow their locks to remain in the middle. The Nirmohis wear the *sheli*, or black anklets made of thread, on their right foot, the Nirvanis on the left, whilst the Digambaras may choose either foot. The *mahaviri*, a vermilion line on the forehead worn as a sign of sectarian affiliation as well as a blessing of Hanuman, rises over the Nirmohis' right eyebrow and over the Nirvanis' left eyebrow; the Digambaras draw it in the middle of the forehead. The banners vary too: the Digambaras' standard carries five colours, that of the Nirmohis is golden and that of the Nirvanis is silver. An upside down *kalas* crowns the staff of the Digambara standard. The other *anis* were entitled to this too until the Sannyasis began carrying it like a trophy (which speaks volumes for the spirit of the *Kumbha Mela*!), the Nirmohis and Nirvanis no longer decorate their standards thus. An image of Mahavir Hanuman adorns each banner, with distinguishing marks on the reverse side in accordance with each sect. Thus the Ramanandi Akhara carries a figure of the sun and the Krishnaites carry one of Garuda. Each *ani* has its own distinguishing kind of music. While all display battle trumpets (*narasimha*) and kettledrums, the sound produced by the Digambaras is said to be so loud that 'it can induce miscarriages' (*garbhagamjani*)! An orchestra, a band, precedes the Digambaras. These characteristics are described in a Nimbarki booklet, edited by R.G. Sastri (2029 VS: 103–5) and I am deeply grateful to Catherine Clémentin-Ojha for drawing my attention to it (see too Ghurye 1953: 208–9).
15. According to Sastri (2039 VS: 101), during the first stage, the *chora* (lad,

novice) or *rakami* (servitor) must serve his superiors, light lamps, fetch water, prepare the bath, wash clothes, sweep, etc., and practise '*shastra-shaastra*'. The second stage, that of the *bandagidar*, involves assembling ingredients from the storerooms, taking charge of the kitchen, kneading the dough, rolling *chapatis*, taking dishes to the temple, lifting the maces and taking care of the Hanuman banners. During the *hurdamga* phase, the pupil must perform *puja*, offer *arati*, remain seated near the oven and give the call for meals ['Harihara': Ghurye observes (1953: 209), 'It is interesting to note that the call announcing the meals is composed of the two words designating the two deities of the Vaishnavas and the Shaivas, namely Hari-hara.'] and prepare the sweetmeat with ghee which is offered to the *panktis* (assembled *sadhus*), cry out *jaya*, raise the banner, and so on. During the fourth stage, *mudathiya*, the ascetic must serve the divinity, cry out *jaya*, keep accounts, supervise *chelas*, continue the practice of '*Shastra-shaastra*'. Only later does one become a Naga and later still aspire to become an *atit*, or master.

16. However, the Sannyasis themselves were to be defeated by the Sikhs at the Hardwar *Kumbh Mela*.
17. The song is attributed to him, at any rate. As Lorenzen has observed, 'The prominent mention of firearms makes it likely that it was written considerably after the Battle of Panipat (1526), when these weapons were first used on a large scale on Indian soil' (1978: 61).
18. Cf. Barnett 1980: 56, 'At Panipat, in 1761, the spectacle made by these troops had quite an adverse impact on the unruly Durrani troops, whom the Shah could barely hold back from attacking them. He prudishly lectured Shuja (the nawab of Awadh) on the impropriety of unrestrained *kafirs*, naked in front and behind (his Persian does not allow a printable translation), parading and lounging in front of Muslims and ordered them be removed to a distance from his camp.' Some words may not be out of place to comprehend the role of the Nagas in this troubled period of the eighteenth century which saw, between the decline of the Mughal empire (that began after the death of Aurangzeb) and the affirmation of British power, the emergence of local powers that shook off the suzerainty of Delhi—Deccan, Awadh, Bengal (at least until the British victory at Plassey in 1757), Rohilkhand (a Muslim principality, ruled by the Rohilas, to the north of Awadh), Bundelkhand (in northern Madhya Pradesh, ruled by the Bundelas), and the Maratha confederation in central India, comprising the Peshwas, the Gaekwads, the Bhonsles, the Holkars and the Scindias. In the north, the Jats began to organize themselves in armed groups and mount periodic ravaging and pillaging expeditions, before being overcome in 1772. Three major powers were in conflict to gain control over Delhi, seat and symbol of the empire: first, the Mughals, theoretically the emperors, but divided by wars of succession: Bahadur Shah (1707–12),

Muhammad Shah (1712–48), Ahmad Shah Bahadur (1748–54), his cousin Ahmad Shah Alamgir II (1754–9), Shah Alam II (1759–1806). Second in the race were the Afghans, under their chief Ahmad Shah Abdali (or Durrani), who laid Delhi to waste in 1756, and their alliance with the nawab of Awadh which triumphed over the Maratha-Mughal coalition at Panipat in 1761. Finally, the Marathas who, despite their defeat at Panipat, managed under the leadersip of Mahadji Scindia to occupy Delhi in 1771, functioning as Regents, until 1803 when Shah Alam called upon the British to come to his rescue.

19. They would appear to have been recruited by a certain Gulabram Aghori who, in 1743, had given Prithvi Narayan a sword imbued with magic powers. As he saw the success of the king who unified all Nepal, which he believed was due to the sword he had given, Aghori sought his share of the booty. When Prithvi Narayan refused, Aghori went over to the Newar camp and offered his services and those of his troops (Baral 1964: 147, 234–5).
20. See Sarkar, Orr, Tod, Thiel-Horstmann on the recruitment of Nagas by the Rajputs. The Vaishnavite Dadupanthi sect seems to have created a Naga wing at the Galta conference in 1756. They themselves trace their origins to Sundar Dass, a Rajput who lived in Bikaner between 1596 and 1680, who was a disciple of Dadu and who is reputed to have placed his weapons at his guru's feet. The guru told him to keep his weapons. Granted a pension by the Maharaja, Bhagavan Dass, he gathered about him a small group of ascetic warriors, who quickly earned a reputation for their loyalty to power. In 1866, there were 6,000 Dadupanthi Nagas among the 14,000 soldiers of the Jaipur army (cf. Sarkar 1959: 226; the Rajputana census of 1891: 53–4 and 1901: 47–8, for which I thank Catherine Clémentin-Ojha; Thiel-Horstmann 1991).
21. What needs to be underscored here is the importance the nawabs of Awadh gave to their Hindu entourage and the liberal donations they made to these Hindus. In Safdar Jung's time, according to Van Der Veer (1988: 144), 'The real administrator of Awadh and Allahabad was a pious Vaishnava, the Kayasth Nawal Rai.' Both the *diwan* and the Chief Minister during Shuja's reign were Brahmins.
22. The Madaris are a heterodoxical Sufi order created by the disciples of Shah Madar, a Syrian, who was buried in Makanpur, U.P., in 1440 (Gaborieau 1984: 111). According to the *Dabistan*, as cited by Lorenzen (1978: 73), 'The Madaris, like the Sannyasis Avadhuts, wear the hair entangled; and the ashes which they and the Sannyasis rub upon their body are called bhasma; besides, they carry iron chains on their heads and necks, and have black flags and black turbans; they know neither prayers nor fasts; they are always sitting at fire; they drink a great deal of bhang; and the most perfect of them go without any dress.'
23. See F. Bhattacharya's introduction to *The Monastery of Felicity* (Chatterji

1985: 7-19), as well as Gordon (1974: 79–82), and McLane (1977: 337). According to the last named, 'In its first edition, *Ananda Math* described a Sannyasi rebellion against the British, but in its later editions it was rewritten to avoid prosecution for sedition by substituting Muslim rulers for the British as the object of the revolt.'

24. On the *akhara* and on 'wrestling as a way of life', see J. Alter 1992.
25. Clearly, however, egalitarianism in the sects and *sampradayas* varied considerably in each case and according to the period concerned. As one has seen, the Dasnami Sannyasis were particularly restrictive in this regard.
26. *Hindu Vishwa*, special bulletin of the VHP dedicated to the 'Second World Hindu Conference', March-April 1979, for which I must thank Christophe Jaffrelot.
27. It is impossible to recount here in detail this episode from India's contemporary history. Of the scores of articles and books on this subject, one may cite Van Der Veer (1987), P.K. Datta (1991) and the compilation edited by S. Gopal (1991).
28. Which happened exactly one year after this declaration, on 6 December 1992.
29. See, too, M. Thiel-Horstmann's observations on the Dadupanthi Nagas, 'The question inherent here and forming part of the issue of this paper is, then, how the nagas reconcile world-renouncing bhakti and warfare. That this should be an issue at all seems, it must be admitted, very outlandish to the nagas themselves. They clearly feel that this issue arises only due to cross-cultural problems caused by the intrusion of the non-Indian student raising the topic' (1991: 256).
30. Cf. Van Der Veer, 'For Vishnuite sadhus, it therefore seems sufficient to be vegetarian and to worship the gods with fruits and flowers, if they want to honour the rule of ahimsa' (1988: 132).
31. One should note, however, of the somewhat contradictory efforts of the Arya Samaj founder, Dayanand Saraswati, who sought to persuade Hindus to return to Vedic Hinduism even as he tried to convince them that 'meat-eating is not necessary for physical strength' (McLane 1977: 284).

REFERENCES

Amatya, S. 1988. 'Pujari Math'. *Ancient Nepal*, 106 (June-July): 1–7.

Andersen, W.K. and S. Damle. 1987. *The Brotherhood in Saffron: The Rashtriya Swayamsevak Sangh and Hindu Revivalism*. Boulder, Co. and London: Westview Press.

Awasthi, D. and S.A. Aiyar. 1991. 'RSS-BJP-VHP: Hindu Divided Family'. *India Today* (30 Nov.): 14–17.

Atkinson, E.T. 1980. *Himalayan Districts of NWP: Kumaun Hills.* Delhi: Cosmo Publications.

Baral, L.S. 1964. 'Life and Writings of Prithvi Narayan'. Ph.D. London.

Barnett, R.B. 1980. *North India between Empires: Awadh, the Mughals, and the British 1720–1801.* Berkeley: University of California Press.

Biardeau, M. and Ch. Malamoud 1976. *Le sacrifice dans l'Inde ancienne.* Paris: PUF and Bibliothèque de l'École des Hautes Études—Sciences religieuses LXXIX.

Bouillier, V. 1989. 'Des prêtres du pouvoir: les Yogi et la fonction royale'. *Purusartha* 12: *Prêtrise, pouvoirs et autorité en Himalaya,* 193–213. Paris: Éd. de l'EHESS.

Brajvallabhasaran. vs 2039. 'Baisnav-ani akhare'. In *Srinimbarka-Sudha,* ed. R.G. Sastri, 96–106. Jaipur.

Buchanam, F. 1934. *Account of the District of Shahabad in 1812–13.* Patna: Patna Law Press.

Chandra, A.N. 1977. *The Sannyasi Rebellion.* Calcutta: Ratna Prakashan.

Chatterji, Bankim C. 1985. *Le monastère de la Félicité,* translated with an introduction by F. Bhattacharya. Paris: Publications orientalistes de France.

Choudhury, M.L. Roy 1951. *The State and Religion in Mughal India.* Calcutta: Indian Publicity Society.

Clémentin-Ojha, C. 1990. 'La renaissance du Nimbarka sampradaya au XVIe siècle. Contribution à l'étude d'une secte krsnaïte'. *Journal asiatique* 3–4: 327–76.

Cohn, B.S. 1964. 'The Role of the Gosains in the Economy of Eighteenth and Nineteenth Century Upper India'. *Indian Economic and Social History Review* I(4): 174–82.

Datta, P.K. 1991. 'VHP's Ram in Ayodhya, Reincarnation through Ideology and Organisation'. *Economic and Political Weekly* (2 Nov.): 2517–26.

Dumont, L. 1966. *Homo Hierarchicus, Essai sur le système des castes.* Paris: Gallimard.

Farquhar, J.N. (1925a). 'The Organization of the Sannyasis of the Vedanta', *Journal of the Royal Asiatic Society,* July: 479–86.

——— (1925b). 'Fighting Ascetics of India'. *Bulletin of the Rylands Library* 9: 1–17.

Gaborieau, M. 1984. 'Les ordres mystiques dans le sous-continent indien'. In *Les ordres mystiques dans l'Islam,* ed. A. Popovic and G. Veinstein, 105–34. Paris: Éd. de l'EHESS.

Ghosh, J.M. 1930. *Sannyasi and Fakir Raiders in Bengal.* Calcutta: Bengal Secretariat Book Depot.

Ghurye, G.S. 1953. *Indian Sadhus.* Bombay: The Popular Book Depot.

Gopal, S., ed. 1991. *Anatomy of a Confrontation: The Babri Masjid–Ram Janmabhumi Issue.* New Delhi: Viking Penguin Books India.

Gordon, L.A. 1974. *Bengal: The Nationalist Movement 1876–1940.* New York: Columbia University Press.

Gross, R.L. 1992. *The Sadhus of India*, Jaipur: Rawat Publications.

Gupta, B. 1969. *Magical Beliefs and Superstitions*. Delhi: Sundeep Prakashan.

Hamid, A.S. 1983. '"Ananda Marga": The Path to Bliss, or the Politics of Social Violence'. *Regional Studies* 1: 19–35.

Jaffrelot, Christophe 1992. 'Le syncrétisme stratégique et la construction de l'identité nationaliste hindoue'. *Revue française de Science politique* 42(4): 594–617.

Kane, P.V. 1968–75. *History of Dharmasastra*. 5 vols. Poona: Bhandarkar Oriental Research Institute.

Kolff, D.H.A. 1971. 'Sannyasi Trader-Soldiers'. *The Indian Economic and Social History Review* 8(2): 213–20.

Lari, M.A. 1990. *Religion and Politics in India during the Seventeenth Century*. Delhi: Criterion Publications.

Lorenzen, D.L. 1978. 'Warrior Ascetics in Indian History'. *Journal of the American Oriental Society* 98(1): 61–75.

Lütt, J. 1978. 'The Sankaracarya of Puri'. In *The Cult of Jagannath and the Regional Tradition of Orissa*, ed. A. Eschmann, H. Kulke, G.C. Tripathi. New Delhi: Manohar.

Mallison, F. 1974. 'La secte Krichnaïte des Svami-Narayani au Gujarat'. *Journal asiatique* 435–71.

McLane, J.R. 1977. *Indian Nationalism and the Early Congress*. Princeton, NJ: Princeton University Press.

Neog, M. 1978. 'A Militant Vaisnava Sect: The Mayamariya'. *Journal of Indian History* 56(3): 417–27.

Olivelle, P. 1980. 'Pancasramaviddhi: Rite for Becoming a Naked Ascetic'. *Wiener Zeitschrift für die Kunde Südasiens* 24: 129–45.

Olivelle, P. 1984. 'Renouncer and Renunciation in the Dharmasastras'. In *Studies in the Dharmasastra*, ed. R.W. Larivière, 80–152. Delhi, Firma KL Mukhopadhyaya Private Ltd.

Orr, W.G. 1940. 'Armed Religious Ascetics in North India'. *Bulletin of the John Rylands Library* 24(1): 81–100

Parry, J. 1989. 'The End of the Body'. In *Fragments for a History of the Human Body*, ed. M. Feher, 2: 490–517. New York: Zone.

Pocock, D.F. 1973. *Mind, Body and Wealth: A Study of Belief and Practice in an Indian Village*. Oxford: Basil Blackwell.

Rizvi, S.A.A. 1978. *A History of Sufism in India*. 2 vols. Delhi: Munshiram Manoharlal.

Roy, N.B. n.d. 'The Early Inroads of the Naga Sannyasis in Bengal (1760–1773 AD)'. *Indian Historical Records Commission. Proceedings* 31(2): 148–55.

Sarkar, J. 1959. *A History of Dasnami Naga Sannyasis*. Allahabad: Sri Panchayati Akhara Mahanirvani.

Sastri, R.G. ed.: cf. Brajvallabhasaran.

Schmidt, H.P. 1968. 'The Origin of Ahimsa'. In *Mélanges d'indianisme à la mémoire de Louis Renou*, 625–55. Paris: Éd. de Boccard.

Sinha, S., and Saraswati, B. 1978. *Ascetics of Kashi*. Varanasi: NK Bose Memorial Foundation.

Thapar, R. 1985. 'Syndicated Moksha'. *Seminar* 313: 14–22.

———. 1989. 'Imagined Religious Communities? Ancient History and the Modern Search for a Hindu Identity'. *Modern Asian Studies* 23(2): 209–31.

Thiel-Horstmann, M. Forthcoming. 'Warrior Ascetics in 18th Century Rajasthan and the Religious Policy of Jai Singh II'. In *Proceedings of the Third Conference on Devotional Literature in New Indo-Aryan Languages*, ed. G.H. Schokker. Leiden.

———. 1991. 'On the Dual Identity of Nagas'. In *Devotion Divine: Bhakti Traditions from the Regions of India*, ed. D.L. Eck and F. Mallison, 255–71. Groningen: Egbert Forsten, Paris: EFEO.

Tod, James [1829] 1983. *Annals and Antiquities of Rajasthan*, 2 vols. Delhi: Oriental Books Reprint Corporation.

Tripathi, B.D. 1978. *Sadhus of India: The Sociological View.* Bombay: Popular Prakashan.

Van Der Veer, P. 1987. 'God Must Be Liberated: a Hindu Liberation Movement in Ayodhya'. *Modern Asian Studies*, 21(2): 283–303.

———. 1988. *Gods on Earth: The Management of Religious Experience and Identity in a North Indian Pilgrimage Centre*. London: Athlone Press.

Van Schendel, W. 1985. 'Madmen of Mymensingh: Peasant Resistance and the Colonial Process in Eastern India, 1824 to 1833'. *The Indian Economic and Social History Review* 22(2): 139–73.

Wilkins, W.J. [1887] 1975. *Modern Hinduism*. London: Lewis.

Wilson, H.H. 1958. *Religious Sects of the Hindus*. Calcutta: Susil Gupta Private Ltd.

World Hindu Conference, *Hindu Vishva* (Mar.–Apr. 1979), Special Number.

Zimmermann, F. 1982. *La jungle et le fumet des viandes. Un thème écologique dans la médecine hindoue*. Paris: Hautes Études, Gallimard, Le Seuil.

On the Rhetoric of Violence

BORIS OGUIBÉNINE

> . . . It is now said that there are special executioners. But do you know how it was with Dzerjinski?
>
> If the judges handed down a verdict of capital punishment, it was left to the investigating prosecutor, he who had made the report and asked for the supreme measure, to execute the sentence.
>
> You seek the death penalty for this man? You are convinced of his guilt, you are certain he is an enemy of the people and deserves death? Then, put him to death with your own hands.
>
> There is a world of difference between signing a piece of paper, confirming the sentence and the fact of killing in person . . .
>
> VARLAM CHALAMOV, *Le premier tchékiste*, in *Kolyma III: L'homme transi* (Kolyma III: *Paralysed Man*)

A Fact of Language

If an Indian specificity must be sought in the conception of violence, it is likely that one will find it in the articulation of the notion of non-violence. In order to demonstrate aspects of this articulation, first it must be pointed out that the term which designates the practice that is contrary to violence (i.e. to murder, to injury, to assault and to bodily harm) has a specific form in Sanskrit. This term, '*ahimsa*', which is interpreted as the 'non-desire-to-carry-out-any-attack' is in fact a privative compound word: it is composed of the privative (or negative) prefix *a-* which precedes the radical *hims-*, a form of the desiderative mode of the radical *han-* 'to assault, kill'. The true import of this form may be gleaned from L. Renou's observation, 'One cannot overemphasize the importance of the mass of negative words in the development of Indian thought. . . . Where but in India could such a purely negative term as *ahimsa* gain currency as a religious injunction, as a politically important term?'[1]

Privative compound words in Sanskrit conjure up an entire world.

Far from being an isolated case, the term designating non-violence is in fact just one of several. Consider, for example, a term like *amrta*. In its primary meaning of 'non-death' it can be used as an adjective ('immortal', 'imperishable', 'not subject to decay'). *Amrta* may also be a substantive, a noun, signifying 'continuity of life, vitality, the fact of attaining an advanced age, protection from premature death' and, above all, 'immortality'. If one bears in mind that the term '*mrta*', negated in *amrta*, merely designates 'death', one realizes that the meanings of negative terms are infinitely more rich and nuanced than and far surpass the monotony of positive terms (Renou 1939). Take a term like *abhaya*, which may be likened to *ahimsa*: it signifies not only 'non-fear' but also 'security, peace, confidence' (whereas *bhaya* merely means 'fear'). Or *adroha*, the 'absence of a stern or non-friendly attitude, i.e. benevolence', while *droha* means 'hostile'. Or yet, *avidya*—'non knowledge, ignorance' (*vidya*: 'knowledge'); *advaita*—'non duality' (*dvaita* 'duality'). *Avyakta*—'non developed, non manifest, invisible, indistinct'—is more interesting yet as the positive term *vyakta*, in the sense of 'the visible world, the world of phenomena', derives from the negative word. Renou's observation, while concluding his study of privative terms, underscores a singularity: negative forms 'do not denote the lack of a quality, or a characteristic but, rather, affirm a state which excludes this quality, demarcating a domain in which that characteristic will not apply'. Compound terms like *ahimsa*, according to Renou, have an 'affirmative' content despite their negative form. Frequently, they are autonomous from the positive terms; in fact, their survival is better assured than that of a number of positive terms which are either derivatives of negative terms or even completely non-existent. Such is the case for example of terms like *akshara* (inalterable), *aghnya* 'which shall not be killed' and *achyuta* 'indestructible'.

The specificity, to my mind, lies in the fact that, whether or not they are in existence, whether seldom used or not used at all, positive terms frequently connote a reality that is sought to be denied or rejected. Do not privative compound words reflect an effort to mitigate an undesirable phenomenon or a state of affairs which is already perceived as negative? Such negation, in a term such as *ahimsa*, sums up the intention to eliminate evil through an entire chain of negations: if the root *hims-* connotes evil inherent in the desire for violence and murder, it is a primary negation bearing on that which is subject to attack; the compound that results from the privative prefix *a-* then becomes a secondary negation, which produces a positive term. The negative form of the term thus derived cannot be dismissed for it is a reminder of that which Indian thought has constantly affirmed: good can only be evil negated, good can only represent the absence of evil; the normal or normalized state makes way for a desired state. It is this which leads O. Lacombe to write, as regards this aspect of Indian philosophy, 'Violence is at the very heart of nature (could that not have been "of the norm"?-B.O.), where it co-exists with spontaneity; death gnaws life away in accordance with the very law of life' (Lacombe 1966: 275).

Thus, even if, as in Renou's definition, the term *ahimsa* itself is affirmative and positive, it continues to bear traces of that which is negated: the desire to kill is offset by the affirmation of another desire, that of not killing. The two aspirations are clearly designated in the very form of the term; it represents the frequent and typical to and fro swing of ancient India, which places opposites, the positive and the negative, on the same plane. To J. Gonda this is indicative of the concern with being as complete as possible. Only such a concern would enable the forging of a fairly transparent term that translates a conception in evolution: murder, evil, all manner of assaults, all these are repudiated by the term's inherent rhetoric; this term seems to express the well known defensive attitude of ancient Indians who dread evil and exorcize it with the sort of imprecatory formulae that abound in the Vedas (of the 'Do not attack!' or 'May death not take me by surprise!' variety).[2] From this, in fact, arises the well known fact that, in the hymns of the *Rig Veda*, verbs and expressions with negative connotations (such as 'to injure', 'to counter the enemy's wrath', 'to prevent', 'to demolish', etc.) are almost exclusively negative propositions (Renou 1939: 1).

VIOLENCE AND NON-EFFICACY DURING THE HIGH VEDIC PERIOD

As an approach to the question of violence and with a view to take into account all the diverse aspects it presents, it would be useful to distinguish the following parameters: the agents of violence; the objects (or victims) on whom acts of violence are carried out; the methods used in violent acts and, to conclude, the finalities these acts aspire to attain.

In the perspective that interests me, accounts of violence in the high Vedic period are relatively meagre but not devoid of importance.

Accounts drawn from the *Samhita* (*Rig Veda*, *Atharva Veda*, *Sama Veda* and *Yajur Veda*) are of interest as they occur at the beginning of what virtually becomes an evolution. Yet, during that period, few cases of violence are clearly distinguished from the counterpart of violence. The reason for this is that 'might' alone counts, in all its forms and varieties. No nuance is possible when the prevailing attitude is that evil reigns everywhere and must be exterminated. Some distinctions, however, are indeed made but these arise from the role played by ritual sacrifices. Good is invariably on the side of those who perform sacrifices; thus violence, especially violence in war, can easily find its justification for the elimination of those who do not perform sacrifices (see Oguibénine 1985: 65–6 *passim*, for specific details). War and violence go hand in hand in the hymns of the *Rig Veda*, and the injunctions addressed to the god Soma Pavamana (*RV* 9.96.4: 'For non-violence, for non-killing, be purified by thyself, for well being . . .!'; see Renou 1955, IX, p. 43), the very god whose qualities as a warrior are eulogized in stanza *RV* 9.96, must be considered exceptional.

The exercise of violence may also arise when there are conflicting sacrifices: each sacrificer attempts to prevail over his rival. Performing a sacrifice is the highest act of merit; to incite the gods to destroy those who do not perform sacrifices is equally meritorious. Violence is also recommended against those who do not perform sacrifices with the requisite excellence: he who sacrifices best may desire the death of an inadequate rival. Thus an entire gamut of violent intentions and acts define the contrast between the good sacrificer and the non-sacrificer or the unfortunate sacrificer.

It may be noted that life threatening violence is exalted in the hymns because and as long as it involves sacrificial acts. The killing of a man is justified in the organization of Vedic worship. Warriors, the only ones who may carry out violence, are exhorted to declare war on those who do not conduct sacrifices. Thus, by the very exercise of their functions they are integrated in sacrificial acts. Moreover, for his own sacrifice is to succeed, an officiant may be driven to use violence against his rivals. In either case, violence is in a way institutionalized, articulated and ritualized. It is an institution in that it enables the smooth conduct of sacrifices. It is articulated, verbalized in that it opposes the condemnable passivity of non-doing that militates against the 'doing' of sacrifice (such passivity manifests itself as avarice, the state of non-awakening, the torpor of an officiant who is isolated from his peers). Finally, it is ritualized because it is indubitably a vital necessity in sacrificial worship: violent poetic jousts between those proffering their best verbal outpourings to the gods, and wars conducted against non-sacrificers, are merely two expressions of a religion revolving around sacrifice.

Although very little material from that period of evolution of the Vedic religion is available for reflection on the concept of violence, it would be noticed that violent acts are clearly distinguished from non-acts, from passivity that is injurious to the efficacy of worship. In such worship, the act (violent, it would appear, by definition) is all, whilst the non-act is nothing. One discerns no trace of an awareness of the moral aspect of killing or of any other violent act. It is a period of unconditional violence or, better still, of a violence conditioned solely by the efficacy of worship and rite.

HUMAN SACRIFICE

In the early Vedic religion, the object of violence is an anonymous mass of men hostile to the Vedic cult, who suffer the consequences of being outside the sacrificial universe. They are not yet individuals. Another form of ritual violence appears in later Vedic times, the object of which is multiple even as it is individualized in enumeration. These, designated by the generic term *pashu*, are animal victims: man, horse, cow, ram, he-goat. In fact, the only really appreciated sacrificial victims are men and horses. According to a hypothesis advanced by W. Kirfel, the fundamental sacrifice, real or imaginary, is the immolation of a man. In Vedic religious history, this would have preceded the sacrifice of a horse, which, though it came later, encompassed and erased ancient and primitive human sacrifice. In Vedic and Hindu thought, universal and immolated Man (*Purusha*–universe), to whom several cosmological references are attributed, includes within himself the entire universe, he is its image, its origin and its point of departure.[3] Allusions are obviously made to the celebrated *Purushasukta* of the *Rig Veda* (*RV*, 10.90), where primeval Man, victim and sacrificial offering of the gods, is dismembered in order to give rise to animals, to liturgical elements (stanzas, melodies, metres), to social classes, to celestial bodies, to space. Verse 10.90.2 tells us that, 'this is the sole universe of the past and of the future'. It is impossible to establish, on the evidence of the texts of the Vedic tradition, whether this immolation of man was real or imaginary. The *Satapatha Brahmana* and the *Taittiriya Samhita* allude more to symbolic offerings of human victims while stating explicitly that men, like wild animals, were released on the conclusion of royal horse sacrifices. Yet it is stated (*SB*.VI.2.1.18) that man is the first amongst *pashu*. It bears reminding that, according to one plausible conjecture, man is the sole authentic victim and that a true sacrifice is one in which the sacrificer is himself the offering, for other animals are merely substitutes for him.[4]

It must be borne in mind that the violence inherent in putting a man to death is justified by a reminder of the model sacrifice, that of the Lord of all creatures, the primeval Prajapati: it is a self-destructive and yet productive sacrifice, 'As Prajapati gave his person to the gods, so exactly do you give your person to the gods' (*SB*. XI.1.8.2–5).[5] The first, basic violence is that which is carried out on one's own person or on one whose person has been purchased for a thousand cows and a hundred horses. Does not the passing from one's own self to the self of another argue, once again, the vitality of the mechanism of substitution? As man is the sole authentic victim and all other animals are just substitutes for him, the principle of substitution continues to create a series of privileged objects for sacrificial violence. Sacrificial practice is thus enriched and the very nature of objects becomes grist to the mill that sustains this practice.

To my mind, we cannot unduly emphasize the decisive nature of the quest for substitutes as objects of violence in sacrifice, a quest which arises, according to S. Lévi, from the repugnance caused by bloodshed.[6] *SB*.I.2.3.7 offers an explanation bearing on the terminal elements of the chain of substitutions: upon the immolation of the he-goat, the animal victim that includes the characteristics of all other animal victims, ritual virtue, the essence of sacrifice (*medha*) transits from one animal victim to another to enter the earth, where it may be found under the form of rice and barley. These grains become offerings and are as much imbued with merit and quality as offerings of flesh and blood.[7] The theologian Katyayana informs us that at one point of time, during this period, there was acute sensitivity to the cruelty and barbarity of human sacrifice. What remedy could be found? The recourse to substitutes was a radical expedient.[8]

Animal Victims in the *Brahmanas*—Objects of Murderous Violence

In the work of G.U. Thite (1975) there is an important synthesis which enables us to touch the core of the problem of violence and non-violence as articulated in the *Brahmanas*. What follows is a brief summary of the conclusions arrived at by the author along with the comments these conclusions inspire.

A consequence of the evolution, whereby ritual killing (of man or beast) was eliminated was that *Purushamedha* became 'almost' symbolic, with animals not being slain but being offered in effigies. In order to understand the motivations underlying that solution, it would be useful to dwell briefly on the very notion of a murder whose object is an animal sacrificial victim. In the Brahmanas, animal sacrifice is part of the solemn Somic sacrifice. As a result, the Soma plant, duly ground and pressed, is offered as a *Pashubandha*, the immolation of an animal attached to the sacrificial stake. However, it continues to be said (*Kausitaki Brahmana* XII.6, *Taittiriya Brahmana* I.4.7.6), that the victim is 'obviously' the king Soma. This is one of several such links made in the context of ritual sacrifice. Elsewhere, for instance, the divinity to whom the animal is offered in ritual sacrifice is identified with the animal itself. Equally, the *yajamana* (he who orders the sacrifice) could be identified with the sacrificial victim (*Aitareya Brahmana* II.11). The *Taittiriya Samhita* 3.1 4k maintains that the rope which ties the animal to the stake also binds the sacrificer. There is a tempting explanatory hypothesis advanced by some writers (Van der Leeuw and Keith among others), which Thite seems to share: the object of animal sacrifice is in fact the sacrifice of one's Self (Thite 1975: 143). S. Lévi more or less echoes this sentiment, 'Suicide would be the only authentic sacrifice. . . . It may not be out of place . . . to believe that religious suicide . . . , known and practised in India through time, may have attracted followers and enthusiasts during the period of the Brahmanas.'[9]

At least two supplementary questions arise from the above discussion. The first question is whether the flesh of sacrificial animals may be consumed, and if so what are its consequences? There was disagreement between theoreticians regarding this question. The *Aitareya Brahmana* II.3 maintains that to consume the flesh of animals sacrificed to Agni and Soma is tantamount to eating the man who has sought redemption through that very animal sacrifice. This view is discounted, however, by the improvised theory which holds that offerings to Agni and Soma are to be linked to the slaying of Vritra, the dragon who obstructed the march of the universe. Agni and Soma had given Indra invaluable assistance in killing Vritra; as just and grateful recompense, the two divinities were granted sacrificial offerings. Thus, to consume the flesh of sacrificial animals and derive satisfaction therefrom was highly recommended. A contradiction, then, seems to exist: whereas the sacrificer is identified with the animal-victim, partaking of the animal's flesh is discouraged. Later, however, certain concessions were made.

The second question is, why replace the animal victim with offerings such as rice cakes? According to the *Aitareya Brahmana* II.8.1, the first victim to be immolated was man (*purusha*). His *medha* left him to enter into the body of a horse. Once the horse was immolated, the *medha* moved into a cow, thence into the ewe and finally into the he-goat. Every time the *medha* leaves a living animal, the gods ensure that the animal in question will no longer be a sacrificial victim and hunt for another that may accept the *medha*. Upon concluding the entire series of animals, the *medha* enters the earth (ready for sacrifice, although the gods do not accept a sacrifice of soil), and then into grains of rice, cooked as special sacrificial cakes. And it is these rice cakes that the *Aitareya Brahmana* (II.9.1) refers to as the equivalent of a sacrificial animal. 'The cake must be immolated exactly as an animal victim would be',[10] says the text, and goes on to explain that the two are one and the same, with similarities in their parts and characteristics. The *Taittiriya Brahmana* (*TB* III.2.8.8) resumes it in a simpler manner, '*purodasha* (the rice cake) is the very image of the victim'. As the final object of *medha* in all its plenitude, *purodasha* is a substitute for all the animate and inanimate objects that can be immolated in sacrifice. It can be offered after an animal, although in rites such as the *haviryajna* or the *isti*, only rice cake is sacrificed. There is reason then to agree with Thite when he affirms that there is no place for slaying (*himsa*) in a context where ritualism is highly developed, as the fruit of an evolution. However, does this exclude violence itself?

As that which finally harbours *medha*, the rice cake enables animal sacrifice in the most complete sense, for it is believed that some parts of an animal (hair, hide, blood, the dewclaws, hooves, etc.) are unworthy of sacrifice. 'How, then, can the sacrifice be considered complete? Since rice cakes are offered during animal sacrifice, the immolation of these cakes enables sacrifice to be complete.'[11] The cake, adds Thite, is as much a victim as an immolated animal.

The *Satapatha Brahmana* (1.2.3.6 and 6.2.2.15) offers another justification for the presence of *medha* in rice and barley. The last in the series of animals in whom *medha* reposes is the he-goat, which may therefore be considered to embody the characteristics of all the other animals. As S. Lévi (1966: 137) points out, 'As early as during this period, a certain repugnance was felt at bloodshed. Doubtless this is the reason why it is imagined that *medha* leaves the he-goat and enters the soil, only for this elusive quality to reappear subsequently in rice and barley.'

If one analyses the two versions (and the fact is that there are two identical plant organisms which serve as a receptacle for *medha*), the conclusion lies that the offering of a rice cake is a variant of the destructive act of animal immolation. As the very last of a series of objects that serve as objects of fatal violence (an act recalled by the use of the verb *a-labh* in the sentence cited earlier from the *Aitareya Brahmana* II.9.1: *sa va esa pashurevalabhyate yat purodasah*), the rice cake attracts a conclusive bout of destructive violence. Inasmuch as the last fraction of *medha* is still vested in it, the rice cake is a substitute for all the other sacrificial objects. In the first phase, to be sure, it is merely an indispensable complement to the violent acts that may have destroyed the immolated animals. The substitution itself is insufficient for the object-substitute is part of the series of substitutions. However, in the second phase, is not the rice cake the image of the victim inasmuch as it would have been a substitute-complement? Aversion to bloodshed may have eliminated the specific objects of violence. Having avoided the slaying of living creatures and shocking established sensibilities (although one may wonder whether the very notion of sensibility is present in the Brahmanas), Brahminical ritualism goes about its quest for objects replete with *medha* and thus appropriate for destruction-consumption. Although there is no question any longer of shedding blood, the fact that the cake is immolated 'exactly like an animal victim' suggests that violence has not been eliminated. Not surprisingly, glimpses of this attitude are to be found in such phrases as, 'exactly like an animal victim', and 'the rice cake is the very image of the victim'.

The awareness that a note of violence persisted in the ritual of substitutions may have prompted the creation of a rhetoric specifically meant to misrepresent violence; violence, no longer obliged to take on the appearance of its opposite, is thus diminished.

The Rhetoric of the Modalities of Killing

Two series of modalities may be observed, although deciding between them may be difficult. The first is founded on substitution of a more or less analogous act for a ritual act held to be violent. More precisely, in the two acts that follow one another, the latter is supposed to nullify or at least mitigate the pernicious aspects of the former.

1. After an animal is immolated, water is sprinkled over it (*Satapatha Brahmana* 3.8.2.8 sq.). The hands must be scrupulously washed clean after the first cut is made into the victim. Water is believed to 'appease' cruelty.
2. Even evil spirits cannot gain access to the victim. A flaming torch is carried around the animal (*Satapatha Brahmana* 3.8.1.6; cf. *Kausitaki Brahmana* X.3), or else the sacrificer (*agnidh*: he who ignites), bearing the flaming torch, walks in front of the animal as it is led to the sacrificial pyre (*Satapatha Brahmana* 3.8.1.9). Evil spirits are warded off by a hedge of fire that protects the animal. Though the animal will be put to death, evil spirits shall in no way tarnish it; immolation will not be the outcome of the play of forces of evil.
3. All traces of violence are sought to be removed since the blood of immolated animals is the province of evil spirits and cruel creatures. Anything that may be linked to the exercise of violence (traces of the animal's hide, blood) is attributed to the forces of evil (*Satapatha Brahmana* 3.8.2.14–15). Evil can be held at bay too by throwing the blood of the sacrificial animal with the *utkara* (waste disposal), with the sacrificer walking on the blood and chanting, 'Thus I squelch the forces of evil, I cast them aside, I cast them into the shadows' (*Vajasaneyi Samhita* VI.16). Evil is negated by creating a gulf between the victim and evil.
4. As one may see, in the choice of objects for ritual sacrifice, only those which can bear *medha* in its fullness are considered suitable. Inversely, only an animal infused with *medha* (through the sprinkling of water, for instance) is worthy of sacrifice and an after-life. The *Satapatha Brahmana* lays down a general principle, 'Ritual possession of an animal (*a-labh*) can only be said to be complete when the act of slaying (*han-*) confers *medha*' (*Satapatha Brahmana* 3.8.4.5).
5. What Thite refers to as 'sophistication in killing' is undertaken in a manner that recalls the technique that has been just described. This also serves to erase the act of killing and to grant life anew to the victim. According to the *Vajasaneyi Samhita* XIII.18, such incantations as 'Hail the very breath of life!' (*pranaya svaha*), sprinkling water on the animal and offerings made by the *adhvaryu* would be appropriate where the intention is to sacrifice an animal 'as if it were alive'.

6. Similarly, the act of strewing pieces of gold along the sides of the victim must be viewed as an adjunct to the act of killing and the acts that follow. Gold is immortality (*Satapatha Brahmana* 3.8.3.26); placed symbolically, gold confers immortality on the victim.
7. At the junction of simultaneity and contiguity, one must also include the act of averting one's eyes at the time that death befalls the victim (*Satapatha Brahmana* 3.8.1.15).[12]

The second series lays emphasis on a reinterpretation of the murderous act. The semantic approach would appear to derive more from the probable or arbitrarily acknowledged similarity between the act of violence and the new interpretation.

1. It is ensured that the immolation itself no longer bears any trace of violent intent. According to the authors of the *Brahmanas*, the animal is not led to its death but to a sacrifice (*Satapatha Brahmana* 3.8.1.10: 'there is no killing, merely sacrifice and offering'; cf. *Manusmriti* V. 39; *Vasishthasmriti* IV. 7).
2. The victim is protected from death by using appropriate techniques: a chip is taken in the stake to which the victim is attached, and this chip is anointed with clarified butter by the *adhvaryu* and then applied to the forehead of the victim. The procedure is repeated with the knife which will be used on the victim. The chip, the knife and the clarified butter, says the *Satapatha Brahmana* (3.8.1.5), hark back to Indra's mace, *vajra*, which offers protection. No evil can be perpetrated with a divine weapon whose function is to ward off evil. The démarche of such sophistication is clear: the specificity of the instruments of death is negated by altering their destination, by conferring a radically different function on them—they will not be used for ill treatment but for protection.
3. Euphemisms are used in the very discourse that follows the ritual act or is concomitant to it. With a view to avoid expressions which directly denote the act of killing, a distinction is drawn between the language of men and the language of the gods. The former would say, 'to kill, to slay', whilst the latter would say, 'to appease, to obtain consent', or yet, 'the victim has joined the gods' (*Satapatha Brahmana* 3.8.1.15).
4. After a detailed description of violent acts, it is stated that this sort of killing is committed in a manner that men do not employ. An animal cannot be killed by being struck on the frontal bone, for that technique is specific to men. Nor can it be struck behind the ears,

> for that is specific to the forefathers. It is recommended that the victim be strangled by obstructing its respiration or by tying a noose (*Satapatha Brahmana* 3.8.11.15). The officiants of the sacrifice are thus enabled to negate the real which would otherwise rock their sensibility. Muzzling an animal softens the sound of its dying laments: similarly, by averting their gaze, the officiants can deny the actual scope of the acts they witness.

Thite is doubtless right in bringing together what he calls the sophistication of killing (or what we have presented here as the rhetorical modalities which modify the very semantics of killing) and certain embryonic ideas about *ahimsa*. He perceives therein a direct corollary of the sacrificer's identification with the victim; the victim obtains a new life and immortality in the lap of the gods, which is exactly what the sacrificer seeks for himself.

Equally, the ritualists do not lay hands on the victim but carry out a series of operations on signs and representations of the victim, which are apt to evoke the victim in various degrees. This, one would be tempted to think, explains the diversity and plurality of signs and representations. The very finality of violence is modified by altering the nature of the acts and materials used in sacrifice, by replacing the object of violence with a substitute for the Self (and let it be borne in mind that the term *havis*, used to denote the sacrificial victim is also applied to milk, butter and even to the very limbs of the victim).[13] Understandably, the signs emerging from this overwhelming need to conceal the all too obvious finality of the sacrifice, were diverse and plural. The signified is replete with such a plethora of distant and proximate connotations of the signifier that the signifier begins to shed its original meaning.

However, the original meaning of the act of immolation could not disappear without distorting the very intent behind the sacrifice of one's own Self in the guise of the sacrificial victim. As it became unacceptable in its more extreme forms of violence, the sacrifice-offering could only survive through the expedient of substitution, which affected the sacrificial act itself, as well as the objects and paraphernalia associated with it. It becomes thus a justification for the rhetoric used. This justification operates on the manner in which the ritual is expressed and not its substance; it fails completely, however, to conceal the inherent violence of sacrificial ritual.

This is also clear in the subsequent evolution of Vedic ritualism.

Violence, Vedic Ritualistic Theory and the Origins of Asceticism

Vedic sacrifice required that the best be offered to the gods—'sacrificing' meant to destroy, wholly or in part, or at least to damage that which was offered. This violence, once perpetrated, is sought to be mitigated by sprinkling water on grains of rice which are then described as 'damaged, despoiled, killed' (*Satapatha Brahmana* 1.2.2.11). The same description is applied to the soil which has been dug up so that a sacrificial altar or stake may be erected (*Maitrayani Samhita* 3.2.3: 3.18.9; *Taittiriya Samhita* 6.3.4.1).[14]

There is a constant concern in Vedic ritualism with preventing violence, or reducing it, or protecting oneself from it. Consider just one of these cases of substitution, drawn from the *Maitrayani Samhita* (3.1.8: 3.9.17 sq.): he who digs up the soil for a sacrifice, it says, shall suffer the same fate as the soil itself. However, through a sacred formula prescribed for the occasion, it may be clarified that it is not the sacrificer himself but the goddess Aditi—the earth-goddess herself—who is digging up the soil. As 'no damage can be inflicted on oneself', no act of evil takes place. The very process of replacing one agent of destruction with another who is defined as one who cannot wreak damage is sufficient to ensure that no harm shall befall the sacrificer.

The disciple who gathers wood in the forest for his guru's sacrifice is instructed not to inflict damage on the trees, for the vow of non-violence covers him too. He may only gather dead branches. During his rites of initiation, his guru will entrust him to the gods so that he may come to no harm. Thus the eventual destructor, agent of violence, as well as the objects threatened by such violence, are made distant from the sphere in which violence is exercised. The disciple does not commit a violent act, since that violence is imputed to the, anonymous death of wood; the disciple is also protected from violence by displacing him towards the realm of the gods.

Schmidt and others rightly believe that non-violence is a tendency taken from the ascetic tradition, principally on the grounds that the role of the perpetrator of violence and that of the object of such violence can be inverted and interchanged. Such substitution, however, is a function of the scale of relationships between this world and the other worlds that Vedic ritualistic theory exploits. The hereafter is an inversion of this world. One of the most radical expressions of this theory is the representation of the devouring of he who devours: that which a man consumes in this world will consume him in the other world (*Satapatha Brahmana* 12.9.1.1). The reasoning is devious, even full of subterfuge. The Brahmin consummates a sacrifice with a fermented drink. However, since a Brahmin may not consume fermented drinks, what he does drink cannot in fact devour him in the hereafter.

Thus, if violence is averted at all it is more on account of the consequences it will inevitably bring. An entire ethical system is still some distance away (for the theory of transmigration still prevails), but every effort is made to soften the law of simple retaliation implied by an inversion of roles. Due reparation must be made, every harmful act or damage (however slight or partial) must be duly appeased, made amends for, thereby ensuring that the perpetrator is spared more severe retribution in the other world. There arises then the problem of the duration of such reparations which, to our mind, would fall in the realm of metaphor and other tropes. Are the powers of appeasement attributed to a chant or to a spell circumscribed in temporal terms? Gradually, the idea emerges that no distinction can be made between evil acts, including those which are cruel and violent, and those that are positive. When integrated within ritual sacrifice, since neither can exercise an enduring influence, they were robbed of their effect. Only detachment, the complete lack of self-interest in an act, whether good or evil, could help avert a new cycle of deaths, of transmigrations.

As M. Biardeau has pointed out in her synthesis of the work of L. Dumont, it is not a matter of chance that non-violence should be first and foremost the handiwork of the renouncer. *Ahimsa* is part of the programme that imposes upon the renouncer the abstemious conditions which will enable the attainment of a state of total detachment, necessary for his final deliverance.[15]

THE FATE OF METAPHORS

A number of elements are common in the behaviour of the Vedic scholar and that of the renouncer. Both are sworn to celibacy, both are mendicants, both recite the Vedas, both carry a stick, neither offers sacrifices and both, above all, subscribe to the principle of non-violence. Obeying one's spiritual master is obligatory to both. In their rites of initiation, whilst the Vedic scholar is first entrusted to the gods so that no harm may befall him, the renouncer (as one who adheres to *ahimsa*) vows never to inspire fear in living beings (*abhaya*, non-fear). These processes, as also the reciprocity that follows from them (the Vedic scholar cannot inflict harm on the gods, the renouncer himself is never overcome with fear), clearly demonstrate that violence is averted through purely rhetorical devices, through the manipulation of signs of the extra-social and divine worlds, through wish-formulation.

However, there is a fundamental difference between the two. While both may refrain from inflicting harm, their motivations for doing so are completely divergent. The student of the Vedas shuns evil because he does not yet know how he must make reparations for it. The renouncer too shuns evil, but only because he knows that the measures of reparation are limited in their impact (and in any case he himself does not apply these measures).

Only renunciation can bring deliverance from the web of acts and their consequences. What advantage does it confer *vis-à-vis* the problem of non-violence? Conceivably, this may be examined in the light of a new kind of rhetoric, where it is not a matter of disguising acts of violence but one of canalizing them towards the very person of the agent of such violence, and not towards the exterior. Several examples of such ways of practising multiple abstention can be advanced as illustration of this aspect. The renouncer is seen as an *atmayajin*, 'one who sacrifices himself, for himself or within himself'. When he accepts food, he sacrifices within himself the sacred fires installed therein by a sacrificer, and which are identified with his very life breath. When he consumes food, he does not derive sensual pleasure, for he consumes it as if it were a medicine, and that too only after sharing it with other living beings (*Baudhayana Dharmasutra* 2.10.18.10, cited by Schmidt 1968: 637, n. 8). As Schmidt points out correctly, 'The entire ritual is reduced and appropriated by the individual.' This can be extended by pointing out that the withdrawal into the Self is further accentuated in a text like the *Chandogya Upanishad* (in which the term *ahimsa* appears for the first time). According to the master, Ghora (*Chandogya Upanishad* 3.17.4), when the renouncer reduces and appropriates sacrificial ritual, by internalizing the sacrificial flames, negating the pleasures of food and displacing these pleasures outwards, there occurs a diminution of the Self in the passage from external to internal sacrifice. As Ghora explains, a man's life is like a continuing Somic sacrifice. The gifts made to officiants must be assimilated with the observance of austerities, generosity through alms-giving, honesty, non-violence and speaking the truth. Ghora, according to Schmidt's reasoning, looks upon all these as variants of the negation of the Self. Austerities enable one who has been ordained (*diksa*) to reduce his body to an emaciated state. To give alms is to shed a part of one's own riches. To speak the truth and to be honest is a constraint, for men are not naturally inclined to do so; the sacrificer, however, as one who moves from the world of men to the world of the gods, must do as the gods do and speak the truth. Since non-violence is an integral part of abstemious practices and since it is the very opposite of natural behaviour (a dictum that spares one the harm which arises from being dependent on others), it attests to the autonomy, the independence and the inward-looking nature of he who has internalized sacrifice.

The fact that the renouncer's sacrifice, by definition individual and autonomous, is a secondary construct needs to be underscored. From this, to my mind, arise all meta-ritualistic and post-ritualistic styles, that is to say, styles of behaviour that are metaphorical in relation to the style of external sacrifice.[16] Such secondary behaviour is built upon and negates the actions dictated by ritualism, which the *atmayajin* has already overcome. Such ritualism is destructive as it makes the sacrificer dependent upon external, worldly elements (officiants, sacrificial victims, offerings, etc.), and necessitates reparatory magic to ensure the sacrificer does not suffer the fate he inflicts upon others. With post-ritualism, or the post-liturgical knowledge arising from rites once they have been practised, the ritual space is not just one in which words and gestures combine to interpret or to reform the world, but the space of acts for which there can be no reparation, even if compensation is made for them either partially or totally, even if the effects of such acts are dissimulated through a variety of stylistic tropes meant to modify the appearance of such acts performed by a non-autonomous sacrificer. Ritualism, even when it includes attempts to make reparations, is looked upon as imperfect. Hence its absorption in the renouncer's sacrifice, a phenomenon that has always been so much a part of India: where the sacrifice of one's Self, individual and singular as it is, is comparable to the offering made to the gods by the primordial Man.

By Way of a Summary, Some Propositions

As a practice, non-violence in opposition to violence is based upon a privative figure of thought which, in its turn, derives from the uncertainty caused by the pursuit of an ideal which calls for the annihilation of any trace of violence. Verbal and stylistic tropes (metaphor and metonymy between which the frontier is so fluid that distinguishing one from the other becomes difficult) become unavoidable, for it is necessary to establish principles for a behaviour that runs counter to customary ritual practices built upon a stock of significations specific to these very practices. Whilst these ritual practices had their own place, they would increasingly be called into question.

The dismemberment of the primordial Man is no mere fantasy that represents the immolation first of a human being and then of an animal. It is, in fact, an attempt to transpose in concrete terms the internal sacrifice which the renouncer must perform. In a way, by sacrificing his self for himself, he announces to the world that he is independent of everyone else, that he needs no longer include others in his sacrificial acts. This is the supreme solitude he exacts from himself, as does the austerities-observing ascetic. In Vedic India, humanity as a collective entity is disjoined in a contradictory way from violence so that violence may operate on the individual who is preoccupied with non-violence. In that sense, man is the non-object of violence. On the other hand, the cow, considered sacred and a hyperonym for all animals if not all animate life, is the privileged object of non-violence: the cow is disjoined from violence.

NOTES

1. Renou 1939: 18. Cf. more recently Wayman 1990: 14–23.
2. Gonda, 'Why are *ahimsa* and similar concepts often expressed in a negative form?' in Gonda 1959: 103, 110, 113.
3. Kirfel 1976: 179–90.
4. Malamoud 1976: 15.
5. From Lévi 1966: 130.
6. Ibid.: 137.
7. Ibid.: 137–8; Minard 1949, I: 198n. 577a.
8. Weber 1868: 58.
9. Lévi 1966: 133.
10. Verpoorten 1977: 338.
11. *Aitareya Brahmana* II.11: *yad evaitat pashau purodasham anunirvapanti/ tenaivaasya tad apuryate* (trans. Verpoorten 1977: 302–3).
12. In fact, the *Satapatha Brahmana* (3.8.1.15) says, 'so that we may not be witnesses when consent is being obtained (to death)'. See Minard 1956, II: 61 for problems of interpretation of this passage.

13. Renou 1954: 174.
14. These and a number of other references that follow have been derived from Schmidt 1968: 625–55: this article abounds in observations relevant to the issue discussed here; some, in fact, have served as food for thought for the ideas I have expressed here.
15. Biardeau 1965: 53.
16. If it is possible at all to understand in this way the term meta-ritualism used by Renou, see Renou and Filliozat 1947, I: 578, and Renou 1978: 109.

REFERENCES

Biardeau, M. 1965. 'L'Inde et l'histoire (à propos de l'œuvre de Louis Dumont)'. *Revue historique* 475: 53.

Gonda, J. 1959. 'Why Are *ahimsa* and Similar Concepts often Expressed in a Negative Form?'. In *Four Studies in the Language of the Veda*, J. Gonda, 103, 110, 113. La Haye: Mouton.

Kirfel, W. 1976. 'Der Asvamedha und der Purusamedha'. In *Kleine Schriften*, W. Kirfel, 179–90. hrsg. von. R. Birwé. Wiesbaden: F. Steiner.

Lacombe, O. 1966. *L'absolu selon le Vedanta*, 275. Paris: Geuthner.

Lévi, S. [1898] 1966. *La doctrine du sacrifice dans les Brahmanas*, 130. Paris: PUF (Bibliothèque de l'École des Hautes Études. Sciences religieuses LXXIII).

Malamoud, Ch. 1976. 'Village et forêt dans l'idéologie de l'Inde brahmanique'. *Archives européennes de Sociologie* 17: 15.

Minard, A. 1949–56. *Trois énigmes sur les cent chemins.* Vols. I and II. Paris: Les Belles-Lettres and CNRS.

Oguibénine, B. 1985. *Essais sur la culture védique et indo-européenne*, 65–6. Pise: Giardini Editori e Stampatori (Testi linguistici 6).

Renou, L. 1939. 'Sur certains emplois d'*a*(*n*)°—privatif en sanskrit et notamment dans le *Rgveda*'. *Bulletin of the School of Oriental and African Studies* 10:18.

———. 1954. *Vocabulaire du rituel védique*, 174. Paris: Klincksieck.

———. 1955. *Études védiques et paninéennes.* Vol. IX. Paris: Éd. de Boccard.

———. 1978. *L'Inde fondamentale.* Études d'indianisme réunies et présentées par Ch. Malamoud, 109. Paris: Hermann.

Renou, L. and J. Filliozat. 1947. *L'Inde classique: Manuel des études indiennes*, I: 578. Paris: Payot.

Schmidt, H.P. 1968. 'The Origin of Ahimsa'. In *Mélanges d'indianisme à la mémoire de Louis Renou*, 625–55. Paris, Éd. de Boccard.

Thite, G.U. 1975. *Sacrifice in the Brahmana-Texts.* Poona: University of Poona.

Verpoorten, J-M. 1977. *L'ordre des mots dans l'Aitareya-Brahmana.* Paris: Les Belles-Lettres.

Wayman, A. 1990. 'The Negative a/an-Prefix in Sanskrit'. In *Sanskrit and Related Studies*, ed. B.K. Matilal and P. Billimoria, 14–23. Delhi, Sri Satguru Publications.

Weber, A. 1868. 'Über Menschenopfer bei den Indern der vedischen Zeit'. *Indische Streifen*, 58. Berlin.

Ancient Brahminism, or Impossible Non-Violence

MADELEINE BIARDEAU

When he made himself the apostle of non-Violent methods, Mahatma Gandhi did not, perhaps, realize that he was thereby effecting a profound transformation of the very meaning of Brahminical *ahimsa*. Discovering *ahimsa* anew, through the prism of Christian values he had gathered in England and in South Africa,[1] he believed that he was rediscovering, formulated in Western terms, the roots of his own culture, and took to it with that much more ardour. *Ahimsa*, it is true, is one of the fundamental concepts whose every aspect was examined by ancient Brahminism. This does not necessarily imply a unanimous presentation of the ideal it proposes. Even if one were to leave aside the *Arthashastra*,[2] one can only be struck by the difference in the treatment of the concept of *ahimsa* in the Dharmashastras [especially in the *Manusmriti* (*MS*)] and in the great epics [essentially the *Mahabharata* (*MBh*)] where it is difficult to know which one preceded the other.

'Non-violence' According to the *Manusmriti*

A quick glance through Chapters V to VII of *MS* offers a useful way of situating the problem posed by *ahimsa*.[3] These chapters deal with rules regarding food and sources of pollution, with the life of ascetics in the forest and with the king respectively. In the first two chapters, the dominant point of view is that of the Brahmin—even at the end of Chapter IV the 'master of the house' is first and foremost a Brahmin—but other social categories are not totally absent (especially when it comes to regulations concerning defilement). Be that as it may, Chapter V, which opens on permitted and forbidden foods, is bound to leave one perplexed. The list of forbidden condiments begins with leeks, garlic, onions and mushrooms that grow on soil that is *amedhya* (impure; literally, soil 'unsuitable for sacrifice').[4] These food items are only forbidden to the *dvija*, or twice-born, although Manu usually applies the term *dvija* only to the Brahmin. The ban is absolute in this case. After a few recommendations regarding the use of curdled milk, there follows an enumeration of carnivorous animals, or, more precisely, predatory and flesh-eating birds, whether in the wild or living near villages, aquatic birds which feed on fish, and practically all kinds of fish. There does not seem to have been a case in which these multifarious creatures were allowed, or a ritual whereby they became edible (V 13–14). The enumeration is punctuated by an enigmatic but peremptory ban on fish (V 15), 'He who eats meat is an eater of that meat. He who eats fish eats every kind of meat: that is why it is necessary to abstain from eating fish.'

The list nevertheless is open ended and the scale of forbidden foods is enhanced by adding wild animals, especially, 'those that are not known' and 'those with five nails' (V 17), with a few exceptions. Finally, however, 'Brahmins may kill wild beasts and birds, so it is recommended, for purposes of sacrifice or in order to feed their household, as Agastya has done so earlier' (V 22).[5] The distinction, therefore, is not one between wild animals and domestic animals (*pasu*). Moreover, its bases remain mysterious, founded on customs and ancient beliefs which escape one entirely. As regards fish, it is tempting to invoke the ever-present *matsya-nyaya* (law of fish), which ordains that fish are impenitent carnivores among whom the small are consumed by the large. In fact, it was something on these lines that Brahma created earlier (V 28-30), 'Immobile creatures are the feedstock of mobile creatures, the toothless ones will be fed on by those with teeth, those without hands will become the nourishment of those with hands, the fearful that of the courageous. . . .'

However, a golden rule is given which, despite taking into account the various forbidden foods enumerated above, still allows the Brahmin to eat meat (V 31), 'Divine injunction holds that meat may only be consumed in the light of sacrifice.' This clause had appeared earlier but here it becomes an imprescriptible injunction; the idea is picked up again in various forms and allows no ambiguity in interpretation (V 32–6),

> Whether he purchases it, whether he culls it from his own livestock or whether it is given to him by another, he who consumes such meat after offering it to the gods and to the ancestors is not soiled. The Brahmin who knows the injunctions[6] cannot consume such meat without adhering to their terms, unless he is in distress. If he so eats without due respect to the

laws, he shall be devoured after his death by the very beasts he himself has eaten, with no recourse open to him. The sin committed by one who kills a wild animal for profit is less heinous in the hereafter than that of one who consumes meat not sanctified as offerings. The Brahmin must never partake of meat that has not been prepared in accordance with ritual formulae, but he must eat meat that has been offered in accordance with the injunction.

The explanation is simple and leaves little room for remorse in the case of one who conforms to Vedic law (V 39–40), 'Sacrificial victims, pasu, were created by Svayambhu himself for the very purpose of sacrifice, for sacrifice works to the good of all. To kill in the course of sacrifice is not to kill at all. Plants, domestic animals, trees, quadrapeds and birds consumed in the sacrificial fire gain access to a higher life form subsequently.'

Until now, the word '*himsa*' has been averted, either as a noun or as a verb. There follow several *shlokas* which speak of killing in cases envisaged by the Vedic injunctions; then it is the form *hims-* which is employed, without however anything being added to what has been so clearly stated. Even in the conclusion (V 44) which calls to mind the verse cited earlier on killing which becomes non-killing in the framework of ritual sacrifice, '*Himsa* as enjoined by the Vedas and applied to mobile and immobile creatures is nothing but *ahimsa: dharma* is made known by the Vedas.' Here, the use of the term '*ahimsa*' is capital: the positive term '*himsa*' must be used so that the corresponding and exact opposite may be gleaned. It is noteworthy, then, that no distinction is made between vegetals and animals. Thus when the text speaks (V 45) of creatures which are *ahimsaka* ('those which must not be killed'), it refers only in fact to plants and animals that may be killed only for purposes of sacrifice.

This seems to produce certain consequences when, as in Chapter VI, there is question of the ascetic in his two forms, as *vanaprastha*, the hermit who inhabits the forest, and as *yati*, the wandering mendicant (the term '*sannyasi*' is practically never used if not completely ignored). The distinction between the two is not well drawn, for Manu affirms (VI 75), 'Owing to *ahimsa*, owing to the detachment of the organs from the senses, owing to Vedic rites and severe austerities—*tapas*—they arrive here and now in that state (Brahman).' Whatever be the conception of deliverance that is articulated here, it links *ahimsa* with Vedic rites and that should hardly occasion any surprise. That *ahimsa* remains intact even if one kills plants and animals for purposes of sacrifice and not out of greed or anger. However, for the ascetic as for the Brahmin 'master of the house', every meal, even if it is vegetarian, is tantamount to a sacrificial offering. In fact, Brahmins even today realise this perfectly well when they place small balls of food around their plate before beginning their meal. Nothing escapes the law of *ahimsa* even as it is being circumvented.

That is not all: the list of forbidden foods began with plants which did not grow on pure soil. Discourse on rules governing food suddenly ceases to make way (in V 57) for rules concerning pollution, ways of being soiled, especially with regard to death and mourning. The most commonly employed terms then are *shuddhi* and *ashuddhi*, *shuddha* and *ashuddha*. It calls to mind the term *amedhya*, 'unfit for sacrifice', used for non-consumable food stuffs. While there is a nuance, since *amedhya* refers to the relationship with sacrifice, the notion of purity and impurity links the two series of terms.

Even as the problem of meat consumption seems to be resolved without great difficulty, new considerations are introduced (V 52–4), just before concluding on the theme:

> None is more guilty than he who augments his flesh with that of another creature without offering it in sacrifice to the gods and the ancestors. The merit of one who never consumes meat is no less than that of one who for a hundred years offers a horse in sacrifice. A diet of fruits and pure roots—*medhya*—and meals like those partaken by hermits confer less merit than abstinence from eating meat.

What else can be eaten then? In the first place, it is merely reiterated that meat may only be consumed within the framework of sacrifice. However, a new dimension is added by introducing the idea that costly royal sacrifices offered over a hundred years and sacrifices involving the consumption of meat bear less merit than pure and simple abstinence from eating meat. Third the diet of ascetics (described as vegetarian) procures less merit than complete abstinence from eating meat. As a matter of fact, it would appear that hermits living in the forest could continue with ritual pursuits, some of which doubtless entailed animal sacrifices. One arrives then at a contradiction whereby ritual activity is forbidden to none, not even to those who seek deliverance; however, abstinence from meat-eating confers the highest merit. While this logic taken in its totality may be difficult to comprehend, it does not detract from the conclusion that vegetarianism had begun to grow into a Brahminical custom. The remark on *ahimsa* seems, at the very least, incomplete, in that on the one hand *himsa* is transformed into *ahimsa* by making the animal sacrifice into a ritual offering to the gods and to the ancestors, and on the other complete abstinence from meat eating is considered superior to all other food—with no reference whatsoever to *ahimsa*. In any case, whether it is the pure or the impure, *himsa* or *ahimsa*, the deepest motivation of the acts they ordain is the protection of the interests of the perpetrator of the act.

With no transition whatsoever, soon after the part on the treatment of human corpses, a new subject crops up, curiously wedged in between the corpses and the rules pertaining to the dead: what of the purity of the king and the rules which govern such purity? The answer is simple and is of interest in that it places the prince alongside holy personages although for reasons specific to himself (V 92–7),

> Nothing is impure amongst kings, nor among those who practise ritual observances or those engaged in a sacrifice. Kings occupy the place of Indra[7] whilst the others are Brahman. The king's sovereign position warrants his immediate purity. The protection he owes his subjects is its cause. As definitively pure are those who perish at the height of a battle, or those struck by lightning or by the hand of a king, or those who die for the protection of a Brahmin or a cow, or yet those nominated by the king (for a particular function). The king combines within himself the eight guardians of the world—the Moon, Fire, the Sun, the Wind, Indra, the Master of Riches and the Master of the Waters.[8] The king is under the aegis of the Lords of the worlds and there is no impurity which attaches to him; otherwise he would never be in a fit condition to act dutifully as a king. Whereas the purity and impurity of ordinary mortals come forth and disappear from the worlds of their own accord. For he who dies in combat in accordance with the *dharma* of a Kshatriya, bearing arms and ready to strike, sacrifice—*yajna*—is a matter of an instant, as is impurity: such is the position.

One may glean two important things from the above account: a king cannot be tainted by impurity, and the first justification offered for that is that his position as the 'sovereign' will not allow him to be impure. He may even instantaneously purify someone whom he designates for a specific task. This concerns him, but also his function. Second, the king's privilege is justified by the fact that the eight *lokapalas* are to be found within him: after all, is he not, on the earth, the guardian of the eight pearls? The justification is a trifle simple. An additional item of information, communicated almost by omission, by preterition as it were, as if one already knows: death in combat is a sacrifice. Obviously, the text, unlike the epic, does not say that war is a sacrifice (for a war has a certain duration), but sacrifice reduced to the act of putting to death is devoid of substance and the impurity of the victim is eliminated at that very instant. This is as important for the victim as for those close to him on the battlefield (although they are never taken into consideration).

It is in Chapter VII that Manu formulates his teaching on the king. He attributes a great deal of power to him, power first controlled by the *danda*—stick, club—which seems to have preceded royalty in the order of creation (VII 14-15), 'This was why the Lord first put forth the *danda*, born of the burning ardour of Brahman, that is to say, *dharma*, his son, protector of all beings. For fear of the *danda*, all creatures, mobile and immobile, are objects and subjects of enjoyment, and say not a word about their *dharma*.' The *danda* is the real king (VII 17–18), 'The *danda* is a virile king, it is the guide, which chastises and, it is said, watches over the *dharma* of the four stages of life. *Danda* ordains, it protects the subjects. When the people sleep, it is *danda* that keeps an eye open. The wise know that it is *dharma*.' *Danda* becomes indispensable because without it people would not know their proper place (VII 20–2),

> If the king did not wield the *danda* without let on those who deserved such chastisement, the strongest would roast the weakest on a brazier like fish. The crow would eat the sacrificial cake, the dog would lick the ghee of the sacrificial offering. Nothing would belong to anyone anymore, everything would be inverted, topsy turvy. The entire world is subjugated by the *danda*, for it is not easy to find a pure man. It is from fear of chastisement that living beings participate in the sensory joys.

This line of thought must be cut off here which carries on, describing endlessly the various categories of creatures at each level of the three worlds. It is as if one had moved from the Dharmashastra to the epic, with one expression that keeps recurring: *bhogaya kalpate*.[9] This is the ordinary world, regulated by *dharma*, whose order it is imperative to maintain. Only the king can do it, and he cannot do it without the *danda*.

The fact remains, however, that the *danda* must be wielded with discrimination, that only those who truly deserve it must be chastised, that violence must not be sought for its own sake. This is applicable as much for policing within the kingdom as in relations with other kingdoms. However, there is no discussion on *himsa* and *ahimsa*: the problem is just not tackled in those terms. There is a sort of royal wisdom that presides over the use of the *danda*. On the part of the sovereign, this calls for self-control, for a domination over his own passions, a specifically royal asceticism. He must seek counsel and his advisers must be chosen from among the families tried and tested for their loyalty to the royal line, and the foremost among these advisers must be a Brahmin of great science. The objective is victory in battle and peace (especially for Brahmins) within the kingdom.

The three basic principles defining the king's duties are: never to flee from combat, to offer protection to his subjects and to respect Brahmins. The rules of combat which a good warrior must observe (VII 90–3) are not specific to the *MS* and are to be found equally in the *MBh* and elsewhere. However, the absence of the term *sharana*, so important in the epic, is noteworthy; *sharana*, implying 'seeking refuge in someone'—the moment a person seeks such refuge, all intention of slaying him must be abandoned, even on the battlefield.

Taken all in all, there is nothing new in the conception of royal power and there is some haziness in the examination of the act of violence and its opposite. The *MS* is a code of laws and not an ideological treatise giving form to a system of socio–religious beliefs and notions. Besides, in its initial cosmogony the text offers a peculiarity which needs to be pointed out. While its cosmogony strongly echoes the great Puranas and the epic, it makes no mention whatever of Vishnu. It does, to be sure, repeat the momentous, 'etymological' stanza which declines the name of *Narayana* (I 10), but it is *Brahma Pitamaha* who is thus designated. Manu pays no attention to or does not know the great gods of epic *bhakti*. It is possible, then, to postulate that his code of laws is meant above all to be 'Vedic', founded on injunctions—*vidhi*—made by texts on ritual, without reference to a supreme divinity nor to that divinity's 'descent' on earth at times of crisis. It could be a possible line for codification of Brahminism which seeks to be closer to Vedic teaching, without however neglecting the organization of the Brahminical society that had sprung from this teaching rather than within it. While it may have attracted fewer followers than the *bhakti* ideology, and may have had less of a future, it was instrumental in shaping a line of specially vigilant and uncompromising Brahmins to whom it owes its reputation for 'orthodoxy'.

The Epic Doctrine

The epic introduces one to a solidly constructed and logically ordained universe. Only those points will be reconsidered which have already been examined in the *MS*, so that one may more precisely analyse what is *ahimsa*. While the *MS* looked at them from the point of view of the Brahmin, the epic, as was to be expected, focuses on problems posed to the functioning of royalty within Brahminism. In other words, the Brahmin retains his pre-eminent status, but the king's duty towards him is carefully analysed and included in the overall Brahminical system. Nowhere does the *MBh* claim that the prince is pure by definition because he must be pure in order to exercise his royal functions.

However, there is no question here any more of Brahminism: the supreme reference is in fact to the supreme god, Vishnu, and to his correlate, Rudra-Shiva, who is complementary to him, while Brahma maintains, at the level of the creation of the world, a creative and organizing function which is a reminder that he is the personification of Vedic revelation. Vishnu and Rudra-Shiva, who were central deities in Vedic ritual, have now become the supreme *Yogins*, the ultimate form of the divine, transcending rites, transcending division into hierarchical *varnas*, promising deliverance from the cycle of births and deaths to all those who practise their own *dharma* on earth. Not that they are disinterested in the fate of the world itself, which transmigrates in its totality with the majority of its denizens vouchsafed to eternal transmigration. This is what prompts Vishnu, duly assisted by the gods in heaven and taking sometimes the form of Rudra-Shiva, consuming the world like the flames of a sacrificial fire, and sometimes the form of Brahma, in order to create, to descend on earth and save *dharma* from peril. It is immediately clear that in essence there is a link between the *avatara*—Krishna, in the *MBh*—and the king who must wield the *danda* to ensure that every subject stays within his or her own *dharma*.[10] In a word, one is in the universe of Brahminical *bhakti*, which introduces the promise of strong nuances to a future that appears more certain and far less constrained than that offered by the *MS*.

Rather than focussing our attention on the *Bhagavad Gita* (*BhG*), the teachings dispensed by Krishna on the battlefield, just before the outbreak of the eighteen day war, to Arjuna, the Pandava who embodies royalty par excellence although he is not a king in name, we shall take up Arjuna's instructions to his elder brother, King Yudhisthira, who wishes to retire to the forest and live as an ascetic in order to expiate the guilt of a bloody conflict fought to preserve *dharma*. Arjuna cannot but highlight the doctrine he has received from the *avatara*, Krishna, and it is he, rather than Bhishma, the great instructor in Book XII, who applies the epic doctrine in all its rigour.

So much does Arjuna's praise of the *danda* echo the *MS* that they even have two *shlokas* in common. The *danda* and *dharma* are practically identical [*MBh* XII 15, 2–4a; id.(*)], 'The *danda* gives orders to all the subjects and also protects them. *Danda* is vigilant while they sleep. The wise know that *danda* is *dharma* itself. *Danda*, O prince, protects *dharma* as well as *artha* and *kama*. *Dharma*, it is said, is *trivarga* (the totality of the three "objectives of man"). It defends the harvest and protects wealth.' *Danda* can only be chastisement in all the diverse forms it assumes according to the circumstances in which it is applied (15, 11–13; id.), 'When the red-eyed, sombre *danda* moves about ready to rain down, then all living beings can no longer remain in a state of confusion if their guides know what is good for them. The Vedic scholar, the "master of the house", the forest-dwelling hermit and the mendicant ascetic, though they may be what they are, will adhere to the right path only through fear of the *danda*.' *Danda* does not only protect *trivarga*, but the four 'stages of life', which to Arjuna seem to mean pretty much the same thing, for the third and fourth *ashrama* are included in the *trivarga* if one takes care to note that *moksha* is 'the desire to obtain deliverance' and thereby includes a desire, *kama*, even as its grammatical form implies.

Danda does not apply to human society alone, or only to the human beings who constitute it, but to their environment as well (15, 36–43),

> If they did not fear the *danda*, birds and beasts of prey would eat up livestock and men and offerings meant for sacrifice. The Vedic scholar would cease his studies, milch cows would not be milked and young women would not marry. Negligence would be widespread, barriers would be broken down and it would be impossible to identify one's own if *danda* did not exist. None would remain in a year-long sacrificial ceremony for the mere fee ordained by law if *danda* did not exist. None would practise the *dharma* which conforms to his own stage of life in accordance with Vedic injunctions, nor even would anyone be interested in knowing them if *danda* did not exist. Only *danda* ensures that camels and bullocks, donkeys and mules consent to be hitched to a vehicle. But for *danda*, neither domestic servants nor little children would obey, nor would maidens observe their *dharma*. All creatures exist owing to *danda* and fear it: the wise know it. In the eyes of man, the heavens like the very earth are founded solidly on *danda*.

In this respect, Arjuna is in agreement with Manu: *danda* is a sort of king who pre-exists the king and which controls absolutely everything on earth. *Danda* is the principle whereby the entire terrestrial world including even animals, is ordained, in accordance with Vedic injunctions. Its power derives from the fear it inspires. And that fear pervades every aspect of human society, from the top to the very bottom of the scale.

Arjuna, however, goes further, not hesitating to emphasize the importance of the capacity to kill as a means of defining the greatness of a king, his *Shri*.[11] Says Arjuna (15, 14–19),

> The King gains no great splendour, no Shri, if he does not strike his enemy at vital points, if he does not accomplish feats, if he does not put unto death as a fisherman does. He who does not kill obtains neither renown nor wealth nor subjects in this world. Indra became the God of gods only by killing Vritra. Only the gods who kill are worshipped here, as Rudra, Skanda, Sakra, Agni, Varuna and Yama. Fatal too, Oh Bharata, are Time, the Wind, Death, Kubera, the Sun, the Vasus, the Maruts, the Sadhyas, the Visvedevas. Those who have known suffering lie prostrate before these gods, never before Brahma, Dhatra or Pusan. Only those who in their own lives are pacific, only they prostrate before gods who remain neutral against all creatures, masters of themselves and resolved in the cause of peace.

There is no question any longer of instantaneous purity or of violence reduced to a minimum. The king's vocation, so to say, is the exercise of force, which can never be better displayed than in laying low an enemy, whether it is the enemy within or without. The gods whose names are invoked are not those who constitute the king (as the *MS* suggests), but those who have given proof of their martial prowess, their capacity to kill, like the fishermen (forever fish on the horizon), and it is interesting to note the denial of worship to Brahma and to his alter ego *Dhatra*, which is in line with well known facts. *Danda* is not just any kind of chastisement. It is most visible in the use of brutal and triumphant strength. One may also note in passing that just a few peace-minded individuals have any consideration for gods with a pacific disposition. Violence and its absence, here, may be directly defined in relation to a certain type of action. No mention is made of what these exceptions are, but what follows hereunder may offer a glimpse. The prince, however, makes no secret of his belief that these people are nursing illusions.

Other passages from the epic demonstrate that the Brahmin is the one who remains committed to peace and to *ahimsa* and to obtain these he must respect the king, the only one who can create the environment of security necessary for him to lead such a pure life. He is the first to realize that if he can lead his life according to his own *dharma*, it is only because someone else exercises violence on his account. In other words, non-violence is never posited as an indivisible ideal: there are agents meant for violence who enable Brahmins, specifically the ascetics amongst them, to practise a *dharma* of peace. The epic goes farther still, without however denying this complementarity.

Arjuna continues his praise of strength and the properly regulated exercise of strength with a plea about the impossible ideal that is *ahimsa*, which does not merely take into account royal duties (15, 20–28),

> I see no one subsisting in this world with the practice of *ahimsa*. As a matter of fact, the stronger live off the weaker. The mongoose eats the mouse, as the cat eats the mongoose. The dog eats the cat as the beast of prey eats the dog. As for man, O prince, he eats everything. See the course of Time and how all creatures, mobile and immobile, become nourishment to him, to living beings. He who knows that all this is preordained by destiny (*daiva*, in the least unacceptable translation) is not troubled by it. Be true then, O king, to the manner in which you have been created. For the foolish ones, who control their wrath and their joy and retire to the forest, cannot, without killing, procure unto themselves what is needed to sustain themselves. For numerous are the beings who live in water, in the soil and in fruits. And it is not true that none kills them: how else could one subsist? Logic teaches us that there are hordes of minuscule creatures who will be slain by a single flap of an eyelid. We see ascetics, free of anger and selfishness, leaving their village and retiring to the forest and then, completely at a loss, beginning anew in the forest the rules of their family lives: they split the soil, pluck plants, mutilate trees, kill birds and animals. Such men celebrate sacrifices and reach heaven.

Ahimsa, then, is impossible: as this evocation of the infinitely small unfolds, can Pascal be far behind? There is, to be sure, no pathos, no mystic terror; it is a matter of logic. And when such a venerable text as the *MBh* preaches thus the impossibility of abstaining from violent acts, it is difficult to gain an overview of a culture which attaches so much importance to *ahimsa*. What is even more interesting, however, is that the negation of this 'non-violence' goes hand in hand with the negation of abstinence from acting at all. The words of Krishna in the *BhG* (III 22–4, IV 5 sq.) still resound in one's ears. Even as he reaffirms the fact that he, as Supreme God, has neither need nor desire, he continues incessantly to act for the betterment of the worlds. He reminds Arjuna of his duty as a warrior. He does not go so far as to deny the eternal *Purusha*, the possibility of non-action, or, to put it simply, abstinence from ritual acts. However, in the eyes of Krishna, to act is to be liberated, if the act is in accordance with *dharma* and if it is detached from the quest for personal gain. The culmination of spiritual quest is neither in abstinence from action nor in ritual exactitude, but in the attainment of complete detachment from the 'fruits' of one's acts, be it even the death of one's own family's adversaries in battle. An act may be committed for the wellbeing of all the worlds, as by an *avatara*, in which case the question of *ahimsa* is displaced. More accurately, it becomes increasingly the province of the Brahmin, whilst detachment from the 'fruits' of one's action confers deliverance upon the non–Brahmin as much as *ahimsa* does upon the Brahmin. The *BhG* does not, in fact, claim to offer a choice between the two paths. It merely indicates both as possibilities which produce the same results in the hereafter. However, it pleads for sacrifice without restraint. Nevertheless, the ideal of abstinence from action must have made some progress among certain Brahmin milieus (at least), going by the fact that towards the end of the *Gita* Krishna feels obliged to emphasize what he calls 'renunciation' or 'detachment' (*tyaga*). This, depending on the context, is the forsaking of that which has been offered to the gods in sacrifice, the gifts one offers (to Brahmins in particular), or the austerities that take the place of the comforts of ordinary life (*BhG* XVIII 4–5). To renounce a prescribed act (*sannyasa*) is incorrect, the fruit of *tamas* or blind ignorance (XVIII 7, to be compared with III 4). The four *varnas*, reminds Krishna, have their own *dharma* (ibid. 41–4) and the golden rule is to adhere to it and to Him, the Blissful One (ibid. 53–5),

> He who is shorn of the ego, of violence (*bala*), of pride, of desire, of anger and of envy, he who has no sense of "mine", "my own", is at peace, becomes Brahman. The pacified soul, on becoming Brahman, is free of worry, of expectation, is placed at the same level with all of creation and acquires supreme devotion to Me. In that devotion, he knows Me, as I am in reality, and thus knowing Me, he enters Me immediately.

These are the last teachings of Krishna, the rest being a *stuti*, or a verse in praise of the text. Devotion unto Krishna encompasses the Vedas (Brahman) and is not meant to be a substitute for it.

The obvious must be accepted: the *himsa/ahimsa* couple is absent in the *BhG*, whereas the dialogue opens with Arjuna's pain on seeing arrayed against him his relatives and masters, whom he will be obliged to kill.[12] In exchange, Krishna offers a clearly articulated doctrine for action: a doctrine which includes the overriding preoccupation with salvation and which is resumed in two terms—*tyaga* and *bhakti*. When he rails about the impossibility of *ahimsa*, Arjuna is by no means betraying the teachings of his master. Conversely, when Krishna uses the term '*naishkarmya*' (non-action) it is in the sense that when action is correctly understood it becomes *naishkarmya* (XVIII 47–8), 'O son of Kunti, even if it bears a defect, the type of act ordained by birth should not be abandoned. Every enterprise carries its own weakness, even as fire shrouds itself in smoke. Detached in mind, with complete mastery of self and freedom from desire, thus we proceed, by renunciation (*sannyasa*), towards the supreme perfection of non-action (*naiskarmya*).' The vocabulary of the renouncer of the Upanishads is thus perfectly translated by the god into an ideal of action for the wellbeing of all the worlds, without attachment to one's self, but with devotion to the supreme divinity.

The Killing (of a Brahmin)

A myth in the *MBh* presents a new dimension to *ahimsa*, although it is not spoken of directly for, as one has seen, this is not what it really sets out to do. However, this is a question for the Brahmins of the epic to grapple with. Thus, it is hardly surprising to discover it in one form or another in this story where the Brahmin players are as important as the kings, for neither can live without the other.

The Brahmin Drona appears in Chapters 130–1 (121–2) of Book I of the *MBh*. One knows he is the incarnation on earth of Brihaspati, the spiritual master of the gods. According to the epic, Drona is born to the apparently unmarried Brahmin, Bharadvaja, a *rishi*. Like a number of other heroes of the epic, Drona too is born *ayoni*, that is without passing through a human womb. His father was quite simply moved at the sight of the *apsaras* Ghritachi, emerging after a bath in the river dressed in the most scanty clothings. Bharadvaja's semen fell to the ground, which he carefully gathered up again in a *drona*, a vessel used in sacrifice (eventually used for *soma*). Thus was the child Drona formed. His father raises him as a forest-bound ascetic, as he himself was. At the feet of the sage Agnivesha, Drona learns how to wield the secret weapon *Agneya*. This, no doubt, was a way of conferring a specific martial power on him. At the same time, Drona also learns the Vedas and the allied texts, along with the young prince, Drupada, son of king Prishata. The two young men become friends, as is inevitable between those who are disciples of the same master. Obliged to return to his royal duties, Drupada swears eternal friendship to Drona who continues to lead the life of a hermit in the forest, even after the death of his father. Drupada accedes to the throne after his father passes on.

Desirous of having a son, Drona marries the pious and ritual-obeying Kripi, daughter of the sage Gautama Saradvat, and twin sister of Kripa. The twins too were born *ayoni*, exactly as Drona had been, only the *apsaras* in question was Janapadi. It would be erroneous not to dwell on how much the very names of the two *apsaras* placed them in opposition to each other. Ghritachi evokes ghee, clarified butter (*ghrta*), essential to ritual sacrifice. Janapadi, on the contrary, derives her name from 'country with its inhabitants', an expression that denotes a kingdom. Gautama Saradvat is one of those redoubtable Brahmins with martial inclinations who prefers the art of archery to Vedic studies, although he has successfully completed the latter. His *tapas* enables him to obtain a great number of magic weapons, until Indra sends Janapadi to tempt him. She produced on him precisely the effect Ghritachi produced on Bharadvaja. However, Gautama Saradvat's semen fell on a clump of reeds (*sharastamba*) and he, the warrior Brahmin, rose again precipitously, leaving nearby his bow, his arrows (*shara*) and his black antelope skin, as a 'signature' of his semen. Twins, a boy, Kripa, and a girl, Kripi, were born of the fertilization of a bunch of reeds and arrows. While Kripa seemed to have inherited the passion for weaponry rather than a taste for royalty, Kripi, the complementary 'Brahmin with martial inclinations', appeared to be more inclined towards royal power.[13]

At any rate, marriage completely transforms the ascetic life of Drona. Soon a son is born to him, who neighs like a horse (a royal animal) at birth, and is therefore referred to as Asvatthaman. Drona desires to possess arms and wealth. He obtains the former from the great Parashurama as that sage, after his feats, prepared to retire to the Himalayas. Then Drona goes to see his old friend, Drupada, now a king. He is given a cold welcome, without even the customary courtesies being extended to him, since Drona had the temerity to describe himself as a friend of the king. Drupada maintains that there can be no friendship between two such dissimilar people, separated not only by wealth and power but also by science. Drona is poor, but he seeks a means to wreak his vengeance. He comes into contact with Bhishma, the great-uncle of the Kauravas and the Pandavas, the cousin-brothers who are to become enemies. Bhishma makes Drona teach weaponry to all the young princes of the lunar dynasty, whom the great warriors of the future war would join.

Quickly, Drona marks Arjuna out as the best of his disciples and places all his hopes in him. He goes to the extent of giving him the secret Brahminical weapon whereby the power of a Brahmin would be conferred on Arjuna although he himself is a Kshatriya and a warrior. Arjuna, however, is too virtuous to misuse the weapon. On the completion of their studies, when it is time to pay the guru his fee, it is Arjuna who, in league with his brothers and cousin-brothers, mounts an attack on Drupada's kingdom. Drupada's capital is occupied, the king himself is taken prisoner and brought to Drona. Drona once again offers Drupada his friendship. However, with a view to reassure his friend about their 'equality', he keeps the northern half of Drupada's kingdom, leaving his friend the southern half, forever bespoiled symbolically.

Drupada, realizing that he did not have the stature to take on a Brahmin who combined in himself *brahman* as well as *kshatra*, i.e. the powers of the Brahmin as well as those of the Kshatriya-king, seeks through an elaborate sacrifice to gain a suitable Kshatriya son capable of killing the Brahmin, Drona. This was a complex sacrifice, which involved normal and legitimate sacrificial activity as well as *abhichara*, or rituals accomplished to obtain the death of someone, what would now be referred to as 'black magic'.

One is now in that context of the epic where *ahimsa* will be declared impossible,[14] although it has not yet been declared thus. The violence of the sacrifice itself is not as much in play as the violence expressed by the master of the sacrifice wishing to kill an enemy through it. Drupada looks for Brahmins capable of celebrating such a sacrifice (I 167; 155: this is the third account one has of the relationship between Drona and Drupada, but the only one of the birth of Draupadi and her brother). In a 'colony' of particularly pious Brahmins, Drupada comes upon Yaja and Upayaja, sons of Tarana ('She who grants Salvation') and Kashyapa. He offers them bounteous gifts and consults them, in order to form his own opinion about them. His choice falls upon the younger Upayaja, of whom he becomes a disciple and devotee. Finally, he asks him what sort of sacrifice must be performed to beget a son who could kill Drona. If Upayaja agreed to be the officiating priest, Drupada would give him ten million cows as remuneration, or whatever else the young Brahmin chose. Upayaja refuses, but Drupada is unrelenting in his services and in the honours he showers upon him. After a year, Upayaja suggests another solution: one day, in the darkest depths of the forest, he saw his elder brother gather a fallen fruit, without bothering to verify the state of purity of the soil and without pausing to check the fruit for defects, which could be interpreted as a grave sin. Yaja studied the Vedas in the home of his master where he was accustomed to consuming leftover food given as alms, singing his praises without the slightest trace of disgust. Manifestly, says Upayaja, his elder brother desires 'fruits' and only evaluates things according to his own desire. Perhaps Drupada should ask Yaja to celebrate the sacrifice.

Overcoming his repugnance at having to address a less 'pure' Brahmin, the king goes to Yaja's hermitage. He comes directly to the subject. Drupada offers Yaja only eighty thousand cows! He narrates his encounter with Drona and his inability as a Kshatriya to avenge himself on this Brahmin warrior, who was instructor to the Kaurava clan. Drona, like Parashurama, could destroy the entire Kshatriya class. Drupada expresses his desire to have a son who could slay Drona. He seeks Yaja's help in performing the sacrifice (*tat karma kuru*), this time promising him ten million cows. Yaja accepts and prepares whatever is necessary for the ritual sacrifice. He promises Drupada that the sacrifice will be performed for the elimination of Drona; in view of its importance, he involves his younger brother, Upayaja, who seeks no profit for himself. Upayaja briefs the king about the sacrifice performed in three fires; the king will have a son, with all the warrior-like qualities, ardour and strength the king could desire (without specifying to what end these qualities will be applied). Thus the 'fruits' sought by the master of the sacrifice is divided into two, between the two people officiating. The king evokes a son in his thoughts as the future killer of Drona and prepares everything for the success of the rite. Yaja, for his part, calls upon the queen to be ready for the moment when the two children will be born, but in vain, for the queen claims she is not ready, and as the time has come to complete the sacrifice, they must make do without her. It is Yaja who pours the offering into the fire. Immediately, there surges forth a young man, as bright and handsome as a god, bearing a crown, a shield and arms and emitting loud battle cries. He climbs aboard a chariot and rides away, acclaimed by the Panchalas. The very earth quivers under this tumult but a celestial voice proclaims that Drupada's worries are at an end: he has a glorious son who will slay Drona.

Yaja had, in fact, announced that there would be twins. At that very moment, from the middle of the sacrificial altar there issues a young princess, Panchali, black-eyed and dark of hue, bearing on her person the fragrance of a lotus that could be sensed even at great distance. The celestial voice announces that this, the most beautiful of women,

Krishnaa, seeks the defeat of the Kshatriyas and she will perform the deed on behalf of the gods. The Kauravas would face great danger from her. The Panchalas scream in joy and the earth trembles. The queen, finally coming along, desires that the two children should know no mother but herself, cloaking their birth in secrecy—a secret perhaps for the two people concerned but an event proclaimed openly by the whole world. The prince is Dhristadyumna, the incarnation of Agni, Fire, and the princess, Krishnaa, becomes better known by the patronymic, Draupadi. She is represented sometimes as an incarnation of *Shri*, sometimes as that of *Indrani*, consort of Indra, king of the gods. As she issued forth from the very middle of the sacrificial altar, she symbolizes the Earth, in its warrior—like and triumphant aspect, even as the Earth itself trembles in terror as signs appear of the impending conflict.

A Brahmin narrates this account of the twin births to the Pandavas by a Brahmin, while the Pandavas are hiding in the forest, after surviving an attempt by their cousins to murder them. The Brahmin exhorts them to participate in Draupadi's *svayamvara*. There, Arjuna, disguised as a Brahmin, wins the contest and marries Draupadi, along with his four brothers (*MBh* 188–9; 179–80). Dhristadyumna kills Drona in combat, with one important qualification: the Brahmin, knowing that his time had come, had already laid arms and assumed a *yogic* posture. When Dhristadyumna chops off his head, he is already dead.

Obviously, the ritual sacrifice sought to be performed by Drupada poses a problem to the Brahmin who worries about purity, but there is no question at any moment of killing, of a desire to kill a Brahmin, of *himsa*. Violence is not the important factor here, although it is of a two-pronged nature (destruction of a sacrificial offering, whatever it may be, and the killing that results from it), but the very impurity of Brahminicide. The fact that the elder of the two officiating priests is less preoccupied with purity enables the sacrifice to be performed in the first place, but the impurity is evidently related to premeditated murder. Only the elder brother is responsible for it, as it is only he who seeks to receive the massive remuneration offered by the king. The younger brother owes obedience to his elder brother, but seeks nothing for himself and is therefore no part of the impurity of the act, although his presence probably adds remarkably to its efficacy. The impurity would be less if the death were not that of a Brahmin. That analysis presupposes that ritual sacrifices made without desire yield no 'fruits' for he who performs them, which is the doctrine of the *Gita*.

CONCLUSION

It could be said that violence in itself does not pose a problem to the most punctilious Hindu conscience, for one is concerned here with high caste conceptions. The doctrine advanced by the *MBh* is a Brahminical creation which hones the interaction between the two highest *varnas* of society. War becomes as pure as ritual sacrifice, for it is indeed a sort of sacrifice which can be perpetrated for the greater good of all the worlds and not for one's own well-being. Some fundamental questions need to be raised: When does a king prosecute a war with no thought to the benefit he may reap from it? Or yet, is it always true that a king must fight wars for the good of his kingdom, to say nothing of all the worlds? However, it is here that the Hindu response leaves no recourse. The Panchalas scream in joy when they learn that Krishnaa will enable the destruction of the Kshatriyas. That is necessary for the maintenance of order in all the worlds, not only for their own wellbeing. The princess' brother must kill the Brahmin warrior who humiliated his father. This would lead the world into a generalized crisis in which the Kshatriyas would be destroyed, the Panchalas themselves included. The very earth quivers in fear, and Draupadi shall suffer from it too, as will her husbands. However, the restoration of order must necessarily pass through that phase. If the question of violence, in its modern and western sense, must be raised at all, then *dharma* must not be the all-encompassing value of the three worlds, which it is in the universe of *bhakti*, where *moksha* is included among the ultimate objectives of man but cannot escape the application of *dharma*. The whole overwhelms the individual. That essential intermediary link is lacking, to which one refers often with some hypocrisy, as the other, or the outsider, or the neighbour, which takes into account the different ethico-religious nuances that go with these terms.[15]

NOTES

* The first number refers to the Poona edition of 1929 and the second to the critical Poona edition.

1. Here, to be sure, is a matter of ideology and one shall take as given that Brahminical and later Hindu non-violence is not more closely related to the actual history of the land of the Bharatas than Christian charity is to the overall history of the West. There is no room, in this short paper,

to take any further the comparison between East and West, for that would lead us to place two philosophies of action in opposition to each other, or nothing less than two world views which place too many things in conflict.

2. See Charles Malamoud's essay elsewhere in this volume.
3. The Sanskrit term shall be used rather than its Western rendition which, as one shall see, is not quite satisfactory and allows for *contresens* (counter-meanings).
4. *MS* V 5.
5. The *Mahabharata* too grants such a margin to Agastya (*MBh* I: 118, 14; 109, 14).
6. One renders, as 'injunction' the word '*vidhi*', a technical term used by the *Mimamsa* to describe all imperative rules of Vedic rituals, which is also synonymous with *codana.*
7. See the scene in *MBh* III 43 and 44, where Indra shares his throne with Arjuna who has just reached heaven.
8. To my mind, this still does not confer divinity on the king, although it is most frequently interpreted thus. The same idea is expressed in the epic where the context indicates that the king is not god, or rather not God, that is to say, Vishnu as an *avatara.*
9. Stanzas VII 18 and 25 are reproduced verbatim by Arjuna in his eulogy of the *danda* in XII 15, 2 and 11; id.
10. This should not lead to hasty conclusions about how the god housed in a temple and the *avatara* are identical, and from there to the formulation of conclusions about the royal nature of *avataras*. However, that is another problem: mention must be made in particular of 'regional' gods (*avataras* like Narasimha, or Subrahmanya, son of Shiva) who have two temples dedicated to them, one atop a hillock, the other at its base, each temple fulfilling different functions.
11. This entire section summarizes briefly pages from *Etudes de mythologie hindoue*, vol. II: *Bhakti* and *avatara,* Paris, EFEO, 1994.
12. There is, as a matter of fact, one stanza in which the term '*himsa*' is used and, a little later, one in which the term '*himsatmaka*' associated with *asuci* (impure) appears (*BhG* XVIII 25 and 27). Violence in that case is the unbridled use of force under the influence of anger or passion. He who is prey to such violence is 'impure'. Needless to say, the act committed by *himsa* is impelled by *tamas.*
13. Among the twins, the Brahmin-prince is the warrior whilst the Brahmin-princess would be the soil of the kingdom in quest of a king. See later the birth of Dhristadyumna and Draupadi.
14. The *Mimamsa* speaks of this kind of sacrifice and forbids it (*Sabarabhasya* I, 1, 2, p. 19, *Anandashrama Sanskrit Series*, Poona, 1943). The commentary *Prabha* (ibid.) cites the *mantra na himsyat sarva bhutani* (see M. Biardeau (1964), *Theorie de la connaissance et philosophie de la parole dans le*

brahmanisme classique, Mouton, Paris-La Haye, index, s.v.); *ahimsa*, 'No harm must be willed unto any creature.' This is an ancient Vedic formulation, given the form of the neutral accusative *sarva* for *sarvani*, which shows that sacrifice quickly raised problems even to ritualists. In this form, it could render the positive *hims-* in order to express slaying or the violence of death. Ritual sacrifice is always linked to a particular desire. Even the *Mimamsa* accept what one would refer to as 'black magic' if someone were really incapable of controlling his desire, though it is said that a ritual sacrifice is meant for the wellbeing of all and cannot target the death of someone. The death in question of course is not that of the sacrificial victim but of the person who is aimed at as the object of the ritual sacrifice. This is the case of the sacrifice performed by Drupada, a clear-cut case of *abhichara*.

15. There are, needless to say, situations defined by *dharma* in which the Other counts, for example, the unexpected guest who cannot be allowed to depart without being duly honoured, especially if he is a Brahmin. On the battlefield, an adversary who avows defeat and seeks grace is entitled to compassion and to the protection of he who has triumphed against him. The other, then, is one who is clearly defined by his situation at a particular moment, and who is treated in accordance with the context governed by *dharma*. The notion of 'human rights as such' simply has no meaning.

The Violences of a Hindu Village

The Suicide of a Young Woman: 'Legitimate Violence' and Dominant Castes in Central India

JEAN-LUC CHAMBARD

In the first week of September 1988, on my way to the village of Piparsod (Madhya Pradesh), which I visit once a year,[1] I halted at the town of Shivpuri, after completing a train and bus journey that had begun at Delhi and taken me through Gwalior. At Shivpuri, a mere 18 km from Piparsod, I have a number of old friends, amongst whom is a lawyer, a native of the village, with whom I spend some days on each of my arrivals. This contact generally yields rich information, for Shivpuri has a whole colony of people from the village. Some are settled there temporarily, mainly for the education of their children, whilst others live there permanently, having first fled the countryside at a time when dacoits in the Chambal valley, the bandit-queen Phoolan Devi amongst them, terrorized the rural gentry. They had decided to remain in the town even after the Sarvodaya Movement led by Jayaprakash Narayan (who died in 1979 before seeing the success of his efforts) had obtained the surrender of the dacoits in the years 1982 and 1983.[2] I had barely entered the office of my lawyer-friend when I noted the presence of a number of people from the village who awaited to give me the bad news: just about a fortnight earlier, the daughter-in-law of the brother of Nathuram the barber, had committed suicide by throwing herself into the Brahmin well. As her body had been discovered only at noon the next day, it meant that those Brahmins who had performed their morning rituals on the curbstone with water drawn from the well, had either bathed in or consumed 'cadaver juice', thus polluting themselves. The *sarpanch* had summoned a general assembly of all the villagers, including the Untouchables, which was unheard of in living memory. In the presence of one and all, with great vehemence he had attacked the barber clan. He made them acknowledge their guilt and accept the task of purifying the well, a task that had been accomplished at a great cost just a few days before my arrival, for it entailed pumping out the water, cleaning the well and then replenishing it with Ganga water specially brought there in a tanker.

I was stunned by this account of cumulative catastrophes, in which I felt morally and financially involved. Ever since my first stay in the village, between 1957 and 1964, Nathuram had been a precious source of information to me. I had taken him with me to France, and he had spent a year in Paris, working with me on the songs I had recorded. As a result, the council of his caste had resolved that on his return he would forfeit the right to practise his profession. Following this, as I continued to get research done by him (to update the genealogies I had collected, for instance), I felt it would only be fair and just for me to take him under my wing by regularly sending him a sort of pension which soon became his main source of subsistence. The residents of the village knew only too well that he received this support from me. It ensured his solvency and enhanced his prestige among his caste brethren, in the village as well as in the region as a whole (which was a great help to him in finding sons-in-law; it may be mentioned that in addition to his other difficulties was the fact that he only had daughters—eleven in all, seven of whom survived and four of those who survived were married at the time of writing this article).[3] Hearing this account, with all the singularly serious implications it had in the Hindu context, I wondered if the support of a foreigner would not in fact complicate matters for Nathuram. I had to take into account the revival in the strength of the traditional ideas, which I had been observing for some years in the village. An increasingly warm welcome was being reserved for activist votaries of Hindu fundamentalism, against the backdrop of the Bharatiya Janata Party's (BJP) campaign for the construction of a temple at Ayodhya, the birthplace of Ram, the great epic hero.

A Vengeful Suicide?

How had this incredible event come to pass? After settling down in the house I have owned in the village for some years, I patiently reconstructed the chain of events relying upon the testimony I gathered. I did not have much time for this inquiry, as my stay would only last for six weeks and I would need to leave in mid-October. However, I had the advantage of already knowing fairly well the characters involved in the drama.

On the evening before the suicide, disputes had arisen in the family of Nathuram's brother. The two brothers' houses adjoin each other and share a courtyard. Disputes though frequent never worried anyone. Nathuram's nephew was called Bhagirath. Having failed to obtain the much coveted job of an office orderly (*chaprasi*) either in the local school or in the town, this twenty–eight year old continued in the family profession, that of a barber. A fine figure of a man, he was also very vain. Frequently, he would ask me to take pictures of him in the most extravagant of costumes—flared trousers, loud colourful shirts, and, above all, the inescapable, large sun glasses that made him look like a hero of a popular Indian film. For eight years, he had been married to a young woman named Baijanti, daughter of a barber in the distant village of Thagausa. She was only twelve years old when they married but did not come to Piparsod until several years later, when she was sixteen. To add to her status, she was also the mother of a handsome, little boy, two and a half years old, though she was no more than nineteen herself. Conditions seemed ideal for the two of them to found a happy home. Yet, husband and wife were constantly at loggerheads. Their loud bickerings, supposedly stoked by the mother-in-law, could be heard by the neighbours. It was no secret that Bhagirath did not look upon his wife as beautiful, describing the slit-eyed, high cheekboned woman as a *junglee*, a 'daughter of the jungle'. A Western film-maker would surely not have shared the husband's opinion. As the customs of his caste allowed him the right to take another wife, Bhagirath was amenable to the idea. Tongues wagged that the disputes were engineered so as to drive the woman into the arms of another man, for she too was allowed the same right. As this was the outcome expected, no one suspected that danger may lurk in that home. The final course of events, however, proved to be completely different—driven to despair, the young woman decided to put an end to her life.

Why in a well? This is the traditional means of suicide adopted locally, by women in particular. On the far western side of Piparsod village, there lies the *Harbavri* well, with its rickety curbstone (*jhonda*), in which the ashes of the dead are thrown (with the exception of the 'flowers' or non-incinerated remnants of small bones, which are carried to the Ganga for immersion; water from the Ganga is drawn and brought back to the village for distribution to all those invited to partake of the funereal feast on the thirteenth day). Albinos, who are not entitled to be cremated on their death, are thrown into the well bound to an animal (usually a goat) which takes the place of the person who is supposed to accompany them on their journey to heaven or hell. This well is where most suicides by women take place (Chambard 1980: 55 and map 41 'Cult sites distant from the village'). Prakash Narayan, son of my late and much revered Brahmin Guru, Gopilal Panditji, told me that this was an echo of the salvation-seeking ritual suicides that used to take place in the Ganga at Prayag (Allahabad)—after all, the Ganga flows in every well and in every body of water in every Indian village.[4] Anyway, the *Harbavri* well had caved in and been without water for at least fifteen years, though funereal ashes continued to be thrown into it.

Why did Baijanti choose the Brahmin well? This raises a serious question and it is difficult not to discern a vengeful motive in the young woman's suicide. Obviously, we must take note of the late hour: at one o' clock in the morning, she may have chosen one of the two wells more readily accessible from her home. However, it needs to be pointed out that she was part of the barber clan that is specifically attached to the Brahmins, one of the village's two dominant castes. (The other powerful caste, the Kirars, have their own 'dedicated' barbers at their service.) Accordingly, the barbers were allowed to dwell in the heart of the Brahmin quarter. As the crow flies, *Manaiya Kua*, where the suicide took place, is not more than 100 m away. This well is incontestably the most prestigious well in the locality. As one enters the village from the northern side, after leaving the bus stop on the main road some 700 or 800 m away, the first constructions that greet one are of the Hanuman temple (the statue of the monkey god is believed to be the foundation stone of the village) and, opposite that is the *Manaiya Kua*. A broad, octagonal, raised, grey-stone paved curbstone ran around the well, punctuated by four pulley frames formed by two stone slabs; a large wooden pulley hung from each pulley frame. As the well lay some 30 m from the path, the pulley frames must have served as an effective hiding place for the young woman, and as a platform for her to leap. This, I was told, must have been foremost in her mind when she chose this well and not the bare *Bangla ka Kua*, which was closer to the barbers' homes and lay right next to the path (Chambard 1980: map 3 'Quartiers et noms de lieux'). At any rate, she could not but have known that many Brahmins still bathed in the water of the *Manaiya Kua* and that some continued to drink its water, even though the district's health authorities had installed a handpump nearby some four or five years earlier. (These handpumps had brought about a veritable revolution by considerably reducing the incidence of typhoid and amoebiasis which used to be endemic earlier.) Had she not deliberately chosen this way to avenge herself on her husband, by gravely polluting his employers and bringing their wrath down on his family? She must have known that the long-standing dispute (which will be dealt with later) between the barbers and their Brahmin clientele would be rekindled.

The dead woman was discovered only at noon the next day by a Brahmin woman who had come to the well to wash her clothes. As the body of the young woman, framed in her dishevelled black hair, rose to the surface, a ray of sunlight was reflected off her nose ring. The village *dai* (midwife), Maya Basorni (of the basket-makers and musicians caste, i.e. the Basors), gave me details of how the drama had unfolded. She, her husband and some Untouchables had been summoned to extract the body, which they had accomplished with a multiple-headed dredger normally used to fish objects out of wells. Maya's account was of a realism calculated to make one's blood freeze. The young woman had bound her ankles with her black saree; this, said my informant, was done to prevent the feet from involuntarily thrashing about which in turn would have brought her up to the surface. Moreover, she continued after hesitating just a little, the sphincter of those who are on the verge of death often opens up; the Brahmins realized only too well then that the water of the well would have been contaminated with human excrement, the worst pollutant in the eyes of a Hindu.

During the meeting of the villagers, held the next day in the presence of the parents of the young woman, the entire family of Nathuram (the eldest of the brothers) was held liable for the purification of the well. The (Brahmin) *sarpanch* had been extraordinarily vehement in attacking them, accusing them of never satisfactorily performing the functions expected of them, and squarely placing the responsibility for the death of his young wife on Bhagirath's shoulders. He had rekindled the fires of a major conflict between the barbers and their masters that dated back to the 1930s; but not all the Brahmins agreed with the *sarpanch* in holding Bhagirath guilty, as they were not keen on losing their barber. Thus, finally, it was the *thanedar*, head of the police post (set up fifteen years ago, near the bus stop), who moved against the husband. He was carrying out instructions received from the central police authorities, following the increasing number of cases in the State of brides being murdered, by burning or by other means, a phenomenon that first became widespread among the middle class of Delhi.[5]

TWELVE YEARS OF EXILE FOR SHORTCOMINGS IN THE SERVICE OF ONE'S MASTERS

The dispute between the barber, Jhinguriya, and his Brahmin masters dates back to 1937. (His eldest son, Nathuram, born in 1933, was then very young.) The regional *panchayat* of the barber caste had just decided that the women would henceforth cease to function as midwives, as that brought about excessive impurity. This would militate against the upward social mobility sought by the caste leaders and for which they had launched a struggle twenty years earlier, obtaining extremely uneven results. Gradually, the different services, traditionally considered polluting, that were provided by barbers would be eliminated: midwifery, minor surgery (of carbuncles, for instance) and washing of vessels. However, fortunately for them, the basic metier of the barber was permitted (though this may have been considered polluting too when it was part of traditional funeral rites such as tonsuring the head of a dead person's son), as were the tasks of masseur, messenger, and matchmaker, which were carried out by both men and women of the caste.

Overnight, therefore, midwifery had to be suspended, and a hefty fine (of Rs. 50, enormous at that time and the equivalent of Rs. 1,500 today) paid to the *panchayat*. The Brahmins reacted with hostility for to them it was a question of purity. No acceptable solution was open to them for childbirth. They decided to exile Jhinguriya and his family.

The 'serving' castes are dependent on the dominant castes who allocate to them not only houses but also tracts of land termed *mafi* (free of cess), naturally in exchange for services. The exiled barbers moved to settle in a village some 60 km from Piparsod, as share-croppers, for there was no question of their becoming competitors to the local barbers. The exile lasted twelve years—a period curiously enough of about the same duration as Ram's exile (fourteen years) in the *Ramayana* and the exile of the Pandavas (twelve years) mentioned in the *Mahabharata*. (Incidentally it takes thirteen years for a young boy to become a man, i.e. the duration of a generation.) The Brahmins' problem would not go away. They could have gone to the hospital in the town for the birth of their children, but even today this practice has not gained acceptance amongst villagers owing to the tradition of placing a new born baby on the bare earth for a few moments immediately after birth. Alternatively, arrangements had to be made with women in the neighbourhood, with widows in particular who are otherwise considered unauspicious. Jhinguriya, probably at the instance of his former masters who missed him, finally found a solution by bringing in from Gwalior a group of people belonging to the Basor (basket-maker) caste. Maya's family was one of them. A little before 1950, the barbers were authorized to return to the village. The father survived only for a year after that and Nathuram, then seventeen, became the head of the family. Tensions with his Brahmin masters continued owing to other decisions taken by his caste *panchayat*. In 1955, washing of dishes was forbidden and fines imposed for offences (though enforcing this ban was more difficult than the one on midwifery). Traditionally, it fell to the barbers to wash the copper plates and tumblers used by their masters to serve outsiders (members of the household use bell-metal ware which the mistress herself may wash without fear of being polluted). *Pattals*, or plates fashioned from leaves, are in widespread use on festive occasions like wedding or funereal banquets because they may be thrown away after being used. These occasions apart, it is not considered polite to make one's guests eat off leaf-plates; hence the use of copper utensils. (It is interesting to note that in the nearby town there is a specialized shop for the exchange of bell-metal ware that may have become impure, for instance by using it to serve outsiders.) Every time the Brahmins had guests, they derived a wicked pleasure by summoning, often by force, the barbers to wash the utensils. When I first came to the village in 1957 and had a barber as a servant, these tugs of war took on subtle forms: how could Nathuram not come himself or not send his wife or mother to do the dishes used by his new master, the sahib, who had partaken of a meal with his Brahmin friends?

Years later, in 1982, when I had been regularly coming back to the village for five years, I asked my Brahmin guru, Gopilal Panditji, about the long exile of the barbers. Advanced in years (he was born at the beginning of the century), his mind was still more alert than ever and was increasingly open to free discussion: he was becoming a sort of renouncer and showed growing confidence in me. For the first time, to my surprise, he approved of the recordings of women's songs I used to make at the home of Dhaniya, the enamel-bracelets maker, when he said to me that 'those people' (which could have meant the women as much as people of low caste) too had a valid culture.[6] I take the precaution of emphasizing the context on account of the importance of what the Panditji told me about the barbers and, in more general terms, about relationships between the dominant classes and the serving castes. According to the Panditji the seemingly severe exile of the barbers was the necessary reaction in the form of 'legitimate violence' (*dharmik himsa*) against servitors who had broken their traditional contract, especially since in this case it had brought considerable impurity to other classes amongst whom birth rituals could no longer be conducted in accordance with the tradition. In the caste system, each one must know his position. If this principle is not applied, those holding power must apply the 'morality of distress' (*apad dharma*) according to which 'legitimate violence' must be exercised so that society would not collapse. Using a commonplace example the Panditji defined *apad dharma*. If a Brahmin wandering in the desert and dying of thirst comes upon a well, where the only person present is an Untouchable with a vessel and a rope, there is no violation of *dharma* if the Brahmin drinks water drawn and served by that Untouchable, for it is a question of survival, not only for him but for the entire social system and for the world to which he belongs. *Apad dharma* is the right (in fact, the duty) to do what one would normally not be permitted to do, in order to ensure the survival of oneself, of one's family or of one's caste. I told the Panditji that something similar existed in the West amongst the Jesuits. He sought an explanation, which I gave him as best I could, but he refuted it most vociferously, saying that there was no similarity whatsoever. To the Hindus, this was not a matter of economic benefit (*artha*), whether considered individually or collectively, nor even a matter of survival for the sake of survival, but a question of order in the world, *visva dharma*. This order exists notably in the definition of relationships between the various castes, dominant as well as serving castes, in such a manner that respect is ensured for all (*parasparik adar ka sthan*).

A reference to the story of the barbers' exile and to the Panditji's exposé of the 'morality of distress' is essential in order to understand the violent reactions of the Brahmins to Baijanti's suicide, and how and why purity and pollution were at the centre of the entire drama. To the barbers it must have appeared to be their *karma*. That the pollution of the well by the dead woman should be connected with the impurity of the birth of Brahmin children, for which they had already paid such a heavy price, was an affirmation of the strange merry go round movement of fate.

How the 'Dharma of Distress' Enabled the Brahmins of Piparsod to Settle There

I knew well how the notion of a *dharma* of distress had facilitated the settlement of the Brahmins at Piparsod as a dominant caste some four hundred and fifty years earlier (Chambard 1975; 1980: 5–9 'Les commencements d'une histoire agraire'; 1984: 8–19 'Piparsod des origines à 1984'). The village, which had sprung up barely fifty years before the arrival of these Brahmins, on a clearing in the forest, is a comparatively "recent" settlement as far as India is concerned, and the events surrounding its origins are still part of everyone's memory. These, along with complementary information gleaned from the village's professional genealogists, enabled me to assemble a fairly detailed account of the village's Brahmins. In the eleventh century, these natives of Gaur Bangal (the present Bengal), from which they derive their name of 'Gaur Brahmins', moved westwards in large numbers, up to Delhi, where they became the court priests of the ruling Rajput clans. Soon after completing a solemn ceremony for the perpetuation of their master's rule, which involved driving a nail, *killi*, which may be at the origin of the word Dilli, as Delhi is known in Hindi[7]—into the head of the serpent, *Ses*, they were driven out of Delhi by the Muslim invaders. They fled southwards. They gave up the priesthood and turned farmers, settling down in a Haryana village where they continued to enjoy a dominant position with no threat to their status (in matters of marriage, for example). In the middle of the sixteenth century, they left once again for the south, arriving in Piparsod just before 1575, which was what the genealogists gave as their date of arrival in that village. There, they discovered that another dominant caste, the Kirars, had been holding sway for the past twenty-five or thirty years. The Kirars had not progressed much in clearing land for the village near the forest and it was probably this that gave the Brahmins a chance, for they realized there was room for everyone. The Brahmins were also helped by the higher status of their caste and by their impressive physical stature (none of them, neither the white-bearded patriarch Manmath nor any of his three sons, was less than 1.80 m in height). The Kirars (Shudras), who were perhaps already preoccupied by their upward social mobility, offered to share dominance of the village with the Brahmins if the latter would consent to partake of a *kaccha* meal with them (with water, the most sensitive object in terms of pollution, which can only be consumed in the company of members of one's own caste or family). The Brahmins found themselves in a cruel dilemma, forbidden as they were from sharing a meal with a Shudra, but they accepted nevertheless in the name of *apad dharma*. (In 1960, Panditji himself had told me about this meal taken in the company of the Kirars, which is more clearly recounted in the records of the genealogists.) The very act of sharing itself appears to have taken place in the most banal manner imaginable. During the meal, the chief of the Kirars took a *chapati* in his hands, split it in two, and gave one to Manmath telling him, 'This *chapati* is the village land. We give half to you, O Brahmins, and we, the Kirars, shall keep the other half.' For the Brahmins getting that land was as vital as the food it produced.

With a view to examining the question exhaustively, alongside this example given by Panditji of the application of *apad dharma* for sheer survival, one must also consider other issues in which the accent is on the idea of the world order or on the notion of danger to the parties concerned from a threat to this order. This in fact is one of the meanings of *dharma*, perhaps even a 'holistic' one. But to translate *dharmik himsa* as 'the violence of order' jars the Western sensibility even more than the term 'legitimate violence'.

The Gardener Who could not Sell His Vegetables in the Town

In 1958, my wife and I witnessed a scene which remains etched in our memory. From a *paur*, or the room overlooking the road, in a house near the village square, we could see, without ourselves being seen, a scene which happened in front of the house of the *sarpanch*. A Kachhi, a gardener, was pushing his bicycle, laden heavily with vegetables (small marrows, brinjals, tomatoes and pumpkins), when three young Brahmins abruptly leaped upon him. They beat him till, half unconscious, he fell to the ground. They damaged his bicycle, twisting its wheels, and, in seemingly the most incomprehensible act of all, systematically destroyed his stock of vegetables. Their explanation was that the Brahmins could not tolerate the idea that Kachhi, a member of the subservient gardeners' caste,[8] should sell vegetables in the town market. The Kachhi should have first tried selling the vegetables door to door. But the Kachhi knew only too well that in the village he would get a measly price for his vegetables, or that extra quantities would be taken away on the pretext that the weights used were faulty, or, quite simply, that he would be asked to give vegetables away for free. That day, the Brahmin masters had decided to 'teach the gardener a lesson'. We found their behaviour deeply shocking although we were the first ones to realize the hardship in travelling all the way to Shivpuri to buy vegetables. We had simply put it down to our not being imbued yet with the philosophy of the country of non-violence! Later, the vegetable trade was to become better organized, with itinerant peddlers bringing vegetables from the town and selling them in the streets of the village, but these were not local produce, and we well understood why.

Two More Examples of the Application of 'Legitimate Violence'

Among other incidents of the same kind, I shall mention two more which would help us give an idea of this sort of violence. They took place at the end of my first stay, in 1961, before my return to France where there was talk of my securing an appointment in the School of Oriental Languages (I did not know then that I would return to the field for six months in 1964, in order to complete the data I had gathered earlier).

The first may be banal, and may appear common-place and hence as 'oft-heard', but is probably a lot less so if it is looked upon as a link in the chain of events I have related. It concerns the misadventure of a Chamar teacher, an 'Untouchable' who belonged to the Great Chamars, those who had given up leatherwork and now worked as peasants or earned considerable money as masons. For about forty years, more than any other vocation, teaching was the one which was most attractive for the educated of Piparsod. There are more than two hundred teachers today, most of them Brahmins, working in schools in the village or in the surrounding areas. Their womenfolk remain in the village to supervise the cultivation of the land in their families possession. The Chamars follow the Brahmins in terms of the number of teachers: there are some fifteen of them. The man we are speaking of was a poet, a great admirer of Tulsidas, author of the *Ramcharitmanas*. He had organized a '*path*' or reading session of the *Ramayana* in his home, during which he is believed to have said that the story of Rama could only be understood in the light of the Vedas, 'which everyone can now read'. The next day, he was taught a lesson when, in a little lane far away from his own neighbourhood, he was beaten up by some young Brahmins duly authorized to do so by their elders. Did he not know that the reading of the Vedas was forbidden even to the Shudras to whom the Chamars are a lot inferiors? Or was he naive enough to imagine that his observations would not be reported to the Brahmins? Nothing can be kept secret in an Indian village, where everything is totally transparent. And this the Chamar knew only too well!

The second example concerns me personally, but I feel no discomfort in discussing it inasmuch as it proved beneficial for me by forcing me to engage in a dialogue with the notables of the village on an important question concerning my work, which I had never discussed: what would be the name of the village in the Ph.D. dissertation which everyone knew I was preparing? I had been seen making maps of the village, carrying, site by site, information drawn from survey documents read aloud to me by Nathuram, documents taken with due authority from the *tahsil* office. Would not those maps reveal sharecropping (Chambard 1980: pls. 60–4) and sale of land, which were forbidden at the time? The villagers, who came frequently to see me and talk to me, were perfectly capable of reading the maps which I fixed on the wall of my workplace; I have always been surprised by the remarkable sense of orientation that my visitors possessed as regards the maps—any question asked about the maps would elicit an unhesitating reply. Anyway, my turn came too to 'learn a lesson'. The occasion chosen was an appropriate one. At the Gangaur festival, Brahmin women carrying images of Shiva and Parvati, move in procession to Shiva's Mango Grove outside the village, where they gather leaves considered to guarantee the longevity of their spouses. During the two days that precede it, they gather in the courtyards and sing songs including the names of their husbands, taking care to evict their husbands from the home (so that the husbands may not hear the wives utter their name, for a good Hindu wife cannot utter her husband's name in his presence). My wife and I had frequently been invited to be present at the ceremony to record the songs and take photographs. It soon became a sort of tradition and the Brahmin women asked me to come to their home on that day even though I was alone, for my wife had by then returned to France. The husbands, pretending to be offended that a wolf should thus be allowed amongst the lambs, foregathered with other Brahmins and it was decided then to send three or four young men to take care of me. They beckoned me from outside the house where I was doing my recording and pounced and rained blows on me the moment I crossed the threshold. I fell unconscious with my back against the curbstone of a well. My tape recorder and camera lay close to me but had obviously received a blow or two (the former continued to function, but the lens of the camera was permanently damaged). The emptiness around me was abnormal—not a soul was in sight! Later I learned why: caste solidarity (and the place chosen) precluded any Brahmin acting against the decision taken. The Panditji explained that to me later. Even though it bothered him, it was impossible for him to intervene by breaking the bonds of belonging and solidarity (*adhinta*, the word also means dependence), which he was bound to uphold as the *grihasth* (or 'master of a household') that he was in the eyes of the Brahmins of the village. (In any case, if he had acted it would have been to the detriment of both of us.) This was also the case with others, amongst them my 'honorary brother-in-law', the husband of my Brahmin 'sister in *dharma*' (*dharam ki bahin*), with whom I had the best possible ties.[9] My servant, Nathuram, was on leave, away in another village. However, alarmed on seeing the situation, his wife was quick witted enough to call my other guru, Bhagatji. Bhagatji, a Brahmin who had recently become a renouncer,[10] was a man who enjoyed a surprising degree of liberty, as much in the realm of ideas and religion as in the sphere of behaviour, where he did not believe he was tied down by anything, having abandoned his family, his caste and his village. I realized, in the very situation in which I found myself, how true it was. He came immediately, only too content to be able to demonstrate his independence to one and all, slapped me lightly on the cheeks to revive me, even as he continued to joke about the dangers inherent in going to women's houses. It ended with a cup of tea in my house—Bhagatji was the only one in the village who ever did that. To me, this was an extraordinarily instructive 'psychodrama'. It was only then that I was able to understand the concrete nature of the renouncer in Hinduism.

However, this misadventure also led to another concrete realization, that it was high time I engaged in a dialogue with the people of the village about my 'book'. Before my departure, we jointly selected the *nom de guerre* that the village would bear: Piparsod. In juridical terms, that would give the village a refuge from any attempt by the administration to use the data published in the book. This solution, satisfactory to all, which was adopted after consulting lawyers in Shivpuri, was proposed by my Brahmin interlocutors, who have an acute legal mind. It was agreed, however, that people's names would remain unchanged in my publications (as the reader of this contribution may have observed). The Brahmins were greatly attached to their genealogies, which would appear therein, and from that point of view, my Atlas (Chambard 1980) is like a *Vade Mecum* to them today. Is it not, as in the case of the barbers, a success for the technician in service?

Happy though I was at the resolution, this incident had one thing in common with the ones that preceded it—aggression had become the normal method for 'restoring order'.

Conclusions

1. In December 1989, Bhagirath, husband of the woman who had committed suicide, and his mother were tried before the criminal bench of the district court at Shivpuri. The case had been filed by the police. The Public Prosecutor accused both of deliberate homicide and charged

them with direct responsibility for the suicide of Baijanti Devi following the violent disputes between the family members and her. The mother and son were defended by my friend Madanlal Gupta, an excellent advocate who had for long years been a Government Pleader. The testimony of witnesses, of the Brahmins in particular, was to prove decisive in the outcome of the case. Without exception, the Brahmin neighbours testified that nothing exceptional had happened on the evening of the suicide. The young woman was described as excessively timid, as one who never talked to anybody. A judgement of 'non suit pronouncement' was delivered.

When I returned to Piparsod, between August and October 1990, I observed that Bhagirath had become particularly active as a barber, cutting and shaving without pause, from morning to evening. I was told that he had committed himself to render these services free to his neighbours for one year.

Let me return to the different acts of violence which one has witnessed. The Brahmins believed, in keeping with their vision of the world, that they were the only victims of violence (by contamination) by the barbers, as much now in the suicide of the young woman as earlier in the stopping of midwifery. However, what of the other acts of violence? To their great credit, the forces of law and order did attempt to bring to book those responsible for the violence that was carried out on the young woman and had brought about her death. No one else, however, seemed to be particularly bothered. Neither the Brahmins, who were too preoccupied with preserving their ritual purity and keeping their barber (for a barber's services are essential for the maintenance of purity or its restoration after funeral rites: the Brahmin world view is consistent from one end to the other). Nor the barbers, who sought to save themselves from a 'modern' justice they barely understood and in the eyes of which they did not really believe themselves guilty, who applied their common law without probably realizing the horror of their behaviour or its fatal consequences—for a woman was involved and it was a society of men (in which the mother-in-law of the victim supported her son). There was, too, the violence the young woman had inflicted upon herself. One is reduced to conjecture about her desire for revenge and, therefore, about the violence she wanted to inflict on her own people. If that was the case, her suicide was futile, for her act was completely erased in the restoration of the *status quo ante* that followed. Obviously, a woman's suicide cannot be taken too seriously! In any case, the barbers seem finally to have emerged as winners, although their predicament might have seemed disastrous immediately after the suicide. In a long term perspective, Bhagirath may be said to have avenged his family for the exile and for all the affronts it had to suffer. The well-known dialectic of the master and the slave functioned perfectly. When, thanks to their Brahmin patrons, the machinery of justice exonerated them, the barbers in some sense became masters of the game and the credit for that went to the system in which they still enjoy their anti-impurity monopoly. Were not the worst 'violences' they suffered the repeated reformatory constraints imposed on them by their own caste *panchayat*, even if these were supposedly founded on consensus? One form of arbitrariness is the desire to propel people towards happiness in spite of themselves!

On all these serious questions, the foreigners are reduced to their Western reflections. My field studies however brought to light elements which are far removed from these preoccupations. I forced myself to stay within the bounds of what was recounted to me. The reader will note, perhaps in surprise, if not in reproof, how little account has been taken of the sort of questions that would strike him as the most important. The cause probably lies in the difficulty in making our point of view converge with that of the Hindus, which in turn arises from the difference in the meaning either side attributes to certain concepts and to the words that convey these concepts: Westerners are too quick to believe that concepts—such as violence and non-violence, for example—are identical in the two streams of thought.

2. Hindu nationalists (through the Rashtriya Svayamsevak Sangh and the Vishva Hindu Parishad, the two grass roots organizations from which the Bharatiya Janata Party derives local support) had been active in the village for a good decade in the mid-1980s–90s and had begun to grow in numbers in the context of the Ram Janmabhoomi movement. The movement reached its peak in 1989 when a dozen residents of the village left for Ayodhya, laden with bricks bearing the name of Ram (only to be beaten up by the police at Jhansi and refused entry into Uttar Pradesh). Four years earlier, a Brahmin family had donated a handsome *haveli* to a private denominational school, called Sarasvati Shishu Mandir. The school fees, fixed at Rs. 30 per month for each child, did not seem to affect the numbers seeking education there. It is true that though education was free in the government schools, only those who took private tuitions from their teachers (for exactly the same price) ever passed.

Could it not be that the Hindu nationalists' remarkable local success came about simply because they knew how to appropriate for their own ends certain conceptions or practices, like 'legitimate violence' and corporal punishment, as means of affirming Hindu values?[11] The reader would have observed that a complete and coherent system of values is in play, which are not only essential to the Hindus of our village, but which one has seen in concrete practice in the events just related. It must not be forgotten that in the Hindu conception of a kingdom, even today very much present, the dominant groups are substitutes for the king. At the village level the dominant classes assume the royal duty to maintain order with the *danda*, i.e. the stick. By applying this principle to their own situation, the dominant classes in our village, who also happen to be Brahmins, concretely integrate violence as a means of maintaining *dharma*, the world order in its totality, when their own status and the social, economic and ideological bases of this status are in question or under threat. As Westerners, we would be inclined to see in this a potentially 'natural' slide from a holistic system to a totalitarian system. To Hindus, however, it is merely conservative pragmatism for the defence of a system which is in fact all-encompassing. The fact remains that one cannot evade the question of the totalitarian nature of the system, not so much *per se* (after all, India has lived with the system for at least two and a half millennia with no more tyrannical excesses than anywhere else, and the system has more often acted upon alien dominant forces than been affected by them) as in the perspective of its use, or likely use, as an instrument of political or punitive action by Hindu nationalists. When militants of the Shiv Sena launch murderous and destructive attacks on Muslim localities in Bombay, it is an example of it. If one went by their official positions, the political formations that lay claim to Hindu nationalism strive to give the impression that they are participants in a Western-style of democracy and that they have not taken the fundamentalist path—the BJP goes so far as to advocate secularism![12] However, the assault on the Babri Masjid at Ayodhya on 6 December 1992, and the killings that followed all over the country during the next three months in which more than three thousand people perished, indicated exactly the opposite. Would the Hindu nationalists look upon the pursuit of such violences as politically fruitful in the four north Indian States of Uttar Pradesh, Madhya Pradesh, Rajasthan and Himachal Pradesh, where their governments were dismissed and President's rule had been imposed? Fortunately, the unfolding and the outcome of the elections of November 1993 gave lie to the fears that the BJP would introduce a fascist note into the Indian polity.[13] The defeat it suffered seemed, on the contrary, to demonstrate a weakening of the potential of religious extremism as a political weapon.

NOTES

* This contribution was initially published in French in 1994.

1. Piparsod lies half way between Shivpuri and Pohri on the road leading to nearby Rajasthan. I first went there in 1957, and then did a long field study (three and a half years) that extended itself up to 1964, with my last visit lasting all of six months. I returned to the village thirteen years later, in 1977, to evaluate the changes that had taken place in the intervening period and include them in my dissertation (Chambard 1980). Since then, practically every year, I have spent a month or two in Piparsod. In 1984, with the consent of the *panchayat*, I became the owner of the house in which we had been living. Owing to this chain of events, I became, and will probably remain, an ethnologist who knows only one village; this situation has not always been easy to live with!
2. The impact of violent crime in the region during that period has been described well in Irène Frain's recent book (Frain 1992), which is the outcome of good reportage on Phoolan Devi, who surrendered in 1983 and met the author in prison. Phoolan Devi was freed on 8 February 1994. [Editor's note = P.D. has been assassinated in July 2000].
3. Readers desirous of knowing more about our setup at Piparsod may consult Elisabeth Andrès' interview with me in the ethnology magazine, *Singuliers* (*Singuliers*, December 1992; Chambard 1992c).
4. These ritual suicides have been described by Eric Newby in the album produced by him with remarkable pictures by Raghubir Singh (Newby 1974) and by P. Olivelle in an important article that appeared in *Wiener Zeitschrift für die Kunde Südasiens* (Olivelle 1978).
5. Though several articles, of uneven quality, have appeared on this topic in Indian periodicals (*India Today*, amongst them), there are just a few books that have been published on the subject. Of the two I know, one (Grover 1990) is a small work which deals with *sati* and with the killing of brides. It is based on press reports and some other documents (letters from the victims, etc.), while the other book (Bhatnagar 1989) is a collection of reports on trials arising from such cases.
6. Increasingly, my work is given to the study of songs sung by Piparsod's women, almost all of which I recorded at the home of Dhaniya the enamel-worker. These include, notably, a feminist and a highly original

version of the *Ramayana* in which Sita plays the principal role (Chambard 1991 and 1992b). Panditji knew this feminist interpretation of the *Ramayana* and had expounded some of its aspects to me before his death in 1986 (to my great regret, I could not see him that year as I arrived in the village a month after his death).

7. *Dilli ki killi*, Delhi's nail, is mentioned in the study of Delhi's dialect by a top-ranking Indian linguist (Singh 1966: 7–9).
8. The practice had existed at the time when the Rajputs, warriors who did not till the soil, occupied the fort in the village, maintaining a small garrison at the disposal of the Hindu king of Narwar (founded by King Nal) whose reign continued during the Muslim domination and only ceased with the Maratha conquest in the eighteenth century. The gardeners at that time were suppliers of farm products to the Rajputs. These Rajputs perished in a combat with other Rajputs; the point of contention being a kidnapped woman (Chambard 1980: 5–6). For a long time before that, the gardeners had ceased to be looked upon as a subservient caste. But that there can be changes in the status of serving castes is illustrated by the case of the Banias, or merchants, of the village. During the rule of the king of Narwar, the serving castes were those who were required to perform specific services to the 'king's court' whenever the king camped near the village, either for an inspection or for hunting. The Banias then were required to function as cooks, for everyone including Brahmins could *partake* of *pukka* food cooked by the Banias. It must be borne in mind that in a village the dominant groups are the representatives of and substitutes for the king and that dominance is in no way related to a superior status in the caste system: the Brahmins themselves, the purest and most elevated in the system, were a serving group in some villages, functioning as temple priests and in return for that service were given *mafi* lands, exempted from cess, as in the case of the barbers. The Brahmins of Piparsod were dominant not because they were Brahmin (they had in fact given up the priesthood), but because they had obtained half the over-riding rights to the land. At the very bottom of the scale of castes, however, there is a co-relation between the caste system and dominance: the fact that it was impossible for the 'Untouchables' (and some other subservient castes) to gain access to the position of dominant caste. This was the case with the Kachhis (Shudras) called upon to serve the king. They could not, however, fill the void arising from the annihilation of the Rajputs. This place was taken in fact by the Kirars, also Shudras like the Kachhis, but with a firmly entrenched position as the dominant group in a number of villages in the area.

   In the case of the dominant castes of Piparsod, an important point that needs to be underscored is that they are looked upon as representatives not only of the king but also of Vishnu (the coincidence arising from Vishnu's two incarnations on earth as king, Rama and Krishna, and also from the fact that to every woman her husband is also king and god). An irrefutable demonstration of this is provided by the course taken by religious processions whose *parikrama* of the village always includes the residential areas of the dominant groups ensuring that these localities lie to the right of the deity in procession (Chambard 1980: map 8 '*Temples et lieux du culte*').

9. The honorific *dharam ka bhai-dharam ki bahin* (brother-sister in *dharma*) is a traditional tie, officially recognized in the caste system. Curiously, this enables a woman (Brahmins included) to select such a brother, even if he belongs to another caste (and even if that caste is lower than her own!), as a gesture of gratitude for a major service rendered. Jagdish's wife conferred the title of 'brother in *dharma*' on me in 1958, when in the middle of the night I had cycled all the way to Shivpuri to buy a medicine that cured her husband of a serious attack of typhoid. Thirty-five years later, this tie is still as strong as ever.
10. Bhagatji was a Joshi Brahmin, different from the Gaurs who dominated the village. He had become a *sadhu* or renouncer, some months before my arrival, following the marriage of his sons and daughters. He lived in a small hermitage, a hut covered with leaves on the banks of a *nala* (a non-perennial body of water, still considered Ganga) which defined the limits of Piparsod. He lived off whatever alms were brought to him for he did not have a home of his own. In 1957, 'on seeing (my) ignorance' after the two or three visits I paid him, he decided to take me on as a disciple. This made him return to the village, where he stayed in a lodging near the Hanuman temple, opposite the *Manaiya Kua*, which was meant for the passing mendicants. For a month, at half past five every morning, he would summon me to listen to his discourses; it was a sort of initiation. It was an exhilarating experience for it was through him that I learnt what liberty meant in Hinduism—the discussions I had with him reminded me of my years at the Sorbonne. Bhagatji passed away in 1966.
11. Christophe Jaffrelot, author of one of the papers included in this collection, has just published his doctoral work on the Hindu nationalists (Jaffrelot 1993). He came several times to Piparsod and was present notably when the denominational school began to take root. He, more than anyone else, would be in a position to comment on the sort of links and distortions that exist between traditional conceptions and those of the Hindu nationalists.
12. The Hindus of Piparsod, in particular those who support Hindu nationalism and approve of the acts at Ayodhya, are openly sceptical of a democratic system. They look upon it as being essentially Western and founded on a dangerous egalitarianism that questions the very notion of a hierarchy and the basis of a Hindu society. Their major

grievance with the present functioning of democracy in India is the excessive importance given to minorities, to Untouchables and Muslims in particular. They go so far as to say that this is an attack on the very egalitarianism in which in any case they have so little belief. This 'ultra' reaction, discernible at the village level, shows how much the problem of reservations (quotas of seats reserved in elected bodies, including village *panchayats*, and government jobs for Untouchables and other social groups considered 'backward classes') served to undermine the chances of success of a democracy that during its first forty years seemed not to have done too badly for itself. To quote a village Brahmin, 'Everyone now, including some Brahmins, wants to have his group recognized as a "backward class" with privileges comparable to those of the others. This is a process without an end. . . .'

13. In an interview given to *Newsweek* (26 April 1993), Mr. L.K. Advani (who in June 1993 once again became the BJP President) was asked, 'Would you like to harness rising Hindu fervour and translate that into political power?' To which he replied, 'I do not want to do that. Ultimately, the Hindu will not support extremism. Extremism never appeals in India. And if extremism is showing an appeal today, it is because my adversaries are totally disregarding the Hindu psyche.' Does not one discern, in this subtly ambiguous response, a trace of the notion of a morality in distress which causes a momentary abandonment of ordinary morality?

REFERENCES

Bhatnagar, J.P., Advocate [1989] 1990. *Cases and Materials on Dowry Prohibition Act, 1961, With State Amendments: Alongwith Dowry Death and Bride Burning Cases.* Allahabad: Ashoka Law House.

Chambard, J.-L. 1980. *Atlas d'un village indien. Piparsod, Madhya Pradesh (Inde).* Paris-La Haye: Mouton-EHESS (Monde d'Outre-Mer, passé et présent XII).

———. 1991. 'La chanson de la terre qui tremble, ou la punition du roi qui avait voulu régner sans sa reine'. *Cahiers de Littérature orale,* n° spéc. 29: *Rêver le roi*, 125–57.

———. 1992a. 'Un curieux dialogue sur l'amour entre un ethnologue et une villageoise en Inde centrale'. *Singuliers* (9 June): 81–3.

———. 1992b. 'Le Râmâyana des femmes dans un village de l'Inde centrale'. *Cahiers de Littérature orale,* n° spéc. 31: *L'épopée dans la littérature orale.*

———. 1992c. 'L'ethnologue, une vocation de rencontres. Entretien avec Elisabeth Andrès'. *Singuliers* (10 Dec.): 76–81.

Frain, I. 1992. *Devi*. Paris: Fayard.

Grover, K. 1990. *Burning Flesh*. New Delhi: Vikas Publishing House.

Jaffrelot, C. 1993. *Les nationalistes hindous. Idéologie, implantation et mobilisation des années 1920 aux années 1990*. Paris: Presses de la Fondation nationale de sciences politiques.

Olivelle, P. 1978. 'Ritual Suicide and the Rite of Renunciation'. *Wiener Zeitschrift für die Kunde Südasiens* 22: 19–44.

Newby, E. 1974. 'Prayag'. In *Ganga Sacred River of India*, E. Newby and R. Singh, 31–6. Hong Kong: The Perennial Press.

Singh, Bahadur. 1966. *The Dialect of Delhi*. New Delhi: South Asia Institute, University of Heidelberg.

Singuliers, juin 1992. *Femmes: maître ou esclave*? 9.

Singuliers, déc. 1992. *Un métier d'homme: traditions et perspectives*, 10.

The Initiation of Devi: Violence and Non-Violence in a Vaishnavite Tale

CATHERINE CLÉMENTIN-OJHA

> Bear compassion towards all beings.
> HARIVYASA[1]

All his life, like the good Vaishnavite that he was reputed to be, Harivyasa respected the virtues of patience, absence of hatred, benevolence, and a friendly disposition bordering on gentleness.[2] Harivyasa, the thirty-first successor to Nimbarka (twelfth-thirteenth centuries) as the head of one of northern India's oldest Vaishnavite traditions (*sampradaya*), lived in Mathura in the latter half of the sixteenth century, when Braj was in the midst of a great cultural and religious renaissance. A widespread theist movement blazed across the region, impelled by a generation of preachers, drawn from every corner of India, who had 'rediscovered'[3] this area associated by Vaishnavite scriptures with the life of Krishna. New traditions began to grow around the cult of the divine cowherd. Moving with the flow, and imbued with a new life under the dynamic leadership of Harivyasa, the old Nimbarka *sampradaya* contributed to the spread of Vaishnavism in Braj as well as beyond the region's frontiers.[4] Although the historic role played by Harivyasa is little known outside the folds of the sect he helped to reorganize, his attributes as a messenger of the word of Vishnu ensure him enduring popularity among Vaishnavites of all descriptions. In their memory, he remains the saint who successfully converted the goddess (Devi).

The oldest source of this oft-told tale is the *Bhaktamala*,[5] the 'Golden Legend' of Vaishnavite saints. The tale begins thus,

> By the power of his devotion to Hari, Harivyasa bestowed *diksha* (initiation) to Devi. That She who moves in air should become the disciple of a man

is extraordinary. But the story is known to all, and holy men do hail it in their songs.[6]

The theme was taken up a century later, in the beginning of the eighteenth century, by the *Bhaktirasabodhini*,[7] a commentary on the *Bhaktamala*, which then offered to the Vaishnavite world at large the standard account of the goddess' initiation by the saint Harivyasa.

They saw a garden in the village of Chatathaval.[8] Pleased with it, they performed their rites there and decided, 'Let us prepare our meal.' At this moment, sombody came with a sacrificial goat and killed it on the altar of Devi. Overwhelmed with regret at the sight, they resolved, 'Let us not drink even water here.' They spent the night in hunger. Deeply distressed by the ardour of their devotion (*bhakti*), Devi, assuming another form, came up to them and pleaded, 'Do prepare a meal for yourselves.' 'Who amongst us could do it? Something has deterred us from it.' 'Then,' said Devi, 'give me that gift, make me your disciple.' Thus he made her his disciple. Having heard the *mantra*, she sped towards the town, where she flung the cot of the great Sardar[9] to the ground. Climbing atop, she said, 'I have become the servant of Harivyasa, and I shall instantly slay he who does not become his slave forthwith.' All came forth and became his servants. It was as if they had assumed a new body. Sin, hardship and unhappiness left. They were released from samsara. Harivyasa and his servants stayed there some days, feasting themselves on varied fare.

Although this curious legend enriches and elucidates the enigmatic *Bhaktamala* with a coherent account of Devi's conversion to Vaishnavism, it does not bear an immediately decipherable message. Or rather, it seems to suggest two contradictory messages. Even as it condemns the violence perpetrated on the animal sacrificed to Devi, it offers an approving portrayal of the threats Devi holds out against the denizens of the neighbouring town. In my view, Devi's attitude appears to be, at the very least, a trifle ambiguous. At the outset, like a good Vaishnavite, she is submissive. Yet, soon after, she manifests the greatest aggressiveness. Consequently, the holy man and his ideal of compassion strike us as ambiguous too. An analysis of this supposedly edifying story will serve as a point of departure for an examination of the respective roles of 'non-violence' and violence in Vaishnavite ideology, and of the place of violence in a religion that encourages the values of compassion.

The first part of the tale, until the initiation of Devi, could be the sort of gloss that illustrates the quotation cited at the very start of this paper. Events flow from the failure to comply with the requirements imposed by the duty of compassion so dear to Vaishnavites. Harivyasa and his disciples began their fast because someone had killed a goat in sacrifice. Devi perceives their expiation for an act that they had not in fact committed as a protest against the food given to her. Her offer to cook for them amounts to an act of reparation, and it is this which prompts her to become a Vaishnavite. Moved by the virtues of the devout Harivyasa, she seeks initiation into Vaishnavism so that she may be cleansed of the deplorable effect produced by the violence of the cult built around herself.

In addition to this particular theme, the eighteenth century commentary on the *Bhaktamala* introduces another important insight. Without detracting from the quality of fable and legend that characterizes this genre of literature, it places the saint's achievement in an identifiable—and historically attested—religious context, that of tensions between Vaishnavites and devotees of Devi (*Shakta*) in northern India. At the outset these tensions must be seen to derive from the fact that the two faiths are based upon ethical systems that invested completely divergent meanings in ritual violence.

Although nothing is said about the precise circumstances in which the animal is offered for sacrifice, or even about the ritual procedure of the sacrifice, the brief description suffices to call to mind the bloody cult of the goddess which prevailed then in northern India and which continued to be fairly widespread even at the beginning of this century. In the Shakta tradition of learning, from which arose the theology and liturgy of such ritual practices, killing an animal as an offering to Devi did not amount to murder. 'In sacrifice,' say the Shaktas, citing the *Kalikapurana* (57.11), 'killing is not murder.'[10] By using, to their own ends, the argument used by Brahmanical tradition (see Manu V. 39) to justify Vedic sacrifice, the Shaktas were merely legitimizing their animal sacrifice by denying its violence.

To Vaishnavites, however, the bloody cult of the goddess arose from *himsa* ('the desire to kill'), which they abhorred as they made *ahimsa* ('the desire not to kill') the pillar of virtue. According to the story, Harivyasa and his disciples are overcome with disgust and depression when they see *ahimsa*, their precious ideal, being flouted. In the beginning of the eighteenth century, this ideal found expression in the complete condemnation of all animal sacrifice, in the fact that Vaishnavite cultural and culinary practices became purely and totally vegetarian.

This had not always been the case, as some examples from ancient Vaishnavite texts would illustrate. The *Bhagavad Gita* (XVI. 2) teaches that *ahimsa*, like compassion and gentleness, is one of the great Vaishnavite virtues. However, what does this entail? A denunciation of animal sacrifices as enjoined by the Vedas? The text *makes no reference* whatsoever to the subject. The first Vaishnavite theologians do not condemn ritual violence either; in fact, they legitimize it by advancing arguments from the *Shruti* and *Smriti*. Thus, according to their commentaries on the *Brahmasutra* (3.1.25), ritual death caused no pain as the animal sacrificed would 'take the easiest path to the gods'.[11] An identical teaching was proffered by the *Smriti* (see Manu V. 40 and 42). It is likely that the first Vaishnavite theologians, who saw no more of the 'desire to destroy' in animal sacrifice than Manu did, also shared Manu's overall conception of *ahimsa*. Like him, they too could have said, '*Himsa* as enjoined by the Vedas must be considered *ahimsa*.'[12] By this token, only the man who perpetrated violence (*himsa*) to satisfy himself must be condemned (V 45). To the founders of the major streams of Vaishnavite Vedanta, he who offered a (Vedic) sacrifice could therefore not be blamed. However, to their successors, Harivyasa, his contemporaries and disciples, every sacrificial act was a part of *himsa*, and therefore deserving of condemnation as any life-threatening act.

They drew their belief from the *Bhagavatapurana*, which made *ahimsa* the supreme *dharma*, consubstantial with Vaishnavite *dharma* itself. This text exemplified another stream of Vaishnavite thought, giving literal interpretation to the notion. In the *Bhagavatapurana*, *ahimsa* implies abstention from (Vedic) sacrifice and from the consumption of animal flesh, whatever be the circumstances, even during the *shraddha* rites (VII. 15.7–8a). This marks deep differences with the *Smriti*. Although Manu favours vegetarianism (III. 227), he allows for the consumption of (sacrificial) meat precisely on funeral occasions.[13] The *Bhagavatapurana* is not unaware of this exception. However, even as it concedes unto those who 'have an irresistible penchant for meat' the right to satiate themselves within the strict confines of ritual sacrifice, it goes on to add that such indulgence is by no means obligatory (XI. 21.29).

The Vaishnavite movements that began to grow in Braj after the sixteenth century made the *Bhagavatapurana* their principal scripture of reference. Unlike the theologians of yore, they did not in any way feel tied down by Vedic injunctions. In fact, there existed then no memory of the very meaning of bloody Vedic sacrifice. Where their forebears perceived violence as legitimate ('To sacrifice is not to kill') since it ensured social and cosmic order, the modern Vaishnavites saw the desire to destroy for sheer personal satisfaction. They only saw 'motivated' violence, or the sort of violence that Indian society had condemned through the ages. In their view, bloody ritual sacrifice was no longer compatible with Vaishnavism. The killing of animals, therefore, could no longer be justified.

These ideas were by no means completely original. The killing of animals, long denounced by ascetics, had slowly begun to be adopted and then disseminated by the Brahmins.[14] The original contribution of the Vaishnavites was not the conceptual creation of *ahimsa*, but the fact that they made devotees of the goddess' the target of their critiques and that they should use the ascetics' arguments against Vedic sacrifice against proponents of the Shakta cult. The Shaktas, as one has seen, used to justify their practices with the Vedic 'to sacrifice is not to kill' argument. Thus, despite the fundamental differences in religious procedures, meanings and contexts between Vedic and Shakta rituals, the latter's adversaries and supporters managed to twist to their own ends the arguments that worked against or for the former.

These were the reasons that prompted the Vaishnavites of Braj during Harivyasa's time to look upon the animal-sacrificing and meat-eating devotees of Devi as abject, impure beings. Their writings bear testimony to this sentiment. 'To frequent the Shaktas,' writes Sevaka, 'is to find oneself in the midst of a raging fire.' To Biharinadasa, 'It is preferable to eat dog meat than to accept the hospitality of a Shakta.' And Harirama Vyasa confirms this when he advises, 'A Shakta brother or relative is an enemy to be abandoned, for it is better to live in hell than to live in their company.' To Harirama Vyasa, 'An untouchable (*chandala*) is preferable to a Shakta Brahmin.'[15]

As an avowed adversary of Vaishnavite ideals, the Shakta was to be isolated. At the same time, he was a tempting target for the Vaishnavite preacher-missionary, the one whose conversion would be truly edifying. Thus, bringing the Shaktas into submission becomes a recurring theme in Vaishnavite hagiography, of which the story about the conversion of Devi is an example. In the context of the frequent tensions between the two sects, the objective is obvious. The Vaishnavite faith, with its emphasis on compassion and *ahimsa*, is pitted against the Shakta faith, which advocates a bloody cult, with a view to reaffirm the supremacy of Vaishnavite values. Its intention is crystal clear: Harivyasa preached with so much zeal that he did not merely convert Shaktas, as so many other saints had done, but Devi herself.

But what were the effects of this conversion? Did the Shaktas lose their Devi? Did they merge their identity with that of the Vaishnavites? The story does not lead one to believe that by bringing Devi to submission, Harivyasa robbed Vishnu's rivals of their divinity. The underlying significance of this to Vaishnavites is brought home, I believe, by a well-known illustration of the conversion legend.[16] It pictures a disproportionately large Harivyasa, his twelve ascetic followers in tow, tying a necklace around Devi's neck, in the customary mark of initiation. A group of women devotees looks on. The goddess, who has left her sanctum sanctorum, stands before him, with two of her hands clasped to show respect. Scattered on the ground around her are the weapons that have fallen from her eight other hands. Henceforth, one is given to understand, Devi has been disarmed.

Understanding the underlying message would entail a brief journey through the religious history of north-western India, where the new Vaishnavite movements first began to grow. As far as can be told, Shakta cults were dominant in these regions until the arrival of the great Vaishnavite preachers. This was particularly true of Braj[17] before the arrival of Vallabha (1492) and Chaitanya (1509). Between the decline of Buddhism (from the seventh century) and Jainism (around the tenth century) and the sixteenth century renaissance of Krishna-based cults, *Nagas* (serpent divinities), *Yakshas* and diverse goddesses had been the principal divinities of the region.[18] As Krishna-based myths themselves testify, Devi had long been worshipped at several sites by pastoral groups.[19] The same situation obtained in the north-eastern part of India as well. For example, Vallabhite writings (*varta*) speak of a cult to Devi in the villages between Prayag (Allahabad) and Benares, and of Vallabha converting Shaktas.[20] The situation in Gujarat and Rajasthan was probably no different, as will be borne out by the fact that to this day Devi and Mata are still very much present in these regions.

However, but here as elsewhere, offerings in blood to Devi were gradually replaced by vegetarian offerings. There are abundant and widespread examples of this evolution, a process that continues to unfold before one.[21] A precise reconstitution of the transformation of the Devi cult, however, may be difficult, for the decline of sacrifices in blood arises from a combination of factors that vary according to the regions and the periods.[22] Besides my purpose is not to reconstitute it but to take up the narrative bearing its manifestation in mind.

The Harivyasa legend, with its account of how Devi was disarmed, leads one to ask whether Vaishnavite movements, which spread to regions in northern India where these bloody practices prevailed, played a part in this decline. The legend seeks to answer the question by demonstrating the influence of Vaishnavite values of compassion and *ahimsa* on the Shaktas. No objective reality need be attached to the supernatural events recounted by the legend, for hagiographic writing has little value in that respect. Seeking essentially to edify, this story seeks to convey the image that a religious group—Vaishnavites, as it happens—seeks to give of itself, as much to its own members as to its rivals, on the socio-religious stage. Even as it was written, the story was the Vaishnavite perception of religious history of that time.

At the beginning of the eighteenth century, when the *Bhaktirasabodhini* was composed, and much before the impact of Western moral values, north Indian Vaishnavite hagiographic tradition associated the propagation of the Vaishnava message with the struggle to eliminate animal sacrifices, specifically those offered to Devi among the Shaktas.[23] The process leading to the pacification of the goddess is spelled out. It is founded on the personal intercession of Vaishnavite preachers whose holiness is edifying and whose exemplary respect for Vaishnava *dharma* is, quite literally, disarming.

However, the Devi is not merely pacified, she is also integrated in the Vaishnava faith. By portraying the goddess in submissive service of the saint, the legend also shows how the Vaishnavites, on arriving in an area dominated by her, take due account of how much her devotees are attached to her. It shows how these are converted by the adoption of their Devi and how her adoption is possible without the Vaishnavites betraying their own ideal of *ahimsa*. The inclusion of Devi shrines and sites[24] in the pilgrim's itinerary of holy Vaishnavite places in Braj (*Braj-parikrama*) is a clear indication of Vaishnavism's capacity to adapt to and to 'Vaishnavize' local conditions.

The two dimensions of 'Vaishnavization', that is, the integration of a goddess following a process of her pacification, appear once again in a text that reflects north Indian Vaishnavite preoccupations during the sixteenth-seventeenth centuries. While describing the different manifestations of the Devi cult, the *Brahmavaivartapurana*[25] qualifies as 'pure' (*sattviki*) that which bears only vegetarian offerings. These are declared to be purer than the sacrifices in blood offered by the Shaktas (*rajasi*), and purer still than those (qualified as *tamasi*,[26] although they are not described) offered by denizens of the forest. Significantly, this vegetarian cult of the goddess is named *vaishnavi-puja*.

The first part of the narrative, written in the Vaishnavite perspective and meant essentially for the initiated, is based on the values that form the totality of Vaishnavite ethics—compassion, *ahimsa*, purity in deed, and abstention from the consumption of meat. By being initiated into the Vaishnava faith, the meat-loving goddess renounces flesh and adopts vegetarianism. However, Vaishnavite 'non-violence' is not shorn of ambiguity, as will be revealed by the rest of the narrative. Despite her conversion, Devi continues to take recourse to violence. Strong arm tactics and threats enable her to bring the others to the feet of the holy man, Harivyasa.

I shall begin by observing that this Devi who places herself in the service of Vaishnavas calls to mind the goddess described in *Harivamsa*, who is so close to her younger brother, Krishna.[27] Myths relating the origin of the goddess (like the *Harivamsa* and the *Devi-mahatmya*) confirm that a necessary complementarity exists between her role and that of Vishnu. In certain situations, especially in the territory under her protection, Devi seems to assume the role of the *avatara*, to act in Vishnu's place. The god is thus spared the need to involve himself, 'lowly tasks are left to the Goddess to keep the purity of God. . . .'[28] The enactment of *Bhaktirasabodhini* borrows and transposes this mythical motif. The Vaishnavite saint is purified of all violence, which is assumed in its entirety by the goddess, whose sphere of action is limited to the 'neighbouring town'. This Devi knows how to be dangerous, and that is in the fitness of things. In myths, the violent action atttributed to her becomes the instrument of salvation of her devotees; in this story, her threats enable those she threatens to be released from *samsara* by adopting Vaishnavism.

The mention of *avatara* leads one to observe that the violence which Vaishnavism absorbed by welcoming Devi into its fold is no different from the violence which the faith had always justified as legitimate. The notion of violent and even life-taking acts is, in fact, at the very heart of Vaishnavite representations of the divine being, the *avatara* propounded as a model of good conduct (*Bhagavad Gita* III. 21–3). The example set by the *avatara* justifies the violence practised by the holy men portrayed in Vaishnavite hagiographies.[29] These holy men, like the *avatara*, take life for the sake of *dharma* (*Bhagavad Gita* IV. 8), for the well being of the world, and not for personal gain or satisfaction. When the divine model inspires them to take on Shaktas, Shaivites or even Muslims,[30] only the desire to defend *dharma* (that is, Vaishnava values) moves them.

In Vaishnava hagiographic literature, these sometimes fatal duels are always founded on the use of coercive magical means (*mantras*, and so on).[31] For, like Shaivites and Shaktas, Vaishnavites too are adept at manipulating the inherent energy of speech to subjugate another.[32] This was particularly true of the hero of the narrative, and of those who formed part of his environment. For example, the eighth chapter of the *Kramadipika*,[33] that compendium of rituals written by Keshava Kashmiri, the guru of Harivyasa's guru, deals entirely with *vashikarana*, or the fact of placing someone under one's own domination.[34] This is particularly evident in biographies, as when Keshava Kashmiri is shown using his dangerous magical powers during an altercation with *Tantrikas* in Kashmir: a single *mantra* from him brings forth a ray of the sun whose flame consumes his adversaries.[35] Svabhurama, one of Harivyasa's foremost disciples, is believed to have acquired mastery over the *Sudarshana Chakra*, the symbol of destruction associated with Vishnu. In combat with the Nathas, followers of a Shaivite cult, he invokes Vishnu's disc, which reduces his enemies to ashes, and the few who survive fall at the saint's feet to beg—and obtain—his forgiveness.[36]

These heroic deeds correspond to transpositions of the *avatara* myth. The *asuras* (i.e. the Nathas, Shaktas or other Tantrikas) rule and the *avatara* (i.e. the Vaishnavite saint) appears to restore order. His act is the fount of salvation.

That, however, is not the thrust of the story which was being analysed, in which Harivyasa never allows himself to commit a violent act. He consigns that task to Devi. As the theme of violence is linked to Devi, this is not only more dramatic, but more instructive as well. Violence, the legend seems to say, is omnipresent, and so is Devi. Thus, both must be attended to. The goddess must be integrated for only she can draw the people at large, who venerate her, to Vaishnavism. Her violence must be accepted, for the Vaishnavite cause cannot advance with compassion, goodwill and *ahimsa* alone.

By using Devi to wreak violence on her own followers, the *Bhaktirasabodhini* introduces a minor variation in the usual tales of conversion which show the saint directly at work. True, the message is no different. To refrain from inflicting harm on another is the guiding principle of the good Vaishnavite, and this is what the first part of the narrative lays down. *Dharma*, however, precludes countenancing those who do not accept this principle (by performing animal sacrifices, for example); hence, violence against such people must be accepted. Thus, Devi's violence is placed in the cause of Vaishnavism and its values, among which is *ahimsa*.

On the basis of the generally accepted hypothesis that Vaishnavite values of compassion and 'non-violence' contributed to pacify Indian society, it is difficult to understand the violence described in the story analysed earlier. The entire objective of the story is to demonstrate, in fact, that *ahimsa* must not be confused with 'non-violence', for not all violence is *himsa*.

Vaishnavite *ahimsa* does not imply opposition to every form of violence. To be exact, the recourse to violence is lawful if it is in the service of *dharma*. Thus, violence against religious adversaries is in perfect harmony with the ideology of *ahimsa*, for such violence cannot be regarded as *himsa* any more than animal sacrifice was in Vedic times. The remarkable continuity in Vaishnavite positions needs to be underscored. Only violence applied to purely personal ends ever meets with their condemnation. However, whilst Ramanuja, Nimbarka, etc., saw 'motivated' violence only in the slaying of animals outside the Vedic sacrificial framework, their successors, like Harivyasa and his disciples, perceived violence in every act of ritual killing. Even as they abstained from such violence, they accepted it to the extent to which it served the ends of *dharma*. In ideological terms, therefore, Vaishnavites of all times have justified violence within a sacrificial framework. In their view, violence is legitimate (within the sacrificial matrix) when it involves forsaking one's self (or a substitute) or one's Ego (by acting without personal motivation) in order to perpetuate the socio-cosmic order.

In ethical terms, this is tantamount to the co-existence of two kinds of morality, each of which grants a different place to violence: the morality of an individual life and that of a community. The first obliges the Vaishnavite to renounce violence and 'bear compassion towards all beings'. The latter permits him to use violence when the interests of his community are endangered. This issues from a sense of responsibility towards the collective Vaishnavite identity and, ideally, would be devoid of all personal motivation. It is the morality of the holy man shorn of the Ego, whose violence is thus justified. His superhuman strength and his use of violence are proof of the intensity of his devotion to Vishnu as to His cause. Thus, it is possible to describe a *bhakta* (devotee) in the following terms, without discerning the slightest hint of a contradiction, 'His indestructible faith in Hari was the axe with which he hacked down the trees of other religions.'[37] It is on the basis of this collective morality that Brahmanic texts enjoin upon the Brahmin, paragon of *ahimsa* in his personal life, to arm himself, go forth and defend the cow and the Brahmin ('*go-brahmana*').[38]

The ambiguity one perceives initially recedes from the narrative when one realizes that it articulates these two moralities on different planes and in different contexts. It is understandable, therefore, that on becoming a Vaishnavite, Devi should simultaneously renounce bloody sacrifice (or the self-satisfying aspects of such violence) and conserve her aggressiveness (or that part of it which is necessary for the Vaishnavite cause); that she should simultaneously display *ahimsa* and violence.

One still needs to consider the objective of the narrative. Must the exploits of Devi and the heroic acts and 'conquests' (*digvijaya*) of Vaishnavite preachers be interpreted only in metaphorical terms? In other words, what part was played in reality by the violence legitimized by Vaishnavite ideology? When they made role models of saints like Harivyasa, who allow themselves to be overcome by violence or who approve of it, were the Vaishnavites of Braj in fact encouraging their devotees to practise violence in real life? The account of Harivyasa's feat seems to indicate that the spread of Vaishnavism to new regions brought with it the decline of another religious tradition. Highlighting the role of Vaishnavism in the propagation of *ahimsa* amongst the Shaktas and presenting the resulting transformation as the fruit of Vaishnavism's civilizing mission, would seem to indicate the existence of social tensions. Yet, history offers no sign that weapons were wielded for the propagation of Vaishnavism.

In that case, what became of Vaishnavite violence? Could it have manifested itself in a different politico-religious environment? If Braj's Vaishnavites had received the support of the local political leadership, could the justified and legitimized forms of violence found in their ideology have been applied to their attitude of exclusion? (By 'attitude of exclusion', I refer to the condemnation of all systems of belief but their own which so fills their didactic works.) Could non-Vaishnavites have been persecuted?

Or must one agree with Véronique Bouillier (whose article appears elsewhere in this collection) that Vaishnavite violence sought refuge in the various ascetic-warrior sub-sects created within the major sects in northern India after the eighteenth century? Though a formidable force at times, under a unified command, the Nagas never sought to impose Vaishnavism on the entire populace. However, viewed as a counter-force to similar Shaivite formations founded earlier, or as a means of defending their co-religionists from the Muslims, they are the very illustration of the group ethic propounded by the narrative analysed: violence, justified in the service of *dharma*, and shorn of motivation by its application to the service of the community.

This legitimation of the use of force led to the abusive application of it against people and property by both Shaivites and Vaishnavites. If motive were the sole decisive factor to determine whether an act is violent or not, it is doubtful whether Vaishnavite Naga *sadhus* ever perceived their acts as violent; since assimilating their acts to *himsa* would have destroyed their very internal coherence, perhaps they didn't reflect on them at all! Does this explain why these acts were perpetrated without arousing reactions and why they remained above criticism?

Be that as it may, in the name of an ideology of religious activism advocated by the *Bhagavad Gita*,[39] the Nagas reconciled *bhakti* with martial virtues; in their midst, the most extreme forms of violence co-existed with the strictest vegetarianism and non-bloody cultural practices. The legend of Harivyasa enables us to understand that, to a Vaishnavite, there is no contradiction whatsoever in that.

NOTES

I would like to thank France Bhattacharya, Véronique Bouillier, Françoise Mallison, Denis Matringe, Chandra Pastor, Gilles Tarabout and Denis Vidal, for their comments on a preliminary version of this paper.

1. *Mahavani*, *Siddhanta sukha* 31.
2. *Bhagavad Gita* XII. 13–14; XVI.2.
3. Cf. Vaudeville 1976.
4. Cf. Clementin-Ojha 1990.
5. McGregor (1984: 108–9) traces this non-sectarian hagiographic Vaishnavite text to the beginning of the seventeenth century.
6. Chappay 77. Pollet (1967: 483) mentions the conversion of Durga as one of the miracles recounted by the *Bhaktamala*, though no comment is offered on it.
7. *Bhaktirasabodhini*: 338–9.
8. This village is believed to be the same as Chatathavar, near Saharanpur, about 250 km to the north of Mathura (cf. *Bhaktagatha-ank*, published by Akhila Bharatiya Shrinimbarkacharyapitha, Salemabad, 2035 VS: 141). Nothing could be more tenuous than this identification, although one of Harivyasa's disciples founded a monastery not far away, at Buriya, on the banks of the Yamuna.
9. A title of Persian origin, used to designate a high dignitary.
10. Cited by Brown 1974: 45.
11. This is the interpretation made by Ramanuja (cf. Thibaut 1904: 598–9) and Nimbarka (cf. Bose 1940: 502–3). It is a revealing indication about the evolution of Vaishnavite ideas that these theologians should base

their approval of Vedic ritual sacrifice in their commentary on a dictum found in the *Mahabharata* (12.9971), 'Let no harm befall any creature.' In the sixteenth century, Harivyasa would interpret this literally. The citation is extracted from *Tait. Br.* 3.7.7.14, 'Thou dost not die, thou art not wounded, thou goest unto the gods by the easiest paths' (cited by Bose, op. cit.: 503).

12. Cf. Manu V. 44, '*Ya vedavihita himsa . . . ahimsameva tam vidyat.*'
13. Cf. Schmidt 1968: 630.
14. Cf. ibid: 642.
15. Cf. respectively, *Sevakavani* 14–15, *Siddhanta ki sakhi* 50–2, and *Vyasa Vani, Siddhanta ki sakhi*, cited by Mital 1968: 496–7.
16. This illustration is reproduced by Mital (1968, opp. page 346), with no observation as to its origin.
17. Vaudeville 1976: 204 and Entwistle 1987: 114–16.
18. Entwistle, ibid.: 115. There was also the cult of *Pashupata-Lakulisa* (Shiva), as is proved by the ancient temples discovered by Growse 1890: 85–7.
19. Krishna's entourage worshipped Devi, cf. *Bhagavatapurana* 22 and 34.1–2.
20. Cf. Mital 1968: 495–6.
21. The older inhabitants of Benares can recall the large number of goats sacrificed at the temple of Durga. This ritual practice is somewhat rare today. Other examples can also be offered (see the following footnote).
22. As a rule, the 'softening' of the goddess' cult through the centuries arises from the continuing growth of vegetarianism in society as a whole (much after it was adopted by the upper castes). *Ahimsa*, thus, could develop in a coherent manner only by affecting cultural practices and food habits (cf. Dumont 1966: 187–93). But local influences could have given an impetus to the overall evolution. In Gujarat and Rajasthan, the Jain influence was doubtless more decisive than any other. Thus, in the kingdom of Mewar, a royal decree in 1693 forbade the slaughter of animals found on Jain estates (cf. Tod 1920, vol. II: 645–6, as also, on this theme, 606–7). A century later, the butchers of Baroda swore to Jain and Vaishnavite Mahajans that they would refrain from practising their trade during the major Jain, Vaishnavite and Smarta festivals (cf. Majumdar 1970: 287). From the sixteenth century onwards, the new Vaishnavite movements lent their support to the cause of *ahimsa* wherever they managed to establish themselves (cf. footnote 24). During the nineteenth century and later, the British, although they condemned sacrifices in blood for entirely different reasons, were an important factor. Animal sacrifice, like child marriage, sati and murder of the girl child, fell into disgrace (see, for example, the case of Himachal Pradesh, in Vidal 1986: 50).
23. While Vaishnavite influence undeniably contributed to the decline of

animal sacrifices, the speed of decline was relatively slow. How else can one explain that in overwhelmingly Vallabhite Gujarat, at the end of the eighteenth century, Swami Narayana should still spend the greater part of his life combating Shakta ritual practices (cf. Mallison 1974: 448)? In fact, as Pocock (1973: 74–6) notes in the case of Gujarat, it is likely that these practices co-existed with vegetarian ritual even after the population had come under the influence of Vaishnavism. The complete renunciation of bloody cults seems very recent.

24. For these numerous Devi shrines in Braj, see Entwistle 1987: 131, 302–3, 335, 338, 377, 382, 395, 396, 420, 473.
25. Cf. Brown 1974: 205.
26. *P. Kh.*, 64.45–9, cited by Brown 1974: 46.
27. The goddess is the daughter of Yashoda, the foster mother of Krishna. Cf. Coburn 1988: 232–41 on the links between the Krishna and Devi cults.
28. Biardeau 1981: 298. On the relationship between the Devi and *avatara*, see 'La Déesse', in Biardeau 1972: 142–56.
29. On this, see Granoff 1984.
30. As in the sixteenth century combat in Mathura between Keshava Kashmiri and the Muslims; cf. Clementin-Ojha 1990: 339–41.
31. Frequently, the use of supernatural power is a strategy employed in the conversion of a religious adversary, cf. Granoff 1985.
32. See too Padoux 1987: 137, n. 87.
33. Cf. *Chowkhamba Sanskrit Series*, 233, Varanasi, 1917. On Keshava Kashmiri and his work, see Clementin-Ojha 1990: 338–42.
34. On this act of magic, see Goudrian 1978: 310–33.
35. Shrikunjvihari Sharanaji; *Shri Acharyacharitavali*, Brindavan, 2036 VS: 109.
36. *Bhaktamala-ank*, Akhila Bharatiya Shrinimbarkacharyapitha, Salemabad, 1956: 610. With the aid of a *mantra*, he transforms another Natha into an ass; see *Nimbarka aur unka sampradaya*, pub. Akhila Bharatiya Shrinimbarkacharyapitha, Salemabad, 1972: 472.
37. *Bhaktamala, chappay* 75, with reference to Keshava Kashmiri.
38. Cf. Kane 1941, II, 1: 123.
39. See Thiel-Horstmann (1991) on the soldier-ascetics of Dadupanth.

REFERENCES

Bhaktirasabodhini, cf. Nabhadasa.

Biardeau, M. 1972. *L'hindouisme, Anthropologie d'une civilisation*. Paris: Flammarion.

———. 1981. 'Devi, La Déesse en Inde'. In *Dictionnaire des Mythologies*, ed. Y. Bonnefoy, 1: 295–8. Paris: Flammarion.

Bose, R., trans. 1940. *Vedanta-parijata-saurabha of Nimbarka and Vedanta-Kaustubha of Srinivasa*, Commentaries on the *Brahma-sutras*. Calcutta: Royal Asiatic Society of Bengal.

Brown, C.M. 1974. *God as Mother: A Feminine Theology in India*. Hartford, Vt.: Claude Stark and Co.

Clémentin-Ojha, C. 1990. 'La renaissance du Nimbarka sampradaya au XVIᵉ siècle. Contribution à l'étude d'une secte krsnaite'. *Journal asiatique* 278(3–4): 327–76.

Coburn, T. 1988. *Devi Mahatmya: The Crystallisation of the Goddess Tradition*. 2nd. edn. Delhi: Motilal Banarsidass.

Dumont, L. 1966. *Homo Hierarchicus. Essai sur le système des castes*. Paris: Gallimard.

Entwitle, A. 1987. *Braj Centre of Krishna Pilgrimage*. Groningen: Egbert Forsten.

Goudrian, T. 1978. *Maya, Divine and Human*. Delhi: Motilal Banarsidass.

Granoff, P. 1984. 'Holy Warriors: A Preliminary Study of Some Biographies of Saints and Kings in the Classical Indian Traditions'. *Journal of Indian Philosophy* 12(3):291–303.

———. 1985. 'Scholars and Wonder-Workers: Some Remarks on the Role of the Supernatural in Philosophical Contests in *Vedanta* Hagiographies'. *Journal of American Oriental Society* 105(3).

Growse, F.S. [1890] 1979. Cf. *Mathura: A District Memoir*, 3rd. edn. North-Western Provinces and Oudh: Government Press. Rpt. New Delhi: Asian Educational Services.

Harivyasadevacarya, *Mahavani* (XVI S.) ed. Akhila Bharatiya Srinimbarkacaryapitha. Salemabad, 1965.

Kane, P.V. [1941] 1974. *History of Dharmasastra*. Poona, Bhandarkar Oriental Research Institute.

McGregor, R.S. 1984. *Hindi Literature from its Beginnings to the Nineteenth Century*. Wiesbaden: Otto Harrassowitz (A History of Indian Literature vol. VIII, fasc. 6).

Majumdar, R.M. 1970. 'Two Gujarati Documents Bearing on *amari* or Non-Slaughter of Animals'. *Journal of the Oriental Institute* (Baroda) XIX (March).

Mallison, F. 1974. 'La secte Krichnaite des *Svami-Narayani* au Gujarat'. *Journal asiatique* 435–71.

Mital, P. 1968. *Braj ke dharma sampradayo ka itihasa*. Delhi: National Publishing House.

Nabhadasa, *Bhakta-mala*, avec la *Bhaktirasabodhini tika* de Priyadasa, ed. Sitaramasarana Bhagavanprasada Rupakala, Lucknow: Tejkumar Book Depot.

Padoux, A. 1987. 'Contributions à l'étude du *mantrasastra*'. *BEFEO* 76: 117–64.

Pocock, D.F. 1973. *Mind, Body and Wealth*. Oxford: Basil Blackwell.

Pollet, G. 1967. 'The Mediaeval *Vaisnava* Miracles as Recorded in the Hindi *Bhaktamala*'. *Le Museon* 80.

Schmidt, H.P. 1968. 'The Origin of *ahimsa*'. In *Mélanges d'indianisme à la mémoire de Louis Renou*. Paris: Éd. de Boccard.

Thiel-Horstmann, M. 1991. 'On the Dual Identity of Nagas'. In *Devotion Divine, Bhakti Traditions from the Regions of India, Studies in Honour of Charlotte Vaudeville*, ed. D.L. Eck and F. Mallison, 255–71. Groningen: Egbert Forsten, and Paris: EFEO.

Thibaut, G., trans. [1904] 1966. *The Vedanta-sutras* with the Commentary of Ramanuja. Sacred Books of the East Series 48. Delhi, Motilal Banarsidass.

Tod, James [1920] 1971. *Annals and Antiquities of Rajasthan*. Delhi: Motilal Banarsidass.

Vaudeville, C. 1976. 'Braj Lost and Found'. *Indo-Iranian Journal* 18: 195–213.

Vidal, D. 1986. 'Le puits et le sanctuaire'. *Purusartha* 10: *L'espace du temple II*, 31–54.

The So-called 'Criminal Tribes' of British India: Colonial Violence and Traditional Violence

MARIE FOURCADE

> Classification is not done because there are things to be classified; it is because classification is done that things to be classified are discovered. This conclusion is not meant to denigrate the activity of classification, or equate it with powers of illusion, but merely to relativise the results obtained and warn against their reification.
>
> JEAN POUILLON, *Le cru et le su*

The double qualification 'criminal tribe' is not specific to Indian society. It has no equivalent in any Indian language and was in fact imported into India by British administrators and jurists in the nineteenth century, who applied it to those whose traditional occupations they viewed as 'predatory' or 'delinquent'. The term 'tribe' is of an ethnic nature whilst the word 'criminal' refers to the criminal code that derived directly from Western laws. Each group's history, social organization and links with other social units would appear to relate it to one caste or the other. The groups become 'criminal' only when viewed in the light of Western notions of marginality. Far from being excluded from social forms specific to societies in the Indian subcontinent, these groups evolve within an ideological universe whose dominant principle is the classification of differences and the absence of exclusion.

Colonial Legislation: Historical Review of a Violence of Terms

British suzerainty introduced a foreign construct to local groups, which drew upon certain features and defined them as characteristics after twisting, deforming and perverting them. Two major trends can be discerned upon analysis. The first is a change in the very conception of the caste system, as the British described castes exercising marginal vocations as 'tribes'.

First, this argues a conception of caste as a separate social entity. Consequently, the overall system derived from this would be a mere juxtaposition of ethnically, professionally and culturally diverse groups. Second, this also indicates a certain idealization of the Brahminical morality which could not accommodate robbery and crime. Such a clarification of the Hindu world view is *borne out* by frequent use of the term 'tribe', rather than 'caste', in the works on criminal law.

The second trend is the emergence of the colonial desire to use social intervention and reform as a means of better control. Pax Britannica enabled a repressive British policy that would correct and prevent criminal activity. Gradually, colonial codes and judicial institutions supplanted traditional means of dispensing justice. From 1830 onwards, the penal repression of earlier decades allied with the spirit of a 'civilizing mission' to bring about the rehabilitation of these groups. A new kind of education, spearheaded by missionaries was imposed on them, with little success as it turned out, owing to two reasons. The foremost one was that the administrators in the corrective settlements, entrusted with the task of correcting the 'tribal' way of life, lacked qualifications and motivation, preferring to keep a watchful eye on their charges rather than understanding them and enabling their rehabilitation. Second, men who had never broken the norms of their own social groups and had in no way repudiated religion were defined as delinquents and outcastes. Thus, the colonial administration widened the gap between facts and the interpretation of facts. The Commission of Inquiry into the 'criminal tribes', formed in the wake of India's Independence, only highlighted the absurdity of the very idea of social reintegration.

The legal provisions applicable to 'criminal tribes' must be viewed in the light of the colonial administration's varied surveying methods, such as the Census and the Gazetteers, for each method reflected Western values and the set ideas of its administrative cadre more faithfully than it reflected observations in the field. Two distinct periods need to be identified. The first, from 1754 to 1871, covers the period when the British were establishing themselves and their power in India, in discourse as in deed. Gradually, there came about a superimposition of Western culture on Indian culture, and in some cases the overlapping of the two. From 1871 to 1947, a number of laws were promulgated on the reform of 'criminal tribes', such as the Criminal Tribes Act of 1871 and the Criminal Castes and Tribes Act of 1911. A critical analysis of the former is the basis of the present paper. The various amendments that were moved to the Act, before it was scrapped altogether, indicate as much the lack of coherence of the colonial dispensation as native resistance to its implementation.

At the end of the eighteenth century, and even at the beginning of the nineteenth century, the East India Company established its rule over India with no concern beyond garnering great profit. The potentially anarchic elements were stamped out. The Company officials needed to examine several factors. The objectionable activities of local caste groups fell within the authority of the regular police. However, since administrators in the hinterland were inclined to be somewhat more respectful of Indian sensibilities and institutions, and in any case lacked the means to enforce Pax Britannica, it inevitably put them on a course of conflict with directives from the Company's London or Calcutta offices.

Change began after the year 1830, as a result of missionary activity and the influence of utilitarianism, which sought justification for its philosophical tenets in political economy. A social policy was derived, which sought to purge the native society of certain 'abuses'. These abusive practices were identified in relation to the Western morality. Among such practices was *sati* (cf. Weinberger-Thomas 1989), or ritual immolation of a widow on her husband's funeral pyre, and the criminality of the '*Thugs*, the well known Kali-worshipping highwaymen who specialized in ritual death by strangulation (cf. Sleeman 1934; Bruce 1968; Gordon 1969).

Until that point, no fundamental break had been sought with the traditional Indian order. The Company's government merely sought to take over a part of the public defence functions that Indian villages were in any case performing. The critical threshold was crossed when Western notions of punitive justice and correctional methods were incorporated in the laws, soon becoming applicable to the social structure as a whole (Pouchepadass 1979: 137). The Criminal Tribes Act of 1871 was that point of departure.

Strengths and Weaknesses of the Criminal Tribes Act, 1871

Under this Act, any group, tribe or class believed to be 'systematically perpetrating' certain kinds of attacks on persons and property could be designated as 'criminal' by a Provincial Government, after obtaining the consent of the Governor-General. Thus, since an entire group could be found guilty without the need for a trial, the authorities could impose a strict regime and give themselves wide powers of detention. While introducing the legislation to the Viceroy's Council, J.V. Stephens, the Council's member (Law) said,

> The caste system is India's distinguishing trait. By virtue of this system, merchants are constituted in a caste, a family of carpenters will remain a family of carpenters for a whole century from now, or five centuries from now, if it survives that long. Let us bear that in mind and grasp quickly what we mean here by professional criminals. We are dealing here with a tribe whose ancestors have been criminals since the very dawn of time, whose members are sworn by the laws of their caste to commit crime, and whose descendants will also be criminal unless exterminated or neutralized as we did with the Thugs. When a man declares that he is a criminal, it must be understood that he has been thus from the beginning and that he will remain thus until the end. To reform him is impossible, for it is his vocation, his caste, I would go to the extent of saying his faith, to commit crimes. (in Sankar 1979: 61)

Such an amalgam of terms—caste, tribe, vocation: a melange of the ritualistic, the ethnic and the secular, all raised to the same plane just for the convenience of British colonial legislation! The inappropriateness of the vocabulary used demonstrates the hiatus between the colonial perception of Indian realities and those realities themselves when twisted out of and placed outside their own context. The very text of the Act lays down a pure criminal jurisprudence which would facilitate the application of an arbitrary law. The British, authors of this law, failed to take into account an essential characteristic of the caste system—its interdependence. The Act was promulgated in 1871, the year of the first census of India's population. The choice of ethnographic and professional categories was to plague the decadal Indian census first instituted by the colonial administration in 1871–2. As they came down heavily in favour of sheer enumeration, the British missed the chance to find a common thread that would have enabled the identification of distinct and meaningful groups (Pouchepadass 1979: 138). Such simplistic, descriptive taxonomy only served to atomize castes and fix them in immobility on a mosaic of juxtaposed characteristics. Issuing from and alluding to the modern universe of the individual, it spirited away any trace of the interdependence and complementarity which held castes together in a single totality.

It was also during the second half of the nineteenth century that land

and property rights were codified and laws formulated on the transfer of property (Galey 1973). This was the essence of the 'legal' structure that Great Britain introduced into India at that time. The law governing 'criminal tribes' was just one aspect of this structure. The surveys of 'criminal tribes' prepared by the British police in each province are a precious mine of information (cf. Gunthorpe 1882; Kennedy 1908; Paupero Naidu 1905). Although the information these surveys provide is rather more sweeping than the official Castes and Tribes compilation of the 'delinquent' population, the fact that they emphasize 'delinquence' and are written in a repressive perspective makes for a wealth of first-hand information which the ethnologist and historian can interpret. The surveys, in fact, are the very illustration of the ideology that underlies the artificial creation of 'criminal tribes'.

To Whom does the 'Criminal Tribe' Tag Apply?

The label 'criminal tribe', in this colonial classification, does not apply to the adivasis, India's first inhabitants, who live in autonomous tribal groups, but rather to other groups whose orbit takes them closer to the mainstream, and whose values and norms are determined by the mainstream. Viewed thus, the term 'criminal tribes' applies to: the groups whose profession was stealing; the groups which occasionally took to stealing (for example, during famine or hard times or natural calamities); to the dissidents who had been ostracized, excluded or outcast by mainstream castes (J. Pouchepadass 1978: 130, notes that sometimes there may be just a minor cleavage within a caste, and the breakaway group may continue to bear the original caste name with perhaps a suffix that would indicate the 'delinquent' nature of the original caste.); and finally to other groups, which bring together outcastes of diverse milieus and become a melting pot for people of different castes and religions. Simple rites governed admission to these groups.

Scholars have long agreed on the mixed origins of these 'criminal tribes', arguing that they openly seek to add to their numbers by recruitment (Bhargava 1949, Chap. I). Indifferent though they are to the need to preserve their purity or an identity, these groups, according to these discourses, nurse their own myths, swear by their own code of honour, internalize their own values in childhood and take to felony as their specific function. Such a characterization have thus made them fit to integrate perfectly with the structure of Indian society as Dumont defined it, 'In a hierarchical schema, the acknowledged difference of a group, which places it in opposition to other groups, becomes the very principle by which it can be integrated with society' (Dumont 1966: 242).

The Criminal Tribes Act in Practice

The law authorized District Magistrates to identify and act against such groups as and when they believed it necessary, to order detention and house arrest, and to corral people into corrective settlements. Until 1910, when philanthropic and missionary organizations such as the London Mission or the Salvation Army took over, these settlements were managed not by the police but by specialized functionaries. According to Pouchepadass, 'The last pre-Independence census listed 198 "criminal tribes", covering a total of 2.3 million people; 77,000 of them had been identified, and less than a third of these had been placed in corrective settlements' (Pouchepadass 1979: 141).

The dismal statistics probably arose from the fact that the law of 1871 was difficult to implement (not least because of the procedure involved in declaring a tribe as 'criminal') and necessitated resources in time, personnel and finance that were well beyond the capacities of the overburdened colonial administration (Radhakrishna 1992: 177).[1] Its own efficacy would have been undermined. Amendments were made to the Act first in 1876 and later in 1897, before a complete overhaul was undertaken in the year 1911. Although Sections 1 and 2 applied to the whole of India, the Criminal Tribes Act of 1871 was meant essentially for implementation in the north-western provinces, Punjab and Avadh. An amendment in 1876 made it applicable to lower Bengal; a subsequent amendment, in 1897, empowered local governments to separate tribal children, four to eighteen years of age, from their parents if these parents were considered undesirable elements. The Provincial Governments were authorized to declare such tribes as 'criminal' and to act against them. According to the provisions of another amendment in 1911, members of such 'criminal tribes' were brought completely under executive authority, thereby depriving them of their rights under common law. Thus, they were obliged to register themselves, record their fingerprints, and notify the administration every time they changed their residence. The Provincial Governments had the power to restrain them from changing their domicile and place any necessary curbs on the movement of such 'tribes' (Shankar 1979: 62).

Converting these 'criminal tribes' to a life of sedentariness and property ownership would have involved winding up the somewhat artificial manner in which they were separated within corrective settlements. (Those who were thought capable of criminality were shorn of their status and placed near the colony's exits. In effect, this meant that they could either recommence their habitual lifestyle or be fully integrated within the colony.) On Independence, the fledgling Indian Republic suspended the application of this law and finally repealed the Criminal Tribes Act in 1952. Offences, if any, committed by members of the erstwhile 'criminal tribes' thus came within the purview of general and common law.

Police figures reveal that 'the repeal of the law did not lead to a significant increase in the criminal activity of the groups in question' (Pouchepadass 1979: 149). However, a law was passed in several states at about the same period (called the Habitual Offenders Act), which stipulated that those held guilty on three or more occasions of offences under certain sections of the Indian Penal Code must register with the concerned authorities who are empowered, if necessary, to intern such offenders. This return to individual-based justice, which was in keeping with the spirit of the new Constitution of India, marked the end of an abusive practice instituted by the British. When the Indian Government restored the notion of individual responsibility and buried Sir J.V. Stephens' idea of the inherent 'criminal heredity' of entire groups, it finally eliminated the simplistic and caricatural notions of caste that had given rise to abusive pronouncements of collective guilt.

Ideological Underpinnings and Perverse Effects of the Criminal Tribes Act

During the nineteenth century, first in the West and then all over the industrialized countries, the poor were criminalized by the very fact of being designated as 'dangerous classes' (Chevalier 1978). Particular attention has been paid to the contextual and historical definition of crime and criminality in recent works seeking to shed light on the different streams of thought that led to the formulation of a systematic policy against the so-called 'criminal tribes'. This policy found expression in special legislations against such groups and was backed with a scarcely disguised and concerted official campaign to ban groups designated as habitual and born criminals. For instance, the Doms were described as 'abominable' and the Kuravers as 'incorrigible', thus, projecting demoniacal qualities onto the Other.[2] In the work of Ranajit Guha and others in Subaltern Studies, it is possible not only to discern the awakening amongst the concerned sections and the manner in which it was repressed but also to distinguish real crime from social crime with some clarity in the ambiguous zone that separates the two. Crime and insurrection, of course, derived from entirely different codes of violence. While insurrections were the point of convergence of a public or community event, crime connoted conspiracy, secrecy and the individual.

A study of the ideological origins of the Criminal Tribes Act (CTA) of 1871 and its subsequent revisions, reveals that they derive inspiration from the definitions of criminality of their times. Further, such definitions of crime as the British advanced were linked to their larger view of the structures and functioning of Indian culture and society, as well as to their Government's ideological imperative to justify the domination and subjugation of India (Cohn 1968). The colonial establishment's legal policies, founded as it was on erroneous and blanket assertions about Indian society, were apt to yield unforeseeable results. The British authorities amalgamated the notion of moral influence with the concept of 'the power of the State' (ibid.: 5, 6, 78). Once designated as Criminal Tribes, the affected groups were left with no legal recourse to rid themselves of the label. As was to be expected with the criminological theories of those times, legislators were quick to accept the idea of 'hereditary crime'. The belief that criminals were biological degenerates was widespread during the nineteenth century, especially as it drew to its close and the writings of Darwin and Spencer reinforced such beliefs. 'In the nineteenth century, the criminal theme was transformed into a social theme' (Chevalier 1978: 144).

As extended to India, the criminal class/dangerous class equation stood the caste system on its head. B.S. Cohn demonstrates that British theories about Indian society were founded on the belief that India was a collection of castes, that India was the sum of its parts and that these parts were castes. Inevitably, this held important ramification for theories about the causality of criminal behaviour. Thus, it was believed, the dangerous castes, which could be easily identified, as well as their criminal tendencies were deep-rooted in the very structure and functioning of Indian society. Taken to the extreme, this oft-repeated logic could not fail to produce texts such as the Criminal Tribes Act. Apart from placing an indelible brand of Criminal Tribe on such groups, criminal social and behavioural characteristics were attributed to them. The official judgement on the Criminal Tribes resulted in many of them being characterized as gypsies, wandering tribes and vagrant tribes. This was very much in line with the belief that vagrancy was 'the breeding ground of crime'.

Entire groups were indiscriminately designated as 'criminal'. Little distinction was made within such 'peripatetic' groups as migrant–shepherds, bards, minstrels, mendicants and itinerant peddlers, or for that matter between castes and tribes. In the case of wandering groups whose very mobility was cause for suspicion, the British made no effort to come to grips with the major features of such nomadism (cyclical and rhythmic variations, even though these could be foreseen; changes of place within territorial limits or frontiers spelled out for each lineage or family, thus enabling a better definition of the migratory group). As a result, official descriptions of 'Criminal Tribes' remained static, shorn of a historic dimension (Nigam 1990).[3]

An exception in officialdom at that time was the Chief Commissioner of the Central Provinces who noted that frequently these itinerant groups were well integrated with the region's society and economy. He wrote, 'Each tribe had its own name, its specific skills and crafts, which were often welcomed in the villages they frequented' (cited in Yang 1985: 144, no. 25).

Unlike the *Thugs*, offences committed by the Criminal Tribes pertained mainly to property. While this did not require the same level of intervention from the state, each case did undermine the Raj's authority; whence the need for draconian measures. The elimination of the *Thugs* became an imperative since the *Thugs* had become a mortal threat to those seeking to establish Pax Britannica; the thefts and dacoities committed by the Criminal Tribes challenged the capacity to maintain law and order.

The content of the Criminal Tribes Act of 1871 was forged as much in accordance with the contemporary ideas on the causality of crime as with colonial conceptions about deviant behaviour. The colonial regime looked upon the police as an agency that could simultaneously be entrusted with surveillance and with enforcement. The resources allocated were meagre, as could only be expected from a regime that saw profit as its sole objective and did not seek to interfere with Indian society beyond the extent necessary to ensure control and consolidation of colonial interests.

W.J. HATCH: VIOLENCE OF A COLONIAL LOOK AT THE KURAVARS, DESIGNATED AS 'CRIMINAL TRIBES'

Consider, by way of an example, a British administrator's monograph, relating to southern India in the nineteenth century (Hatch 1976 [1928]). Published in 1928, it bears the following title: *The Land Pirates of India: An Account of the Kuravers, a Remarkable Tribe of Hereditary Criminals, their Extraordinary Skill as Thieves, Cattle-lifters, Highwaymen and their Manners and Customs.* The author specifies that its purpose is to recount the 'romantic' aspect of the lives of the Kuravars, who are mentioned in the Government's regional gazetteers as well as in E. Thurston's *Castes and Tribes of Southern India* (1909). Hatch based his book on these two sources as well as on documents made available by the Board of Revenue of the Madras Government.

In geographical terms, the by and large nomadic Kuravars were mainly to be found in the Madras Presidency, in the Tamil and Telugu speaking areas, as also in the princely state of Mysore and parts of the Bombay Presidency. An observation is called for on the very first chapter, Who is the Kuravar? Hatch identifies this caste with a collective individual without postulating the existence of a system that would enable the study of the group in its totality. The word 'Kuravar' derives from *kuram*, the Tamil word for divination. Many Kuravars, in fact, do practise that art. There exist several variations of the term '*kuravar*', such as the word '*Kaikaries*', used essentially in the Bombay Presidency, which derives from the Tamil *kai* (hand) and *karan* (man). Obviously, the word is related to palmistry, to chiromancy. The Kuravars are either itinerant or apt to be found on the fringes of villages. They face great difficulties in earning a living when many of them come together in a single locality. The 1891 census evaluates their number at around 135,000.

According to Hatch, Indian criminals fell into the following typology: the ordinary criminal; the habitual offender; the hereditary criminal and the incorrigible criminal. The Kuravars were believed to combine the last three types.[4] Incorrigible criminals could be divided into two sub-categories. The first covers those who, owing to a defect in their nature or owing to a lacuna in their upbringing, lose the capacity to distinguish between right and wrong and therefore steal compulsively. Such a criminal if captured and then released would almost immediately recommence his thefts. The second sort of incorrigible criminal is one who seldom or never steals on his own account, but is never averse to directing others in their efforts, since he loves the risk, the pleasure and the thrill of the game. The fact that society opposes him merely serves to add some spice to his existence and to sharpen his astuteness. As the organization's thinker, he occupies a place of eminence within the 'criminal tribe' and is entitled to honour, respect and obedience. Hatch justifies the very discourse of Stephens that has been examined earlier, 'As the Kuravar tribe includes all these types, the Government was called upon to designate the Kuravars as a Criminal Tribe' (Hatch pub. 1976: 20), and goes on to add, 'The Kuravars belong to a known caste. They have a community spirit, caste privileges, practices which cannot be transgressed and a tribal law that must be obeyed. A man does not become a Kuravar because he is a thief. He is a thief *because* he is a Kuravar. *It is a matter of birth and blood . . .*' (ibid.: 27; emphasis added). The author uses the term 'caste' as much to denote similarity with other groups as to define specificity. The shift from 'caste' to 'tribe' reveals the implicit movement that took place even as a definition of the caste system was emerging. This shift makes synonyms of terms that initially had, and still now have their own defining characteristics.

The Kuravars: Myths about their Origin and their Religion

Several myths exist about the origins of the Kuravars. In a ninth century poem, there is a reference to *kurammakal*, or children of Kuravar, but no other precise allusion to the caste. The group is said to have been founded by a god; or, beings from another world are believed to have played an important role in establishing them within society. In E. Thurston's account (1909, III–K: 445), drawn from sacred books, it is related that,

> Venudu, son of Agneswathu, a direct descendant of Brahma, reigned over the world but could not have a son. He, like other mortals, passed on. His corpse was neither cremated nor buried, but embalmed. The seven planets could not leave the land ungoverned. From the thigh of the embalmed king, it was decided to create a man, who came to be called Nishudu. Uncouth and ungainly, he was believed to lack the necessary regal bearing. A second effort was made to produce another man, this time with happier

results; when Proothu Chakravarthi came forth, he was duly installed as monarch. The enraged Nishudu prayed to the gods to give him the right to rule, as he had in fact been created for that very purpose. However, since Chakravarthi had already been crowned, Nishudu was sent into exile, though he was given the title of Governor of the Forests. He it was who was the forefather of the Kuravars. As he kept a vow of silence so that he may know the spirit of the gods, some of his descendants go by the name of 'Yerukulas', which derives from the Telugu word for 'knowing'. Yerukulas and Kuravars are branches issuing from a single trunk.

Here, as in the case of several other myths pertaining to the 'Criminal Tribes', one is dealing with an usurped myth about royal origins. It would appear to be a defining characteristic of these groups to claim descent from deposed royalty. Another such myth traces the origin of the Kuravars to the *Mahabharata*, as descendants of Dharmaraja (Biardeau 1981: 71, 73).

In historical terms, Paupa Rao Naidu (1905), who studied this caste from the point of view of the police, established that at the outset the Kuravars were attached to temples in south India as servitors, before a higher caste evicted them. Hatch, however, believes there is insufficient grounds for this thesis which was founded only on the fact that the Kuravars had a *gotra*, or clan. The *gotra*, one is inclined to think, indicates that they had a special role to play in temples and in certain rites related to processions (cf. Reiniche 1979: 60). Hatch attempts to refute Paupa Rao Naidu's hypothesis by arguing that, 'Those who served the gods abandoned these temple services and went away to become marauders' (Hatch 1976: 36). Could this not, in fact, be interpreted as an extension of their surveillance function? Is it not possible that by losing their assigned function they would have also lost their specific position *vis-a-vis* the gods? And that this led them to adopt activities which were forbidden to them earlier by divine control but which fell within their *dharma*?

He further argues that the names replete with religious significance are advanced as a sort of custom, without taking into account their origin, which may have been religious in nature. Hatch is inclined to think that these names with religious echoes were included in the *gotras*, 'with abusive intent and engender the belief that they were a group of devotees rather than a band of robbers. By moving within the region and pretending to be temple servitors, they were received and tolerated. This was a splendid Kuravar ruse to lead people to believe that they belonged to an honourable profession' (loc. cit.).

To Hatch, it was only the Kuravars' wiliness that prevailed upon them to select *gotras* whose names bore religious overtones. Equally, however, it could be argued that the Kuravars took these names not with a view to mark their identity *vis-a-vis* other castes but in view of themselves and their own original functions. Whether this is unfounded is yet to be demonstrated.

According to Hatch, even as children the Kuravars are filled with accounts of warring gods in the higher world, of devils in dispute in the lower depths and of spirits that inhabit 'the space in between'. Prayers are offered at the temples before the start of each expedition as well as when offerings are made. The Kuravars in the south worship Subrahmanya, patron of thieves. In the decorated interior of the *kavadi* that they bear on their shoulders are the offerings that they give to the temple—to the recitation of *mantras*, consecrated groceries, food, fowl are placed before the god. The best known shrines are Chidambaram in south Arcot and Tiruttani in north Arcot. While Ganesh is worshipped at marriages, Mariamman, goddess of small pox, commands her own following (cf. Thurston 1909, III–K: 462). Doubtless it is from their double function as thieves and guards that the Kuravars' worship of Aiyanar derives. Aiyanar, the lord protector of fields and houses, is the sworn enemy of thieves. The worship of Mudevi, goddess of the shadows, gains clear preference over the worship of Sedevi, goddess of light. There is also a bloody tradition for the worship of Kali.

Social Organization and Justice of the Kuravars

In ancient times, the Kuravars split into two major branches, one sedentary and the other nomadic. Members of the sedentary branch settled down in huts on the outskirts of a hamlet or village. They busied themselves in a variety of small jobs (such as basket weaving) or made tidy profits from robbery and 'blackmail'. If the village's regular residents began to take a lean view of them, they would move on to another hamlet. Only a few professional thieves could survive within a defined geographical area. The others necessarily had to adopt a nomadic lifestyle. When he was made the victim of frequent and systematic crime the Indian landholder's tolerance began to fray at the edges. He then had no recourse but to get together with his caste brethren in the village and organize dissuasive resistance to the Kuravars. Imprisoning the Kuravars merely brought subsequent reprisals.

According to Thurston (1909, III–K: 451 sq., cited by Hatch 1928: 62–3), the four important classes amongst the Kuravars are founded on a division of ritual work along the following lines: *Sathepati*, a corruption of the term *Sathupati*, this includes adorning a god with flowers, jewels and clothes. Second class was of *Kavadi* was a small, semi-circular arch borne on the shoulders, carrying offerings to a temple god. The *Manapati* sang the praises of god in a temple. The fourth class was the *Mendraguti* which is a corruption of the term, *Menrikutti*, implying the stitching of footwear and offering it in a temple (a custom that is still prevalent in Tirupati, apart from other shrines).

The major sub-divisions, according to Hatch (ibid.), derived from different kinds of professional specialization among the Kuravars: Kaval Kuravar: sentries, scouts; Uppu Kuravar: salt sellers; Thappai Kuravar: bamboo workers and basket weavers; Karuvepillai: term used to designate curry leaves; Pankaikarie: snake charmers; Parukiyerukula: ear piercers, tattoo artists, also known as Pachakuti Kuravar; Koot Kaikaries: dancers; Bhan Santree Kuravar: musicians; Ram Kaikaries: stone workers; 'Nari' Kuravar: those who eat jackals, foxes and eagles; Koonachi Kuravar: brush makers; Sadepati Kaikaries: denizens of the jungle (basket weavers); Koodekatti: belt, net and basket workers.

There existed other divisions, generally related to occupations, sometimes not those actually exercised but to the vocation assigned to the clan at the very origins (Hatch, loc. cit.). Unlike the Kallars studied by L. Dumont (1957), however, nothing in the case of the Kuravars would lead one to discern a direct relationship with robbery which, according to Hatch, was their principal function.

Loyalty and mutual assistance were primordial among the Kuravars. Although pressure from the police led to divisions, there still existed a rock solid fraternal feeling born of ties of blood and shared lifestyles. Prison terms were preferred to the weight of being subjected to everyday discipline and loss of liberty. As caste brethren were always at hand to provide an alibi, it was practically impossible to establish guilt. Sometimes, the very perpetrator of a crime would happily 'assist' the police in their efforts to find the offender. According to Hatch their cunning was a by-word. Their capacity to lie was quite out of the ordinary.

In their robbing methods, they clearly followed enunciated principles. For example, they would not kill even if a life taken would enable them to achieve their objectives. Varied processes were used; drugs were used to induce sleep, or a beggar's guise was adopted, or a stealthy use of the scissors was considered necessary. When they burgled, first they flung sand pebbles or another object into the house to ensure its denizens were sleeping. Then a hole was dug in the wall, just large enough to enable a child to crawl in and open the door. Most raids were mounted in groups. The chief, chosen on the basis of his knowledge of the Indian Penal Code, was entitled to twice as large a share as that of any other member of the gang. Women members whose menfolk may be in prison were entitled to a half-share. Retired members may draw a one-eighth share and sometimes a minor share may be set aside for those who did not take part in the attack. A final one-eighth share was reserved for the god. Not all gangs were governed by a single set of strict rules on the division of the spoils, and it was possible to observe considerable differences between districts.

'Kuravars' quarrels,' says a south Indian proverb, 'are endless.' The quarrels could be on just about anything, about women in particular. Disputes, according to Hatch, were settled without recourse to the judicial machinery established by the government. A *panchayat* (Council) presided over by a chief, investigated the reasons for disputes. The *panchayat's* decisions were simple and/or cruel. Judgement by ordeal was uncertain in nature. No elaborate system existed to collect proof, nor was any interest shown in how evidence was procured. However, by instinct the judges were experts in assessing character and their knowledge of the tribe's thought processes was so deep and so sharp that they rarely erred in their final verdict. Hatch maintained that the specificity of the Kuravars was that no other group in conflict with the colonial police had so thoroughly organized and so frequently practised gang robbery. Nowhere else was it so difficult to neutralize such activity as with the Kuravars. Reorganized earlier to combat the *Thugs* (Fourcade 1989; Freitag 1991), the Madras police drew inspiration from the same policies to deal with the Kuravars. But, in fact, many members of the old police force belonged to the 'Criminal Tribes', and those who did not were fearful of organized burglar groups. It would appear, therefore, that belonging to the police actually worked in their favour and, far from hindering their banditry, it conferred, in fact, an advantage on them. This apart, the distinctive feature worthy of attention was their role and function as sentries and protectors.

PROTECTORS-THIEVES, THIEVES-PROTECTORS: NON-VIOLENCE AT THE COST OF PROTECTION

A Well Organized System

Among the Kuravars, the Kavalgar (*kavalkaran*) is one who was entrusted with the security of a village and its property. Wherever the Kuravars were to be found, the villagers seemed to require the services of a watchman. Every landowner worth the name had to pay his share to the Kavalgar if he was to benefit from the protection provided by the Kuravars. The watchman could live far afield (about 5 or 6 km away) and his task could possibly consist merely of coming by to collect his dues. While the size of the contribution varied, the gift of a herd of sheep once a year was customary, as was the transfer of a stock of foodgrains at the time of the harvest. An additional sheep was needed to be thrown in if there should be a marriage in the sentry's family. A Kavalgar with a certain number of villages under his purview could earn fairly hefty sums. To the British, this protection was just blackmail. To be fair to the Kavalgar, he was required by tradition to restore lost sheep or stolen foodgrains or to pay for them in cash. It was not uncommon for a sentry to receive ten sheep for his services and yet 'owe' twenty for those that had been stolen from him. Kavalgars needed to be on good terms with one another to avoid turf battles. Areas were clearly demarcated so that no unnecessary calls were made upon the lives and means of the landholders who sustained them year in and year out.

If a Kuravar discovered that one of his own group had committed a theft, he immediately informed the chief. If a suspect was not named right away, every effort was made to identify the culprit. 'There must be honour among thieves,' says Hatch (1976: 106), 'without which the caste system would be shattered and serious conflict would follow amongst the tribes.' Men, women and children alike joined in the search for the guilty one, especially if the Kavalgar concerned was a person of standing within the community. For then it would be an insult to him, a personal affront, if other tribals could enter his jurisdiction with impunity and make off with goods entrusted to him for protection. 'Did a Kuravar in the village possess a sheep? Was a sheep's hide sold to the Muslim merchant? Has a member of the caste been a bit of a spendthrift lately? Has someone purchased a new set of garments?' (Hatch, ibid.: 107). To find the guilty one was a matter of duty. 'Tribal' laws enjoin that there shall be no theft amongst them and that those laws must be defended by finding the perpetrator.

The chief called for a meeting of the oldest members of the caste. After secret deliberations, they decided upon a course of action. If a particular person was suspected, he was summoned and given an opportunity to prove his innocence. If the accused acknowledged having committed the crime, the stolen object was to be produced and, if possible, thrown into the courtyard of the rightful owner. If the stolen object was a sheep or a bullock, the animal was to be tied up and left in a lonely spot for the owner to find before the break of dawn. Where the stolen object could not be found, compensation in cash must be made to the owner though the identity of the thief was protected. With reference to his peers in the caste group, the offender had to make amends by hosting a feast. When a guilty person failed to confess, he was subjected to an ordeal. If he refused to submit to this test, he was driven out of the fold and placed in isolation. As a rule, the suspect acknowledged guilt rather than expose himself to such punishment, for such acknowledgement and a modest fine paid to the *panchayat* or the tribal court entitled him to continue as a member of the 'tribe'.

In such fixed and formalized caste justice, one may observe the presence and application of such notions as ostracism and banishment in relation to actions that contravene norms.

Hatch explains this phenomenon as follows:

> There was no organized police force. Those who had vast landed interests were called upon to evolve a system whereby their lands could be watched and protected. As a matter of principle, then, they decided that it would be best to entrust the task to a thief, by selecting men with criminal inclinations to perform the watchman's job, in the knowledge that just as a dog does not eat another dog, a thief does not steal from another. This came to be recognized as an appropriate form of protection wherever tribes of thieves were to be found. (Hatch 1976: 109)

In this explanation, based on the logic of totemic taboos so dear to those times, one sees the ambivalence of the function of the watchman as opposed to that of the thief, both recruited for the same reasons.

As a corollary to the *kaval* system, which was basically meant to remunerate the watchman, there arose another, related, system for landholders who did not employ a Kavalgar. Such landholders were required to pay *tuppukuli* (or, money for detection)[5] when they sought to find lost or stolen property. This practice arose from the fact that many landholders did not pay the watchmen. Consequently, the security of herds lying outside each Kavalgar's geographically designated area could not be guaranteed, especially since Kavalgars were only liable unto those who paid them. A defaulting landholder could receive a night call from the Kavalgar or one of the latter's representatives so that reparation could be made instantly.

Where the *tuppukuli* system prevailed, the person responsible for the theft called on the owner and promised to restore the stolen object at a suitable time and place, provided an appropriate amount of money was paid and provided the deal was kept secret. The police must never be involved in such transactions, as the following account of an incident demonstrates:

> A farmer who had lost two bullocks was willing to pay the tuppukuli so that the bullocks may be restored to him. Secretly, he informed the police. An inspector and a contingent of policemen arrived at the spot where the bullocks were to be restored. When the robbers brought the bullocks, the police moved in, arresting two robbers and capturing the animals. The other cattle rustlers escaped, sought out their caste brethren and returned in strength to the spot, where they took on the police, recaptured the bullocks and released their comrades. (cited in Hatch 1976: 110)

Tuppukuli usually amounted to half the value of the stolen object, though this was consolation enough. Several efforts were made to break the system and it is true that the influence of the system waned in many places. But a break with the system often brought confusion and distress in the community. When certain European householders (notably a case in Trichinopoly) refused to employ a Kavalgar to watch over their home and property, they were subjected to a series of burglaries of their vessels and furniture. The moment a Kavalgar was employed, the burglaries ceased, as though by magic, and the objects were restored.

The Kuravars' Condition under the CTA

All Kuravars claimed to be employed. If they could not prove the legitimacy of their sources of income, they were charged under the Indian Criminal Procedure Code and required to provide a surety or go to prison until such time as someone was willing to guarantee their good behaviour. Kuravars were entitled to a piece of land and became cultivators. While the men were away thieving, the land was cultivated by their wives and young sons. In earlier times, some of them had turned to herding but in more recent times most have taken to farming.

Only during the last two decades of the nineteenth century did the Madras Government awaken to the lacunae in the Criminal Tribes Act of 1871, as amended in 1876 and 1897. The new Act of 1911 enabled a better means of circumscribing and controlling the Kuravars. Not only did this affect the other Criminal Tribes, but also those who associated with such groups in any manner whatsoever.

At statutorily designated intervals, every man registered under the law was supposed to present himself to the police or to the village headman, with a view to justify his movements or change of residence. Frequently, they spent the night at the police post and worked at home during the day. Sometimes, this movement involved distances of 5 to 6 km. The other villagers were invited to spy upon and bring to the authorities' notice any suspicious movement by these 'known depredators'. However, this expedient seldom worked and the police themselves had to go to the spot. The number of Kuravars registered as 'known depredators' was legion. Hinduism's complexity prevented the British from promulgating the sort of religious morality that would have prevented the divorce of the legal space from the spiritual space. The fortunes of various 'missions' operating special schools among the Criminal Tribes were apt to fluctuate as did the short-term results they obtained (Radhakrishna 1992). According to the 1911 Census, six out of every thousand members of the Criminal Tribes could write their name and read a simple book.

Kallar/Kuravar: A Comparative Example

According to the 1931 Census, of the Kallar caste there were 5,10,000 members of the Pramalai Kallar sub-caste in the southern districts of the Madras Presidency. It was amongst these Pramalai Kallars that Louis Dumont did his research (1957).[6] In Tamil, the word '*Kallar*' is the plural of '*Kallan*', which means 'thief'. The Kallars enjoyed, and continue to enjoy, such a reputation. Most of them looked upon themselves as descendants of warriors and claim the status of Kshatriyas. There existed a definite relationship between theft, the major caste function highlighted by the British, and the Kallars' own claims to a martial function. Although its origins are not clear, the caste's more recent history as well as some of its characteristics would appear to bear out the martial vocation. From the eighteenth century onwards, not only did they fight to retain control over their own lands, they also refused to submit to the suzerainty of the nearby sovereigns. Further, they took part in the armed skirmishes as local allies of those resisting British or French occupation. Nowadays the Kallars seem to be small-time farmers eking out a subsistence from the land.

They had two supplementary sources of income—the right to thievery and, as a corollary, the right to provide security, as with the Kuravars. The traditional 'watchman' status legitimized the use of force and also enabled them to claim the privileges of domestic service. Thus, under

Pax Britannica, they sought to intervene as arbitrators, thereby consolidating their position and laying claim to additional prerogatives.

Their offences were usually in the form of pillaging expeditions mounted outside their own region, thus illustrating the law of retaliation. According to Nelson (1868, II: 41, 56), 'One Kallar, seized by a violent fit of anger, slashed his own ear lobe just so that his adversary may do the same unto himself, as a sort of honourable reparation.' In the account of the missionary, Father Martin (cited in Nelson, ibid., I: 53), 'For a trifling offence, a man put his own wife and children to death, just so that he could have the satisfaction of forcing his adversary to do the same.' In Dumont's interpretation, these acts of self-mutilation (as extended to the family) 'arise from the final playing out of aggression, when the self counts for little if it helps to wound the opponent; thus, even today, a ruinous and futile litigation will be initiated only to reduce the adversary to rack and ruin' (Dumont 1957: 285). As behaviour was extrovert amongst the Kallars, the results were immediate, often manifest in physical forms. They were also translatable under Kallar law in terms of value–price–money. Thus, if two men slashed each other's ears, he who acted first was condemned to pay two and a half rupees, which were divided accordingly. As Dumont notes, 'Death is the unit of the currency of reparations. As death is the complete annihilation of the body, indemnities arising from the amputation or elimination of parts of the body are rationalized as fractions of this unit. If the head is worth one unit, the eye is believed to be worth half a unit, the nose and the ear a fourth of the unit and so on' (Dumont 1957: 304).

A sliding downward scale of tariffs thus existed and included even the minutest injuries. To what could all this counting be attributed? It would appear to correspond to the fact that the Kallars extended to the social body their vision of the physical body. At the same time, it should be set against the process of indebtedness (which L. Renou 1978 and Ch. Malamoud 1980 have studied), and against the law of tit for tat retaliation referred to earlier.

From 1871 to 1947, the Pramalai Kallars were governed by the Criminal Tribes Act of 1871 and the Criminal Tribes and Castes Act of 1911. As the registration of the population had been completed by the year 1921, efforts were made to constitute a *panchayat* in each village, elected by the inhabitants and controlled by the police, which would be responsible for the good behaviour of the population. The *panchayat* was entrusted with the tasks of eliminating the watchman system, bringing to the authorities' notice any case of flight or absence, and identifying and bringing to book those guilty of crime. A village that fulfilled these duties was exempted from application of the Criminal Tribes Act. When this Act was officially repealed in the Madras Presidency in July 1947, by the passing of the Criminal Tribes Repeal Act, there was a concerted effort to ally policing with a number of economic and educative measures. A report prepared by Labour Commissioner T.E. Moir (Government of Madras, Law General Reportment, G.O.: no. 96, 6 June 1961), was accepted by the government. The report detailed those of the caste's activities which could be looked upon as the vestiges which had survived from the anarchic guerrilla wars of the eighteenth century, but which could also be considered the core of the Kallar character and thus formed a base for a rehabilitation policy. While economic development was necessary, it was by no means sufficient in itself to put the brakes on criminality, for it was not only the poor who resorted to illegal activity. In the corpus of India's religious and literary texts, there abound examples of the prestige that attaches to those who commit illegal deeds, for example the praise of the thieving abilities of Sharvalika, the thief, in Sudraka's *Mrichhakatika* (*The Clay Cart*), and an echo of this can even be heard in the works of Apollinaire (1965: 304).[7] A concerted effort was therefore made to raise the overall level of education. The objective of entrusting law and order to the chiefs was to make the criminal unpopular and to offer new career opportunities to the young people. Crafts workshops were held, surplus land distributed, emigration was encouraged towards plantations, and new schools were built. For some time, a special Kallar Reclamation Officer working under the police was charged with the implementation of this policy, before the police were given the complete responsibility for it in the year 1932. In 1949, the policy implementation was given first to the Harijan Welfare Department and then to the Rural Welfare Department. A major effort was made in schooling, with scholarships being offered to young Kallars to be trained in teachers training establishments. However, in terms of results, these policies would appear to have been only moderately successful, despite a decline in banditry and despite their caste receiving a moral education from missionaries. Kallar students graduating from Kallar institutions seldom derived benefit from their studies. Even after several years, many could only read with difficulty and could barely write.

The Kallars, according to Dumont, 'show no taste for culture'

(1957: 20), and, characteristically, did not understand how it could benefit them. Doubtless the major cause for this was the syllabus that derived from British educational models and not from their own lives. While some took advantage of the state's efforts to improve their lot, and there was an undeniable normalizing movement, the objective of empowering them to open new horizons for themselves remained distant. All in all, it amounted to the activity of a few bureaucrats who maintained the life of diverse institutions, with little or no participation from the people concerned. As Dumont observed, 'At the village level, one does not note the presence of progressive, young leaders keen on informing and stimulating their community; young teachers are distant from such a role, for authority is always vested in the old lines of leadership, in the arbiters of the villages' destiny' (ibid.: 22).

British Justice: The Violence of Ambiguity

Several points need to be borne in mind when touching upon the British legal system, for it, according to the context, either functioned as a substitute for or as a supplement to a caste's internal justice mechanisms. British legal provisions, systematic and uniform, sometimes introduced new and revolutionary principles to traditional practices. Traces of this impact remain discernible to this day in Indian society.

In the first place, the Kallars' *panchayat*, unlike others elsewhere in India, continued as before to deal with all manner of disputes, although some were referred to the benches set up by the administration. As a matter of fact, there was some degree of overlapping, especially with regard to homicides and the innumerable cases of loans against collateral. In the latter category, where documents were registered officially, the matter would be referred to a bench. If, as was more often the case, it were a transaction inscribed merely on a palm leaf, the matter would come before the *panchayat*. According to what was likely to prove more beneficial to him, it was upto the plaintiff to select the appropriate forum for justice. A trial presented the advantage of potentially ruining the adversary; *panchayats* were too anxious to reconcile warring parties to contribute to the 'romanticism of the dispute' (Dumont 1957: 306). The choice offered to the Kallar was not between the bench and the *panchayat* but between direct action and judicial recourse, between killing and the pitiless grind of a trial. The police intervention was frequent in cases of collective conflict. The police served only to enforce the decisions given either by the *panchayat* or by the official bench. Sometimes, the combination of the official apparatus and that of the Kallars themselves was apt to be less than happy, notably when the former overran the latter, as was inevitable in the case of homicides within the sub-caste. In such cases, the police were entrusted with the investigation and the judiciary with pronouncing judgement. As a rule, the conflicting parties would agree to sabotage the functioning of the official machinery and pursue their own parallel processes for compensation: agreement was reached on the amount of the fine (*bali*), which was deposited with a third party, the *panchayat*, until the official investigation was declared closed. False declarations by the plaintiff and his witnesses would ensure in any case a speedy end to the official investigation. Then the compensation was handed over to the next of kin of the victim, though the prosecution may still attempt to pursue the case before the bench.

The colonial police was expected to combat crime, protect property and generally serve the colonial power by keeping a close watch on the indigenous people and functioning as the administration's eyes and ears. To British administrators, the security of the Raj and the safety of the Europeans counted for far more than that of the Indians themselves. Thus, for example, the police force of the Madras Presidency was completely centralized, under the direct authority of the Provincial Government. Its titular head, the Inspector General, had very little independence in the running of his department. The control exercised at headquarters by the Governor and his Council was replicated in the districts by making the Superintendent of Police subordinate to the Magistrate or Collector. The police was completely absorbed within the administrative structure of the state and was frequently strapped for funds.

Overlapping Structures: Collisions and Consequences

A necessary concomitant for keeping the police away from the village was the role of the village headman and of the village watchman, the lowest ranking member of the police force. Although neglected and poorly utilized by the British administration until the end of the nineteenth century, subsequently the role of the 'man on the ground' began to be highlighted as that of one who was not official enough to become foreign or hostile to the villagers and yet sufficiently part of the official dispensation to be trusted on professional matters. It fell to the headman to dispatch the watchman to the nearest police post to report a crime. The headman's preliminary reports were the base for the entire official investigation. This of course would leave the door open for abusive practices, for the headman and watchman often worked in cahoots. European police officers were apt to complain that headmen offered dacoits protection in return for a share of the dacoits' booty (Genet 1993: 170). Thus, the gulf between the colonial police and the village began to grow with no effective institution being able to bridge it.

As long as the villagers paid their taxes and crime did not attain ungovernable levels, the colonial administration paid little attention to the villages. Consequently, a number of violent incidents, such as the killing of an unfaithful wife, the drowning of a suspected witch or yet female infanticide and human sacrifice, went unrecorded in official statistics since the villagers did not look upon them as criminal acts. Not reporting crimes is in itself a pointer to the manner in which the villagers perceived the police and the administration. Corruption, torture, incompetence and tyranny on the part of the police were good reasons to strengthen means to 'police the police'. Many villagers justly looked upon the police as agents of exploitation and of external oppression, rather than as impartial protectors of the law. To the backward classes, moreover, the police appeared to be hand in glove with the local elite.

In the pre-colonial period, the Kavalgars were the highest law enforcement officials in the region, receiving remuneration (*kaval*) for the protection that they offered to the village. The system had begun to collapse towards the end of the eighteenth century, as military chiefs used *kaval* rights as a means to spread and strengthen their power in the rural hinterland. Under the British, the Kavalgars became master blackmailers, extorting their wages through threats, murder and burglary. The British sought to retire the Kavalgars or to absorb them in the police force. Such was the power of the Kallars, however, especially in southern Tamil Nadu, for instance, that many simply refused to give up their *kaval*.

Group attacks and Kavalgar related crimes alarmed the colonial regime owing to the general climate of insecurity that it bred and the challenge—whether implicit or explicit—that it seemed to hurl at the government. If banditry were neglected, it could well burgeon into pockets of rural revolt and anti-colonial resistance. The *kaval* system could become a danger to the colonial administration's interests. In 1861, a colonial police officer noted, 'There may be great difficulty in reducing these "robber police", incompatible as they are with a just and enlightened administration, to controllable limits, but sooner or later the obstacle must be faced and surmounted' (C.S. Hearn, *Memorandum on Tirunelvely Village Police*, 1861, MJP, no. 97, Dec. 1870).

The persistence of the *kaval* system and the police's belief that certain castes and communities were intrinsically disposed to commit crime were ancillary factors in the clamour for increasingly strict measures against 'habitual and professional offenders'. An effort to eradicate crime could well translate itself into a way to recast the offenders in the colonial mould, to garner productive effort for the colonial economy from hitherto unproductive communities; provided, of course, this effort came under the yoke of the law. The Kallars, for example, worked in tea or coffee factories and in textile mills to become respectable small farmers. Crime and criminality became convenient expedients to label bothersome or unproductive lifestyles, like those of small time itinerant peddlers. At any rate, they justified the brutal and crude imposition of a rash of reformatory measures on the part of the police. It was not as a matter of chance that entire sections of the indigenous population came to be designated as Criminal Tribes or Dangerous Classes, but as a fundamental component of perceptions of control prevalent in the nineteenth and twentieth centuries.

The British, like other Europeans, looked upon the population as composed of communities of virtually autonomous districts. Defined in terms of race, religion, language and even by caste and sub-caste, these community identities were believed to offer a clue not only to models of social organization but also to behavioural and personality traits. It was to the advantage of the colonial regime to divide the society under its control into different social blocs. Several of these were perceived as potentially useful to the regime, the 'martial races' being a prime example (Arnold 1984). It was among these classes that the British hoped to recruit their soldiers and their clerks, thus co-opting prosperous and influential men who could be valuable collaborators or intermediaries *vis-a-vis* the masses. Yet, even to the colonial administrators, the brutal sociology of control was not free of paradox or ambiguity. Thus, even as the Kallars in their totality were categorized as 'criminal' and 'dangerous', irrespective of sub-caste, they were also waiting to be recruited in British ordnance depots. Labelling and categorizing sections of society was integral to the preservation of British control. Apart from the identification of friends and enemies of the regime, it also enabled the British to concentrate the efforts of their meagre human resources, including the police, on those sections which seemed most likely to threaten colonial interests. In 1874, the Lieutenant Governor noted in the N.W. Police Administration Report, 'More than all other categories of crime, the expression of open and declared contempt of public authority by groups of armed men gathered with violent intent must be rigorously and remorselessly suppressed, and no effort must be spared to detect and bring to book the parties concerned' (*Report of Police Administration of UP*, 1872, pp. 9–10).

Despite their fulminations against the dubious role of village chieftains who supported, if not encouraged, criminal activity, colonial administrators recognized that their own position as foreigners made the inclusion and reinforcement of indigenous control structures inevitable. As early as the eighteenth century the British realized the difficulties arising from using watchmen who owed loyalties to two masters at the same time, on the one hand, the landholders who remunerated them and provided leadership to their community, and on the other the Raj, which expected them to prevent or at least report and detect crime. Although the British attempted to supplant the authority of village headmen by raising that of watchmen, by and large they conserved the skeleton of the earlier system, in which the watchmen were linked to rural power networks whose functioning was ensured by local chieftains.

When observers pointed out the fact that the police and the criminals were frequently drawn from the same social groups, a conscious effort was made to include the most turbulent elements in the police force. By treating Indians as members of immutable groups bearing specific characteristics, some of which were even believed to be genetically determined, the Raj reduced India's social mobility and fluidity. It was this which brought to a halt the integration of marginal groups within the folds of settled society, which had been going an until the early nineteenth century.

CONCLUSION

The artificial 'Criminal Tribes' label was merely an expedient to club various groups living off criminal activity, without paying heed to the underlying organizing principles of Indian society as a whole. This was to be a stumbling block subsequently in every British effort, whether in the government, in the dispensation of law, in the economy or in education. It is through this conflict as also through the interpenetration of British and Indian cultures that one can hope to discern the sociological reality which is most tellingly illustrated by the foregoing examples of forms of violence, notably that of the watchman being the corollary of the thief, in full collusion with the Raj's own institutions. Between pure repression and the 'strategy of condescension' between colonizer and colonized (Bourdieu 1992: 118), is the power relationship between the actors in the arena, each in his own universe and in a certain position *vis-a-vis* the others, but not to be stigmatized either through a surfeit of exoticism or through an excess of ethnocentricity. What Kipling put down as an improbable encounter between East and West could be attempted by relativizing the selection of our operational parameters, 'by founding the study of different cultures on the categories which are specific to them' (Vidal 1992: 188).

Even today, all over India, either dispersed over an entire region or grouped in a single place, often at the very site of the old British reformatory settlements, erstwhile 'Criminal Tribes' continue to exist on the strength of meagre subsidies granted by the Government of India; for example, the Kanjarbats of Solapur in Maharashtra (Zauberman 1989). These peoples have internalized two centuries of British colonization in their memory and have sanctified for themselves the belief that they were and will always be held as thieves (Mayaram 1991: 69). In this respect, the Indian police seems merely to have taken up where the British left off. Police interests are greatly served by having a set of pre-designated offenders the moment a crime is committed in a zone where the erstwhile 'Criminal Tribes' are known to move. Rarely do these people, known to be physically or tacitly subjected to violence, manage to shed the contemptuous label, to find release from a universe shorn of hope: eternal victims of the seal of infamy which is only reinforced by the complicitous accusations of ordinary Indians.

From the work of young historians, mainly Indian (Nigam 1990; Mayaram 1991; Radhakrishnan 1992) and British/American (Yang 1985; Freitag 1991), one realizes more about these men and women, whose identity-defining references were in great measure shaped, deformed or reshaped by the *officials* of the Raj. One realizes that new references can only originate in their own history of which they have been deprived for so long. They have much to gain by a 're-indigenization' of their history which would be part of the history of those who count for little but have a lot to say, those who still remain, at a mythical level, in the very depths of collective memory as also in the reality of criminal investigation, objects of suspicion in the view of the Indian Government and in the eyes of their fellow men.

NOTES

This paper reproduces in part arguments developed for the defence of a doctoral thesis on Indian social anthropology, submitted to the Ecole des Hautes Etudes en Sciences Sociales, under the guidance of Jean-Claude Galey, Dean of Studies at the EHESS. I thank him for encouraging me to work on this subject which derives its inspiration from the writings of Jacques Pouchepadass, Research Director at the Centre National de la Recherche Scientifique, to whom too I would like to express my deep gratitude.

1. Consider the following example quoted by Radhakrishna:
   Sometimes, the police administration would notify a group as criminal because of its alleged insolence. The Superintendent of Police, Tirunelvely, while making out a case for the criminality of Koravars cited the fact that they had adopted a system of ranking among themselves, as a parody of the police administration. He was piqued by the fact that one was called Inspector, another Sub-Inspector, and so on. 'This along shows what class of persons they are', he complained. (Judl. GO 2494, 12.10.1915)
2. These labels can, in fact, be found in the Judicial Reports and the Police Committee Books in the Archives at Egmore, in Chennai (Madras). To be sure, this forms part of the colonizer's imagery as applied to the colonized; surprisingly, this vocabulary was taken up in the 1960s and again in the 1980s by rock and roll groups (The Abominables, The Incorrigibles, The *Thugs*) seeking to paint themselves in these colours. A popular art form enabled them to personify the demonic 'other', the extremes of fantasy, which majority-driven societies use to slake their deep thirst for transgression.
3. 'The category of criminal tribes was stereotypical in the sense that its defining characteristic though seen to be rooted in Indian society and its past were brought together in an ahistorical and decontextualised form' (Nigam 1990).

4. In Hatch one discerns the obsession with classification that was so close to denizens of the eighteenth and nineteenth centuries. It highlights the introduction of a criminal typology based on a direct import from Western mental categories which in turn were being applied to a just germinating criminal anthropology in the West. More so, it draws attention to the danger inherent in applying the measures of punitive justice and a prison structure that the West has constructed through its own cultural history to a colonial population whose major religious and social characteristics are so different from those of the West (cf. Foucault 1975).
5. *tuppukuli*: more precisely, was a provision or deposit made for the conduct of an inquiry.
6. It must be specified, though, that Dumont's study did not make a special effort to study the Pramalai Kallas in the context of 'criminal tribes' or their belonging to such a group.
7. 'I remember the evening of that Indian drama
   The Cart of a Child a thief burst forth
   Who reflects before piercing a hole in the wall
   What form must he give to the cut
   So that beauty may not lose its rights
   Even at the moment of a crime.' (*Apollinaire* 1965: 304)

REFERENCES

Apollinaire, G. 1965. 'Calligrammes. Poèmes de la paix et de la guerre (1913–16)'. In *Oeuvres poétiques d'Apollinaire*, 304. Paris: Gallimard.

Arnold, D. 1984. '"Criminal Tribes" and "Martial Races"; Crime and Control in Colonial India'. Paper presented to *Seminar on Comparative Commonwealth Social History.* London: University of London.

Bhargava, B.S. 1949. *The Criminal Tribes: A Socio-Economic Study of the Principal Criminal Tribes and Castes in Northern India.* Lucknow: Universal Publishers Ltd.

Bourdieu, P. and L.J.D. Wacquant, 1992. *Réponses.* Paris: Seuil.

Bruce, G. 1968. *The Stranglers: The Cult of Thuggee and its Overthrow in British India.* London: Longman.

Chevalier, L. 1978. *Classes laborieuses et classes dangereuses pendant la première moitié du XIXe siècle.* Paris: Librairie générale française.

Cohn, B.S. 1968. 'Notes on the Study of Indian Society and Cultures'. In *Structure and Change in Indian Society*, ed. M. Singer and B. Cohn. Chicago: J.L. Aldine.

Dumont, L. 1957. *Une sous-caste de l'Inde du Sud. Organisation des Pramalai Kallar*. Paris-La Haye: Mouton.

———. 1966. *Homo hierarchicus. Essai sur le système des castes*. Paris: Gallimard.

Foucault, M. 1975. *Surveiller et punir. Naissance de la prison*. Paris: Gallimard.

Fourcade, M. 1989. 'La légende noire des adorateurs de Kali'. *L'Histoire*, 123: 78–81.

Freitag, S.B. 1991. 'Crime in the Social Order of Colonial North India'. *Modern Asian Studies* 25(2): 227–61.

Galey, J.-C. 1973. 'Les conceptions relatives à la tenure foncière dans l'Inde avant l'Indépendance'. Thèse de 3e cycle. Paris X-Nanterre: EPHE-VIe section.

Genet, C. 1993. 'Banditisme et répression dans l'Inde coloniale: les "Dacoits" et la police de l'Inde centrale (1857–1947)'. *Journal asiatique* 281 (1–2): 139–84.

Gordon, S.N. 1969. 'Scarf and Sword: Thugs, Marauders and State-Formation in 18th-Century Malwa'. *The Indian Economic and Social History Review* 4(4).

Gunthorpe, E.J. 1882. *Notes on Criminal Tribes in the Bombay Presidency and the Central Provinces.* Bombay.

Hatch, W.J. [1928] 1976. *The Land Pirates of India. An Account of the Kuravers, a Remarkable Tribe of Hereditary Criminals, their Extraordinary Skill as Thieves, Cattle-Lifters, Highway Men and their Manners and Customs.* Delhi: Concept Publishing Company.

Kennedy, M. 1985. *The Criminal Classes in India*, Delhi: Mittal Publication. (1st published in 1907: *Criminal Classes in the Bombay Presidency.*)

Malamoud, Ch. 1980. 'Théologie de la dette dans le brahmanisme classique'. *Purusartha* 4: *La Dette* 39–62.

Mayaram, S. 1991. 'Criminality or Community? Alternative Constructions of the Mev Narrative of Darya Khan'. *Contributions to Indian Sociology*, n.s. 25(1): 57–84.

Nelson, J.H. 1868. *The Madura Country, A Manual Compiled by Order of the Madras Government by . . . in five Parts.* Madras.

Nigam, S. 1990. 'Disciplining and Policing the "Criminal by Birth" Part 2: The Development of a Disciplinary System, 1871–1900'. *The Indian Economic and Social History Review*, 27(3): 257–87.

Pouchepadass, J. 1979. Délinquance de fonction et normalisation coloniale: les 'tribus criminelles' dans l'Inde britannique'. In *Les marginaux et les exclus dans l'histoire*, 122–54. Paris: Plon.

Reiniche, M.L. 1979. *Les dieux et les hommes: Étude des cultes d'un village du Tirunelveli, Inde du Sud*. Paris-La Haye: Mouton.

Radhakrishna, M. 1992. 'Surveillance and Settlements under the Criminal Tribes Act in Madras'. *The Indian Economic and Social History Review* 29(2): 171–98.

Renou, L. 1978. *l'Inde fondamentale*. Études d'indianisme réunies par Ch. Malamoud. Paris: Hermann.

Shankar, G. 1979. *Born Criminals*. Varanasi: Kishor Vidya Niketan.

Sleeman, J.L. 1934. *La secte secrète des Thugs. Le culte de l'assassinat aux Indes*. Paris: Payot.

Thurston, E. [1909] 1975. *Castes and Tribes of Southern India*. 7 vols. Madras: Madras Government Press.

Vidal, D. 1992. 'Le gandhisme en écho'. *Cahiers de Sciences humaines* 28(2): 187–207.

Weinberger-Thomas, C. 1989. 'Cendres d'immortalité. Crémation des veuves en Inde'. *Archives Sciences sociales des Religions* 67(1): 9–51.

Yang, A.A. 1985. *Crime and Criminality in British India*. Tucson: University of Arizona Press.

Zauberman, Y. 1989. *Caste criminelle* (documentary film, 70 mn). Paris: Les Films du Paradoxe/La Sept.

Non-Violence in the Country of Violence: Lessons from the Dhanbad Mining Belt

GÉRARD HEUZE

Contemporary violence as well as practices and theories of non-violence are easily excluded from old (or more 'classical' or 'noble') perspectives. This is particularly true when violence is placed in an urban or industrial world where continuities with 'tradition' are, to say the least, abused. With a view to examine critically these conceptions, one will confront several types of discourses and practices of violence and non-violence, as evidenced in one of India's most tormented mining belts. One shall attempt later to explain the extent to which the rural hinterland of this industrial area uses non-violence as a symbol of identity: a symbol that serves to demarcate it from that which is indispensable to it and at the same time threatens its very existence.

Where Men are Wolves

Since the nineteenth century, the mining belt of Dhanbad, 250 km west of Calcutta, has acquired a reputation for violence that has only been reinforced since the nationalization of coal mining in 1971. Not surprisingly, popular stereotypes make this out to be the place for all kinds of crime, brutality (with the exception of war) and corruption. Indian newspapers, never afraid to be sensational when it comes to the Dhanbad area, speak of 'pits of horror', of 'the inferno of crime', of 'the power of the hoodlum', of 'mafias' and of 'unspeakable horrors'. After a century-long industrialization, this undulating stretch of land, about 600 sq. km in area, is now perforated and ravaged by more than four hundred mining centres, where live some two hundred thousand miners holding permanent jobs, and tens of thousands of coal 'scroungers' and workmen with precarious jobs. These miners in turn are providers to a population some three times their own number.[1] All around the zone of extraction, an overpopulated and sorely underdeveloped hinterland contemplates the mining belt with increasing envy and rancour, as a growing proportion of jobs in the area go to migrants. The fact is that despite its execrable reputation, Dhanbad attracts a workforce from all over India, from the populous Gangetic plain, in particular.

Early on, the region saw the concentration of numerous factors apt to provoke violence. Since its very creation, the zone has been marked by the presence of migrants from manifold *jatis* and dissociated groups.[2] Many of these attach a great deal of prestige to the war-like ideologies. A heavily concentrated workforce has to live in and cope with structures that are not as familial as those it has known elsewhere. The conditions of living are appalling.

The mining belt has not been spared the usual kinds of violence of the present times. These, which revolve essentially around matrimonial alliances (dowries) and inheritances, are of a complexity that defies description. However, this common or garden variety of violence is hardly what gives Dhanbad its reputation. Even the violence born of sexual frustrations, low wages, appalling working conditions, accidents, poor or unspeakably foul housing in horrifying neighbourhoods, or the muscle power of usurious moneylenders who resort to various sorts of deceit, can be found in India's other industrial centres, especially its mines. In any case, it cannot explain the superlatives conferred plentifully on Dhanbad. When a local or a national observer speaks of violence in the mining belt, he speaks normally of something else. By simplifying the situation enormously, one can discern three kinds of 'extraordinary' violence, that adjective signifying either that people are killed or that they are sought to be terrorized.

The first cause of the 'extraordinary' violence arises from the institutionalization of state-sponsored 'plunderers' and their tumultous relations with corrupt managers and administrators. Scores are often settled with armed henchmen. The inclusion of the mining industry in the political and social context of Bihar is at the root of a first type, whose equivalents in fact may be found in mining concentrations the world over. The state and certain migrant groups play the most active role therein. One can observe in this framework the manner in which conflicts of interest and confrontations between rival political factions combine. Bharat Coking Coal Limited (BCCL), the nationalized company that exploits most of the mines, sub-contracts a part of its activities.[3] Besides, coal is a controlled commodity and there exists a great demand for it in the parallel market. The politicians of northern

Bihar wield enormous influence amongst the public sector enterprises of the region. Over the last twenty years, certain trade union activists originally close to the Congress, but now much more diversified, began to see in this situation the chance to enrich themselves and launch a political career, the two being intimately linked. Building upon groups composed of committed people, they organized entire networks, complete with their own laws and codes, before extending their control to society at large.

The second kind of extraordinary violence is linked to rackets run by lower echelons of these 'crime companies'. Not everyone can attack the state, whether to lay it to waste or to use it. 'Private sector crime' faces competition from an underpaid police force. Towards the end of the 1970s, the increasingly stiff resistance from the victims of these rackets was in itself an important cause of violence. The third category of extraordinary violence derives from the state-as-employer itself, which has embarked since 1975 on a rationalization of open cast coal mining. Entire villages have been displaced and confrontations have arisen, as the displaced people demand jobs at the mines with increasing vehemence. In the final analysis, this kind of conflict is akin to struggles for control of land (particularly for land controlled by tribals in the surrounding rural areas), that in past decades has led to frequent police excesses.

So diverse are the forms and the causes of violence that it may strike the reader as absurd to associate them in an ensemble which could help characterize a society. The exact magnitude of violence remains to be determined. It would appear that a great number of the people and institutions involved in it overstate its dimensions. Their reasons are different and variable but cannot in any case be limited, however real it may be, to the impact of popular belief, which naturally inclines towards exaggeration. Deaths have scarred Dhanbad and there can be no getting around this fact.[4] This essay shall proceed from the hypothesis that since violence in the mining belt is also an everyday social index of status and power, it is also subject to reinterpretation. In some measure, it would be a constructed reality. Invoking it enables the articulation of the discourses of the most diverse social forces. In relation to the outside world, some inhabitants of the region, in particular those driven to assume the status of the elite, are constrained to define themselves in relation to the image of violence that others have conferred upon the mining belt. A great part of this image has been created by the regional and national media.

Mythical violence and real violence are not the only elements in play: non-violence, in a more or less articulated form, is also frequently invoked here, a dimension that is completely neglected by outside observers. This essay shall attempt to show what happens on two essential levels—the trade union organizations of the belt and the rural society close to the mines. Both these are often called into question when it comes to violence in Dhanbad.

SOCIAL ORGANIZATION FACED WITH VIOLENCE: CLIENTELISTS AND RENOUNCERS

INSTITUTIONAL NON-VIOLENCE AND ITS ARRANGEMENTS

The ups and downs of various kinds of violence can be easily imagined in the mining belt merely by reading the press and listening to conversations. Violence is daily and omnipresent. Yet the region's principal social and political forces are as one in condemning and rejecting the phenomenon. The belt's population is so disparate that it would be difficult to set down here in detail the social forces present and the manner in which they are organized (Heuze 1989). However, by simplifying outrageously and by taking into account only the organizational forces that dominate this industrial world, one may distinguish between the political class (and the local administration of Bihar which is feudally linked to it), the business-class bourgeoisie, the (central) public-sector bureaucracy, and what I would call secularized Renouncers. Whilst there is no great mystery about the first three categories, the last would require a word of explanation. Secularized Renouncers are a group of individuals, generally placed in opposition to the powers that be, who militate for a society free of exploitation and violence in the name of moral principles, articulated in Gandhian or Gandhian-socialist (Jayaprakash Narayan) or Marxist-Leninist (a legalist(ics) derivative of Naxalism) terms. One may call them thus for, despite their indifference or opposition to religion, they bear a striking resemblance to certain other types of renouncers and are in fact largely looked upon as such by people.[5] This categorization of relational practices does not in any way detract from the well-known and acknowledged autonomy, radicalism or modernity of their explicit discourse. They lead unions or small parties or local associations. Their importance derives from the intense support they enjoy amongst certain sections of the population. Whilst all these sections condemn violence, they do not all do so in the same manner, in spite of borrowing one another's methods and ideologies concerning violence.

Until 1989–91, most politicians in the mining belt generally belonged to the Congress (the BJP and the Janata have since picked up the baton, but this may probably be a mere episode). Alongside old *zamindars* like Shankar Dayal Singh (a legislator from Katras), one finds union activists of the INTUC (B. Dubey or D. Pandey) and representatives of the Gangetic plain-centred political system of Bihar. Dhanbad was included in the new born state of Jharkhand in Nov. 2000. Violence, in various concrete forms, is deeply ingrained in the politics of Bihar, where more than a third of the members of the Vidhan Sabha have a criminal past (robbery, rape, graft, murder, etc.). The elections are the occasion for settling scores in blood. The ballot boxes are known to be stuffed. The power of politicians in the north derives less from acts of violence than from the setting up of clientelisms, therefore from the more or less inegalitarian relationships often associated with ideologies of consensus or social harmony. Concretely, this means that the legislators shower favour to the extent they can on their kith and kin, on the networks of allegiance based on caste and, notably in urban areas, on more heterogeneous groups of clients. They try to distribute government jobs, licences, contracts (to the more affluent) and various grants. For the poorer and the weaker, there is the promise of the status quo, of the state's non-intervention against illegal activities or unauthorized shops and homes situated on the public land. Political clientelism functions through a system of intermediaries, 'community' chiefs, merchants, usurers, unscrupulous public servants or labour contractors, who benefit from a share of the loot and have a personal relationship with the politicians. This relational model was imported into Dhanbad, which was part of West Bengal until 1956, and grew apace during the 1960s.

In the extractive industries zone, however, there exist certain peculiarities. The INTUC-affiliated mining union (Rashtriya Collieries Mazdoor Sangh, RCMS) is a fairly typical element of this landscape.[6] Officially, its membership runs into tens of thousands. Since the 1960s, it has been engaged in a sort of co-management with the entrepreneurs, a trend that has become more pronounced since nationalization in 1971. The leaders of the RCMS play important political roles. Two of them were in fact named the Minister for Labour in Delhi, whilst several others obtained posts in Patna. Viewed as politicians, they are not very different from their colleagues in the Gangetic plains. As union leaders, they are obliged to take into account the importance of competition (there exist at least a dozen unions), and the reactions of workmen, who, despite a great deal of dependence, are still more successful than the peasants in extracting themselves from systems of subjection.

The INTUC is a clientelist organization which, at a local level, exchanges security of employment and housing for allegiance, though it is not only that. The union is preoccupied too with training, assistance and purchasing power. At the national level, it tends to pressurize the government in order to obtain certain advantages which it redistributes, like sinecures, through its institutionalization and its privilege of representativity. The union is a path to power even as it is a power centre in itself. Its support is taken to enter into negotiations with other political forces. Voting patterns in the mining belt have long been determined by union loyalties (this perhaps has ended with the irruption of the BJP and preoccupations related to quota-based hiring).

All this apart, in a manner that is inextricably linked, the organization is a source of profit for its leaders and cadres. It entered into business in the 1950s by selling social harmony and by participating in the recruitment of labour. As the labour contractors and racketeers entered the market in increasing numbers, and as the union gained in economic and political influence, this trend became more pronounced. During the 1960s, sub-contracts in the mines became the rage, with usurious loans being given to the better-paid and therefore more solvent workers. Matters were aggravated by the institutionalization of the union and by the uncontested hegemony of the Congress. After nationalization, sub-contracting became even more profitable: promotions and recruitments were up for sale and these businesses have become essential with rising unemployment. Alongside certain cells of the union which have a more or less professional leadership not concerned with the rackets, the INTUC in the mining belt also harbours diverse parasitical classes that live off clientelism and use the organization for their own ends. A certain symbiosis exists between these elements, along with some contradictions. Subjected to very strong internal and external pressures, more often than not the Congress-led union appears in the final analysis to be a greater producer and user of violence than the majority of ordinary political men and structures in Bihar.

The INTUC's notables, whether they are of the bureaucratic variety engaged in the formal game of collective negotiations or of the racketeering variety infinitely less attracted by formalism, profess unanimously to detest violence. Beginning with a consideration of the professional bureaucracy, the organization's official ideology is founded on the negation of contradictions between what it calls 'the different partners in industry'. The INTUC in the mining belt (affiliated to the ICFTU) has never directly confronted the state (or private entrepreneurs). It has supported all the Congress governments. The prospect of violent clashes in the relations between the employers and the employees is looked upon with particular suspicion. Violence at that level is not excluded for primarily cultural reasons. Strikes and other forms of open conflict that could lead to violence, notably *gheraos*, would be 'anti-national' and 'economically damaging'. Petitions and hunger strikes are the only accepted forms of expression. The INTUC counts on the support of the state, in a climate of calm, to improve the lot of the miner. The events since 1971 seem to bear out the wisdom of this strategy.

In relation to violence, the bureaucrats of Dhanbad's INTUC have ideological convictions that can be very serious. These derive from Gandhism, which attributes to them the role of 'trustees' of labour. Yet, the INTUC in Dhanbad is very distant from Gandhian experiments in trade union activity, like the Mazdoor Mahajan (or TLA) of Ahmedabad, the sole organization in which the Mahatma really took some concrete interest. Gandhi and Vinoba Bhave are cited here, as and when the circumstances require, in order to justify legalism and moderation in the workers' struggle and to underscore the horror of conflict (and not merely of violence). In the meanwhile, it is in the name of Gandhi and Bhave, and with the authority conferred in this regard by the combination of their upper caste origins, their education and their affluence, that union leaders affirm their intention to 'reform' and to 'elevate' a mining milieu abased and sullied by alcoholism, promiscuity and domestic violence. The sheer efficacity of these themes is more or less nil, as these leaders themselves recognize.

They are opposed to violence too for materialistic reasons. These are the mediators who live rather well off their capacity to keep order and to express what the miners feel. Open confrontation would signify not only their obsolescence as a more or less docile instrument of government policies, but also their failure as conscious promoters of trade union (and political) paternalism. Finally, they fear violence: violence from other union organizations seeking to enhance their following—the INTUC has an institutional monopoly that strikes many as illegitimate—and, since the beginning of the 1980s, violence between rival politicized factions within the union. The last kind of tension in fact has become the most important. In 1986, revolvers were drawn and fired by supporters of the ex-Chief Minister, Jagannath Mishra, and those of B. Dubey, who was to become the chief minister, in a clash to gain control over the union's office, an immense cement structure in a suburb of Dhanbad.[7] Several local chiefs were killed the same year. Quite apart from precise ideological references, the invocation of non-violence is of a piece too with the need to survive when confronted with the internal disintegration that characterises the local society, for it is discernible too in the political, religious and 'communal' spheres.

Even the racketeers solidly entrenched in the union's structure, are opposed to violence and know how to make use of citations from Gandhi. Originating in the same upper castes and belonging to the same political networks as those who are 'pure' unionists, they draw from the same ideological sources. Less learned and concerned with legalism than the bureaucrats, their attitude towards violence is sometimes more pragmatic; violence only bothers them in relation to their own power and their own personal and material interests. As a rule, though, their practice is to keep peace in their fiefdom by all means—including violence. They have organized diverse, usually precarious, systems of clientelism that ensure allegiance, votes (for themselves, or for their bosses higher up in the echelons), and profits. Violence in working relationships implies an interruption in the sub-contracting operations, rackets and usury that guarantee the very economic foundation of these relationships. Violence creates tensions and polarizations that threaten systems of allegiance and necessitate the intervention of the police, and it is not always easy to get around the police. The racketeers are ardent advocates of social harmony. Violence is condemned in the name of 'workers' unity', 'popular unity', or 'loyalty to the leader'. Everything is done, besides, to ensure that the workers do not gain access to the brutal methods used on a day to day basis by their union representatives. The idea of a 'large family of workers', or of loyalists of some local chieftain or the other, is customarily the underpinning of the discourse of non-violence employed among themselves by the clientelist and the racketeering leaders. The dominant local ideology in terms of familial ties would preclude an uprising against one's father (whom the union chief uses as a symbolic reference) or one's elder brother (usually to denote the men at arms or subalterns of the clientelist ensemble).

Concretely, this sort of representation implies that violence is inconceivable or abominable within a group, and that it cannot express the permanent contradictions that exist between the miners and the moneylender-unionists or the recruiting agent-unionists. If the miners were to revolt, the symbolic violence used by the father (or rather, of the elder brother) would be totally legitimate. It means too that violence, inconceivable within a family (the clientele of a chieftain, also sometimes of the INTUC-Congress), is by no means incongruous outside it. Only, there cannot be any talk of it for it does not fit in well either with the Gandhian reminiscences of the bureaucrats nor with the interests of the racketeers, who do not wish to attract the attention of the law.

Extreme Violence Invokes Non-Violence

Since nationalization, new varieties of racketeering unionism have mushroomed which pose the problem of violence in the mining belt in a slightly different manner. This, however, is not in contradiction with the practices of the INTUC, from which most of them in any case originate. The most popular movement is the Janata Mazdoor Sangh (JMS) of Surajdev Singh, founded in 1977. At the time of writing, the JMS had more than 30,000 members and had become the second biggest union organization in the mining belt (Heuze 1989). The JMS cannot be reduced to the person of Surajdev Singh, for it has survived him. However, one cannot imagine its growth without this charismatic leader, who died in 1991 and whose popularity far exceeded that of the ministerial notables of the local INTUC. Singh, a former security guard at the mines, arrived here from his native Bhojpur in the 1960s. Soon after, he entered the INTUC. By the end of the decade, he had become the bodyguard of the most important leader, whom he probably eliminated in 1971 (for which there was no trial), before launching his sub-contracting business in the coal mines. Nationalization gave a great boost to this business which, along with the corruption of certain BCCL managers, enabled this strongman felon to become an important racketeer-unionist, combining control over sub-contracts and tenders with control over labour.

Following his arrest during the Emergency, and wearied by the remonstrances of the few principled officials in the Congress organization, he left the INTUC and founded the JMS in 1977, affiliating his fledgling union to the new party in power (the Janata Party). The new organization kept the clientelism of the INTUC but shed the weight and the relative control exercised by Gandhian moralists and specialists in collective negotiation. The JMS has no major institutional responsibilities (it took part in collective negotiations as part of the Hind Mazdoor Sabha, to which it is affiliated (Heuze 1993), and got no state support after 1980). Yet, it has become the richest union in the mining belt. Its growth initially came at the expense of the INTUC, generally through violence. Apart from exacting higher than average contributions from the workers and subjecting them to all sorts of rackets (more often than not disguised as subscriptions or as fees for taking part in lotteries), the regular business lines of recruitment and promotions ensured for the organization total control over several sectors situated at the very heart of the mining belt.

These activities, carried out in complete symbiosis with subcontracting and speculation in the real estate, were the first reasons that led journalists to evoke the 'Mafia of Dhanbad'. Certainly the union (to say nothing of the gangs that are more or less associated with it) is at the root of an ensemble of violent practices. The rackets (even octroi was levied by the union during the Janata's rule) have aroused popular resentment, especially in the rural fringes of the mining belt, where local people outnumber migrants from the north. The JMS tends to repress individual revolt with greater resolve than what the INTUC ever displayed. In minor cases, the 'offenders' are beaten up and their homes are looted.[8] When a potential leader emerges, retired hooligans and racketeers converted to trade unionism break his limbs and leave him in that state in order to make an example of him. In the early 1980s, the sight of some of these individuals, reduced to a larval state and begging at the gates of Jharia, became the most telling propaganda. It was not uncommon for death to befall those who blew the whistle. With what remained of the INTUC and with small Marxist and regional organizations, the JMS fought a long and ruthless war in order to protect or increase its territory. The union has been relatively calm since 1989, when it became the target of a New Delhi-driven campaign to cleanse the gangs' morals and to put the miners back to work.

Finally, in relation to the state-as-employer, the JMS broke with the consensual practices of the INTUC, without quite being at the same time in a situation of radical opposition. Surajdev Singh, a Janata member of the state assembly, often invoked his humble origins in order to exact wage increases (which only fed his rackets) and to increase the recruitment of unproductive manpower.[9] The JMS seldom resorts to strikes but it takes recourse to other means of pressure, utilizing its criminal know-how to circumvent the management and the forces of order. As his chieftains protect or organize various widely practised activities, from the theft of scrap and spares to the diversion of coal and illegal coke making, that take place at the expense of the mines, they are in permanent contact with the police, taking the side of the 'common man' when the state's employees are not in association with them.

It was all the more remarkable then to hear Surajdev Singh affirm, with regularity and conviction during the 1980s, that he abjured violence. Towards the middle of that decade, he was officially involved in 110 criminal acts, including 27 murders. True, Congress (and also Janata Dal) politicians do tend to use charges and trials, often completely fabricated, to immobilize their opponents. However, a great number of these acts of violence have been authenticated by private investigations. The man was constantly financing violence and was in fact surrounded by it in the form of his vigilant bodyguards. His assistants acknowledged to him that the end justified the means; his effectiveness was in fact one of the well known reasons for his popularity. Well informed local political observers, like A. Beg, set him up as the very illustration of the fighter untouched by either scruples or morals (Heuze 1989).

Why, then, did the 'Godfather of Dhanbad' attempt to pass himself off as a non-violent figure? The response is by no means simple. At a certain basic level, it derives from a discourse that seeks to rebut his opponents' propaganda. The union chief used to deflect violence onto his opponents, explaining that he merely allowed himself, in the most passive way, to be subjected to it. He did not hesitate either to refer to Mahatma Gandhi.[10] This criminal's non-violence, however, manifested itself more concretely and more deeply. Surajdev Singh lived in a palatial mansion north of Dhanbad, forever surrounded by his guards; but he lived there like an ascetic. He did not drink, nor did he smoke; he lived a life of chastity and followed a strict vegetarian diet. The mores of most other Bhojpuri migrants from his *jati* (Rajput) and milieu, known for their unrestrained pursuit of alcohol, their brawling ways and the assiduous regularity of their visits to the brothels of Bokaro, are rather different. The Godfather detested firearms and could not stand the sight of the very violence he organized and which he had known well when he was the chief bodyguard of B.P. Sinha in the INTUC.

The invocation of non-violence by this specialist of terror arises, it would appear, from the particularities of charismatic 'leadership' in the mining region and in India at large. Without always being necessary, it is however an integral part of such leadership, where one evokes the other. This is especially true of the populist versions. Despite his regular use of violence to settle conflicts, Surajdev Singh was a popular man. He was regularly re-elected from 1977 to 1991 and coercion does not seem to have been the main reason for the voters' attitude. From time to time, he held massive meetings. He represented a movement, a sensibility; the sensibility of the rural poor who had migrated from the north of the state to work in Dhanbad. Thousands worshipped him and declared their willingness to lay down their lives for him. When he was arrested in 1985, more than 15,000 people protestors confronted the police. Surajdev Singh's charisma is not extraordinary in the Indian context. He relied on the *mise en scène* of the chief's moral superiority, whence the white clothes, the vegetarianism, the references to purity in all forms, and, in his meetings, to the existence of personalized links between himself and the atomised crowd. Within the framework of the mass-based political culture of a mining region, there could be no question of 'Rajput virtues', or Bhojpuri or warrior-like qualities, or any other sectorial culture. Besides, if the union leader had come before his followers with revolvers and flashy clothes, the process of identifying the chief with the religious guru (so widely propagated and upheld by the Congress), which is so large a part of charismatic leadership, could not have worked. He would also have been put in question if he had sullied his hands (for that is the question here) in his home even as he eliminated violence from the public sphere. These actions can be carried out by the leaders of the INTUC as they are backed up by a powerful bureaucracy and by the state, but they lose in the local elections.

Non-violence, and this is important, is not non-recourse to force in absolute terms, but the absence of direct contact between degrading realities and a chief, who is organically linked to his supporters. The chief's followers, or rather the structural influence of the sort of popular leadership in which his action unfolds, dictate that he should not stoop so low as to indulge personally in violence, adopting the depraved behaviour that goes with it, for the two are intimately bound up. Doubtless, violence then becomes synonymous with defilement. It must not appear for it annihilates the relationship between the chieftain and his followers and the somewhat magical efficacity of the former. By refusing violence, as he does other practices ordinarily judged as low or unclean, the chieftain in the Gandhian manner elevates his followers whilst in the Surajdev version he makes them more strong. 'Strong' has been the watchword at Dhanbad for the last twenty-five years but it would appear that both perceptions of the utility or necessity of a certain quasi-ritualistic *mise en scène* of non-violence, have been deep rooted since long. It may not be entirely absurd to distinguish between a Brahminical model of interpretation (that of elevation) and a 'Kshatriya-tribal' model (that of instrumental efficacity), bearing in mind, however, that the reality is a lot more hazy (for large numbers of Brahmins supported S. Singh).

The people of Kustor and Jharia (where the JMS has its fiefdom) were not blind to the fact that their chieftain approved and ordered acts of violence. However, it was considered part of a sort of 'community' solidarity, likened to family conflicts in which everybody considers it normal that authority should be imposed with some severity in order to maintain a certain cohesion. When required, it was pointed out that Bhojpuri culture and the culture of the mining belt legitimize the recourse to violence in many cases (attacks on one's honour). That brought into play less elevated but more widely-held values. This violence could be separated from the purview of the effort, believed to be of a higher order, to act upon the entire social body. Neither the relationship with the *neta* nor collective affirmation was in question. There existed alongside this, a forgotten, in some part accursed, violence, related to the functioning of business. When challenged, Surajdev Singh acknowledged the existence of this violence though he, like his followers, would not attach the slightest importance to it, unlike their attitude to non-violence. This sort of violence was looked upon as a sort of slag of the terror of life at Dhanbad. It was devoid of any ethical meaning.

Besides internal violence was abjured, for the very clientelist reasons that inspired the racketeers of the INTUC, though with much firmer resolve. Contrary to what happens in the INTUC, where the assimilation of the trade union or of a faction of the union to a family is essentially symbolic, global and rather abstract, Surajdev Singh's clientelism was founded solidly on family and, by extension, clannish practices. There were no factions within the organization and the presence of a charismatic chief willing to adopt the worst methods in order to remain uncontested chief doubtless accounted for it (to many, the man's unity seemed to have a magical quality). At all levels, this leader had devoted and motivated followers. They would address one another as 'brother' at that level. Frequent meetings would be held at the home of Surajdev Singh, who would regale the gathering, calling each man by his first name. When an underling was killed, for example in clashes with the INTUC or with the extreme left, the Godfather would offer the widow and children shelter in his home for extended periods and arrange later for a sort of pension. He never forsook one of his own. Unlike the leaders of the INTUC, who often allowed their men to fall into the hands of the police, Surajdev was looked upon as the very personification of fidelity, of indestructible links. In this context, warding off internal violence, which is forever smouldering and being stoked from the outside with great efficacity, relied upon efficient practices. Those likely to attack the chieftain or the management would be excluded from the family and would invite a legitimate violence upon themselves, never explicitly evoked but always formidably obvious. By extension, all the inhabitants of the mining belt where the JMS dominated were frequently considered a part of the family. As everyone knew the legend of the 'Godfather of Dhanbad' (in its saintly and in its not so saintly versions), the miners knew where they stood.

The Renouncer and Legitimate Violence

There is a shift in the theory and practice of violence, without undergoing any radical ruptures, when it comes to certain extreme-left opposition groups and Jharkhandi nationalist and tribal movements. The regions bordering the mining belt account for a major part of the labour force. The population is composite: a substantial tribal minority (Santal, Munda, Bhumij), various lower castes that have come here from the north in order to escape from upper caste masters (Bunyas, Mahtos), upper caste moneylenders and landowners who came here from the north during the nineteenth and twentieth centuries, certain members of the upper castes of Bengal (Bengali being the spoken language in the countryside) who are very dominant in cultural terms. The Jharkhand movement,[11] founded just before the First World War, is based upon the tribal people and their specific consciousness in relation to their soil. However, after this district was included in the state of Bihar, it has also become the product of fairly variable political alliances between diverse autochthonous groups against rural and urban migrants from the Gangetic plains. Laying claim to varying degrees of autonomy for the southern region of Bihar and certain adjoining areas, the movement has begun to carry considerable electoral weight since the 1970s. Several parties have emerged, like the 'Jharkhand Party' (1950) and the 'Jharkhand Liberation Front' (Jharkhand Mukti Morcha, or JMM, 1974). It would be interesting to reassess the situation after the creation of the state of Jharkhand under BJP patronage (2000). These parties have generally tended to legitimize violence by local people against the state and against the more affluent migrants. After several years of radicalism, their practices have begun to veer towards those of the Congress and, in terms of union activity, those of the INTUC. The communists, who are popular amongst the Bengali-speaking people and who exercise a fairly lively union activity, are torn between a sub-clientelism, akin to that of the INTUC without however the means of the latter, and anti-government propaganda; moreover, they are fundamentally legalists. At the conjunction of these two types of movements, those that are founded on 'ethnic groups' and those that lay the emphasis on 'class', developed one of the mining belt's most singular and most typical praxis, that of A.K. Roy and the Bihar Collieries Kamgar Union, or BCKU.[12]

Founded in 1968, the BCKU attempts to bring together class grievances, radicalized by recourse to Marxist-Leninist ideology, the emancipatory discourse of the lower castes and Dalits and ethnic and regional claims.[13] The implementation of this perspective of all round liberation, concretized through a peculiar organization and practice, is primarily bound up with the personality of Roy, an engineer from East Bengal who is its principal theoretician and who is the effective link between fairly disparate factions. Roy is a charismatic leader, though he is surrounded by intellectuals and his union functions on more democratic lines than most others. By his supporters as indeed by his rivals, he is believed to have the essential qualities of a renouncer, or even a saint. He does not drink or smoke and lives the life of a celibate. He lives alone and gets around on a bicycle. He is poor and sleeps on a *charpoy* in a little hut close to the people. He spouts theory as others read sacred texts. These are not secondary elements in the making of Roy's reputation, a reputation that has usurped nothing from anyone. They are the very foundation of the BCKU's success, its moving away from a lowly-considered communist bloc to a situation where it now draws great popular support in the Chas region, some 40 km to the south of Dhanbad. Roy was elected member of Parliament for the third successive time in 1989, though he was defeated by a BJP candidate in 1991. The vow of poverty is all that separates A.K. Roy from Surajdev Singh in day to day life. Roy typifies the charisma of an educated urbanite talking to the rural poor. The Don of Dhanbad, like his peers from north Bihar, came to the mines in order to make money. As a rule, in the mining belt, migrants from the north (which is much more heavily populated than Dhanbad), appreciate models of economic success, tending merely to dissociate honour and wealth, whereas local people are inclined frequently to place the two in opposition.

Roy himself never commits an act of violence. Nor indeed does he organize acts in which others bloody their hands on his behalf. That would certainly have detracted from the spell he casts as a perfect man, untouched by the ties, corruption and compromises of the world. However, as one who has facilitated the birth of a new consciousness and as the bearer of a message of liberation for the poor and the weak (which is how he looks upon himself), he must deal with violence. He is in complete contradiction with all other discourses in this regard. He relies on his clean morals and his oft-affirmed and constantly-lived commitment to non-violence to justify certain acts of violence by the Just oppressed; that is to say, in his interpretation, poor peasants, Adivasis, Dalits,[14] and wage-earners exploited by the state or by intermediaries like labour contractors.

Violence is sometimes a means of survival in these sections of society on whom Roy confers superior value (though not a higher status). He declares, doubtless repetitively, that violence is more often than not exercised by the rich on the poor, by the police on the common citizenry, rather than the other way round (and statistics prove him right), and there is no question of giving violence in general a transcendental value. However, there exist numerous cases of legitimate violence and of different degrees of legitimacy. Dalits violence is legitimized because it is exercised by those who suffered violence for so long without demur (the idea of violence undergone that must be repaid in full measure for the moral order of the world to be restored). The 'Oppressed' classes are perceived as the future (a modern vision), but also as the country's purest people (turning around the classical Brahmanical argument in a sectarian logic). Certain kinds of violence bear within them a special legitimacy for they are magnified and quasi-sanctified by the ritual of 'correct theoretical interpretation' and, finally and above all, by the fact that they are purified by the mediation of Roy (or the organization) and his own incorruptible dignity. While it is true that he abstains from participation in violence, in accordance with a logic of renunciation which he shares in part with Surajdev Singh, he participates nevertheless in the transformation of brutal and meaningless violence into pure and liberational, more or less transcendental, violence, by using modern eschatological perspectives as much as concepts and relationships derived from the world of caste.

The BCKU practically never, therefore, takes part in public fasting and other ritualistic actions of the Gandhians, the JMS and the communists. As its management has always supported direct action and been opposed to the omnipresent judicial mediation that characterizes industrial relations in India, it has been involved in several conflicts ever since its creation. There were clashes with the mines' management and with the police over wages and working conditions. There were campaigns against the 'hoodlums of the JMS'. Attacks were made on liquour and moneylending outlets (both of which are closely linked). Since the mid 1980s, the union has been opposed to rackets in recruitment and has led an uphill struggle against mechanization of mining operations and against open-cast mining (which has displaced thousands of peasants). All these activities, founded on mass mobilization, have involved a certain degree of coercion *vis-à-vis* its adversaries, a kind of violence whose nature is dependent upon the moral judgement that is made on them. The 'hoodlums' were beaten and in some cases lynched. Liquour vends were pillaged. Mine managers were sequestered. The reaction on the part of BCKU's rivals and the management was extreme and severe; several were martyred for the organization's cause, beginning with Sadanand Jha, killed in Gomoh in 1973 by INTUC racketeers.

The martyr, proof of the violence that 'illegitimate forces' (and not the illegitimacy of force) inflicted upon the organization of the Justs, represents an essential theme, a cultural property if one wishes to call it that, of the BCKU. In this respect it is distinct from most other organizations. By attributing such an exalted status to the sublimated concentrate of violence undergone, which lays the fraternal foundation for a hierarchy-free community, it utilizes not only communist references but draws close to the ideological world of Muslims. There are in fact a fair number of Muslims in the organization, as there are in the constituency of Chas as a whole, from where Roy has been elected several times. It is unlikely, however, that this arose from a particular motive. The BCKU's management seldom speaks of the concrete dimensions of collective affirmation (the dalits being an ideological creation), except in order to condemn in the strongest possible terms the 'divisive' practices of 'religious fanatics' of all kinds. These practices are considered impure even as they are looked upon as theoretically unsound. Besides, the members of the BCKU have no explicit discourse relating to a 'family', and the paternalistic or filial practices that hold sway are given neither any credence nor any recognition. The sole reference that is accepted is to the 'oppressed' as a whole. Violence amongst sections of the oppressed is taboo, very much as violence within the family is taboo for members of the JMS. This arises from rational considerations (political defeat, the failure of strikes), intimately linked with the idea of the virginal purity (primitive, in the sense of the very first) of the dalits and their allies. By turning their backs on the familial symbolic, and the ideological ready-to-think capacities that go with it in this region, the BCKU's management may have allowed the risk of factional conflict (of which there is no shortage) and the shadow of disintegration to fall upon their organization. It is only through perpetual conflict with mightier external forces and thanks to the cult of martyrs that the union has managed to keep its unity. Despite its prestige and electoral success, this sect, and it is indeed one in a way, does not attract a very large following. The BCKU has five times fewer members than Surajdev Singh's organization.

Violence—A Notion Constructed from and Interpreted by Social Practices

It will be noticed that there are several manners to be violent in Dhanbad, capital of contemporary Indian violence, and that within the restricted framework of perspectives opened out by workers' organizations, the problem may be dealt with in various ways. Between a violence that is shunned in principle as it divides the nation even as it is accepted elsewhere because a national consensus dictates coercion, a violence abhorred because it endangers business even as it is constantly used to snuff out competitors, a violence exorcized because it is apt to be divisive within a family even as it is used the moment one is excluded from that family or leaves it, and finally a violence sanctified by a certain social and programmatic framework but eliminated otherwise as a rule, one discerns the multiplicity of interpretations of violence among those who represent or organize mining workers. A Brahmanical perception of non-violent action, of a 'holy man' who believes he can influence others (by 'fasts unto death' that last all of a few hours) is only discernible amongst the bureaucratized and 'honest' sections of the INTUC and legalistic communists. Beyond that, the scene is marked by the pragmatism and diversity (at once hybrid and complex) of cultural references. Few organizations, not even Roy's BCKU, are beyond the temptation to play on insecurity in order to impose their protection, perpetually evoking the crudest forms of violence. Non-violence, a non-violence that largely exceeds the boundaries of explicit references to Gandhism, still occupies pride of place in the discourse of the majority and inspires a number of practices. The manner in which Hindu models of relationship with the guru and sectarian figures of renunciation influence practices and representations of violence within greatly 'secularized' worlds, is truly remarkable. In this context, it is these figures and relational models that evoke non-violent practices and ideologies and not the other way round. Specialists in hired violence and apostles of liberational violence alike draw upon these in order to enhance their own status, to strengthen the cohesion of their cohorts and to wage the battle against those who contradict them.

The consensus in this regard is not about the nature of violence in Dhanbad but about the desire to get rid of it. Violence in Dhanbad is always done by 'the other' and the field of legitimacy of violence is as restricted and ideal as its practical and concrete expression is widespread and banal. The 'mafia', an expression invented by journalists in the 1970s, has become a metaphor usable in all cases to designate others, including supporters of the BCKU. The state plays a big part in this never ending game of words with a violence that each one passes to the other as if it were something unclean and degrading, even as its omnipresence is recognized. The state, in Dhanbad, means the mines' management and half a dozen police companies completely devoured by corruption, involved in racketeering and crime, whether or not these are controlled by the unions. Holding a monopoly on legitimate violence, the state, by virtue of its characteristics, is completely devoid of any credibility *vis-à-vis* its subjects. Violence by the state has on several occasions seemed partisan and excessively cruel, since the time of Sadan Gupta.[15] These are not the only elements that lead to the delegitimization of state power and violence; there are other—subnationalist or regional—claims for diverse causes. In the main, however, these are the factors responsible for the unquestioning acceptance by the miners of 'gangster power',[16] such as that of the JMS. The JMS, in fact, replicates the state, though its violence seems more legitimate in the final analysis. The discourse of the BCKU's revolutionaries, promising the brief and liberational generalization of the transcendental violence of 'the Big Day', appeals rather to those who have managed to escape the clutches of the clientelist structures and the pressures of the mining belt; that is to say to specialized workers and to workers coming from the villages. The state functions like a lightning rod to all, as a sort of receptacle into which violence may be poured with no moral compunction whatsoever, in spite of the close links it has with two of the organizational forces described above. Members of the INTUC denounce each rival faction of the INTUC for state-driven degeneration, rather than the organization as a whole, although the same phenomena appears in all factions.

Towns and Countryside: Violence, Non-Violence and the Creation of Collective Identities

Let us take a look at the violence in Dhanbad from another perspective, that of the villages which surround the mining belt, which provide a major part of its work force, villages who owe to Dhanbad their survival as well as their economic stagnation.[17] The villages do not constitute a homogeneous society which, in its culture and mode of life, may be placed in opposition to the mining region. The disparate nature of a process of settling that took place in several waves of migration from often distant regions has already been emphasized. Class differences are less visible in the countryside, but they combine with ethnic dimensions and with the residue of old hierarchies to remain every bit as cruel and real. The long standing and high degree of economic interpenetration between the mining basin and the neighbouring areas cannot be unduly emphasized. Between 1970 and 1990, 'the villages' (some two thirds of the district's population) stood out for their relative political unity; whilst the mining region favoured the Congress or the strong-armed, racketeering unionism of Surajdev Singh, the villages preferred either the movement led by A.K. Roy (himself based in town) or the autonomy-seekers of the Jharkhand Liberation Front (who are based in the villages), and between whom, in any case, there had long been electoral understandings.

The villagers' discourses *vis-à-vis* violence are in remarkable unison. Violence is looked upon as an exclusive peculiarity of the mining region but, in getting to this conclusion, due account is not taken of all the forms of violence. 'Surajdev the bandit does what he pleases', is the most characteristic example over the last decade. It is a symbol, frequently accompanied (or illustrated), but never rivalled, by the frequently recurring image of the hoodlum who snatches women's chains outside cinema halls. There follow, in no particular order, the treatment meted out by the gangs to those who defy them, strong armed tactics for fund collection, intimidation for hijacking elections, rival union leaders killed in gang warfare. On the other hand, inter-community massacres (for instance, 47 Sikhs were killed in Bokaro in 1984) have been forgotten, as have acts of violence related to work,[18] to the exploitation or despoliation of the environment, none of which is considered particularly meaningful. Surajdev Singh is violence made man, a demon, if one goes by what the rural folk of Dhanbad (and even those who become part of his clientele on leaving the village) believe of him, and is looked upon in a curious manner. In order to make it appear that he was capable of any crime, it is put about that he refused assistance to his own near and dear ones and that he 'spat upon his father'. To the villagers, absolute evil is manifested in Bihar's politicians who, immediately on occupying an official post, deny their own relatives, friends and acquaintances access to the gravy train. To destroy the family is to destroy society. Surajdev's bodyguards, who squeeze the populace and serve to keep competition out, are described as buffers between the leader of the BMS and his family. To the villager, his 'family values' are in confrontation with the drifting anarchy, in the sense of an absence of links, of the mining region.

This is curious, or revealing, because if there was a man who placed the family above everything else, who gave family ties a sacred character, it was indeed Singh. He gave his parents regular sums of money and inducted his brothers into his organization-enterprise. In fact it was his elder brother who took over the union, though he could not keep the family's grasp on the assembly seat. Without quite sharing the same culture (for the Bhojpuri world is unique), the villagers and the 'black hero' of Dhanbad broadly share the same values. The growing conflict of interests between the local people and migrants from the north (especially sensitive during the last fifteen years in terms of the job market) would prevent the attribution of any qualities at all to the most aggressive representative of the migrants—but why are such falsehoods invented about him? In the eyes of those who live in the rural areas, the greatest violence is the breaking of links, the interruption of blood ties, whether or not these are sanctified by a hierarchical context or ideology. Caste hierarchies, which are never clear, have lost a great deal of their consistency in the region. Castes bring pressure groups into play on an equal footing and therefore lead to violent conflict. The family (several kinds of family) is still the unit which enables the concentration of hierarchical behaviour, which becomes the matrix that enables the perpetuation of such behaviour, despite the intensity of disputes (linked to egalitarian perspectives). The withdrawal of the social into the familial in a context of penury tends to place families in positions of rivalry, of constantly increasing competition. The consensus on the interpretation of violence is construed as one of the rare signs of a harmonious, often idealized or even invented, past.

If the debate has focussed on this question and if a negative image of Surajdev Singh has been spread, it is because of the widespread sentiment that there must be unity for survival, as the villages, belittled by the new masters of the mines and looked upon as a single block, are laggards in the race for jobs and sinecures. The new element is not violence but the hunt for increasingly rare jobs. The sole advantage local people have is the fact of having been there before the others, for at all other levels they are handicapped, and this advantage can only be effective if they present a united political front. It is important to define a local 'rural identity' from the pieces of an unstable jigsaw puzzle of communities, cultures and divergent interests. It is even more important to claim a link with the soil that goes beyond time (though the region has been inhabited only for a few centuries), thus reactivating relation-based ideologies without however, forsaking the creation of new factors of loyalty (modern sub-nationalism). The Jharkhand movement has stuck to this task for the last fifty years, with noteworthy success. Constructing an identity in a time of crisis necessitates an enemy, a counter model; the mythical violence of the BMS' leader, and that of the mining belt as a whole, serves this purpose at the deepest and also at the most commonplace level.

The symbolic assimilation of violence to severed links finds expression at numerous levels. It corresponds to some everyday practices which, when interpreted in the light of what is happening today in the mining belt, enable the conceptual opposition between the two worlds to be founded upon the way violence comes into play and the construction (or modern reinterpretation) of the village identity. There has never been a consensus on the region's social order, but there exist enough common cultural elements that could serve to create an illusion thereof, *vis-à-vis* the outside. For example, those who live in the countryside do not use knives frequently, especially in homes (though bows and arrows are in everyday use). A blade mounted on a base, which seems to make a euphemism of the gesture of cutting, is employed (Heuze 1989). Things are not very different in the mining localities, where women and juniors are the ones who cook, and where all the symbolisms in play, without exception and in most milieus, do not allow them the implements of liberation. That vegetables are cut in the same manner in Jharia (in the centre of the region) as in Chandi-ankari (a town in the south), is a fact that is overlooked by the villagers who keep evoking the switch knife (freely sold between 1977 and 1988 and a somewhat rare sight in the countryside) as the characteristic implement of the mining belt. The opposition between those who hack human flesh and those who refuse to use violence even on vegetal matter may strike us as caricatural, but this in fact is the characteristic of this identity constructed in extremis.

The ideological references invoked, for the refusal of violence and for the association of the peasant-miners of the villages with a radical and all-encompassing non-violence, are rather varied. They change according to caste, culture and origins. Bengali Brahmins and Kayastha invoke Ramakrishna Paramahamsa Dev or their gurus (Goswami); the lower castes invoke Ambedkar or Gandhi; the Santals, Mahtos and almost all the others are influenced by the Bauls, by Kabir and by gurus of the Beosnab caste.[19] The renouncers in the region's numerous Bhakti sects are generally opposed to violence and to its orchestration. Their great popularity may have paved the way for charismatic figures like Roy. Finally, the CPI(M)'s members, whose influence, exerted from their bastion in neighbouring West Bengal, have a well-founded reputation for their legalist approach and practices. Ever since coming to power (1977), they have tried to exorcize political violence. It is certainly important, perhaps decisive, that non-violent references and discourses expressing themselves in several social perspectives were available in the local cultural context, as indeed they are elsewhere in the mining belt. A multiplicity of authorities, learned and sacred in varying degrees, are one in structuring and legitimizing the widespread sentiment that violence cannot be a characteristic of villages, which are solely inhabited by 'the poor' who are bound together by a shared destiny of exclusion and injustice. Often, there is a tendency to look upon the villages in relation to the mining belt as one family, with its limitations and its honour that must be defended *en bloc*. This is the meaning that must be read into the frequent allusion to assaults on women outside cinema houses (which are actually very rare), because snatched necklaces are easily assimilated with the honour of the woman and with that of the collectivity to which she belongs. 'They rape our women', goes the insinuation, so that the ranks may be closed, but that is not the principal element in identity construction.

This general movement, obviously subject to contradictions, regressions and highly diverse variations (the countryside has its share of those who admire Singh and his 'efficiency'), takes its place in a world scarred deep and early by violence. From the Santal insurrection of 1855 and the 1973–5 movement for the restoration of land expropriated by usurers,[20] violence has frequently erupted in confrontations between the rural people and the external world (the state included); this violence includes violence amongst the rural people themselves. Crime-related mortality is high, as it is in all of south Bihar, and is doubtless higher than in the mining belt where, all things considered, the inflow of wealth is enough to prevent a man from killing just to take the shirt off another's back; for this, in fact, often happens just 30 km outside Dhanbad. From the nocturnal exploits of *dakus* (bandits) to alcoholism-related accidents, most of these incidents of internal violence seem devoid of meaning and do not threaten the general conception of their society. The situation is different when it comes to agrarian conflict, which threatens to set the entire stage afire, as it does in north Bihar, and which can only be contained by employment in the mines. If migration is to be stopped (which is a generally shared objective) and the explosion of internal conflicts is to be avoided, it is essential to show and to communicate the idea that the villager is the prototype of someone assaulted in his very home by external forces, of someone who has never known violence because he has always been one with the soil. This purpose is served by the orchestration of the non-violence of the poor of the countryside and by placing this in opposition to the opulent anomie of the mining belt. Some upper castes (Bengali Brahmins), former landowner-occupants, play a singular role in this respect, but all big landowners[21] as a whole are noteworthy for their attachment to this myth of non-violence. In the present context, doubtless it is in the interests of the richest amongst them to defend the idea of a pacific and aggressed community, but, as the political game is fairly open, it is certain that the majority of the poor and landless will accept to be mobilized around certain landed elites.

To expel internecine factional violence and to form a homogenous entity defined by a social vision associating ties and non-violence—these are visions and practices that are related but very diversely realized. The form of these concrete perceptions, of this identity-founding non-violence varies according to the milieu, local conditions, proximity to the mining belt and the community culture. At this level, the Bengali Brahmins and Kayasthas do not merely defend agrarian interests, they fight for status and political pre-eminence. In numerous places, the rural communities include Brahmins from Bihar and Uttar Pradesh alongside upper caste Bengalis who practise the cult of the goddess. Owing to their strict vegetarianism, they believe themselves superior to Bengali Brahmins, for the Mukherjis, Chatterjis, Bannerjis and Chakravartis eat fish and sacrifice goats. Non-violence as well as ritual purity are on the side of Brahmins from the outside, but that does not enable them to derive any profit from it in terms of influence or effective social prestige. The majority looks upon them as outsiders (they came here in the nineteenth or the twentieth century, at the same time as the lower caste groups which now refuse to be associated with them) and enemies. A reputation for abominable violence, attributed to them by the Bengali Brahmins, who are associated with the lower caste groups that were once their clients, has been appropriated by the majority and has sufficed to destroy their prestige. Their crime is the expropriation of land, often interpreted symbolically as a rupture, a break in ties. In many cases, upper caste families from the north and their Marwari allies, have never, or have not since long, indulged in land grabbing. They are, quite simply, large, cohesive families who know how to take advantage of family ties and modern laws. The law, like the state as a whole, is perceived as an agent of separation (of men from the soil, of men from one another), thus as a factor in violence and chaos, the two being inseparably linked.

In the final analysis, one has a situation in which the members of a caste that does not practise *ahimsa* and whose status is relatively low when indexed according to generally accepted Hindu principles, enjoy a prestige, an overall reputation for non-violence that enables them to ensure their pre-eminence *vis-à-vis* their more exalted competitors. Like anywhere else, violence and non-violence are linked to status, to religious rituals in particular, but as regulatory agents of the social space, they take on their most decisive expression at the political level.

It is the illegitimacy of the Hindi-speaking Brahmin and Bhumihar migrant groups that is signified by attributing to them a reputation for violence in spite of their more rigorous mores. Symptomatic of this is the fact that a reputation for non-violence is conferred too on the low caste Mahtos, hunters, warriors and 'hit men' in everyday life. This derives neither from their acts nor from their mores but from the fact that they are not said to have stolen other people's land and that they seldom refer to the Law of the Land.

One discerns thus the endlessly growing importance of violence as a stake and as a constantly exchanged symbol, as a foundation for identity and as an object for permanent social debate in this over-populated countryside forever haunted by the spectre of unemployment. In a complex, multicultural society, with several claimants to social 'leadership' (though the special case of the Santals has not been discussed), for so long overrun with a city and an industry that live solely for their own ends, ritualistic and religious notions of violence, although very much prevalent in personal discourse, do not operate greatly in the social space. The spirit of systems of relationships pre-dating industrialization, amongst which are very ancient conceptions of social unity, continues, however, to be maintained, unless it is in the throes of a 'revivalism' expressing itself in various forms: traditionalism, Marxism, or the Jharkhand movement. The essential perception is that if the members of a society are de-linked or linked merely by economic interests, the most dangerous violence will unfailingly ensue; this is what one may call anomie and what the Bengali Brahmins refer to as *Kaliyuga*, when they are not more specific in their allusion to the mining belt and its hoodlums. The non-violence of the countryside, now emblematic, sprang forth naturally in relation to this most widely shared culture, from a substratum of practices and conceptions that frequently overlap and contradict one another but to which this reference brings a semblance of unity.

Violence, Non-Violence, Framework and References of Social Recomposition

At Dhanbad, as it appears elsewhere in other industrial regions of India, an overall relationship of opposition between town/country has emerged, which derives from a multiplicity of cultures in both milieus and from the colonizing nature (class-driven, dominant and exploitative) of the industrializing town. A deep rooted internal differentiation, now made unbearable in the face of modernization, has exploded the remnants of overall relationship systems and erased common reference points; it appears to be inspiring undercurrents for recomposition and unification. It is not always possible, especially at Dhanbad, to brandish community symbols, although that has been done greatly in the case of the tribal and autonomous Jharkhand movement. The tribals are in a minority, and highly divided. If the two worlds, the rural and the industrial, are linked, and they are linked in an extraordinarily intricate manner, it has become important for them to be linked by dissociation: the rural must pit its 'moral virtue' and its poverty (the reduction to the lowest common denominator, so dear to populists) against the easy money and the perceived destabilizing influence of migrants. As far as the city is concerned, this growing desire to separate the two worlds rests on an exasperation with modernist ideologies, on contempt for the 'backward' countryside, and on the wish to be rid of a lowly-qualified but clamorous work force. The exploitation-seduction model of relations begun at the end of the last century between the mining belt and its hinterland continues, but the bulwark of rural and Jharkhandi identity, which owes its existence in great part to the invocation of rural non-violence and urban violence, contributes a new element. Few have theorized locally on non-violence in the present socio-economic context. It is not a subject for debate. It came rather into the reckoning from pre-existing relational and reference systems from which it 'spilt over'. By explaining the nature of the adversary outside the restrictive framework of familial practices, it serves to interpret and to rationalize, especially the conflicts. It is a 'social' ideology that goes beyond family ties and offers an explanation and an action plan in unforeseen situations.

The two worlds have a lot in common, including their analyses of violence, which is interpreted in reference to social links that need to be forged or reinforced. Though clientelism does not assume visible or mass proportions in the countryside (as a result of which there is little talk of a mafia), it nevertheless continues to hold sway. The recent drifting of the Jharkhand Mukti Morcha shows that the political mores of rural south Bihar do not in any way lag behind the relational systems of migrants from the north.[22] It cannot be said that there is a cohesive society in the countryside and anomie in the mining belt. When one sets them against each other, the two kinds of violence in Dhanbad, rural and urban, there is a throwback to the evolution of the popular Hindi film since the 1950s. The metaphor is relevant for the film has become by far the premier cultural element in the mining belt, as in fact it is a major reference point in the countryside. In the rural areas, they continue to see films from the 1950s. Violence is an everyday phenomenon: men are battered and die quickly, but often attacked by nature (the famine of 1967 is still frequently evoked) or by old world exploiters, like the village money lender. These visions of confrontation with powerful but surmountable, and in fact partially surmounted, forces may explain the continuing progressivist impulsion of the rural areas as opposed to the mining belt, which does not believe in it very much any more. In Dhanbad, there is a representation of the post-1980 period. Here each one is pitted against all the others. Penury is as extravagant as abundance. Violence and hoodlums thrive because the mad release of desire has destroyed all links, hierarchies, fraternities, and, most concretely, families. Many rural observers do realize however that even in the mining belt, fraternities, hierarchies and family ties (especially amongst the Bhojpuris) continue to occupy pride of place, as in the rural areas. They know too that the migrants know how to close ranks within the unions or when faced with natural disasters (which are as bad for the mines as for the countryside). These sparks of lucidity do not suffice, however, for them to question the image of a world of anomic violence that concentrates in the mines and in the migrants the very traits that they do not want to accept in themselves.

Particularities of Contemporary Violence

The violence that occupies Indian newspapers—and that in Dhanbad, foremost of all—often seems to belong to a world of relationships or, more broadly, to a culture which is that of modernity and class conflict imported from or stimulated by the outside. Going by the usual analysis (though it is customary to speak of violence without seeking to analyse it), what happens in the mining belt derives from conflicts of interest and political contradictions that have their equivalents everywhere in the world.[23] In that case, it may be justified to wonder whether the region's cultural specificities need to be invoked to analyse violence. Over and above the fight for monetary gain and power, which has certain 'international' aspects, the present approach enables some light to be thrown on other dimensions of these phenomena, particularly the autonomous nature of these relational and social representation systems *vis-à-vis* the economic context. Interests are expressed and derive their meaning from reference to social notions, to collective identity and to value systems. Violence serves at this level as a mediating and revealing agent. The empirical approach seems particularly apt in order to apprehend what happens on this plane. There is in fact a notable corpus of doctrine on violence in Dhanbad, but what are the texts of Gandhi, of the Jains (for long influential in the area) or of Ramakrishna, when torn away from the concrete context of their application and the peculiar trajectories they then underwent? Beyond written references, often oversimplified in the quest for coherence, the various discourses on violence are of fascinating complexity and would deserve specific approaches. However, is not what they dissimulate—a propensity to mobilize and hierarchize loyalties to subserve certain types of social relations—or attempt to relativize more important than what they proclaim? This is only discernible by comparing the attitudes of the diverse protagonists. Contemporary social practice in relation to violence is strongly influenced by references, attitudes, ancient, but still more or less extant, relational systems, all of which were already defined *vis-à-vis* the problem and had conceived the foundation of an order or a praxis for it. In all frames of reference, something important—religion, vocabulary, familial culture, political tradition—legitimizes or facilitates the idealization of non-violence. At that level, there is a deep-rooted interference in this violence, which seems economic and exogenous, from India's cultural system, from her entire history. To place acts of violence (and references to non-violence) that are considered 'traditional' and of a cultural nature in opposition to a more 'modern' violence that ignores the social particularities of South Asia, or just isolating the former, strikes us as an error.

Dhanbad, the seat of crime, invokes non-violence with unanimity, setting aside spaces, distant or secondary in accordance with the beliefs of the protagonists, for the exercise of legitimate violence. One has observed that non-violence is intimately linked with mass clientelist systems for which it becomes an ideological argument in relation to other symbolic references. However, there does not appear to be an overall link, in the entire region, between systems founded on patronage and the absence of individual choice on the one hand, and the invocation of non-violence to create or to ratify a consensual atmosphere, on the other. Rural clientelism does not utilize references of this kind and rural non-violence serves to affirm collective choice and to enlarge the possibilities for family and individual actions. In this respect, rural and urban non-violence are fundamentally at variance. The reference to non-violence does not legitimize clientelism but the social link, whatever it may be, and, in the case of the local people, the link between societies and the soil that bears them. Dhanbad's non-violence does not seek to reach a specific goal and is largely dissociable from the moral discourse and concerns of spiritual elevation so dear to Gandhi. Non-violence is the symbol, just moderately effective as far as the outside world is concerned but strongly operational *vis-à-vis* the protagonists, of a certain commonality of beliefs on the values and practices of social organization. The fact that the (atheistic) saint can more or less resemble the (near-fanatical) gangster where certain aspects of this question are concerned, is illuminating. Non-violence and violence alike, in all their concrete manifestations and symbolic expressions, set forth and characterize a certain state of society, a system of relations. Dhanbad's non-violence is generally dissociable from notions of collective status, usually so important in such cases. This does not mean that it does not play a role at this level. However, the influence of the overall framework of confrontation between town and country in a world of collectivities in the quest of Being, gives these dimensions a subsidiary, at all events localized, reality.

NOTES

1. The 1981 Census indicates the existence of an urban population of 1.044 million and a rural population of 1.070 million. Given the peculiarities of the mining industry, many villages have been included in urban zones, whilst rural populations outside are also concerned with the mines. *Census of India*, 1981, Series 4; Bihar, Parts XIII, A and B. Also see Heuze 1989.
2. According to our views, it is difficult to name the entities organizing and 'disorganizing' the coalfield societies by using a singleword. This is true regarding the rural society as well. 'Community' is particularly dim and confusing but 'group' is even more unprecise. 'Community' may concern any type of collectivity, the endagamous *jatis* (various levels), the official categories of the Indian State (Scheduled Castes, Scheduled Tribes . . .), any type of social setup related to kinship and lineage and the various movements associated with nation and nationalism.
3. Since 1973, India's coal mines (Coal India Limited, or CIL) comprise seven nationalized companies, BCCL amongst them.
4. There is talk of 400 to 2,000 victims in 1979-80, a period of great violence. All the organizations combined, irrespective of their affiliations,

do not revere more than some thirty martyrs, but doubtless there were numerous, unknown victims. See Dhar 1979: 690–1, or T. Ghosh (1979), 'The Mafia Still Rules', *Sunday*, 2 September, or yet A.S. 1980: 2046; Srivastava 1979: 550.

5. Trade union activists of this kind are present in other regions as well. The best known in recent times are Swami Agnivesh (stone quarries to the south of Delhi) and Shankar Guha Niyogi who led a movement in the iron mines of Madhya Pradesh. The latter was slain by hired killers in September 1991. Read Bandhua Mukti Morcha 1981 and Sen 1992: 271–90.
6. The RCMS was founded in 1949 by the INTUC. Currently it claims a membership of 2,50,000 among the 5,60,000 mine employees. Its influence has never been ratified by elections (which the union refuses to hold) but merely estimated by the management. The union held the absolute privilege of representability until 1974. Since then, every four years, it prepares and signs the National Coal Wage Agreement alongside the other trade unions (AITUC and HMS in 1974; AITUC, HMS, CITU and BMS after 1977), without however losing its primacy.
7. Jabbar Alam (1986), 'Dubey thrown out from INTUC Union', *New Age*, 22 June 1986; 'Bihar INTUC Rift Widens', *Amrita Bazar Patrika*, 27 August 1986; and author's testimony.
8. Sinha 1982 : 111–36.
9. Since its inception, the BCCL has accumulated losses arising from poor working results that can only partially be attributed to heavy investments. It is estimated that BCCL employs 50,000 unproductive, frequently absent persons. Hundreds never report for work and live off *rangdari* (racket, patronage) that exceeds their wages. For details see, 'Rangdari ko khuli chhut', *Janmat*, 15 April 1986, or K. Kethar (1979) 'Gangsterism in Dhanbad', *Economic Times*, 5 March, or yet 'Bihar ke udyogpati Bihar kyo nahin rahna chahta?', *Bhubharti*, May 1986, or Roy 1984: 1699–1702.
10. Interviews of the author with Surajdev Singh in November 1986 at 'Singh Mansion' and in the Janata Mazdoor Sangh office at Jharia; Heuze 1987a; S. Singh (1984), 'I will continue to fight', *India Today*, 15 February. Surajdev Singh died in the spring of 1991, following cardiac arrest in the midst of an election campaign. His brother took over the union but was defeated in the (local/assembly) elections by a woman Janata Dal candidate supported by the left.
11. Read in this context: Weiner 1978; K.L. Sharma 1976: 37–43; Sengupta.
12. Read Pradeep and Das 1979.
13. Works consulted include, notably: Roy 1983, *Kis Aur? Dhanbad*, BCKU; id. 1984, *New Dalit Revolution*, Tribal Documentation Centre Chaibasa.
14. This term, which designates all the 'oppressed' in present-day society by referring to dimensions of caste and class, has recently grown in

currency from its origins in Maharashtra and movements such as the Dalits Panthers. It is yet fairly new in Bihar. Read *Dalit Voice*, published from Bangalore by R. Shetty, which sets out well the themes of the movement.

15. Sadan Gupta, a union leader in many respects similar to A.K. Roy, founded a combative union in 1947. Following the murder of a businessman by the miners, he was sentenced to death in 1953, but reprieved in 1967. He then communicated his experience and his spirit to A.K. Roy. There were several police massacres during the mine-workers' strikes in the early 1950's; notably, 40 to 80 miners perished in a single incident at Amlabad.
16. *Gunda Raj*, in 1977, this became a popular expression and slogan.
17. D. Rothermund makes the opposition between the stagnation of the countryside and the economic development of the mining belt an essential datum and characteristic of the region. He is often right, but relations and points of resemblance between the two universes seem to be underrated in his somewhat economist perspective. D. Rothermund 1986, 'Enclave Economy of Dhanbad', *Times of India*, 28 December.
18. The Chasnalla catastrophe (456 were killed in 1975 following the collapse of a water pocket) is still fresh in people's minds as a reminder that the mines and the preoccupation with production at all costs devour men. This sort of violence takes on an entirely different note and plays a muted part. It must be acknowledged that since 1977 the management of CIL (Coal India Ltd., of which BCCL is a part) has done what it can to limit the number of accidents.
19. A sect created by the disciples of Chaitanya, the Bhakti philosopher born in Bengal in 1486. Initially composed of people from diverse humble social situations, the Beosnabs are now a caste from whom priests (performing 'secondary' pujas) and gurus of the lower castes are drawn.
20. Iyer and Maharaj 1977; D.N. and G.K. 1989: 1505–6; Sengupta 1988.
21. Peasants with small holdings are dominant and big landowners are somewhat rare. See Heuze 1989; Mundle 1979.
22. Since 1988, the JMM has split into several factions, some of which have rejoined the Congress with whom it had an electoral pact. A new generation of Jharkhandi organizations was born from student movements. Accusing the former leaders of corruption and nepotism, they have nibbled away at the JMM's popularity.
23. To illustrate this trend: (anon.) (1984), 'Dhanbad Mafia', *The Illustrated Weekly of India*, 4 April; A. Bose (1979), 'The City of Terror', *Sunday*, 11 March; A. Singh (1983), 'Mafia in Coal Belt', *National Herald*, 18 April, and numerous other newspaper articles as well as the collection edited by Sengupta (1982).

REFERENCES

Bandhua-Mukti Morcha. 1981. *Bonded Liberation Front, an Introduction*. New Delhi: Special Editor.

Bondurant, J.Y. 1958. *Conquest of Violence*. Princeton: Princeton University Press.

Dhar, H. 1979. 'Gangsters and Politicians in Dhanbad'. *Economic and Political Weekly*, 14(15): 690–1.

Erikson, E.H. 1969. *Gandhi's Truth*. New York: Norton.

Heuzé, G. 1987a. 'L'épilogue du voyage'. In *Philographies: Mélanges offerts à Michel Verret*. Saint-Sébastien-sur-Loire: ACL.

———. 1987b. 'Travail ouvrier et consciences communautaires. L'évolution des mentalités des travailleurs de la mine en Inde contemporaine'. *Cahiers de Sciences humaines* 23(2): 245–60.

———. 1989. *Ouvriers d'un autre monde*. Paris: Éd. de la Maison des sciences de l'homme.

———. 1993. 'Inde'. In *Histoire générale du syndicalisme des origines à nos jours*, ed. J. Sagnes. Toulouse: Privat.

Iyer, K.G. and A.N. Maharaj. 1977. *Agrarian Movements in Dhanbad*. New Delhi: National Labour Institute.

Karnik, V.B. 1978. *Indian Trade Unions: A Survey*. Bombay: Popular Prakashan.

Kumar, R. 1981. 'Nationalisation by Default. The Case of Coal in India'. *EPW* 16(18): 824–30.

Mundle, S. 1979. *Agrarian Relations in a South Bihar District*. New Delhi: Indian Institute of Public Administration.

N., D. and K., G. 1989. 'Some Agrarian Questions and the Jharkhand Movement'. *EPW* 24(27): 1505–6.

Pradeep, P. and A.N. Das. 1979. 'Organisation of the Future? A Case Study: Bihar Colliery Kamgar Union'. *Human Futures* 2(3).

Rothermund, D., E. Kropp and G. Dienemann. 1980. *Urban Growth and Urban Stagnation*. New Delhi: Manohar.

Roy, A.K. 1984. 'Cleaning the Coalfields, Limitations of the Gujral Way'. *EPW* 19(39): 1699–1702.

S., A. 1980. 'New Aspects of Coalfield Politics'. *EPW* 15(49): 2046.

Sen, I. 1992. 'Les femmes, le travail et la mine au Chhattisgarh'. *Purusartha* 14: *Travailler en Inde*, 271–90. Paris: Éd. de l'EHESS.

Sengupta, N. 1980. 'Class and Tribe in Jharkhand'. *EPW* 15(14): 664–71.

Sengupta, N., ed. 1982. *Fourth World Dynamics: Jharkhand*. New Delhi: Author Guild Publications.

Sengupta, N. 1988. 'Reappraising Tribal Movements'. *EPW* 23 (20), (21), (22), (23).

Sharma, K.L. 1976. 'Jharkhand Movement in Bihar'. *EPW* 11 (1–2): 37–43.

Sharma, U. 1978. *Violence Erupts*. New Delhi: Radhakrishna Prakashan.

Sinha, A. 1982. 'Struggles against Bureaucratic Capitalism'. In *Fourth World Dynamics: Jharkhand*, ed. N. Sengupta, 111–36. New Delhi: Author Guild Publications.

Srivastava, A. 1979. 'Trade-Unions Murders in Dhanbad'. *EPW* 14(10): 550.

Weiner, M. 1978. *Sons of the Soil*. Princeton: Princeton University Press.

Remarks on Dissuasion in Ancient India

CHARLES MALAMOUD

Of the fifteen books that constitute the *Arthasastra*, that great Indian treatise on the art of governance, eight (i.e.VII to XIV) are given over to foreign policy.[1] Foreign policy is a matter of applying, in relation to circumstances, one or the other of the *sadgunya* or 'Six Measures': peace, war, abstention, marching orders, the quest for protection, a two-pronged policy (VII, 1, 2). In this context, war and peace are not simply antithetical terms; they are, in fact, the extreme poles of a continuum of processes. Peace is not defined merely as an absence of warfare: in the *Arthasastra*, peace is referred to as *sandhi*, which should strictly speaking be rendered as 'accord', and is characterized by a positive link, a treaty (*panabandha*). We have translated the term *asana* as 'abstention' (and sometimes as 'expectation'); literally, *asana* is applied to the 'seated posture' and may only be considered pacific to the extent that it is devoid of active hostility. The sign of war itself (*vigraha*) is the harm one seeks to inflict to someone (*apakara*). What is called 'marching orders' (*yana*) is the building up of forces. The quest for protection (*samsraya*) is recourse to the assistance of another power to whom there is temporary submission. The 'two-pronged policy' is the simultaneous practice of war and peace: the text is not clear about whether the two-pronged policy is in fact, as is most likely, a double game played on a single partner (peace in the open; war on the sly); or whether, as claimed virtuously by some Indian scholars, it refers to a quest for peace with one power and acts of aggression against another. The text wonders if the 'Six Measures' should not be brought down to two: is each case not a variant of either war or peace, as the ancients described? No, answers Kautilya, the master whose doctrine is expounded by the *Arthasastra*; six processes, six attitudes must in fact be distinguished, for each of these has its specificity.

While it is true that foreign policy cannot be reduced to a mere choice between war and peace, is it possible to discern in the complex of 'Six Measures' a peculiar combination of war and peace that approximates to what we call dissuasion? It is tempting to seek that in the 'marching orders' process, where forces are visibly, even ostentatiously, built up in order to intimidate the enemy, persuade him that any aggression from him would inevitably lead to a very costly defeat. The *Arthasastra* does not deal separately with dissuasion thus defined, but one can attempt an explanation for this absence: the *Arthasastra* does not lay it down as a principle that peace is preferable to war. The text is a compilation of precepts addressed to the king, a king of whom it is expressly and repeatedly said that his nature, his vocation, his very *raison d'être* mark him out as *Vijigisu*, 'he who is imbued with the desire to conquer'. That 'conquest' refers to the entire planet. It is hardly surprising, then, that the greater part of these precepts should cover offensives.

Defence is not looked upon as that which is necessary to resist an attack or maintain a given situation, but as a totality of potential retreats that enable regrouping prior to a fresh offensive for conquest (refer in particular to Book XII). As very little theorizing is done about defence, the problem is less a matter of dissuading the adversary from attacking than a matter of wearing down his resistance. Terror (*vibhisana*, *vibhisika*, *trasana*) is a potential way of deterring him. Dissuasion is not a strategic option but it could be good tactics. In battle itself (as opposed to the manoeuvres designed to prevent battle), the task of terrifying the adversary to the point of paralysing him falls to the elephant division. (Elephants, one should not forget, are the primary 'arm' of Indian battle formations. The others, in hierarchical order, are the cavalry, the chariots and the infantry.) Terrifying the enemy is part of the totality of tactics deployed in *kutayuddha*, 'combat by ruse'. This is looked upon as a form of disloyal or contemptible combat in texts that are somewhat more gallant in inspiration than the *Arthasastra*. *Kutayuddha*, 'combat by ruse', includes, in addition to terror, surprise attacks when the enemy has been weakened through natural calamities, as well as feigned retreat that lull the adversary into relaxing his vigilance, following which a fresh attack may be mounted on him. In the *Arthasastra*, 'combat by ruse' is merely held out, with no moral judgement attached, in opposition to 'open combat' (*prakasayuddha*), and distinguished from 'silent combat' (*tusnimyuddha*), which entails the use of secret agents (*apasarpa*) and agents provocateurs (*upajapa*).

With 'silent combat' we leave the realm of confrontation between two armed groups on a battlefield and enter operations that are carried out in the enemy's territory. Here, more than anywhere else, dissuasive terror comes into its own. The bluff, that singular form of fiction, is the backbone of this terror. Doubtless, no king 'desirous of conquest' would overlook the usual ways to inflict real damage on the enemy and demoralize him—setting camps on fire; dropping soldiers disguised as ascetics and mendicants behind the lines, so that they may surge forth when necessary and put men and beasts to death; assassinating key members of the enemy's court, etc. What the *Arthasastra*, however, describes in great detail are the magic spells which would lead the adversary to believe that the king seeking conquest is imbued with supernatural powers and, more importantly, is on terms of some familiarity with the gods. Crude in their essence, brutal in their effects, but complicated in their mechanism, these so-called wondrous exploits (in which, for instance, the statues of divinities would come to life and speak) involved the deployment of a phalanx of secret agents with the most diverse specialities, all related in some way or the other to the conjurer's art. Incidentally, it is disturbing that even as the *Arthasastra*, a seemingly rational text, cynically reveals how the religious credulity of the enemy must be exploited, it lays down a long series of precepts in which magic and religion are taken very seriously: charms and extravagant black magic spells, interspersed with instructions on rites and prayers designed to make the adversary perish or just to ward off misfortune, are the essence of Book XIV (the book of 'esoteric practices'). Apart from recourse to the prestige of the supernatural, the arsenal of 'silent combat' includes the use of a more earthly fiction roughly equivalent to what one calls 'intox' (disinformation)—assail the enemy with disastrous (and false) news that begins to acquire substance from the reaction it engenders. The following sentences from the book (X, 6, 48–50) summarize and comment upon the manoeuvres and manipulations of 'silent combat',

> The conquering king must strike terror in the heart of his enemy with his machines, with his use of occult practices, with hired assassins who kill the non-vigilant, with magic, with manifestations of his proximity to the gods, . . . with diversions created by agents masquerading as messengers who will tell the rival king, 'Your fortress has fallen or has been set afire; this or that member of your family has risen in revolt against you; this or that tribal chief, your ally, has switched sides.' An archer's arrow can at best kill one man, or perhaps none. Intelligence put into action by a wise man could even kill children at their mother's breast.

A process that is akin to dissuasion is the taking of hostages as a preventive measure. This is discussed in Book VII, 17. Whenever the king leaves on a campaign, he must make sure to take with him, under close surveillance, the sons or brothers of his allies, as a guarantee of their loyalty.

This observation on allies, that is to say on alien elements forming part of the royal camp, allows a neat transition from foreign policy to domestic policy. In war and in diplomacy, as one can see, dissuasion is a part of the tactics deployed for what is essentially a permanent offensive by the conqueror. The dominant theme of domestic policy, however, is defence. Within the kingdom, it is by no means the duty of the king to carry out or institute reform (the problem of newly-conquered territories shall not be considered here). The royal task lies solely in preserving the social order, or in restoring it if it has been taken apart. There is no question, let it be emphasized, of founding, or inventing or even discovering that just social order which is in harmony with the cosmic order: it is an order that is contemporaneous with genesis itself or at least with the coming into being of the world (though that may have come at various stages, depending on the school of thought), it is enshrined in the very nature of things, even if it is endangered by the overall decadence of humanity or comes under the cloud of the ill-will of men. The king has no other function than to prevent such alteration by vigilantly ensuring that each individual and group remains confined within his/its specific status and system of observances.[2] *Dharma*, the socio-cosmic order, can only remain intact and stable if each one remains faithful to his own *dharma*. Social defence, or rather the social 'defensive', does not necessarily exclude a political offensive. It is remarkable, however, that the *Arthasastra*, believed by tradition to have been composed by a minister who helped his master usurp the throne by driving away the incumbent, should have no wisdom to dispense on the art of capturing power. It constantly adopts the point of view of the power in place, which is legitimate by definition and therefore obliged to defend itself against attacks by others. Dissuasion is an essential element of the effort required to maintain the *dharmic* order, which cannot be separated from the effort the king must make to preserve his own power.

Like Yama, god of death, king of the dead and the very prototype of all mortals, the king's emblem is the staff, the *danda*: so much so, 'politics' is often referred to as *dandaniti*, or the 'art of wielding the staff'. The *Arthasastra*, however, does not share the recommendation made by certain 'ancient masters' that the king must constantly brandish and wield the staff. On the contrary, the very art of politics consists in using the stick with discernment, in ensuring that *dharma* is preserved (and the king obeyed) without recourse to repression (I, 4, 3–16). Even as large sections of the *Arthasastra* are given over to techniques that may be employed 'to eliminate thorns' (notably in Book IV, entitled *kantaka-sodhana*), the text gives every indication that an efficient and just administration would prevent the king's subjects from feeling discontented and enable the king to hold out the threat of chastisement but not its reality.

In the task of wielding the staff moderately and judiciously, the king is greatly aided by the fact that in theory what he seeks to impose is not his personal will but something that is perceived by all as the natural order. Though it only falls to the king to impose *dharma*, by force if necessary, the constraints of *dharma* are internalized by everyone and defended by all institutions of society. In the last resort, it is indeed the king, or the judge who speaks in his name, who pronounces or ratifies the punishment a delinquent must undergo. However, before reaching that stage, the criminal would have felt, in potential if not in fact, the singularly dissuasive but not directly violent reactions of his family, his caste, his village: exclusion from a caste is not less daunting than the most cruel corporal punishment inflicted by the king's justice. Moreover, the fear of consequences in the after-life for crimes committed here and now functions perhaps far more concretely in India than in any other traditional civilization. To those who believe in retribution (*karma*) and in the perpetual cycle of births and deaths (*samsara*), it would appear a self-evident truth that the manner in which one behaves in this life determines, in a foreseeable and inescapable manner, the form of one's human (or animal) existence in the next life. However, in the *Arthasastra*, which is a political treatise, this kind of argument is rarely invoked. The values and beliefs which form the base of Indian society are only alluded to in this text, doubtless because they are taken for granted. One may go so far as to say, with regard to dissuasion in domestic policy, that the king's principal weapon in dissuasion is the very existence not only of political science but of the book that contains it. Unlike the codes and laws of *dharma* (like the compilation of the Laws of Manu, for example), which merely define possible violations and recommend suitable punishments (inflicted either by human justice or by the mechanism of *karma*), the *Arthasastra* describes, with extraordinary pedantry, the means the king must employ to detect criminals, among whom must be counted all 'opposition', rivals, usurpers or potential conspirators: tortures, provocation, subtly specialized traps set to test the loyalty or just the solidity of character of the king's subjects, of the minister as well as of the merchant.

The *Arthasastra* teaches that apart from the regular penal code, the king may take recourse to 'silent punishment' (*tusnimdanda*) whereby he can eliminate, through poisoning or some other equally rapid procedure, those who stand in his way. By definition, the techniques of the police are meant to be secret. The *Arthasastra*, however, reveals that they exist, that these agents are omnipresent and that, thanks to their efforts, the king is omniscient and omnipotent. The notion, shadowy though it may be, that the king is in possession of all these powers inspires in his subjects a wholesome terror that spares the king the exercise of those very powers. That, strictly speaking, is dissuasion. It is to be noted, in passing, that the repression recommended by the *Arthasastra* does not spare those charged with dissuading or repressing the subjects: judges, policemen and jailers who may be negligent in their duties, or too cruel with their prisoners, are warned that the king has the means to detect and punish their misdeeds. The enormous phalanx of supervisors and auditors, both public and secret, are themselves supervised and audited, publicly and secretly.

The kingdom's cohesion is ensured by two distinct dissuasive ensembles: the general system of *dharmic* values, or, speaking schematically, the religious norms that structure each social institution and even each individual; the royal staff, or *danda*. There is no incompatibility, even in theory, between these two ensembles. Problems of adjustment arise nevertheless, in forms that vary according to the epochs or texts concerned.

A convenient way to approach them in such a manner as to highlight the specificity of ancient India in this regard, would be to pursue an inquiry on non-violence. *Ahimsa* (a term ordinarily translated as 'non-violence' but which should strictly speaking signify 'the will not to kill') is a virtue enjoined by the tenets of *dharma* upon all men, whatever be their condition. Curiously, the *Arthasastra* formulates the same doctrine. In Book I, 3, 13, for example, it is said that, 'non-violence, truth, purity, absence of malice and compassion' are 'common to all'. The list of virtues enumerates a superlative of *ahimsa*, *abhaya*—the fact of being neither a threat nor a danger to anybody, of being, on the contrary, the centre of a circle of peace and security. The inversion of this attitude, or the spread of fear around oneself by one's words and gestures, is expressly condemned (in Book III, 18).

Undeniably, the desire not to kill and not to be a danger or become cause of terror to others is of religious, even ascetic character. However, there can be no gainsaying the fact that these ideals are re-commended to society, with varying degrees of seriousness and emphasis, not only by Buddhists and Jains but also by Hindus. (The Jain fear of taking life may sometimes strike one as a near phobia.) It does not follow therefore that in its reality the history of traditional, Hindu, Buddhist and Jain India has been notably less violent than that of other peoples (though tortures, mutilations and massacres seem to have been less widespread than elsewhere). However, the cultural consequences of the exaltation of non-violence have been considerable. What follows here is the outline of an enumeration to be read in conjunction with the above examination of dissuasion.

Religious circles as well as the various schools of philosophy in ancient India had pondered deeply upon ways to make the obligation to practise *ahimsa* compatible with a king's duty to preserve the prosperity of his realm through threats, violence and even open war. The most eloquent and the best known of such philosophical reflections is the *Bhagavad Gita*. On a theoretical plane, it leads to a distinction between the actual act of violence, which is frequently inevitable and before which there can be no retreat especially if it is required by duties of state (such as the royal *dharma*, as in Arjuna's case), and the spirit of the person who acts, who must be shorn of selfish desire as to the outcome of the act. The critique of violence as much as the art of coming to terms with it form an integral part of an overarching theory on the act in general: in either case, detachment as to the outcome is indispensable. In terms of social practice, such doctrines reinforce the idea that the only kind of legitimate violence is that which is exercised by or in the name of the king.

If, as one has seen, violence is condemned when it occurs in relationships between men, it is equally held to account when used against animals. Gradually, it would be eliminated from ritual sacrifice. Even during the Vedic period, and much before the elimination of animal sacrifice (not that it ever was totally eliminated, although sacrifices without death would continually gain in prestige and dignity), Brahmins were applying themselves to devising ritual procedures that would thwart or neutralize the violence inherent in such killing. These procedures, which took the form of soothing words and not threats, were meant essentially to dissuade the victim from seeking revenge against its executioners in the hereafter.

As it does not act upon others, the capacity for violence may be turned upon oneself. The most excruciating and outlandish bodily exploits go hand in hand with the minutiae of theories on how to renounce the world. Once the desires that propel one towards the world have been checked and the violence one is capable of has been spent in controlling one's own body, one acquires, according to Indian philosophy, extraordinary powers in which the prestige of attaining the other-worldly combines with the purely physical prowess of the ascetic's look and speech. Legends and myths abound with examples of the ascetic's terrifying wrath. In such cases, as one can see, non-violence is transmuted into violence, an eminently dissuasive violence.

Not all ascetics are Brahmins, much less are all Brahmins ascetics. More than any other social group, however, Brahmins have a sort of vocation of non-violence. Thus, they refrain from working directly on the soil, so that they do not snuff out the life that may breathe within it. They are more naturally inclined to be vegetarian than others. Their status and their singular association with ritual sacrifice enable them to adopt that peculiar combination of violence and non-violence known as asceticism. As a matter of fact, the means they adopt to exercise pressure on others, on royalty in particular, when it comes to defending their own rights and immunities, are directly drawn from the ascetic's sphere of influence. Thus, the individual or collective fast in protest (*praya*) is a favourite non-violent weapon dreaded by kings. Royalty, in its turn, conjures up ways to make such weapons inoperative or to dissuade Brahmins from wielding them. If one is to believe the *Rajatarangini*, which is more like a historical chronicle, the king would have officials in charge of fasts. If he had the strength to withstand the consequences of a face off, the king could refuse to allow the cremation of the body of anyone who died fasting for an unjust cause. An escalation, or *traga*, was also possible on the part of those who undertook the fast. Apart from the protester himself, his son and cattle too could perish in the fast.

Returning, by way of conclusion, to the specificity of the *Arthasastra* and the (relative) autonomy it confers upon the political in relation to the religious, to be sure, Kautilya's treatise frequently affirms that the ultimate objective of the king is to protect the system of the four *varnas* and the four *asramas*. It is also emphasized, besides, that the king may take recourse to expedients such as surreptitious war and silent punishment only to the extent that he finds justification for them and gratification in *dharma* (for the king must be *dharmaruci*). In other words, violence as a means of deriving pleasure is forbidden.

Equally, though, the author of the *Arthasastra* attempts his utmost to analyse the king's objectives and action in worldly terms. A striking example of this desire to remain in the here and now, in the march of the world (*lokayatra*), in the world as it is and which is the province of royal action, is offered by the passage (IV, 13) which sets down the reparations the king must make when he is unjust, when he inflicts his *danda* (by way of fines) on his *adandya* subjects who may not be thus punished. Such reparations take the form first of rites, an offering to be made to the deity Varuna, for Varuna chastises kings whose conduct towards men is erroneous (*mithya*). The sin-purifying offering (*tena tat puyate papam*) is immersed in water, which is Varuna's element. However, what is this offering composed of? It is a sum of money equivalent to thirty times the amount of the unjustly collected fine. After being thus presented to Varuna, it is distributed among Brahmins, that is to say, re-introduced in the social circulation of material goods. Penitence takes the concrete form of a fine that the king imposes upon himself.

On a wider plane, one may observe a unifying strand that may guide us in our reading of the *Arthasastra*, the classification of *bhayas*, or dangers (and the fears that these dangers inspire, for the term '*bhaya*' may be used both in a subjective and an objective sense), from which the king must protect the kingdom or, more precisely, the constitutive elements (*prakrti*) of his power (VI, 2, 6–12, as also IV; 1, 3 and VIII, 1, 2). Calamities are one of the various kinds of events that may come to pass. Calamities are of two kinds: those that arise from *daiva*, from the will or pleasure of the gods, and those which are human in their essence. The former are the handiwork of misfortune (*an-aya*). In the case of the latter, however, it is the king's bad policies (*a-naya*) that would be incriminated. But it is these essentially human calamities, according to the text, which are the outcome of thought (*cintya*) and to these alone that the author of the *Arthasastra* is willing to apply his mind. From what is conceivable arise the various kinds of conduct and the totality of dissuasions that would be appropriate to the system of ends and means which is the specific domain of *artha*.

NOTES

* Reproduction of the text of a verbal communication made at a colloquium on Dissuasion and Culture, organized by J. Charnay, at Paris-IV University's Centre d'études et de recherches sur les stratégies et les conflits, from 28 to 30 January 1982.

1. Indian tradition holds that the *Arthasastra* is the work of a Brahmin known as Kautilya, a minister in the court of Chandragupta, founder of the Maurya dynasty, and grandfather of the emperor Asoka, who ruled over Magadha (Bihar) during the last quarter of the fourth century BC There is no solid foundation for this belief. It is generally and more credibly believed now that this text, at least in the form in which it has been handed down, goes back to the first century AD. There exists an exhaustive English translation of the text by R.P. Kangle (Bombay, 1963). In French, a highlight was the annotated and translated extracts in M. Dambuyant's *Kautilya, l'Arthasastra, le Traite Politique de l'Inde Ancienne* (Marcel Riviere, Paris, 1971).

   After being re-discovered, at the beginning of the twentieth century, the *Arthasastra* has been the subject of a great number of studies and analyses. In the impressive bibliography that has thus resulted, mention must be made of H. Scharfe, *Untersuchungen zur Staatsrechtlehre des Kautilya*, Otto Harrassowitz, Wiesbaden, 1968 and T.R. Trautmann, *Kautilya and the Arthasastra*, Brill, Leiden, 1971.
2. R. Lingat, *Les sources du droit dans le système traditionnel de l'Inde*, Mouton, Paris, p. 249 sq., 1967.

Magical Violence and Non-Violence: Witchcraft in Kerala

GILLES TARABOUT

> Vedic India, for so long the torch bearer of art and science, is also the land of *fairy-like enchantments* as well as *perfidious magic*. Both are taught by the Vedas and both were revealed by Brahma himself.
>
> DR. PARAMANANDA MARIADASSOU,
> *Médecine traditionnelle de l'Inde: la magie noire*
> [*Traditional Medicine in India: Black Magic*]

OVERVIEW*

Kerala is a land of enchantment in two ways. Its natural beauty and the refinement of its inhabitants, the Malayalis,[1] would charm the traveller sensitive to the tranquil rhythms of rural life, enabling him to partake of the quietude which Pierre Loti felt nearly a century ago about Travancore:

> [It is] a region of happy tranquillity, cut off from the frenzied denizens of this century, isolated and spared beneath coconut palm arches.' (Loti 1920: 36)

But Kerala is also 'pre-eminently the land of magic and sorcery' (Padmanabha Menon 1937: 204), a reputation firmly established all over Southern India and Sri Lanka. Rare is the family that can claim never to have been the object of occult attacks by an enemy (though this does not make it a perpetual obsession either). Such suspicion is rooted in a climate of envy, scandal mongering and low blows, poisoning frequently social relationships. Kerala may offer few examples of openly violent conflict: but passions express themselves in more discreet, but no less fearsome, modalities (cf. Obeyesekere 1975, in the context of Sri Lanka).

The aim of this paper is to present some facts and discourses pertaining to witchcraft in Kerala, particularly in Southern Kerala (the former kingdoms of Cochin and Travancore). The paper will have to limit itself to rather general indications, for two reasons: firstly, as far as South India is concerned, little has been done on the subject; and secondly, the present inquiry is still at a preliminary stage. Fieldwork was done as an external observer: I was in no way linked to the Powers or the stakes involved. True, the need for and the wealth of possibilities offered by 'participatory observation' have been highlighted by the work of Favret-Saada (1977) and Camus (1988) on witchcraft in France. The situation here is different: a European's presence at a ritual might possibly enhance its reputation in the eyes of those who participate in it, for it means its fame has spread beyond local confines. But apart from providing occasionally such an involuntary guarantee, the alien observer in Kerala is perceived usually as being outside the sphere of action of local occult powers. He 'does not belong' to the place, which makes him both immune and inoffensive. In order to become what Favret-Saada (1977: 23) calls 'a power-endowed-one (a sorcerer, an exorcist)', you need here a pedigree, or divine legitimacy, neither of which the present writer can claim to possess.

A terminological clarification needs to be issued. Following Evans-Pritchard's (1937) work in Zande country, anthropology in the English language has sometimes distinguished between 'witch' and 'sorcerer'. The first term is used to designate people who are supposed to possess a particular power by themselves, while the latter term describes practitioners whose efficacy is essentially technical. Since then, this distinction has become relative. Lewis (1986: 11) considers it to be more the exception than the rule and speaks, doubtless in humour, about 'Zande cultural imperialism' in anthropological theory. To Favret-Saada (1977: 27), these concepts applied to the French cases she studied are 'as different as Tweedledum from Tweedledee'. In Kerala, too, a more or less similar situation obtains, so the distinction seems unnecessary.

The Malayalam term *mantravadi*, or 'expert in mantras', can be rendered according to the context as 'exorcist', 'magician' or 'sorcerer'. *Mantras* are verbal or phonic formulae which are said to have the capacity to act when properly uttered, murmured or just evoked in the mind. Mastering *mantras* is the core of some initiatic disciplines ('tantrism'), enabling the practitioner to acquire extraordinary powers (*siddhi*) and spiritual awareness. At the same time, it is the very foundation of routine cult praxis. In this particular technical respect, *mantravadam* ('magic', 'sorcery', 'witchcraft') cannot be always clearly distinguished from these ordinary practices.

This paper aims to study the ideological and social conditions that enable magical non-violence to be culturally constructed as a value, in opposition to occult violence. It begins by examining accusations of witchcraft within the framework of explanations for misfortune. Then, a few examples will point to the social context in which such accusations are articulated. In the final part of the paper, witchcraft will be studied as a theory of spiritual power, both at the level of the person and at the level of society. To begin with, let me recall briefly some characteristics of Kerala society.

Society in Kerala

According to the 1991 Census, Kerala had at that time 30 million inhabitants. The dispersed settlement pattern, characteristic of this region, and a very high density in population (744 people per square kilometre, nearly 3 times the national Indian average) entails that there is no notable rupture between towns and the countryside. Most city dwellers, in fact, maintain their rural links.

Malayalis are justly proud of the high literacy rate in the State—more than 90 per cent of the population. There are periodicals, daily news-papers, weeklies and other publications in great number; a highly evolved political culture; significant levels of unionization; widespread awareness about hygiene, and effective birth control. In a word, this predominantly agricultural society, while remaining deeply conservative in certain respects, is widely open to the modern world in many others. In addition, the high density of population has led to emigration overseas and to other parts of India. It has fed, too, an intense local competition for everything, from acquiring land to getting seats in universities and white-collar jobs (more than half of those who have completed secondary school are unemployed).

About a fifth of the population is Muslim, a similar number is Christian, the remaining three-fifths being Hindu. The three faiths have coexisted for centuries in harmony, which does not preclude occasional prejudice or even, sometimes, conflicts. Among the Hindus, the traditional caste hierarchy can be simplified and represented as follows (excluding all that is not relevant to this paper):

Brahmins, of 'pure' birth, with access to Vedic Revelation. They are few in number (less than 1 per cent of the population) and divided into several sub-castes, among which we may mention for the present purpose:

(a) the Nambudiris, formerly organized in patrilinear Houses which held often superior rights to land.[2] In economic and political terms, their power is now a thing of the past, though several Houses continue to enjoy local prestige. Nambudiris are still the foremost in ritual hierarchy. Some Nambudiri Houses are known to practice *mantravadam*.

(b) Tamil Brahmins settled for centuries in the former kingdom of Cochin. They take little part in the ritual life of Malayalis, but some are astrologers (they are mentioned here for this reason).

—A one time martial caste, the Nayars, who have an elevated local status. Though they do not have access to Vedic knowledge and are, at least in theory, part of the pan-Indian Shudra category, they were formerly considered the 'lords of Kerala'. Significant in numbers, the Nayars were organized, until the beginning of this century, in matrilinear Houses. With the power to bestow life and death on the lower castes, the higher among them used to control both land and men, under the overall authority of Rajas or of Nambudiris. They continue to play a decisive part in present-day rural and urban Kerala society, where many have gone in the liberal professions.

—Numerous castes of lower status, considered 'polluting' and therefore 'untouchable' by the upper castes. The acts of public discrimination that they used to suffer have now disappeared, forbidden by the Constitution of India. Many of these groups continue, however, to be held in contempt. Yet, the situation is not uniform. The Ezhavas, whose 'caste-activity' is toddy tapping, are in fact often peasants and small merchants. Since the beginning of this century, they have taken great strides up the social ladder, now even rubbing shoulders with the Nayars, especially in towns. The Kaniyans, or astrologer-exorcists, despite their science, are still considered with prejudice. The Pulayans and Parayans, essentially agricultural workers who were bonded slaves in earlier times, continue to be victims of ostracism.

Explaining Misfortune

Multiplicities

A single misfortune can be explained in several simultaneous ways, at different levels. Take for instance Gopal, an educated young man from an affluent Nayar family in Trivandrum, who tells how his father, an official in the Forest Department, died of cancer a few years ago. Some time before his death, when apparently still in good health, he had been to see his astrologer, a common practice in Kerala. The astrologer informed him that death was not far away. In a corroborating sign, an owl perched on his bed a few days before the fateful day. Besides, Gopal and his family believe that the father's colleagues, motivated by jealousy about his successful career, brought about his death by calling upon the services of a sorcerer.

As can be seen, three levels of interplay are made explicit here:

1. an overall determinism, where stellar positions are simultaneously cause and symbol, giving mathematically the moment of death (with other signs coming as confirmation);
2. human malevolence springing from envy, which calls upon invisible forces and brings forth the peculiarity of the event: why did this man, enjoying full health and prosperity, die suddenly in this particular way?
3. a medical aetiology, seen clearly as the immediate cause of death but, at the same time, reduced to be only a manifestation of the other two causes.

At a still higher level of explanation, some people might invoke retribution for past deeds, referring to the 'doctrine' of *karma* (Skt., 'action, deed'), although more often than not it appears a rather abstract discourse.[3] For instance, K.N.B. Asan, a Kaniyan astrologer whom we shall meet again later, cites a Sanskrit verse attributed to the sages of yore (*acharya*):

purva-janma-krtam papam
vyadhi-rupena jayate

'The fault done in a previous birth finds rebirth in the shape of disease in this life.'[4]

However, in his commentary of the above verse, Asan underscores that one's own deeds in a preceding life are not necessarily the decisive elements: 'What enables the astrologer to conclude whether the diseases in the present life are the consequences of the wicked deeds of the person concerned in his previous birth, or done by his father or his paternal ancestors, or done by his mother or his maternal parents, is the position of the stars [. . .]. The deeds of an ancestor can therefore ruin the life of a person.'

Even at this level of scholarly discourse *karma* is not, then, a mere 'personal' matter. Transferable along both matrilineal and patrilineal lines, it is the result, and an affirmation, of kinship solidarity.[5]

The various levels of explanation for misfortune complement one another without difficulty, and their simultaneous multiplicity, with a corresponding multiplicity of treatments and specialists, has been underscored elsewhere in India.[6] This indicates that it would be erroneous to imagine that the fear of occult forces is incompatible with 'modernity'. As a rule, astral influence is regarded as scientifically founded, so that, for instance, a well-esteemed psychiatrist in Trivandrum bears on one of his fingers a ring with a red sapphire meant to avert the malefic influence of Saturn.[7] The possibility that occult or magical forces are at play exists therefore within the accepted order of things. This does not mean, of course, that every practitioner of magic enjoys the Malayalis' confidence. And, for some people, witchcraft is definitely a superstition of the past, a thing of charlatans meant for the credulous. In a few cases, however, such a scepticism will have to be appreciated in context.

Finally, it must be borne in mind that witchcraft is a fact of subjective experience ('To those who have not been caught, this does not exist!' Favret-Saada 1977: 137). As a matter of fact, sorcerers are feared not only in rural areas but in urban zones as well, as has also been observed elsewhere in India (see, for instance, Pandya 1982, on Lucknow).

OCCULT SOURCES OF MISFORTUNE

All misfortunes and illnesses are not necessarily explained by supposing that invisible forces are in action. And when it is indeed the case, witchcraft is only one of the many reasons that can be put forward. In this respect, specifying the context will be essential.

There does exist a learned discourse on the topic, which is developed in particular by astrologers. They are at the very core of the process of determining the occult causes of misfortune in Kerala, although they are not the only specialists, for people under divine possession may be consulted as well. Their views on the subject offer a rather 'rationalised' presentation of what are in Kerala widely-held opinions (but in an unsystematic way). In the present case, information was gathered from S. Jyotsyar, a Tamil Brahmin from Trichur, whose very name means 'astrologer'. Jyotsyar uses the standard, local texts on astrology. On this particular topic, he elaborates upon the 15th chapter of the *Prasnamarggam* ('The path of questions'; Govindan 1987), an astrological work which deals with the elucidation and resolution of crises.[8]

The term commonly used in Malayalam to denote afflictions resulting from occult causes is *upadravam*, 'trouble, torment, blow, wound, attack, destruction'. Such afflictions are therefore clearly perceived as acts of violence, of aggression perpetrated on their victims. Relying upon the *Prasnamarggam*, Jyotsyar lists eleven possible sources for such aggressions. They are all identified—in this astrological discourse—by analysing the position of the planets at the moment of consultation, an analysis complemented by taking into account other signs, too, such as the physical posture and behaviour of the person seeking consultation, as well as numerous various other events occurring in the surroundings (e.g. noises by animals)[9]:

1. The wrath (*kopam*) of a god or goddess (*deva*).[10]
2. The wrath of the family deity—as distinct from other gods or goddesses—capable of inflicting 'torments', *badha*. This latter term is particularly used to denote cases of affliction by possession.
3. The wrath of serpents (*sarppam*), whose occult powers manifest themselves in nightmares, female sterility, or skin and eye diseases. Here too, such afflictions are spoken of as *badha*, but can be as well said to be *dosham*, 'fault', 'illness' (lit. 'defect'; in Ayurvedic medicine, it means 'humoral constituent'—see Zimmermann 1989). 'Fault', in this context, is more of a ritual order than of a moral one, for in that latter case the term papam would be preferred.
4. The wrath of one's forbears (*pitr*), including the father (the text of the *Prasnamarggam* includes in fact also ancestors in the maternal line, including the mother). Irrespective of whether they are living or dead, the displeasure of these forbears finds expression as 'anger' or 'curse' (*sapam*).
5. The wrath of a Master (*guru*), whether living or dead: one has to fear his curse.
6. The wrath of Brahmins (similar peril). Jyotsyar, himself a Brahmin, notes with a touch of humour that afflictions due to a Brahmin's curse belong now to the past, since no Brahmin is imbued anymore with the sort of spiritual power required to produce effective maledictions.
7. The influence of planets: they have potentially their own malefic effect (*grahapidha* or *grahadosham*). Let us recall that the Sanskrit word *graha*, or planet, literally means 'hold, grip, abduction'. The term is used in ancient texts, medical ones in particular, to denote malefic beings of whom the chief is Skanda (Thite 1982: 11ff., 41).

8. The wrath or acts of unsatisfied deads, *preta*. Popular imagination distinguishes between various kinds of such evil deads and incorporates them all among the *bhutam*, those dangerous beings which form turbulent hordes and constitute the armies of various divinities. They often torment their victim through possession (*badha*).[11]
9. The evil eye, called in this context *drshti*, which inflicts *dosham* or *badha*. According to S. Jyotisyar and the *Prasnamarggam*, the term denotes the influence of various invisible entities. The treatise lists eighteen of them (such as *Rakshassu*, *Gandharvan*, *Bhutam*, etc.) which can possess their victim. This learned discourse differs from popular usage which draws clearly a difference between the afflictions caused by such entities (who act very much in the manner of *pretas* with whom they are often equated) and the evil eye proper. The latter, in Malayalam, is termed *karimkannu* ('black eye, incendiary eye, eye that desiccates'). It is an ill-defined malefic influence borne by some people, often unbeknownst to themselves. For instance, a single word from them in praise of a mango tree would suffice for its fruit to rot and perish. Apart from *karimkannu*, there is also a 'black tongue' (*karinakku*), to say nothing of a special term (*koti*, 'ardent desire') for denoting the envious look of those who, starving, are contemplating others' food.[12]
10. 'Hand poison' (*kaivisham*): this is a mantra-charged substance which, when absorbed or merely touched by one who has been taken as target, destroys his victim or brings him under the magician's absolute control.[13]
11. The act of an enemy (*satru*), who asks and pays a magician for inflicting *dosham* or *badha* on his victim with appropriate spells. In Kerala, several words are used to describe this specific kind of occult aggression: *abhicharam* (magic, sorcery, witchcraft), *kshudra-karmmam* (foul deed), *maranam* (murder), *marrumaranam* (murder by deceit).[14]

As an occult source of misfortune, therefore, witchcraft forms part of a system of representations which links together various symptoms of different nature, the living and the dead, benefic and malefic Powers, perceptible and occult actors, without placing them in opposition with one another. The eleven categories enumerated above do not by any means exclude one another. The eleventh, in particular, overlaps with several others. Thus, one's enemy could well use 'hand poison'

(Category 10), bring unsatisfied deads into play (Category 8) or send various Powers (Category 9).[15]

A Few Narratives

CONFLICTS

One of my friend, a Tamil Brahmin of Trichur retired from a pharmaceutical business, told me that, once, his son faced 'problems' at work with his superior. Brahmins were then summoned to perform a *homam* for protection. A *homam* (or *havanam*) is a sacrificial ritual in which offerings are poured or thrown into the sacred fire, but without any actual killing of animals in most of its contemporary Kerala practice. Such rituals have the reputation to be extremely powerful. In my friend's case, the *homam* involved 1,008 recitations of the *Sudarshana mantra* (named for Vishnu's discus), which is a *mantra* 'for attacking'. Soon, the son's situation improved, for his boss was promoted and transferred elsewhere! This came as an elegant triumph for 'non-violent' Brahmins who, in order to defend themselves, had to take recourse to occult arms—very literally, for the Word is their weapon as the sword is that of the warrior. Further, my friend pointed out humorously that their enemy had not been harmed in any way.

He had in store another, equally edifying story. Prey to a *Cattan* (a violent deity, see *infra*) unleashed on him by a close relative, a man rushed to a wise Brahmin for relief. The Brahmin advised the man against performing complicated and onerous rituals, arguing that evil must not be sent back to the enemy: 'Who are we to dispense punishment? God will take care of that! Protecting oneself is simple enough. Recite the *Gayatri mantra* [*mantra* invoking the sun and learned by Brahmins at the time of their initiation], a thousand and eight times each day. That requires no money, just a little time.'[16]

Accusations of witchcraft aim frequently at close relatives, as is often the case elsewhere in the world. This contrasts though with the observations of J. Favret-Saada who notes a counter trend in the area she studied in France: 'Rarely does the exorcist accuse a relative of the victim, for the objective of the treatment is in fact to divert the bewitched person's violence towards non-relatives' (Favret-Saada 1977: 107 n.17). In Kerala, the tensions made explicit by accusations of witchcraft cut across families, lineages, Houses.[17] Thus, the son of my friend evoked the case of 'someone close': she was a woman unable to bear the prosperity of her own brothers, and she was seeking to ruin them by having recourse to 'hand poison'. However the brothers, multiplying prayers and rituals, could resist the onslaught. Finally, the woman was unmasked by her own husband and mother-in-law, following the diagnostic of an astrologer.

Exorcists with whom it has been possible to speak make similar statements: most accusations made by victims focus on members of their families, who are believed to have employed evil *mantravadis* to gain the upper hand in disputes on land, money and inheritance. On the contrary, strangers are seldom suspected of anything more than being able to cast the evil eye. And in conflicts between people of very different social status, accusations of paying a sorcerer for inflicting occult aggressions are rare.[18]

Published accounts confirm this. In the only case of Kerala ethnographic literature in which the precise relationship between accuser and accused has been spelled out, a young woman is said to have been bewitched by her husband's family (Panikkar 1918b). More recently, in an unpublished psychology thesis dealing with people claiming to be possessed (Jagathambika 1968), some of the victims trace the source of their affliction to occult action initiated by enemies, and in each case these are close relatives.[19] Here are three instances:

For six years, Sarasa, a young Hindu woman of 25, has been possessed by *Arukola* ('Massacre'), identified here with the spirit of a woman who had hanged herself to death. Sarasa's parents believe that the possession is the consequence of spells cast by close relatives with whom they have a property dispute (pp.155ff.).

Anna, a 35-year old Catholic belonging to a low-status caste, is possessed by *Cattan*, *Kutticattan*, *Covva* (all three known as *durmurtti*, or 'cruel' divinities), and by the spirits of three dead people: a young Nambudiri, a Christian girl (Thressia) and a Parayan boy, the latter two being unfortunate lovers who committed suicide. When Anna is in a trance, these divinities and spirits take turns to speak. They explain they had at first hidden themselves in her body by taking the form of illnesses. Later on, they were 'forced' to reveal their true identity when Anna was taken to a church well known for exorcising the possessed. They claim that it is the wife of Anna father's brother, together with this woman's brother, who sent them to afflict Anna and ruin her family, as these relatives felt they did not get a fair share at the time of some property division (pp.117ff.).

Mathai's story, cited in the same book (pp. 211ff.), is different in that he says he became possessed quite accidentally, without intervention by an enemy. However, the spirits said to inhabit him are those of his sister-in-law (elder brother's wife) and her mother, who claim that when they were alive they had indeed plotted to use 'hand poison' on Mathai with the help of a *mantravadi*. The spirit of the *mantravadi*, too, is possessing Mathai, not out of any animosity towards him, but because he needed to recover his fee from the two women who omitted to pay him!

Possession and witchcraft, therefore, are not mutually exclusive, and they may well combine. Both transpose and take forth tense and conflicting situations on the plane of invisible forces. But compared to possession, accusations of witchcraft are much more explicit expressions of existing antagonisms, as Lewis already pointed out (1970; 1986, Chap. 3).

As for the motives said to be behind such accusations, they arise typically from envy, resentment, jealousy, hatred, all passions unleashed and exacerbated by an environment of acute competition (for land, for degrees and for jobs) which permeates this society, where social relationships are at the same time still largely contained within local antecedent networks.[20]

ATTACK AND DEFENCE

Accusations of witchcraft express more the fear than the reality of an attack. An enemy is identified, against whom steps must be taken. Legitimating action in the name of defence, it allows then for radical measures if these are deemed to be necessary. It entails that aggression is usually seen as the other face of protection in most *mantravadis'* activities, as is the case, too, with a lot of deities invoked for their mundane efficacy (Claus 1973).

Let us consider the example of *Cattan*, a god already mentioned and called often also *Kutticattan* ('small, baby *Cattan*'). He may be worshipped either as a lone figure, or as a pair, or yet as hordes of *Kutticattans* (10, 12, 336, 390, 400, or more still), in which case he is the leader of the horde and represents simultaneously its totality. This child of Siva, brought up by a Parayan woman (or, according to some claims, a tribal woman in the mountains), has a dubious reputation throughout Kerala. He may routinely display his power by polluting food with hairs or bits of finger nails, by transforming water into urine, by polluting statues of gods, by provoking spontaneous combustion of clothes or hay-stacks, and by various other mischievous acts in bad taste. Though his deeds are here rarely fatal, he definitely knows how to make life miserable (read Krishna Ayyar, 1928, for a lively description).[21]

Cattan, with all his affinity with impurity and violence, is worshipped as a major god not only in many of the lower castes, but by *mantravadis* of higher status as well, including Brahmins—in the latter case, it is a personal worship limited to the magician. The fact is that *Cattan* is typically thought of as a god used by *mantravadis*, at least according to intermediary and upper castes: at this level of society, the god is not known to act at his own initiative. Instead, he must be dispatched by an enemy and will act only upon the orders he is given (as in Anna's case). The best way to eliminate him is then to consult another *mantravadi*, who will either invoke more powerful divinities to subjugate *Cattan*, or plead directly with him to leave, or yet try to return him to the sender.

A number of temples to *Cattan*, managed by Ezhavas ('toddy-tapping' caste), flourish in the Trichur region and offer most publicly their services. These are family shrines where the divinity is regularly incarnated in the body of a possessed man, as a rule a member of the family. During such possession séances, the god himself is supposed to speak, and diagnoses and acts directly for the benefit of a large and varied clientele that often comes from distant places. There is for instance this woman from Karnataka, who has come following a series of deaths in the family, and whose alcoholic son constantly shows her disrespect, all of which she attributes to her husband's family seeking to enrich itself at the expense of her own family by unleashing malefic influences. There is this businessman from Andhra Pradesh who is merely interested in increasing rapidly his wealth—*Cattan* is known to be efficient in that respect. All séances are held in public.

In these temples, participants assert that the god is invoked for defensive purposes only, not for reprisal. However, from the outside, this image is contradicted somewhat by the Kattumadam House, a Nambudiri House of *mantravadis*, which claims to be the only one to use Cattan in such a pacific way: Kattumadam alone has the 'good' *Cattans*, the members say, because these *Cattans* are vegetarians and are offered vegetarian equivalents of blood sacrifices, at the most. On the contrary, they add, the *Cattans* worshipped in the Ezhava temples are fed on sacrificed fowl, and are therefore violent ones, apt to be used for destruction. The Ezhavas' ritual practices, which are in fact most usual at this level of society, are therefore interpreted by the Brahmins in terms of occult violence, attributing evil motives to the Ezhavas which the latter, of course, totally deny.

These opposing discourses are obviously dependent on the respective positions of both parties, a fact which has been put in evidence elsewhere (Favret-Saada 1977; Augé 1979). Here, however, these positions draw sustenance from objective variations in ritual, linked to caste, and hierarchically contrasted. What the Nambudiris attribute to the Ezhavas can be denied by the latter as far as they themselves are concerned. They, in turn, can attribute the same to others of similar or lower status than themselves. But they cannot return the compliment to the Brahmins.

Besides, in spite of the nice declarations of the officiating priests or the consulting parties, the god himself is of a very dubious reliability. Inevitably, this rebounds on his clients, even those of high status. This appears clearly, for instance, from the following situation: when the affliction is serious, the victim is given a statuette of *Cattan* which he has to worship every day at home. When the devotee dies, embarrassment ensues for the family, for nobody else may be privy to the real purpose of this worship. Was the statuette used to attack an enemy ? Because there is always a doubt, the best solution is to get rid of the statuette by taking it back to the temple, where it is disposed of with appropriate rituals. Thus, while those who flock to *Cattan* temples present themselves as 'victims', outsiders tend necessarily to look upon them as potential aggressors.

Moreover, the efficacy of the protection which a magician is supposed to be able to grant is often judged from what he is deemed to master in terms of attack. This dual role can be publicly obvious. For instance, possessed by a goddess, one Ezhava lady practitioner in central Travancore receives two supplicants in succession. The first is a woman afflicted by a skin disease. Amma ('Lady'—the habitual mode of address for the goddess) reveals that the woman's enemies have placed a malefic object in a cleft somewhere in the south-western part of the dwelling. The object must be removed. The woman is given a black string for protection. A mixture of sacred ash and saffron is applied to her arms, afflicted by the skin disease. Then the woman is followed by a man. He complains that his wife has stolen his money and has an affair with another man. Amma draws then a diagram (*yantram*) on a metal plate, infuses the diagram with *mantras* and gives the man the plate, asking him to place it on his rival's path or in his rival's garden, so that it may cast its (attacking) spell on him.

Malicious tongues wag and claim that it is the very same *mantravadis* who are casting evil spells on people before proceeding to exorcise their own victims. Such accusations are of a piece with the 'blackmail' and 'cheating' attributed sometimes to low caste *mantravadis* (see below). As a counter to the violence, or at least the ambiguity that is attributed to their magical deeds, some *mantravadis* take care to stress their own ideal: aggression against a human being is to be considered a perversion, a deviation from duty. As K.N.B. Asan notes: 'These acts of witchcraft (*abhicharam*) are meant to be employed only against evil spirits and demons. The *Acharyas* have ordained so. But nowadays, people employ this black magic for the realization of selfish motives. Whenever it is found difficult to subdue an opponent by the power of money, physical strength or numerical superiority, men exhibit a tendency to employ *abhicharam* against him . . .'. He adds: 'It must be understood that it was by practising austerities for a long time that *Acharyas* came to possess the knowledge of witchcraft. This knowledge is intended to be used for good purposes only. But the lust for money makes man stoop to the level of employing it against fellow human beings. . . .' So, according to him, 'the aim of *mantravadam* is to ensure the prosperity of all human beings. Its aim is also to afford protection to all against adversity. The sages have said that astrology and *mantravadam* are meant for good purposes only.'

This is then the image that one *mantravadi* would like to project about his own role. Let us take a look at what else he may have to say on the subject. This will enable us to understand how discourses on witchcraft partake of a wider vision of society, as locally expressed.

Spiritual Power

The Qualifications of a *Mantravadi*

K.N.B. Asan is a Kaniyan astrologer of Trivandrum, who also practices *mantravadam*. Let him be our guide. According to him, a *mantravadi* is said to possess extraordinary mental strength (*manasakti*), which is the result of several converging factors:

—Belonging to a line of transmission (*paramparyam*): in this case, transmission is mostly thought of in terms of heredity, you have to be born in a family where it is a part of tradition.

—Training with a guru: the guru is often one's own father, who must guide the disciple to gain mastery of the mantras. They will be honed later to perfection under the guidance of other erudite people. All the interviewed *mantravadis* stressed the necessity for such a direct, oral guidance during the training, and condemned without appeal any unguided study of mantras directly from books.[22] Only *mantravadis* with evil designs would learn thus from books, with the additional risk besides that they may not be able to control the forces they unleash.

—Exertion and personal courage: the combination of *mantra*-recitation with meditation (*mantrajapadhyana*) on a chosen god, and ascetic rigour over a long period, enable the neophyte to be progressively transformed into a 'divine being'. Tantric techniques (breath control, rites for placing the divinities on one's body) come into play. Isolated in the forest, the neophyte faces various occult dangers during this initiating transformation. If he fails, he might lose his mind. If he is successful, he can compel the chosen divinity to appear and obey his orders (Asan calls this *devatasiddhi*, or 'power over a deity').

Asan concludes:

> If a person is prepared to concentrate his mind and thoughts with single-minded devotion on [the goddess] *Yaksini*, and meditates while chanting the *Yaksini-mantra* the prescribed number of times, *Yaksini* will definitely manifest before him. She will further execute whatever the devotee commands. If an assignment is given to *Yaksini* to inflict harm on a particular individual born in the house of a particular star, the command is bound to be executed. Similarly, there is *Cattan seva* [service of *Cattan*]. *Cattan seva* means pleasing *Cattan* and thereby getting control over him. Strict austerities for a period of about 2 to 3 *mandalams* [one *mandalam* is a period of 41 days] are to be observed to win the favours of *Cattan*. As a result of the chanting of *mantras* with the attendant rituals, one will achieve a state of inner purity. This purity will be perceivable only to the five sensory organs of the person concerned. Others cannot have any idea about it. *Cattan* actually manifests before the person who wins his favour. He can see *Cattan* when his mind is concentrated in meditation. In case the person who wins mastery over *Cattan* sends the god on a mission for inflicting harm on a person or for bringing a person before his master, *Cattan* will obey the commands. But if the opponent is also in possession of magical power and mental strength, *Cattan* will be incapable of inflicting harm on him. [. . .] In short, evil spirits can do little harm against a person having strong mental power.

Thus, Asan says,

> the man in meditation succeeds in propitiating a particular god because he is able to concentrate his mind in meditation unmindful of the distracting sounds and sights. If he becomes nervous, his attempt will end in failure. If he loses self confidence in the attempt of joining with the deity through meditation, there is every possibility of his becoming a victim to insanity. Several persons have become insane thus.[23]

Mental power, *manasakti*,[24] is at the very heart of ideas about sickness and health, about occult aggression and defence—as well as at the heart of normal cult practices and initiatic disciplines. Troubles of any kind are likely to affect first those who are not strong in mind (same observation in Deliège 1992). Such strength varies from person to person and may differ, even for a single person, according to the point of time, for it is frequently related to degrees of purity. There are several categories. Women, for instance, are said to possess less mental strength than men; people of low status are deemed to be generally defective in that respect too. On the opposite, the most prestigious Nambudiri House in all of Kerala, the House of Azhuvanceri Tamprankal, Brahmin amongst Brahmins, has a reputation of such a purity and spiritual power that unsatisfied deads could never once afflict its members.

Acknowledging a *mantravadi's* innate and acquired mental powers is an important aspect of the debate on the 'reality' of witchcraft. Brahmins in particular, voice some scepticism about its contemporary existence because, they say, nobody is anymore able in the present age to attain the spiritual strength required—for lack of time, lack of spirituality and for the fact that people are growing weaker by the day. But the foundations of such power and its past reality are never questioned. According to one Nambudiri who specializes in the consecration of divine idols and in the exorcism of temple sites:

> In the past, things were different. There was for instance Chemmangat Nambudiri. He achieved the recitation of *Rig Veda* a thousand times in thirty-six years. At the end, he had become almost divine. All he had to do was to place his hands on a person possessed [by an unsatisfied dead] in order to cure him. He had already conquered the world of mantras, and did not need any more to chant them. [for an exorcism]

The 'near-divine' ascetic is the sorcerer's ultimate refinement, beyond mantras for he has mastered their very quintessence, the *Rig Veda*. Fortunately, there exists a palliative to contemporary decline: for 'though no one possesses enough spiritual power any longer, the ritual system is so perfect that it will still work anyway' (K.P.C. Anujan Bhattatiripad).

A CHOICE OF ACTS

Strict adherence to rites is said to be imperative if a *mantravadi* wants to be successful: technical perfection is the other source of his power. The terminology applied to the rituals in *mantravadam* stress clearly their quality of 'actions': *karmmam* (action, ceremony), *kriya* (action, ritual), *krtya* (prescribed act, sorcery), *prayogam* (application, manipulation).[25] These acts are classified according to their way of tackling problems. K.N.B. Asan enumerates the Eight Acts (*ashtaka-rmmankal*) of witchcraft (*abhicharam*) thus:

— immobilization (*sthambhanam*)
— attraction(*akarsanam*)
— enchantment (*mohanam*)
— conquest, seduction (*vasikaranam*)
— demolition (*bhedanam*)
— expulsion (*ucchatanam*)
— creating enmity (*vidvesanam*)
— breaking (*oti*), the most dreadful of these acts.[26]

Asan offers an example of Immobilization:

> If Immobilization is performed, the mobility of the victim will immediately come to a standstill. The person will cease to be in possession of his faculties including the faculty of speech and work. The prosperity of the person will also wither away. He may even lose his job. [. . .] Suppose the opponent is a trader. As a result of Immobilization, the trader may lose interest in his business and eventually, the business may come to a standstill. In the case of an industrialist, the persons who cooperate with him in his venture may quarrel with him and cease cooperating with him with the result the industry will perish eventually. These are the results achieved by employing *abhicharam*. Moreover, there is the Immobilization of speech, of sight, of hearing and of the nervous system. It can be seen thus that by employing Immobilization, the functioning of any faculty can be impaired.

Not all the Eight Acts are acts of violence. K.N.B. Asan reminds us that the nature of the divinities employed by *mantravadis* varies in accordance with the proportion of 'clarity, serenity' (*sattvam*), 'activity' (*rajasam*) or 'darkness' (*tamasam*)—three qualities referring to classical speculations about the manifestation of the perceptible world.[27] Asan explains thus that

> it is the purpose that determines which deity or *Bhutam* is to be employed. Suppose the purpose is Seduction. Then deities with *sattvik* qualities only are employed. If the purpose is Immobilization or Expulsion, deities with high destructive powers are employed to achieve the desired results. But deities with *sattvik* qualities should not be used for the above purpose. But a deity with *sattvik* qualities can be directed against another one with destructive powers with the intention of seducing the latter. In case the attempt to seduce the deity fails, then Immobilization could be employed. Or Expulsion could be employed.

There is therefore within witchcraft theories a dialectic between soft and hard methods, between appeasement and expulsion. This echoes what Zimmermann (1992) highlights in the case of ayurvedic medicine, or the dialectic that prevails in the art of governance. As a Tamil Brahmin once pointed out, there are four methods to obtain the obedience of a human being or of an invisible power. They are, in order: appeasing words, gifts, threats, and blows.

Since a *mantravadi* mobilizes a divinity to attack his victim, a reprisal against such aggression would involve combating, or 'seducing' the divinities themselves. This is why K.N.B. Asan could affirm that the primary mission of witchcraft is an action against invisible powers. The operations which enable such relationships to be established with the divine are in essence no different from those of ordinary worship at each level of society.[28] *Mantras* form the base, whether it is to propitiate or to command a divinity, or yet to breathe power into a talisman, a poison or a protective device: and each *mantra* is linked to divine powers by esoteric interpretations. Together with *mantras*, other practices may come into play—the use of mystical diagrams, acts of worship (*puja*), possession, and sacrifice. Sacrifices are of two kinds—bloody sacrifice, with actual killing of animals or with the use of vegetal substitutes; and oblations poured in a sacred fire (*homam*), ascribed to Vedic Brahminism, whose secrets are supposed to be known to Brahmins alone (in fact, *mantravadis* of all classes do perform *homams*, though Brahmins would deny their validity).

Not all practices are so harmless. Those which have been cited are, needless to say, more easily observable amongst (and acknowledged by) the specialists I met. We shall examine later what is said about rites performed by *mantravadis* of very low status, although it is difficult in their case to separate rumour from fact. Before coming to this aspect, the following example would attest to the existence of quite violent—and, in this case, secret—practices, when compared to routine cults performed in Kerala society. In her autobiography the poet Kamala Das narrates how, being back to her native House after living for many years in other parts of India, her enemies (presumably, the village notables and a few of her own relatives) took recourse to witchcraft: 'They [my enemies] buried an urn somewhere in my yard, hoping to kill me with the rites of sorcery. I chose to ignore the warnings given by my servants. One day I found on the ledge of our well a decapitated cat and on inspecting it minutely, I found my name engraved on a copper piece, an egg, some turmeric and a lot of stuff that resembled vermilion stuffed inside its body.' (Kamala Das 1988: 200ff.; later, on page 205, she explains how she lost nerve and came to ask a sorcerer—was it the same?—to protect her and her sons.)

WITCHCRAFT AND STATUS

As we have seen, in Kerala as elsewhere, witchcraft is perceived through a range of contrasting viewpoints. Protection from an enemy could well be interpreted by the latter (and by others) as attempted aggression. This divergence in perception, arising from one's situation in an interpersonal relationship, also combines with a judgement related to the caste status of the *mantravadi*. Thus, Nambudiris affirm that *Cattan* temples maintained by Ezhavas 'return evil' (to the supposed enemy). Such statements are made without qualifications, without distinguishing between one *Cattan* temple and another, on the sole basis of the contrast between Ezhava and Nambudiri ritual practices. This sort of 'social image' is what will be examined now. With a view to simplify, the discourses about only four castes will be presented—about the Nambudiris, about the Ezhavas, about the Kaniyan astrologers and about the Parayan agricultural labourers.

NAMBUDIRI BRAHMINS

Mantravadam is the traditionally recognized specialization of several Nambudiri Houses (we have already referred to one of them, the Kattumadam House). Popular opinion, among various castes, believes that the Brahmins 'know all the *mantras*, even the most cruel ones (*durmantram*), but they use only the good ones (*sanmantram*)'. As masters of Vedic knowledge and texts, and as points of reference in matters of ritual, the Nambudiris see the good image they have of themselves by and large accepted (in this respect) by other castes. It is an image that includes:

— An all-embracing (occult) knowledge, only a fraction of which would be known to *mantravadis* of lesser status. The higher spiritual power of the Nambudiris is borne out in many ways: once, some *Cattans* were subjugated by a Nambudiri and cheerfully abandoned their low-caste master to serve their new one; in an Ezhava temple it is the use to invoke Brahmin ghosts (*Brahmarakshassu*) in order to exorcise unsatisfied deads, for Brahmin ghosts are deemed to be the most powerful among the deads.

— A high level of purity, which enables their brand of magic to enjoy a reputation for non-violence (at least against human beings): let us recall how the *sudarshana homam* performed by Tamil Brahmins led to the advancement of their own enemy! Witchcraft practised by the intermediary castes, described as 'rajasik' (active), are somewhat more ambiguous. As for the '*tamasik*' (dark, gloomy) castes, it is said that they can only indulge in black magic. (see, too, Kapur 1983: 95ff.)

But individual variations are possible even within ascribed Nambudiri 'non-violence'. An Ezhava temple in Trichur includes a small shrine dedicated to the spirit of a dead Nambudiri, a powerful *mantravadi*, whose links to terrifying goddesses are highlighted. In the same perspective, a member of the Kattumadam House does acknowledge the existence of 'bad' Nambudiri *mantravadis*, but does not wish to cite names (though there are textual traditions in Kerala in which names are given).

KANIYAN ASTROLOGERS

Although their caste status is relatively low, in certain respects Kaniyan astrologers have a somewhat variable social position. Many of them are farmers working on small holdings, poor and often held in contempt. Others, like K.N.B. Asan living in the state capital, get some prosperity out of their specialized profession and enjoy the respect of society at large.[29] The members of the caste, as such, are supposed to have some powers for practising exorcisms. From the origin, according to one of the caste's myths, they have been magicians. However, no standard practice exists. In some parts of Kerala, Kaniyans make terrifying masks and wear them while performing dances like the *kolam tullal*.[30] Asan and others like him, however, are *mantravadis* whose practice is based upon meditation, worship and sacrificial rituals.

Their mastery of astrological findings makes the Kaniyans an important node in the social network of specialists dealing with misfortune. This is particularly true in the case of misfortune occurring among those whose social status is comparable to, or higher than that of the Kaniyans themselves, and this includes Muslims and Christians. Not always do the Kaniyans themselves dispense treatment to the afflicted. Frequently, after setting down the astral characteristics of the problem on a paper, they will refer their clients to other specialists who will dispense the actual treatment—these range from exorcists and temple priests to doctors and psychiatrists. And in the overall discourse dealing with the causes of misfortune, it is the astrologer who determines—or confirms—the existence of an enemy.

Their science, and sometimes their Sanskrit knowledge, points explicitly towards the model of the Brahmins. One of the caste's myths holds, in fact, that they are descendants of a fallen Nambudiri (Padmanabha Menon 1933: 448ff.), the cause of this fall being, as is often the case, a misalliance. At the same time, the practice of astrology is locally recognized as intrinsically ambiguous. Another myth tells us that Subrahmanyam, the son of Siva, founded this discipline, and predicted that his father would one day be reduced to beggary. The enraged Siva promptly cursed this newly born science and consigned it to eternal discredit (ibid.). The gods (like our own contemporaries?) do not seem to distinguish between the capacity to predict misfortune and the capacity to provoke it. In any case, the Kaniyans are believed to possess knowledge as well as power, although, unlike the Nambudiris, they do not enjoy the reputation of using either only for good purposes.

MAGICIANS IN A 'PERSONAL' CAPACITY: THE EXAMPLE OF EZHAVA SHRINES

The managers of the *Cattan* temples in the Trichur area do not get from the fact they are Ezhavas any particular reputation, be it for their knowledge or their ritual ability in *mantravadam*. With a view to legitimate their power, they are then driven to highlight mainly two characteristics.

Firstly, at the origin of each of these family temples is an ascetic who was able in days of yore to obtain both the *mantra* and the vision from the god. This ascetic, central to the lineage cult, is believed to have not died really but to have attained *samadhi* ('meditation, accomplishment') instead. His body has been buried into a pit, in a seated position, and the pit covered with a stone slab. Such covered pits (called equally *samadhi*), which can be observed in many *Cattan* temples in the Trichur region, serve here in actual ritual as altar for the sacrifice of fowl. The prestige of such *samadhis* is such that one *Cattan* shrine, which calls itself *matham* ('monastery'), has even two of them (Chaitanya Das 1987). Thus, transmission of a power derived from ancient, distant asceticism contributes to legitimating these Ezhava *mantravadis*. Anchored in the past, constituting a permanent specificity of the lineage, it dispenses today's practitioners from the need to submit themselves really to similar austerities—a mere initiation to the *mantra* suffices.

Secondly, these temples base their efficacy on the living presence of the god. The *Cattan* shrines we have seen operate as shrines for cults of possession. *Cattan* becomes incarnate, elucidates himself the problems of his devotees, promises them his direct assistance. He has elected for life the one in whom he incarnates, provided the man has shown some 'inclination'. Such divine manifestation becomes a second manner of legitimating the practice of *mantravadam*, by referring to a contemporary, personalized and periodically renewable divine election.

Neither form of legitimisation benefits the Ezhavas as a caste. The same applies to all those *mantravadis* who act in an 'individual', or just 'familial' capacity. These practitioners cannot rely on a caste reputation for *mantravadam* and have a problem of legitimacy to solve, either by taking recourse to the two above-mentioned methods, or through other modalities, such as spiritual affiliation to a *guru* or knowledge of treatises. Their role is perceived in a somewhat ambiguous manner, too, being neither 'completely good' nor 'completely bad'. But their very existence is significant, calling to mind what P. Brown wrote about the late Roman Antiquity: 'Such sorcery is very much a *carrière ouverte aux talents*. A man of occult learning could placate, manipulate, even threaten suprahuman powers to his advantage. If a society gets the sorcery it deserves, the Late Antiquity sorcery is a tribute to the learned and competitive spirit prevailing in the fluid areas of society in which it was most rife' (Brown 1970: 34ff.).[31]

THE PARAYANS

As far as the Parayans are concerned, they are branded with a decidedly negative image. Early twentieth century compilations describe them as bonded agricultural labourers, mats and baskets makers, of very low status. They were said to be dirty, backward, carrion-eating practitioners of exorcisms and necromancy, personifying the qualities of *tamasam* (darkness) in the eyes of others.[32] Curiously enough, at this devalued pole of society, we find a complementarity between castes similar to the one that exists among the upper castes. Thus, when the Pulayans, who were also formerly bonded agricultural labourers of similar status, claim to be descended from fallen kings, the Parayans look upon themselves as downgraded Nambudiris—and the funeral rites which they perform for the Pulayans ensure that the latter are forgiven for their sins and saved from everlasting hell (see Thaliath 1956: 1035ff.).

As dark images of the luminous Nambudiris (whose very name evokes light), the Parayans are said (by others) to provide for the sorcerers of the worst kind, those who will stop at nothing in terms of occult aggression perpetrated at their client's bidding, those to whom the bloodiest of practices are attributed. Actually, some may today acknowledge that they perform rituals for attack. However, the effective level of violence involved in these sacrifices seldom seems to go beyond the sacrifice of small animals, most of all of fowl (though we must recall Kamala Das testimony of the witchcraft done by killing a cat).

This image of the Parayans was even stronger in earlier times. According to general opinion of the time, some Parayan sorcerers, called in this particular case *otiyans*, were believed to be adepts of the eighth and worst category of the witchcraft acts, the Breaking (*oti*).[33] Using specially made oils, one of which being prepared from a human foetus extracted alive from its mother's womb (if possible a high caste woman), then put to death and submitted to complex processes of preparation, *otiyans* were able to become invisible or to assume the form of an animal of their choice, such as a cat, a dog or a bull. The more attentive observer would notice, however, the absence of a tail or a similar deformity, apart from the fact that invariably their cry is that of the jackal (Unni Nayar 1952: 65; Kapur 1983: 19ff.). The *otiyan* wanders thus at night, ready to aggress his victims in an isolated spot-shattering their vertebrae or strangling them by squeezing their neck between two sticks. Anthropologist Ananthakrishna Iyer noted at the beginning of this century (1969, I: 81): 'This cult has been practised by the Parayans some twenty years ago, to a very large extent [. . .] and even now, it has not quite died out. [. . .] The records of criminal courts attest the power and prevalence of this persuasion among the more intelligent and higher classes.'

Iyer observes further (ibid.) that the Parayans were quite reticent to elaborate on the topic. According to him, they 'keep the cult a dead secret, and profess total ignorance owing to their fear of punishment'. There were definitely good reasons for that, as Thurston and Ranga-chari reported:

> In 1834, the inhabitants of several villages in Malabar attacked a village of Paraiyans on the alleged ground that deaths of people and cattle, and the protracted labour of a woman in childbed, had been caused by the practice

of sorcery by the Paraiyans. They were beaten inhumanely, with their hands tied behind their backs, so that several died. The villagers were driven, bound, into a river, immersed under water so as nearly to produce suffocation, and their own children were forced to rub sand into their wounds. Their settlement was then razed to the ground and they were driven into banishment. (Thurston and Rangachari 1909, VI: 130ff.)[34]

The occult violence of which Parayans are deemed capable of is but one aspect of the abjection which higher caste people attribute to them. But such an ascribed violence cannot really constitute itself as a counter-power in society, though it may be sometimes imagined as such. Its affinity with 'darkness' brings it close to dangerous divinities and to misfortune itself, making it the negative pole of religious practice and representations in Kerala. However, it is always completely contained and controlled by the real physical violence used by the upper castes. And in ideological terms, the Parayans' attributed violence is reduced to be merely a part of Brahminical knowledge, which is universal *ex hypothesis*.

Therefore, notions about occult aggressions cannot be dissociated from Kerala's traditional power structure, especially in the agrarian context.[35] This may well be illustrated by the following story about the death of a low-caste necromancer at the hands of the members of a Nayar House, Manakampat House—of whom the narrator is a scion (Unni Nayar 1952: 61ff.):

It was a very subtle but sinister form of blackmail. In the beginning, perhaps he poisoned a few cattle, and having thus established his reputation he sat back to enjoy the fruits of his cleverness. No calf died, no child fell ill after that, but our necromancer was sent for in a hurry. For a consideration he agreed either to cure the existing ills or prevent future ones according as (shrewd man that he was) he judged the seriousness of the condition of the patient. A recurrence of the disease in a home which had bought immunity did little to lower his reputation, as everyone, in fairness, owed that he was a cheat as well as a scoundrel. His clientèle increased, his business flourished, and he prospered.

He seldom tried conclusions with the men of Manakampat, whose steel [of their swords] was an argument he knew he could not beat. But some arrogance, some impish devilry, made him once or twice proclaim to admirers that he had cast his spell on Manakampat and the family would soon realize his power. The men of Manakampat bided their time and one day they struck. The sorcerer was brought before them bound hand and foot on a charge of stealing cattle and of various similar activities, including murder, none of which he could deny. He was taken to the platform [for execution] . . .

The beheading of the sorcerer shifts then the balance of powers onto another plane:

It appears that the man when dead became even more of a nuisance than when alive. His head, the legend says, sprang up to the topmost branch of the tree, the eyes rolling in a frenzy and the face ringent. The bloody head then hurtled through space and alighted, the face still working, on the cattleshed of a neighbouring farm. The farmer in terror gave the soul sanctuary by building a memorial for the head. Thus Kandath Raman [the sorcerer] was installed in the Mannat family. [for worship]

In death, Kandath Raman became worshipped by those who were either seeking his favours, or merely desirous to be spared the wrong kind of favours. One day, incarnated in the person of a possessed member of the Mannat Nayar House, he confronted the Manakampat House's Goddess, herself incarnated in her usual man. Side by side, they both danced in the courtyard of the Manakampat House. As they strode to and fro, each one (in accordance with the practices of the region) whacked his forehead with his sword 'until blood streamed down their faces and blinded them'.

Finally Raman, with an abjectness which gave Manakampat satisfaction, asked for forgiveness, and swore he never would show his manifestations on Manakampat estate or [his repentance making him large of promise] in the estate of anyone related to Manakampat; he fled howling, never to darken our doors again.

The Manakampats, certain of their own power over men and of the power of their goddess in the invisible world, could allow themselves some amusement over the pretensions of the 'scoundrel', whether in life or in death. As Augé said (1982: 257), 'Pretensions of power, when not reflected in social or political position, must meet their end in ridicule or in blood.' Scepticism itself appears then as an integral part of power relationships, as much on the human plane as on the divine. We must bear in mind that the Brahmins, at the very summit of the social hierarchy, are amongst the most open of 'sceptics'. But what they refute is not the efficacy of *mantras*, but only the spiritual power of low-status *mantravadis*. Thence comes the somewhat paradoxical affirmation that those who practise 'black magic' are in fact 'charlatans'.[36]

CONCLUSION

Within the discourse on witchcraft, 'non-violence' is constructed at two levels—that of interpersonal relationships, and that of social groups.

In interpersonal relationships, involving an accuser and his enemy (with the former being the one we usually come to know), the occult violence of 'the other' is a given. This violence is thought of as a conjunction of the violence experienced by the accuser as his misfortune, and of the violence of the passions he attributes to his enemy. Any reprisal is legitimated in advance: it is merely a defence. Others, of course, could easily interpret such a defence as an attempt to use witchcraft, especially since the reputation of the *mantravadis* possess that same ambivalence which is attributed to the divinities they manipulate. Unlike the *mantravadi*, the accused—the enemy—is frequently someone close to the victim, a relative or a colleague. The pattern of accusations reveals tensions between a socially mobile and competitive context, and older forms of loyalty and social equilibrium. Viewed thus, the number of accusations between brothers and sisters seems particularly significant. The conflict that is played out through accusations of witchcraft reconfigures indeed interpersonal relationships without necessarily taking recourse to physical violence.[37]

When considering social groups, it is the *mantravadi* (and not the enemy) whose image is involved. The practice of witchcraft is part of a complex of representations about spiritual power, knowledge, 'innate qualities', which are inseparable from caste hierarchy. In this respect, two stereotypical poles are defined. That of the Brahmins (knowledge, purity, occult power, non-violence) and that of Parayans (ignorance, impurity, fraud, criminality). Doubtless, the reality of discourses may be more complex, as much owing to nuances in what is said within either pole as on account of the existence of stray specialists and castes of intermediary status. The 'socio-moral' polarity thus established is nonetheless self-imposing in the local society. In this way, the occult violence attributed to the untouchables must be re-situated in the context of their repression, and should less be seen as a symbol of revolt than as an additional mark of infamy—an image firmly grounded in the local power structure.

By personifying the violent and impure pole of religious representations, and despite accusations of exploiting the ignorance and credulity of their clientele, low caste sorcerers are feared nevertheless by those who can flourish neither the scriptures (the *Vedas*) nor the sword. In fact, more often than not, it will be divinities worshipped among low castes (as in the case of *Cattan*) who will be invoked for *mantravadam* by upper-caste practitioners. Pragmatic arguments may doubtless be given in justification, among them the fact that such divinities are closer to ordinary human activities than higher gods in the pantheon. But there is, too, a kind of implicit recognition that occult power may come from two related sources: one corresponds to the inherent strength of misfortune, as represented, caused and frequently even remedied by these divinities; and the other arises from the menace to the social order which lurks from the darkness at its margins, as is imagined here to be the case with the Parayans (or, elsewhere in Kerala, and for other reasons, with Christian or Muslim sorcerers).

To get back to the example of *Cattan*: while the god may be worshipped by Nambudiris as much as by untouchables, such worship is offered in extremely contrasted ways. Thus, unlike the lower castes, the Kattumadam House subjugated *Cattan*, and twice over at that, first through an ancient forebear and then through the goddess of the House. The god's malefic power is subordinated and thereby transmuted. When upper caste *mantravadis* thus control and manipulate inferior deities which are the fount of misfortune, they reaffirm a global order in which they posit themselves as masters, and in which these very deities, once subordinated, become protective and beneficent. Out of a violence viewed as part of a state of anomie, comes a violence founding an order which is eventually at the service of a certain ideal of non-violence: this provides for a dynamic of power structuring the divine world, human beings, and society.

By establishing 'a continuity between the biological and the social order, whereby the former becomes a signifier of the latter' (Augé 1982: 224), the discourse and practice of witchcraft explicit a certain notion of spiritual power and its 'qualities' which orders social relationships. In Kerala, as elsewhere in India no doubt, misfortune and violence are more to be circumscribed than to be erased—the crucial question in that respect being one of control.[38] True, non-violence might still be proclaimed as a supreme and all-encompassing value. But it is constructed, openly and ceaselessly, on actual violent power-based relationships—between castes with stereotypical attributes, and between individuals with conflicting points of view.

NOTES

* The French version of this paper was written in 1992. Since then, important relevant studies have been published or have come to the author's notice, which the present English version, being a mere translation, does not include.

I would like to thank J. Assayag, C. Clémentin-Ojha, G. Colas, C. Ghasarian, M.-L. Reiniche, A. de Surgy and D. Vidal for their friendly reading of a first draft of this paper and for their observations. In India, fieldwork was made possible due to the support of Professor V.I. Subramoniam (International School of Dravidian Linguistics). Caroline and Filippo Osella, in addition to numerous friendly discussions on the topic, kindly introduced me to some specialists in their own fieldwork's area. Most decisively, I benefited continuously from the indefatigable assistance of N. Rajasekharan Nair and L.S. Rajagopalan, from the affable willingness to be available of all the specialists interviewed, and from the help of M. Sivasankaran Nair for a first translation of K.N.B. Asan's interview.

1. Transcriptions are based on the Malayalam spelling of words; exceptions are marked 'Skt', denoting Sanskrit.
2. An analysis of traditional Nambudiri and Nayar aristocracy is presented elsewhere (Tarabout 1991).
3. U. Sharma's article (1973) underscores the contrast between the systematic recourse to the theory of *karma* when the reasons for misfortune are sought in the abstract, and the explanations put forward in specific cases of misfortune. 'Perhaps the commonest mode of accounting for misfortunes, especially illness or injury, is not in terms of *karma*, but of the malice of some other persons, deity or personalised agent' (Sharma 1973: 354; see too similar observations in Babb 1983; Nichter 1992).
4. Asan did not indicate the text from which he drew the citation, nor could this be traced subsequently. Thite (1982: 17ff.) quotes several classical texts in which comparable verses can be found, the *Satatapasmrti* in particular, where there is a quite similar formulation.
5. The 'transferable' nature of *karma* is debated at length in classical texts (O'Flaherty 1980a-b; compare with the transfer of sin in the *Rig Veda*, in Siqueira 1933: 181). What Daniel (1983: 291) refers to as 'parental *karma*', as opposed to 'ethical' *karma*, is visible too in popular notions in different parts of India (Carstairs and Kapur 1976: 59ff.; Hiebert 1983; Sharma 1973; Nuckolls 1981; Nichter 1992). Speaking of Bali, Boon suggests that the importance of ritualism, ancestor worship in particular, cannot be reconciled with a fully evolved ethical doctrine of *karma* (Boon 1983: 187). That viewpoint could apply in Kerala, where upper caste Houses are firmly rooted in widely-acknowledged ancestry, and

where ancestors are at the very heart of lower caste cult practices. However, the existence of comparable notions on *karma* in other parts of India suggests a need for cautious interpretation.

6. For textual studies, see Thite (Chaps. 2 and 3); Balodhi and Roy Chowdhary (1986). Among ethnographic observations: Carstairs and Kapur 1976: 58ff.; Hiebert 1983; Nichter 1979, 1992; Sharma 1973; Weiss et al. 1986; Wirz 1954. See also Kakar 1977; Jaggi 1973.
7. On the concept of 'superstition' as it has appeared in modern Hindu discourse, see Bharati 1970.
8. An English translation of this text has been published by B. Venkataraman, IBH Prakashana, Bangalore.
9. Indian astrology usually takes into account nine 'planets'—the Sun, the Moon, Mercury, Venus, Mars, Jupiter, Saturn, *Rahu* and *Ketu*. *Rahu* and *Ketu* are invisible. When *prasnams*, or questions, are to be solved in Kerala, astrologers take also into consideration the malefic *Gulikan* (or *Mandi*), a son of Saturn originated as a small ball of dirt from the latter's body. The planets are looked upon as divinities and, during the *prasnam*, come under the authority of *Dakshinamurti*, or Siva in his ascetic form dispensing knowledge. For the most elaborate *prasnams*, such as crises affecting a temple (equated with a 'body' that can be afflicted), it is particularly important to take additionally into account the omens provided by all the events occurring in the surroundings.
10. The text speaks of 'wrath' under several listed categories, but there could be other motives too. A god, and invisible powers such as *Bhutam* and *Rakshassu*, could inflict harm, shorn of all resentment, with a view to get their power recognized by humans, and to be then 'seated' in a shrine and worshipped. Others, like the *Gandharvvan*, may affect their victims just out of love for them.
11. On Kerala's *Bhutams* and unsatisfied deads, see Tarabout 1986; 1992.
12. Panikkar (1918 a–b) specifies that the words of praise must be spontaneous if they are to produce their malefic influence. Compare with Pocock's excellent chapter on the evil eye in Gujarat (1973) and with the studies of Spooner (1970) and Foster (1972) about other parts of the world. A similar relationship between the praise expressed and the malefic influence felt can be discerned in Favret-Saada (1977: 186), when she quotes what is said about the acts attributed to the sorcerer: 'When he says, "It's beautiful, your garden!" That's done, the evil is done.'
13. On accusations of witchcraft by poisoning, in Karnataka, see Epstein 1959. According to the author, some witches are compelled to poison others in order to avert their own death or misfortune. As far as Kerala is concerned, I have heard of no similar case until now .
14. *Abhicharam* (in Sanskrit, *abhichara*; literally, 'moving towards, approaching') is explained in classical texts as being an occult aggression, especially an

act done with a desire to destroy (*himsa*), murder in particular. In his remarkable study, Türstig (1985: 81ff.) identifies three meanings for the word: (1) any malefic practice; (2) a particular kind of spell; (3) a rite forming part of Tantric tradition that can be used on oneself as a means of spiritual advancement, rather than as a means of aggression on others. In mediaeval (vaishnavite) Vaikhanasa texts, the term *abhicharika* qualifies either an 'anti-rite' or merely a rite so poorly performed, even involuntarily, that it can have only bad results, either by being ineffective, or by benefiting the *Asuras* (cf. Gérard Colas, personal communication).

15. Magicians in Rajasthan are believed to be able of provoking snake bites (Gupta 1979: 194ff.). Keshavan et al. (1989) point out that accusations of witchcraft could attain epidemic proportions in certain areas (as for example in Karnataka in 1980).
16. The *Gayatri mantra's* ability to protect is widely accepted in India; S. Kapur even cites the case of a Muslim exorcist who uses it along with the performance of homam (Kapur 1983: 115ff.).
17. A similar observation has been made in Karnataka, in Epstein 1959: 239ff.
18. See Evans-Pritchard (1937: 105): 'Commoners bear ill will against commoners and princes hate princes.' In the same vein, G.M. Foster (1972: 185) suggests that the caste system fragments society into small groups, between which envy is minimized. On the contrary, Rao (1986), following upon Gough (1958), interprets witchcraft in Kerala as a means used by the lower castes to seek vengeance from the higher castes; Gough writes thus that witchcraft 'seems to have been confined to relationships between low and high castes' (Gough 1958: 472). For want of space, it will not be possible to discuss here in details the stand taken by these two writers; in brief, though, it would appear that they might have confused between the one who pays for witchcraft and the one who does the job.
19. As a further instance, Kapur (1983: 84ff.) narrates how a Malayali taxi-owner in Mumbai claimed that his sister, who lived in Kerala, had cast a spell on him.
20. The sort of tensions that would give rise to accusations of witchcraft abounded in former society, too, especially among its aristocracy organized in Houses: there could be tensions with affines (Gough 1958: 469ff.), or tensions arising out of court intrigues (Shungoonny Menon 1983: 310) or out of rivalry for positions of honour (Venni Vasupillai 1983, narrates how a prince was said to have taken control of a temple after murdering by occult means its legitimate owners).
21. *Cattan* is often mentioned in literature but, as a rule, without much details (Fawcett 1915; Ananthakrishna Iyer 1925: 197; 1969, I: 70ff.; Panikkar 1918a-b; Krishna Ayyar 1928; Dare 1940: 192ff.; Thaliath 1956; Gough 1958; Kapur 1983: 76ff.; Kottarattil Sankunni 1974). Some temples

in the Trichur area have published booklets (e.g. Chaitanya Das 1987). See also the *Indian Express*, Cochin edition, 2 March 1991.

22. The *Atharva Veda* may be the ultimate reference in terms of magic, but the manuals customarily used are tantric treatises (see list in Padmanabha Menon 1937: 215); K.N.B. Asan mentions three treatises: *Dattatreyam*, *Merutantram*, *Saradatilakam*. There are also numerous recent works, and even cheap booklets sold in the street, which provide the reader with the indications for various charms and spells. For one in French, picked up in Tamil Nadu, see Mariadassou 1937.
23. A lively account of the terrifying dangers that mark the path to tantric power can be obtained in the apologetic publication of Shrimali (1988). See also Rosin 1983.
24. English-speaking Malayalis render *manasakti* as 'spiritual power' or 'mental power', as well as 'will power'.
25. In classical texts, *Krtya* (Skt.) is a terrifying goddess, created by or personifying spells (Turstig 1985: 7ff.).
26. Published lists sometimes differ from Asan's list in respect of certain details, in the number of categories and, occasionally, in the meaning attached to their label. For instance, from *Saradatilaka* Türstig (1985: 101) lists Six Acts (*satkarmani*): peace or pacification (*santi*), subjugating (*vasya*), restraining (*stambhana*), exciting hatred (*vidvesa*), expelling (*ucchatana*), killing (*marana*). See also Gopalacharlu on the *Mantra Sastra*, as cited in Padmanabha Menon 1937: 207; also, the *Dattatreyatantra*, a frequently consulted text in Kerala, cited by the same author (pp. 216ff.); Mariadassou 1937: 21–9.
27. Other classifications of divinities in relation to witchcraft are possible. As regards northern Kerala, Fawcett (1915), quoted also in Padmanabha Menon (1937: 212ff.), describes a binary opposition between 'pure and serene forms' (*satmurtti*) and 'cruel forms' (*durmurtti*).
28. Poisoning, burying charms, sticking needles in statues or setting a 'cruel' divinity or an unsatisfied dead on one's enemy would not of course constitute 'ordinary worship'. However, the process by which this is activated, which makes this efficacious, is a rite that can hardly be characterized as different. This perception is confirmed by a journalistic report on sorcery (Mohan 1981), despite its sensationalist dramatization.
29. Many earlier travellers allude to the Kaniyans, notably Barbosa in the sixteenth century (Thurston and Rangachari 1909, III: 187), Visscher in the eighteenth century (Letter XXIV in Padmanabha Menon 1933), and Buchanan in the beginning of the nineteenth century (Buchanan 1988, II: 528ff.). On the caste itself, see Thurston and Rangachari (1909, III: 178–99), Ananthakrishna Iyer (1969, I: 185–230—the most complete account); Padmanabha Menon (1933: 448–55); Panikkar (1918a–b); Fawcett (1915).

30. Panikkar (1918a–b), Thurston and Rangachari (1909, III: 192), and Varma Raja (1940: 98ff.) refer to the *kolam tullal*. Similar dances are presented as homage to the goddess (Tarabout 1986: 211–61).
31. Also see Pitt-Rivers 1970: 184.
32. On the Parayans, see Thurston and Rangachari (1909, VI: 120–39), Ananthakrishna Iyer (1969, I: 68–86), Padmanabha Menon (1933: 512–23), Krishna Iyer (1939: 82–111).
33. Fawcett (1915); Ananthakrishna Iyer (1969, I: 77ff.); Unni Nayar (1952: 65ff.); Kapur (1983: 19ff.). According to a *mantravadi* cited by Mohan (1981), there are still *otiyan* practising their trade.
34. With regard to Europe, Cohn notes that 'to accuse people of being Satan's servants was a very effective way of releasing huge potentials of hatred, and of enabling people to support and engage in one-sided killing without qualms of conscience.' (Cohn 1970: 16). See Gupta 1960 for Indian examples of accusations of witchcraft leading to murder.
35. Unni Nayar's autobiography (Unni Nayar 1952: 66) speaks of how, with the help of counter magic, one of his ancestors easily vanquished an *otiyan*. This triumph was commemorated by an annual rite of allegiance to his Nayar House, performed by people whom the narrator calls '*otiyans*'. As this rite of allegiance comprised 'a dance, gay in step and lively in manner, by men who carry harvest offerings in their hands', it may well just have been, in fact, the usual regular homage paid by bonded agricultural workers to their landlord.
36. 'Society in general, though it fears their "art", considers them charlatans.' (Panikkar 1918a: 108; 1918b: 282). According to a Christian nun who practises exorcisms in Bombay (cited in Kapur 1983: 106), 'most fakirs and sadhus are hoaxes—and are more often than not, black magicians, seeking to control unsuspecting souls'.
37. This problem has been dealt with extensively outside India (see for instance Bleek 1976). In a perhaps too functionalist perspective, Mary Douglas (1970: xxv) sums up: 'Witchcraft beliefs are essentially a means of clarifying and affirming social definitions.'
38. For similar conclusions in other areas, see Nichter 1992 and Zimmermann 1992.

REFERENCES

Ananthakrishna Iyer, L.K. 1925. *Lectures on Ethnography*. Calcutta: University of Calcutta.

———. 1969. *The Cochin Tribes and Castes* (2 vols.). New York: Johnson Reprint Corp. (1st edn. Madras, 1909–12, Higginbotham/Govt. of Cochin).

Auge, Marc 1979. 'Ici et ailleurs: sorciers du Bocage et sorciers d'Afrique', *Annales ESC*, 34(1): 74-83.

———. 1982. *Génie du Paganisme*. Paris: Gallimard ('Bibl. des Sciences humaines').

Babb, Lawrence A. 1983. 'Destiny and Responsability: Karma in Popular Hinduism', in C.F. Keyes and E.V. Daniel (eds.), *Karma. An Anthropological Inquiry*, Berkeley: University of California Press, pp. 163–81.

Balodhi, J.P. and J. Roy Chowdhary 1986. 'Psychiatric Concepts in Atharva Veda: A Review', *Indian Journal of Psychiatry*, 28(1): 63–8.

Bharati, Agehananda 1970. 'The Use of "Superstition" as an Anti-Traditional Device in Urban Hinduism', *Contributions to Indian Sociology* n.s., 4: 36-49.

Bleek, Wolf 1976. 'Witchcraft, Gossip and Death: a Social Drama', *Man* n.s., vol. 11, no. 4: 526–41.

Boon, James A. 1983. 'Incest Recaptured: Some Contraries of Karma in Balinese Symbology', in C.F. Keyes and E.V. Daniel (eds.), *Karma. An Anthropological Inquiry*, Berkeley: University of California Press, pp. 185–222.

Brown, Peter 1970. 'Sorcery, Demons, and the Rise of Christianity from Late Antiquity into the Middle Ages', in M. Douglas (ed.), *Witchcraft Confessions and Accusations*. Londres, Tavistock Publications, pp.17–45.

Buchanan, Francis 1807. *A Journey From Madras Through the Countries of Mysore, Canara and Malabar* (3 vols.). London (rpt. 1988, New Delhi: Asian Educational Services).

Camus, Dominique 1988. *Pouvoirs sorciers. Enquête sur les pratiques actuelles de sorcellerie*. Paris, Imago.

Carstairs, G.M. and R.L. Kapur 1976. *The Great Universe of Kota. Stress, Change and Mental Disorder in an Indian Village*. Berkeley: University of California Press.

Chaitanya Das 1987. *Kanadi Madam. Ancient Traditional Centre for Chathan Cult*. Peringottukara, Kshetrarangam Publications.

Claus, Peter 1973. 'Possession, Protection and Punishment as Attributes of Deities in a South Indian Village', *Man in India*, 53(3): 231–42.

Cohn, Norman 1970. 'The Myth of Satan and his Human Servants', in M. Douglas (ed.), *Witchcraft Confessions and Accusations*. London: Tavistock Publications, pp. 3-16.

Daniel, E. Valentine 1983. 'Conclusion: Karma, the Uses of an Idea', in C.F. Keyes and E.V. Daniel (eds.), Karma. *An Anthropological Inquiry*. Berkeley: University of California Press, pp. 287–300.

Dare, Paul M. 1940. *Indian Underworld. A first-hand account of Hindu saints, sorcerers, and superstition*. New York: E.P. Dutton & Co.

Douglas, Mary 1970. 'Introduction: Thirty Years after *Witchcraft, Oracles and Magic*', in M. Douglas (ed.), *Witchcraft Confessions and Accusations*, London: Tavistock Publications, pp. xi–xxxviii.

Epstein, Scarlett 1959. 'A Sociological Analysis of Witch Beliefs in a Mysore Village', *The Eastern Anthropologist*, 12(4): 234–51.

Evans-Pritchard, E.E. 1937, *Witchcraft, Oracles and Magic Among the Azande*. Oxford: Clarendon Press.

Favret-Saada, Jeanne 1977. *Les mots, la mort, les sorts. La sorcellerie dans le Bocage*. Paris, Gallimard ('Bibl. des Sciences humaines').

Fawcett, F. 1915. 'Nâyars of Malabar', *Madras Govt Museum Bulletin*, III(3) (rpt. from the 1901 edn.).

Freeman, J.R., Jr. 1991. 'Purity and Violence: Sacred Power in the Teyyam Worship of Malabar'. Philadelphia: Univ. of Pennsylvania (Ph.D.Thesis).

Foster, George M. 1972. 'The Anatomy of Envy: A Study in Symbolic Behavior', *Current Anthropology*, 13(2): 165–202.

Goudriaan, T. 1978. *Maya Divine and Human. A study of magic and its religious foundations in Sanskrit texts, with particular attention to a fragment of Visnu's Maya preserved in Bali*. Delhi: Motilal Banarsidass.

Gopal Panikkar, T.K. 1983. *Malabar and its Folk*. New Delhi: Asian Educational Services (rpt., 1st edn. *ca* 1900).

Gough, E. Kathleen 1958. 'Cults of the Dead Among the Nayars', *Journal of American Folklore*, vol. 71, no. 281: 446–78.

Govindan, Krishnalayam M.K. 1987. *Prasnamarggam (purvvardham)*, Kottayam: N.B.S.

Gupta, Beni 1979. *Magical Beliefs and Superstitions*, Delhi: Sundeep Prakashan.

Gupta, R.K. 1960. 'Witchcraft Murders in the Duars', *Man in India*, 40(4): 307-19.

Hiebert, Paul G. 1983. 'Karma and Other Explanation Traditions in a South Indian Village', in C.F. Keyes and E.V. Daniel (eds.), *Karma. An Anthropological Inquiry*. Berkeley: University of California Press, pp. 119–30.

Jagathambika, R. 1968. '*A Case Study of Multiple Personality or Possession-syndrome. Its Aetiology and Treatment*'. Alwaye: Union Christian College (unpublished Ph.D. Thesis).

Jaggi, O.P. 1973. *History of Science and Technology in India*, vol. 3: *Folk Medicine*. Delhi: Atma Ram & Sons.

Kakar, D.N. 1977. *Folk and Modern Medicine (A North Indian Case Study)*. Delhi: New Asian Publishers.

Kamala Das 1988. *My Story*. New Delhi: Sterling Publishers.

Kapur, Sohaila 1983. *Witchcraft in Western India*. Bombay: Orient Longman.

Keshavan, M.S., H.S. Narayanan and B.N. Gangadhar 1989. "Bhanamati" Sorcery and Psychopathology in South India. A Clinical Study', *British Journal of Psychiatry*, 154: 218–20.

Kottarattil Sankunni 1974. *Aitihyamala*, Kottayam: Kottarattil Sankunni Memorial Committee (1st publ. serially, 1909–34).

Krishna Ayyar, K.V. 1928. 'Chathan: a Devil or Disease?', *Man*, 28: 151–3.

Krishna Iyer, L.A. 1939. *Travancore Tribes and Castes* (vol. 2). Trivandrum: Government Press.

Lewis, I.M. 1970. 'A Structural Approach to Witchcraft and Spirit-possession', in M. Douglas (ed.), *Witchcraft Confessions and Accusations*, Londres, Tavistock Publications, pp. 293–309.

———. 1986. *Religion in Context. Cults and Charisma.* Cambridge: Cambridge University Press.

Logan, William 1981. *Malabar* (vol.1). Trivandrum: Charithram Publications (1st edn. Madras, 1887).

Loti, Pierre 1920. *L'Inde (sans les Anglais)*. Paris: Calmann-Lévy.

Mariadassou, P. 1937. *Médecine traditionnelle de l'Inde: la magie noire.* Pondichéry: the Author.

Mohan, Lakshmi 1981. 'Voodoo and Black Magic. Exorcism in the back-waters of Kerala', *The India Magazine*, 6 (May 1981): 52–60.

Nichter, Mark 1979. 'The Language of Illness in South Kanara (India)', *Anthropos*, 74: 181–201.

———. 1992. 'Of Ticks, Kings, Spirits, and the Promise of Vaccines', in C. Leslie and A. Young (eds.), *Paths to Asian Medical Knowledge.* Berkeley: University of California Press, pp. 224–53.

Nuckolls, Charles W. 1981. 'Interpretations of the Concept of Karma in a Telugu Fishing Village', *The Eastern Anthropologist*, 34(2): 95–106.

O'Flaherty, Wendy Doniger (1980a), 'Introduction', in O'Flaherty (ed.), *Karma and Rebirth in Classical Indian Traditions.* Berkeley, University of California Press, pp. ix–xxv.

———. 1980b. 'Karma and Rebirth in the Vedas and Puranas', in O'Flaherty (ed.), *Karma and Rebirth in Classical Indian Traditions.* Berkeley: University of California Press, pp. 3–37.

Padmanabha Menon, K.P. 1933. *History of Kerala* (vol. III). Ernakulam: Cochin Government Press (rpt. 1984, New Delhi: Asian Educational Services).

———. 1937. *History of Kerala* (vol. IV), Ernakulam: Cochin Government Press (rpt. 1986, New Delhi: Asian Educational Services).

Pandya, Mukul 1982. 'Occultism in an Urban Community', *The Eastern Anthropologist*, 35(4) 319–22.

Panikkar, K.M. 1918a. 'Religion and Magic among the Nayars', *Man*, 18: 104–10 [included in 1918b].

———. 1918b. 'Some Aspects of Nayar Life', *JRAI*, 48: 254–93.

Pitt-Rivers, Julian 1970. 'Spiritual Power in Central America. The Naguals of Chiapas', in M. Douglas (ed.), *Witchcraft Confessions and Accusations.* London: Tavistock Publications, pp. 183–206.

Pocock, D.F. 1973. *Mind, Body and Wealth. A Study of Belief and Practice in an Indian Village.* Oxford: Basil Blackwell.

Rao, M.S.A. 1986. 'Supernatural Possession in Kerala', *Man in India*, 66(1): 1–22.

Rosin, R. Thomas 1983. 'Notes on Dread and the Supernatural in Indian Society', *Man in India*, 63(2): 115–40.

Sharma, Ursula 1973. 'Theodicy and the Doctrine of Karma', *Man*, n.s., 8(3): 347–64.

Shungoonny Menon, P. 1983, *A History of Travancore from the Earliest Times*, Trivandrum: Government Press (1st edn. Madras, 1878).

Shrimali, Narayandutta 1988. *The Power of Tantra*. Delhi: Hind Pocket Books.

Siqueira, T.N. 1933. 'Sin and Salvation in the Early Rig-Veda', *Anthropos*, 28: 179–88.

Spooner, Brian 1970. 'The Evil Eye in the Middle East', in M. Douglas (ed.), *Witchcraft Confessions and Accusations*, London: Tavistock Publications, pp. 311–19.

Tarabout, Gilles 1986. *Sacrifier et donner à voir en pays malabar. Les fêtes de temple au Kérala (Inde du Sud): étude anthropologique* (vol. cxlvii), Paris: E.F.E.O.

———. 1991. 'Au "royaume" des brahmanes, les guerriers sont rois. Souveraineté, pouvoir et statut au Kérala', in J. Pouchepadass and H. Stern (eds.), *De la royauté à l'Etat. Anthropologie et histoire du politique dans le monde indien*. Paris: EHESS ('coll. *Purusartha*', no. 13).

Thaliath, Joseph 1956. 'Notes on Some Pulaya Customs and Beliefs', *Anthropos*, 51: 1029–54.

Thite, G.U. 1982. *Medicine. Its Magico-Religious Aspects According to the Vedic and Later Literature*. Poona, Continental Prakashan.

Thurston, E. and K. Rangachari 1909. *Castes and Tribes of Southern India* (7 vols.), Madras: Government Press (rpt. 1965, New York: Johnson Reprint Corp.).

Türstig, Hans-Georg 1985. 'The Indian Sorcery Called *Abhicâra*', WZKS, XXIX: 69–117.

Unni Nayar, M.K. 1952. *My Malabar.* Bombay: Hind Kitabs Ltd.

Varma Raja, M. Raja Raja 1940. *Selected Essays.*Trivandrum: Kamalalaya Book Depot.

Venni Vasupilla 1983. 'ampalanatayil: mammiyur sri ambasivan', *Malayalanatu*, 8(5): 56–60.

Weiss, Mitchell G. et al. 1986. 'Traditional Concepts of Mental Disorder Among Indian Psychiatric Patients: Preliminary Report of Work in Progress', *Soc. Sci. Med.*, 23(4): 379–86.

Wirz, Paul 1954. *Exorcism and the Art of Healing in Ceylon*. Leiden: E.J. Brill.

Zimmermann, Francis (1989), *Le discours des remèdes au pays des épices. Enquête sur la médecine hindoue*. Paris: Payot ('coll. Médecine et sociétés').

———. 1992. 'Gentle Purge: The Flower Power of Ayurveda', in C. Leslie and A. Young (eds.), *Paths to Asian Medical Knowledge*. Berkeley: University of California Press, pp. 209–23.

The End of a Feud

DENIS VIDAL

It is still difficult today to evaluate the role that violence played in traditional contexts of Hindu culture and society, owing to the successive concealments and distortions, which have baffled its interpretation. Yet, recent researchers have progressively unveiled a different image of Indian society, in which violence and conflict are increasingly reintegrated within the logic of culture and society.[1] The following analysis should be considered another step in this direction.

This is a two-part account: first, of the manner in which local feuds that deeply affected the identity of entire communities, were perceived and lived; and second, of the manner in which these perceptions changed under the impact of ideas that brought with them new modes of social behaviour in the latter half of the twentieth century. This paper, however, is not only about mere tales of killings and feuds, violence and insecurity. Nor is it simply about practices linked with social, political or territorial domination. It is rather about complex cultural arrangements, and social as well as psychological confrontations and negotiations, in which Gods and ancestors play their part alongside immediate human protagonists. Hence, it was a whole way of life that found expression in feuds between rival clans living in the wooded highlands of Himachal Pradesh, adjoining Uttar Pradesh.[2]

In earlier times, Chaupal district was part of the small Hindu kingdom of Jubbal, and, at least in name, the people paid allegiance to the raja and also acknowledged the pre-eminent status of the Brahmins. Real power, however, was wielded by some fifteen 'warrior' clans (Khunds)[3] whose writ ran in the wooded hills and valley slopes dotted with their terraced homes. Each of these clans had its dependents (*ghara*).[4] When a conflict arose, all those who lived in a particular clan's territory (*its khaut*) were bound to support that clan. Power was wielded by a Council (*kumbali*) composed of the elders (*siyana*) of the various families, the priests and the mediums serving the clanic divinities, and representatives of the lower castes. This was the institution, which took decisions essential to the life of the clan.

Khunds were large, patrilineal clans (*dhai* or *biradari*), comprising anywhere from a few hundred to several thousand individuals, who acknowledged a common ancestry and were divided into several lines of descent (*al*), sub-divisions (*khandan*), families and homes.[5] They were exogamous and generally married among themselves, although they could make alliances with clans of proximate status in the neighbourhood.[6] However, the notion of a 'clan' must not mislead one here. It is certainly true that the common reference for all members of a *biradari* was their common ancestry which conferred a single name on the entire clan.[7] The existence of such genealogical lineage, however, should not be viewed too literally. Terms like *biradari* and *dhai* more closely signify brotherhood. The sense of a collective fraternity binding members into a single unit is, indeed, central to *biradari*. A shared ancestry was not however always at the origin of such a brotherhood. Ancestry as well as extended fraternities were rather those factors which the local society could equally manipulate and bring into play.[8]

In one's understanding of the region's social morphology, one must also be wary of an excessively classificatory perspective. The colonial administration, for example, lumped most of the population under the term 'Kanets'; in the valley studied here, they were referred to more precisely as 'Khaush Kanets'. However, as often the case elsewhere in India in comparable situations, it would be wrong to invest the term with any deep sociological meaning and still less with any ethnic connotation. These appellations, now fallen into disuse, served mainly to distinguish the bulk of the local population from a handful of dynastic lineages (Mians and Thakurs) related to the rulers of the region's small Hindu kingdoms and who sought exclusive use of the title of Rajput. Thus, among the so-called Kanets, one could find, in fact, groups of different status and diverse origins. The warrior-clans (particularly so, the Khund), for example, looked upon themselves as Rajputs, adopted Rajput values and sought treatment as Rajputs. Other lineages whose members acted as *pujari* for the local Gods, enjoyed a status comparable to if not exactly similar to that of Brahmins.[9] Yet, other lineages of 'Kanets' were assigned the equivalent of a lower caste status. Apart from the 'Kanets', practically every other caste can be found in the region, from Brahmins to Untouchables, to say nothing of the various artisan castes, although the mercantile caste was virtually absent until recently.[10]

A final point needs to be made before embarking upon a study of feuds. The clans' religious practices revolve around incarnations of Shiva (Mahadev, commonly revered in the region as Bijet) and of the Goddess[11] in various local incarnations. The Goddess is generally identified with the territory of dominant clans for whom she becomes a family deity (*kuldevi*), playing a vital role within the community, expressing her opinions and desires through a medium. However, the local incarnation of Shiva, acknowledged as the spouse of the local goddess and the master of the clan's territory, is not necessarily the clan's *kuldevta*. Other deities too—whose temples are to be found on the territory of these clans—are either worshipped by the entire clan or solely by the members of certain castes.[12]

Archery Contests

Archery contests (*thotha*) are held in succession at various sites in the district from April to June each year; at the time of my fieldwork, they were still the major events in festivals revolving around the gods worshipped by clans and associated with Shiva Mahadev. The host clan would challenge another warrior clan from the valley. A couple of young men would be designated to venture by night into the chosen clan's territory. The exercise was perilous. Their mission was to place shrubs over the wells and doorsteps of the clan's elders. Then, from a safe distance, they would call out to the members of the households concerned, challenging them to come to the festivities. If the young men were captured, they would be beaten up or simply ridiculed, depending upon the relations between the two clans. If, however, they succeeded in their mission, the families concerned would not be entitled to use their wells and doorsteps, which were symbolically barricaded until the festival, when all the members of the challenged clan were received by their hosts in the traditional form of hospitality.[13]

Without going into all the implications of these archery contests,[14] one aspect stands out: a dominant feature of the symbolism that came into play was the challenging, albeit in jest, of the very ancestry that conferred its identity on the clans. This was evident even in the manner of the challenge. Elders were considered as living links with the clan's ancestors. An ancient Hindu tradition held that wells were votive offerings tended by the living in memory of the deceased. More significant yet was the unfolding of the contest itself, which took the form of duels in which champions among the guests could challenge anyone from the host clan. Each took turn shooting arrows (without arrowheads) at his rival's legs, the only authorized body target. The recipient would turn his back on his adversary and dance, axe in hand, weaving his body this way and that to avoid the arrows shot at him, and heaping ridicule and gibes on the archer every time an arrow missed its mark, calling him unworthy of his ancestors. Equally, if an arrow struck him, he was expected to acknowledge his adversary's merits. The 'target' would then become an archer in turn. Yet, the contest ended the moment any blood was shed, and the champions were then required to change opponents.

In a social and cultural context where feuds played a paramount role, such a parody of combat is especially meaningful because it reproduced, in a theatrical microcosm, the structural logic of the antagonism between clans. Note, however, that such a logic did not mesh so well with the concept of a caste-bound society in which roles and status are hierarchically defined, once and for all (Dumont 1966). On the contrary, the alternation of roles was the salient feature of these contests, and it is precisely such a situation of alternating dissymmetry that prevailed—in a dramatic mode—between warring clans in feuds.

Feuds

How does a feud start? At the outset, one finds generally a spat, a quarrel between families, usually concerning women, herds, or access to water resources and grazing grounds.[15] However a feud would only happen if the dispute ceased to be a private one and turned into a recognized and institutionalized conflict between two dominant clans.

The decision to turn a personal dispute into a conflict involving the entire clan could only be taken collectively at a clan council meeting. The outset of a feud was usually solemnized by a ritual (*chhinga*), after which any form of convivial relations with members of the rival clan would be theoretically forbidden. Such a sundering of relations had painful consequences, especially for the women, when, as often the case, the two clans were previously linked by intermarriage. From this moment on, a feud may be roughly described as a series of hostile acts traded by the feuding clans. A good illustration of it is a feud that I studied more in detail during my fieldwork, which involving the Manai and Sajaik clans and lasted nearly a hundred years.

A woman born to a family living in Sajaik-controlled territory was given in marriage to a man living in Manai territory. During a visit to her parental home, the woman apparently committed adultery with a Sajaik. Her husband, a member of the Manai, turned to them to avenge his humiliation, which they readily agreed to do.[16] There followed a series of incidents, of which I shall describe the most important one here. First, the Manai challenged the Sajaik (a *paukh*) to engage in open combat at a designated spot on Sajaik territory. Some of their warriors moved towards that spot, or rather made as if to do so. In fact, they tried to occupy other areas in Sajaik territory but they met on their way a solitary Sajaik warrior who managed apparently not only to kill one of the Manai but also to beat back the would-be occupiers.

In reprisal, the Manai persuaded a Manai woman married to a Sajaik to betray her husband.[17] On a day when the hapless Sajaik would be alone in the fields and therefore ripe for ambush, a white cloth was lowered onto his roof from the Manai watch tower, as a signal. After the Sajaik had been thus killed, reprisal was swift from his brother, who, along with his accomplices, torched the small fort where his brother's murderer had seen the signal and killed the murderer as he sought to escape the flames. Two violent episodes followed in quick succession: one in which Sajaik children were killed, and another, in revenge, when Sajaik disguised as Gujar nomadic Muslim herdsmen mowed down some Manai children.[18]

Today, these incidents have assumed locally near epic proportions and are best known through songs. The feud moved into a latent phase with the decades passing between the episodes recounted above and those that followed, which are anchored in more recent history and about which several accounts, some conflicting, can be obtained. The *status quo* was suddenly shattered in the following manner. A number of Sajaik were attending a traditional Manai festival, proof that the feud had receded in the background. However, a fresh dispute arose between Manai and Sajaik during the festival, and the Sajaik managed to withdraw without any losses. In the course of the scuffle, however, they destroyed (or took away, according to some accounts) a silver drum from the temple built to the Manai's god. Some time later, the Sajaik organized a festival peculiar to the region, a ceremonial fishing expedition (*maun*) to which several clans were invited. The host clan erected a small platform and placed thereon a large quantity of *timbar*, a kind of plant poison. Young warriors from the host clan were designated to guard the *timbar* as attempts would be made to steal it in hand to hand combat by young men from the guest clans.[19] The combat would cease the moment one of the invading party managed to reach the poison and place a small quantity of it in his mouth. The poison itself would then be thrown into the river and a sumptuous feast cooked for all and sundry with the fish killed by the poison.[20]

The river where the festival was organized was the borderline between Sajaik and Manai territory. As they had not been invited, the Manai observed the proceedings from the hill slopes. Suddenly, one of them crossed the river and, exploiting the element of surprise, climbed the platform, grabbed some poison and put it in his mouth. He then succeeded in returning to his clansmen, safe and sound. His offence was double—an affront to the Sajaik as well as to the guest clan. He had 'polluted' the poison by his act, thereby obliterating the sanctity of the festival and forcing the Sajaik to sacrifice a quantity of goats to propitiate their guests.

The Sajaik then decided to invite the Manai, openly this time, to an archery contest. In accordance with the custom, two of their number did venture into Manai territory and drape shrubs on Manai wells and dwellings. Then they hid and challenged the Manai to come to the contest. The Manai did indeed come, but proceedings took an ugly turn, with several injuries and one death. The final incident occurred when the Manai organized a ritual (*Shant mela*) for their Goddess. On such occasions, custom demanded the offering of an enemy's head. A commando of youths was assigned by the clan to find a suitable victim. The commando raided the home of a Sajaik where a Brahmin was staying as a guest. On revealing his identity, the Brahmin was spared. The Sajaik was decapitated and his head offered to the Goddess. This incident took place in the year 1940. The killer's identity was known; in fact, he took no pains to conceal the facts. He was arrested by the ruler of the area, judged and imprisoned, only to be granted amnesty when the kingdom's jubilee was celebrated, just a few years before India's independence.

Since the events that follow do not arise from the same context, I would like to interrupt this account to analyse feuds first in their more traditional setting. When a conflict causes loss of life, the first and foremost issue is the impossibility of performing the last rites in such a way that the deceased becomes an ancestor, for the victim of a feud is looked upon as 'ill-dead', or *bhut*, who might well turn against his own if not avenged. Only when vengeance is wreaked is he placated. In the course of a feud, both sides are, therefore, forever on the lookout. From one death to another, both sides trade the form of danger that each alternately poses to the other. The clan that perpetrates the latest killing faces danger from a human source in reprisal, whereas the latest victim's own clan faces an equally daunting threat, although of a different order: that of being encumbered with an 'ill-dead', crying out for revenge.

This is the paradox that generates the internal dynamics of a feud. On the one hand, the tradition allows that one man is worth another, that the killing of an adversary is a sufficient condition for the previous victim to cease to be 'ill-dead'. But on the other hand, the only fact that one man' death should be compensated by another death can only result in a vicious circle: its consequence is to perpetuate indefinitely the feud because it means also that it will always be a last death having to be avenged.

Propitiation can palliate however an unavenged death. The clan elders gather around the Goddess' temple. One of them is possessed by the victim's spirit, then indicates where a shrine should be built to him. As a rule, it is the very spot where the man was killed, or in a nearby field. That spot becomes forbidden to all; if a field, then its cultivation must cease. A wooden figurine clad in precious metal is subsequently placed in the shrine (*sog chaura*) built on the spot. Yet elevating the victim to sacred status does not waive the necessity of revenge. On the contrary, it becomes official. Only when actual vengeance has been wreaked does the 'ill-dead' completely cease to exist as a malevolent entity. The field where the shrine is erected can then again be open to cultivation. The dead man becomes a minor divinity, like the other divinities who stand guard at the entrance of temples and whose identity is characterized by certain ambivalence.

How can one grasp the status conferred at different times upon the victim of a feud? His lot is believed to differ from that resulting from an ordinary death. Unlike some other cultures, any notion of proximity between the living and the ordinary dead is considered with the greatest suspicion in the Hindu tradition. Funeral rites are in fact aimed to ensure that the dead transit from a deceased state (*pret*), a perpetual threat to the living, to that of an ancestral spirit (*pitr*). This transition gains its very sanctity from its capacity to give the dead access to the hereafter, where they will be alongside the gods. It is also the ideal way for the living to rid themselves of the dead, consigning them to the anonymous mass of ancestors. By contrast, the 'ill-dead' continue to haunt the living, in the literal sense, by remaining close to them; in the figurative sense, by refusing to shed their individuality. The ghost of a victim, who is held responsible for all the ills that befall the clan, also visits the dreams of the living. The erection of a shrine to the 'ill-dead' is then designed to acknowledge the inevitable and also thereby to contain the damage. True, as long as the victim of a feud remains unavenged, he retains his very specific identity. It is only once vengeance is accomplished that he becomes just one of a host of minor divinities.

There is, however, one ritual possibility of genuinely stopping a feud; but according to local people, this rarely happened. It supposes that the murderer's clan seizes the initiative to deify the victim from the rival clan by erecting a shrine in his honor on its own territory, Theoretically, this is the only way to genuinely terminate a feud. However, even in the case where the spirit of the last victim has been appeased and deified, there remains the question of restoring links between the rival clans, although that now becomes possible. At a ceremonial rite performed atop a sacred mountain in the region, two acts are performed. First, the vow to cease all convivial relations between the clans is repudiated through the *sauri katnau* ritual. Arrows from either side, shorn of their heads, are broken then bound together into fascia. Then a bard of the Chanal caste is appointed to compose a song that recounts the story of the feud.

A sort of impartiality distinguishes these songs allowing both sides to identify with them since it is indeed a necessary condition for them to be enshrined in the collective memory. Thus, each incident is addressed in such a way as to valorize alternately the action of the erstwhile victors, and this satisfies all in that it also justifies the defeat of the vanquished. In this light, it becomes easier to understand how the most sinister ruse or perfidy alternates, seemingly unperturbed, with the exaltation of valour. Like in many other epic traditions, cowardice is perceived as the true opposite of bravery but stratagems and perfidy are ranked with epic values. So, the winning clan of the moment does not need to be ashamed of its victory; but the losing one needs not blush in defeat and can, like the other clans, sing the same song.

I would now like to relate the consequences of this particular feud to approach the issue of the present-day relationship with this tradition.

The Challenge of the Tradition

The last victim of the Sajaik clan had no son. The duty to avenge him fell on one of his nephews, the son of his eldest brother. Flouting tradition, this man refused to avenge his uncle, and also forbade anyone else to act in his stead. He plainly announced that he would not pay the ceremonial price whose disbursement traditionally made official the vengeance, should anyone go against his wishes. Since in symbolic terms, this was tantamount to invalidating the murder that should have been perpetrated in his name, a grave crisis arose in his clan. He was threatened with ostracism, especially since the Goddess herself, via a medium, had clamoured for a death. Worse still, she decided that if such little heed were paid to her wishes, she would speak no more through her intermediaries, whatever the circumstances.

If, despite these warnings, the man refused to budge, it may have been due primarily to the fact that he was not only an obstinate man but also a member of one of the clans' most prestigious families. However, what really strengthened his resolution was the fact that he had had several sons in the years since the murder, whereas his cousin's murderer, a man of the same age as he, only had daughters and no male descendant. According to him and his immediate relatives, this was the one most important proof that he was in the right and that greater gods approved his behaviour, despite what people thought and despite the local Goddess' obvious disapproval. The cogency of this form of reasoning cannot be underestimated. As I learned during the course of several interviews on these traditions, the lack of progeny was very frequently the motivating cause behind a new step in a feud.

The Manai also rejected any compromise despite the lack of unavenged deaths. They insisted that the Sajaik first restore the silver drum dedicated to their god, which had been stolen or damaged during one of the incidents. That was a heavy demand, which the Sajaik, who still had an unavenged death on their hands, naturally refused to satisfy. In this impasse, however, two men took unexpected initiatives, almost simultaneously: on the one hand, the Manai murderer, afraid that he would beget no descendants; on the other, a Sajaik who functioned then as the medium of the Goddess, who himself had no male heir, and who believed this was because the clan had failed to wreak vengeance. The irony is that these two men, with identical motives, should have reacted in such diametrically opposed ways. To the general surprise, the Manai murderer announced that since the members of the victim's clan had so aberrantly refused to avenge him, he, the murderer, would personally perform the funereal rites to appease the victim. Although he was part of a community of people who generally hated even the idea of venturing into the plains, this man actually made a pilgrimage to the four most sacred Hindu shrines in the subcontinent. His pilgrimage lasted a whole year. At each shrine, he performed funeral rites to appease the victim's soul, as he would for his own father. His acts appear to have borne fruit, for upon his return he had, to his great joy, a son.

The heirless Sajaik who was the medium of the Goddess pursued a completely contrary logic. He went off with a nephew to the neighbouring state of Uttar Pradesh, where he slew a man belonging to a family distantly related to the Manai clan. He brought his victim's head back home and offered it to the Goddess in a secret ritual.[21] The family of the formerly unavenged Sajaik victim could barely contain their fury at being thus avenged against their own wishes, but as they explained to me, they had ultimately no choice but to have a minimal participation in this ritual which they had done their best to avert. Owing to the circumstances, this final murder assumed nevertheless a peculiar connotation. While it was no doubt more or less in keeping with tradition, a number of details did not fit with the tradition. For a start, the victim was merely a distant relative of the clan proper, whereas tradition dictated that victims be drawn from amongst a clan's leading families. Second, the victim was a simpleton prone to disappear for long periods of time. Thus, no immediate concern was aroused when his body was thrown in the river: and when his relatives began to worry, they ascribed rather his disappearance to the possibility of an accident.

Everyone in the valley where the Manai and the Sajaik lived had acquired some knowledge about the murder, but no one on either side would take any account of it. While I was doing my fieldwork, the Manai continued to reject any compromise, continuing to invoke the silver drum dedicated to the divinity. However, no reference was made to this last murder. As to the Sajaik murderer, he never fathered a male heir. Moreover, whenever he alluded too directly to what he had done—as he was doing it from time to time—he was gently advised to hold his liquor as well as his tongue. Therefore, if one considers the problem raised by the emergence and the spread of new values in a context where an unresolved contradiction exists between specific clan values and those of society as a whole, the behaviour of each of the three major players in the latest incidents illustrates in an exemplary manner the various issues at stake.

The act of killing an enemy in the course of a feud occasioned no guilt in the murderer, especially since he claimed to act not on his own account but on the direct commands of the Goddess.[22] However, when the last murderer killed a simpleton, though he believed his view to be backed by tradition, it had already in fact become untenable, with an entire set of circumstances appearing to conspire to change the meaning of his act. By contrast, the victors in this, so to speak, Darwinian-like logic, since they were blessed with progeny, were those who altered the significance of existing values by their acts: first, the brother of the last victim who, by justifying his break with tradition through theistic and non-violent arguments, held out a vision of reform of existing practices; and also the first murderer, who very clearly enlighted me as to his own perception of his act,

In those times, people were stupid. If disputes arose and if they were unable directly to take revenge on their enemies, they would steal their women or cattle. And so hostilities would never cease. We were that stupid. But now we are less ignorant. When we read the *shastra*, we know that killing a man is equivalent to killing sixty cows. Whether you kill sixty cows or a man, the crime is the same and you must bear the consequences.[23]

THE SOCIAL CHALLENGES OF VIOLENCE

All things considered, what do these feuds really mean? And what distinguished effectively the clans that practiced these traditions from the rest of society?

I shall first consider the place of these clans in the social context of these valleys in order to understand how and why their traditions gave to the concept of caste a slightly different content from the one prevailing in the plains. Admittedly, the division of society into castes and into *varna* constituted there—like in many parts of India—the standard frame of reference that served to define the social order. Also, like elsewhere in India, the Brahmins, the Rajputs and all the other castes had their status quite clearly defined in such a hierarchy. The Khunds also considered themselves an integral part of the same framework, defining themselves, as one has seen, through the ideals of the warrior class (their *dharma*). Though for them, a distinction must be drawn. Instead of looking upon their identity as an inherited status and *fait accompli*, their traditions converged to give their status both the strength and fragility of something won and kept through constant trials. No doubt, their status was by and large institutionalized. However, it remained nevertheless linked to a sense of their clanic superiority in relation to their dependants, sustained by their constant willingness to risk violence and regularly put to test in the context of feuds,

> Imagine us, the Khunds, setting out to fight, arriving with our bows and arrows. We want to know how they feel. If we pick one out, he bares his chest and says, 'Kill me if you like, but my clan brothers will avenge me.' But if he tries to run away and we catch him, we put a bow string into his mouth and make him swear never to fight the Khunds or let anyone from his family fight the Khunds. We would call him Khanara. And no one would associate with him or his family.[24]

Conversely, examples exist of members of the warrior clans who, having taken Brahmin wives and acquired their status, renounced violence and any future involvement in feuds after a solemn ritual and a collective oath sworn before the gods. Thus, one can see how the status of these clans, and even their very caste roots, were defined, whether historically or mythically, by their attitude in situations involving violence.

There are no doubts that the first consequence of the feuds was to divide profoundly the people of these hills between themselves. However, at a local level, it was also a powerful means of aggregating them altogether with their neighborhood. A warrior clan's protection encompassed its entire *khaut*, i.e. everyone who lived in the territory it controlled. In fact, it would be accurate to say that feuds and the state of continuous tension they caused were at one and the same time the cause and the justification of the role assumed by these warrior clans. Thus, with few exceptions, during a feud, not only the Khund but also the whole populace became involved, in some way or the other. This was the lot of most of the local clans, as well as other castes, living in Khund territory, which ended up fighting alongside the Khund. Even Brahmins and wandering *sadhus*, although not directly engaged in combat, frequently played an important role by indicating the most appropriate time for action or by supplying varied panoply of fearsome magic weapons.[25]

Relatively recent historical examples throw also some light on how relations between these clans and the kingdoms in which they lived were played out. One clan, for instance, refused to change the date set for a festive celebration it had organized, although a death had just occurred in the royal family, which habitually meant collective mourning and a strict ban on animal sacrifice. The breach of custom was tantamount to a rebellion. The king ordered other warrior clans to punish the erring clan. Quickly, however, the conflict degenerated into yet another feud between rival clans. A similar situation apparently arouse from the border disputes between the kingdoms of Jubbal and

Sirmur, which adjoined Chaupal district. Disputes between rajas rapidly deteriorated into confrontations between neighboring rival clans and consolidated, paradoxically, their importance.

All things considered, the local predominance of the warrior clans was both weakened and strengthened by the royal power. The earlier administrative division of the district into *parganas* overlapped more or less, for example, with the territories dominated by each Khund. Many elders had long held such administrative functions as *zaildar* and *lambardar.* It is not impossible to argue that the origin and continuance of the Khunds' influence could be traced historically not only to their own interaction with the rest of the population of these valleys but also to their ambivalent participation in the maintenance of the authority, the administrative structures and the political borders of the region's Hindu kingdoms.

Feuds threatened the survival of the clans involved, but their interpretation must be qualified. As one saw earlier, the decisive nature of the relationship that bound people together in these clans was more evident in the quotidian awareness of the 'fraternal' ties than in the more theoretical consciousness of a common ancestry. But an analysis of the feuds also reveals the necessity for the living to find an effective means to appease the spirits of ascendants waiting to be avenged, and enable them to join the relatively benevolent and anonymous host of ancestors. Until this was done, the very presence of the ghosts of the victims of the feuds posed a threat to the living in manifold ways and threatened to jeopardize their prosperity and their prospects of progeny. One also saw that the very existence of the feuds complicated relations contracted by marriage, with the serious danger that one's relatives by marriage could well join the enemy ranks. It is probably no accident that the term used to denote a sister's husband (*mitr*), the closest ally in the same generation, also means friend. In this overheated context, there was no guarantee that a brother-in-law would forever remain a friend.

A feud questioned then the very fundamentals of the benevolence of a world in which death offered the promise of accession to ancestral status, where young adults offered hope of a plentiful progeny, and in which every man of comparable status was potentially a friend and ally. The networks of interaction on which the past, the present and the future depended as well the relations that linked one to one's ancestors, to one's allies and to one's descendants, were shaken up or reassessed during a feud. However, at the same time, and in fact for precisely the same reasons, feuds served to tighten bonds between clan members and their dependents. Welded together as they were by the dangers, these clans were formidable fighting machines, particularly since all were prepared to sacrifice their dearest interests for the sake of a common cause. Young warriors had to be ready to lay down their lives. However, the sacrifice asked of elders was no smaller, since they had to name the clansmen, more often than not mere adolescents, who would join in a sortie. Nor was it less daunting for brothers, who had to call upon sisters to betray their husbands.

Clans involved in feuds were thus apt to find their identity reinforced rather than undermined. This is proved to some extent by the fact that the most populous clans were often the one most involved. Feuds were an ordeal that served to strengthen the feeling of belonging to a single entity. Relations between the individual clan members were reinforced, thus forging the elements of a common history, highlighted by the twists and turns of each feud. This peculiar historiography, bringing collective entities rather than individual heroes into play, was transmitted through the accounts of the clans' elders and also through the songs sung on festive occasions and night watches. All were raised to be prepared for any sacrifice and all were aware of the dangers they faced due to their very identity.

This makes it easier to understand how the traditions of these clans distinguished them from those of Rajput clans more directly associated with kingship. Amongst these, clan solidarity was also paramount in a crisis, but the relative egalitarianism prevailing within the 'warrior' clans made way in this latter case for hierarchies defined by differences in status within the kingdom.

Vengeance and Sacrifice

In an enlightening essay on vengeance in ancient Hinduism, Charles Malamoud stresses the contrast between vengeance and sacrifice,

> Vengeance does not enter into the scheme of sacrifice. A close examination of the relationship between executioner and victim reveals that vengeance is the very opposite of sacrifice, for the avenger hates his victim and wants to make him suffer, while the true sacrificer feels gratitude towards his victim. The sacrificer sees in the victim his Alter Ego, offering redemption. He wishes to spare his victim pain; he promises his victim the heavens he himself craves. So strongly indeed does he empathize with the victim that he seeks assent before killing him. (Malamoud 1989: 204)

Paradoxically, however, the anthropological study of feuds in this Himalayan region shows a much closer proximity than expected between the attitude that characterizes people involved in a feud and the one which is expected of people engaged in a sacrifice. Thus, at least in theory, only those who gave their consent engaged in hostilities. As one has seen, Brahmins, as well as those who refused combat through cowardice, were exempted from participating in the feuds. Theoretically in the battlefield also it was possible for either party to hang fire if so desired.[26] Similarly, when clandestine expeditions went forth seeking a victim from the rival clan, tradition dictated that even if the victim-to-be did not actually consent, he should at least be informed of the fate that awaited him, 'In the night, a man came to the river. We decapitated him after a short fight during which we told him, "We're going to cut off your head." We said to him, "Brother, we are Sajaik and you are a Manai. We must take revenge, so be prepared." He tried to throw me into the river. He was strong and brave as a lion.'[27] Not only did the killers seek, if only in theory, the consent of their victims; but they did not hesitate either to emphasize their closeness to the victims, or the great repugnance they felt at the act they were about to perform. They knew too well that by acting thus, they were condemning themselves, but the reasons were overwhelming. Having been designated by their clans, they could only refuse to act on pain of ostracism and reduction to the status of pariahs. As a matter of fact, they did not consider it to have any real choice—this was their fate, they had to accept it and bear the consequences.

I was just seventeen, without even the shadow of a moustache. When I was taken to Jubbal, King Bhagat Chandra said, 'He is still a child, he could not have killed anyone.' I was told to admit nothing, but answered that I would tell the truth, that I would not lie, it was not in the tradition of my *khandan*. Someone said I would be hanged. I responded by saying I would accept that. Because in any case I was expected to bear the sin of killing a man. By not confessing, I would also have to assume responsibility for anything that happened to my family. They said, 'What makes you think that you must feel guilty for the killing? He was our enemy.' I said he had been like a father to me, I would never have killed him; God only knows why things happen. As for the man killed because of our hostilities, I told my companions, 'You'll see that I shall refuse to kill him, come what may.' But they forced me to do it. Brave men it was after all, they said, who killed new-born babies, how could I be so blinkered, simply because this man had once let me warm myself by his fire. I must kill him or consent to

> leave the village and the valley and have no contact whatsoever with my clan. 'You will no longer be part of the clan and we will be nothing to you.' Finally, I agreed. I shall not lie. When I have committed a murder, why lie?[28]

Thus one finds, among the killers, the very ambiguities Charles Malamoud describes as characteristic of the sacrificer. By putting their deepest emotions into play, they identified at least partially with their victims. But the comparison is not uniformly tenable, for in several respects, the mission of the warriors was closer to that of an officiant at a sacrifice, rather than to that of the sacrificer himself. As one sees in the foregoing account, warriors did not act on their own initiative, but were assigned their tasks by the clan Council. They were duly rewarded by ceremonial honours tantamount to a sort of *dakshina*.[29] The receipt of such a ritual honorarium exonerated them from any personal involvement in the act that had just been accomplished.

This is why although a reference to the logic of the sacrifice may help to understand the ideology of the actors of these feuds, fundamental distinctions remain. One should not forget, in particular that, in contrast with more orthodox forms of sacrifice, the collectivity as a whole did not assume in equal measure the inherent benefits as well as the dangers of an act of vengence. Instead the social universe was temporarily divided by a new act of vengeance between those who benefited provisionally from it and those who assumed the stigmas which went with it. Defined thus, vengeance is a sacrifice whose dangerous remains are deliberately used against one's adversaries instead of being neutralized through ritual. Such a perspective is perfectly illustrated by the victim's fate. His mutilated corpse is that of an 'ill dead' who will haunt his clansmen. However, if the rival clan has absconded with his head, it could regard its trophy as an auspicious offering to the Goddess. This is attested by the last two episodes in the feud described earlier. The man who regretted his act made it a point to stress that the victim's body was intact, 'No, the head was not taken, just a few hairs from the top of his head. If the head had been taken, how could they have performed the cremation? A headless body cannot be burned. In earlier times, the Khunds did not take their enemies' heads, for the head was needed to make cremation possible.'[30]

The other killer, however, insisted with equal force that he had in fact decapitated the victim.[31] As one has seen, however, a middle way could be found by making the victim whole and divine. This infact was what the victim's clan did, with clan members making a wooden effigy covered with precious metal, in the victim's name. This tradition of sanctifying a dead warrior was often explained to me with references to the *Mahabharata*,

> When the Kauravas and the Pandavas fought, millions died in battle. The heads of the dead laughed and said, 'Neither the Kauravas nor the Pandavas were our enemies. We lost our lives for nothing.' When the heads laughed thus, an unknown voice was heard, 'Take these heads and throw them in the direction of those hills.' Myriad gods (some 36,00,000) are worshipped in India. The heads said, 'We shall be sent to the hills, where we shall become idols (*murtis*) and be worshipped by the people. But we wish to reach Heaven, when can we do that?' Then they were told, 'When the eight planets become one, then you shall be free and reach Heaven'.[32]

References to the *Mahabharata* are indeed a dominant feature of the region's culture. Warrior clans were that much readier to cite the epic as many elements in their tradition derived legitimacy from it—feuds and their dilemmas, of course, but also, for example, marriage practices like polyandry and the social emphasis put on the notion of brotherhood. Thus, the Khunds liked to present themselves as successors to the heroes of the *Mahabharata*, offering as evidence, *inter alia*, the division of society into Shatis and Panshis, corresponding, according to themselves to the ancient division into Kauravas and Pandavas.[33] Besides, during the ritual at which a head is offered to the Goddess, the *pujari* recites a lengthy chant to salute the Goddess' arrival, the gist of which speaks of Bhima's adventures in the Himalayas, when he ascended Mount Kailash to secure the Goddess' support in the impending battle with the Kauravas.[34] Thus, the feuds animated a system of relationships and an ideology, which succeeded in fracturing continuously an otherwise homogenous social and cultural space. Moreover, it would not be wrong to say that the feud could be defined, in the cultural perspective of Hinduism, as one of the forms, if not the supreme form, that the logic of ritual sacrifice could assume within a divided social space.[35]

Only a true sovereign could transcend clan antagonisms and the cycles of vengeance they bred, by becoming the guarantor of a global order that covered the totality of the social space, which feuds tended to fracture. That, in fact, is the ancient Indian logic for royalty and for all the sacrificial rites associated with royalty. Charles Malamoud clearly demonstrates the contradiction that exists in ancient Hindu values between vengeance and the order or *dharma* as incarnated by the sovereign. He also shows that the very existence of revenge could only be interpreted as a failing in the exercise of royal power.

The awareness of such a contradiction was not lacking in the case under study. However, in the absence of a human sovereign capable of personifying effectively the *dharma* for the inhabitants of these valleys, the ideology of sovereignty was devolved upon a local divinity, Bijet, a manifestation of Shiva, identified by the local people in particular with Yama, the God of Death. It was in fact atop the mountain where his shrine lay that ceremonies to effect reconciliation between warring clans took place, there that the songs commemorating the feuds were composed.[36] It was also in the honour of this deity that the mock combats parodying the feuds and celebrating the friendship between the clans were organized; unless, of course, these mock combats themselves degenerated into a *casus belli*. Only recently, it would appear, has awareness grown of the contradiction, which, earlier, was an integral part of the very logic of these traditions. Only recently does it seem to have been considered that this contradiction was reason enough to call for a halt not to one particular feud or another but for a more radical and definitive rupture with tradition.

At any rate, that was the opinion of Amar Singh Singta and his father (the Sajaik who refused to wreak vengeance) and their friend, Om Prakash, of the Manai clan: they helped me gain an understanding of their culture, to which they remained deeply attached, although this did not prevent them—quite the contrary, in fact—from putting an end to feuds and the serial sufferings they caused. This was the feeling too of the old man who, like so many others of his generation, had been deeply involved in feud conflict. When, in my presence, the old man met his victim's nephew for the first time, he explained,

> If you saw things in the light of the Khund tradition, you had wreaked vengeance and accomplished a great deed. But if you looked upon your deed in the light of the Dharmashastras, you discovered that you had sinned. Today, when you refused to drink tea in my home, and you said you felt uneasy when I offered it to you, you knew you should not have entered my home. But you are a wise man, for you did nevertheless consent to have a cup of tea. Now that, you see, is the real difference between now and then, when we came to your feast. Now, a compromise is possible, but earlier this was not possible for those in favour of compromise. Yes, today you have come, but there are others who will still refuse to come. I have prayed at the four holy pilgrim centers; 'I looked upon the victim as if he were my father, and I have become his son'. I have worshipped him, as I would my own father. Now, go and tell your father: 'What happened was inevitable, forget it.' If he accepts food from an enemy, then a compromise can be found.[37]

NOTES

1. See, for example, Bayly 1983, Kolff 1990, or the impressive series of works done under the label of Subaltern Studies.
2. Field studies for this research were carried out in 1983. Without the kindness of Amar Singh Singta and Om Prakash Dafraik, and their families, my view of the traditions described here would have forever remained superficial. While I respected all other details in the accounts of these feuds, the names of the clans involved are fictitious. Thanks also to Gerard Lenclud, Gilles Tarabout and Raymond Jamous for their comments on an earlier version of this paper. The translation from the French has been done by K. Chandrasekar and revised by Nissim Marshall.
3. Local opinion holds that the term '*khund*' derives from *khun* (blood). In everyday conversation, it applies only to the warrior clans and carries a 'brave' connotation. Curiously, ethnographic literature does not contain, at least to my knowledge, any analysis of the traditions described herein. The sole detailed reference I could find is from the Jubbal State Report (M. Douglas 1907), 'In the first place, there are two classes of Kanets, superior and inferior. The former is generally spoken of the Khas Kanets, or real Kanets, a term which has been at times confused with the word '*kash*'. Many of the *khels* of the first class trace their descent from the old *mawis*, and it is said that they are still clearly distinguishable by the quarrels and unruly temperament of their members. Bashahr is said to have 25 *mawi khels*, Jubbal, 24, Keonthal, 10, Kothkai and Kumharsain 6 each and other states, one or two. In Bashahr, they are collectively referred to as Khund Kanets, and other Kanets are Ghara Kanets. Certain religious ceremonies such as the *Bunda* and *Shand* sacrifices are only performed in villages where there are Khund Kanets'.
4. Convention puts the number of warrior clans in the kingdom of Jubbal at eighteen. Fourteen of these were in the Chaupal district.
5. The division into clans, dynasties, sub-divisions, families and homes is common to many castes, although the denomination of each level may change. It is the overarching sociological tenor, however, that is most apt to vary from one region and from one community to another. Thus, in the neighboring valleys of the same state, one frequently comes across comparable clan structures, whose implications, however, are generally confined to a sociology of kinship, a diffuse sense of collective identity and common practices of worship, but without enabling the clans to maintain a true 'political' identity.
6. Traditional forms of marriage vary greatly, since the clans practiced monogamy, polygamy and polygynandry (a fast disappearing mode of marriage in which a group of brothers married a group of women, usually sisters).

7. Thus, Manu was the ancestor of the Manai, Saju the forebear of the Sajaik, and so on and so forth for each clan.
8. On the importance of the brother-sister relationship in Hinduism and of ego-generation in defining ancestry, see Jamous 1993.
9. On the status of priests in the area, see Vidal 1989.
10. According to the 1901 Census, the kingdom's population was 21,172, comprising 16 per cent Brahmins, 51 per cent Kanets, 2 per cent Rajputs, 21 per cent Kolis and others 10 per cent.
11. Local religious practices were greatly marked by Shaivism and Shaktism. The influence of Vaishnavism was limited to circles close to royalty. Perhaps the most important difference *vis-à-vis* the religious practises in the plains is the persistence of blood sacrifice and the limited influence of vegetarianism. Few Brahmins were vegetarian, with the majority readily consenting to consume those parts of sacrificial animals that were exclusively reserved for them. For an analysis of Hinduism in a neighboring kingdom, see Vidal 1986: 31–54.
12. For more details on these practices of worship, see Vidal 1987.
13. On the morning of the festival, for example, they would be served *sidku*, a sort of wheat-flour pancake laced with opium seeds, steam-cooked over a bed of leaves and then covered with ghee, or clarified butter.
14. Thus, for example, in the fact that the thigh was the only part of the body that could be aimed at, one may be tempted to see the image of a combat whose symbolism calls to mind the duel between Bhima and Duryodhana in the *Mahabharata*. Bhima, it may be recalled, shattered his adversary's thighs, in violation of the ethics that governed duels between Kshatriyas. On this, as on other questions related to the possible symbolism of these feuds, one may consult Madeleine Biardeau's interpretation (1985) of the *Mahabharata*.
15. Although these groups appear to have practiced slash-and-burn cultivation from time immemorial, the tending of sheep, which even until recently was a dominant activity among them, has begun to decline rapidly, in favor of polyculture and now horticulture.
16. The Manai are relatively few in number but are considered a prestigious clan, with a well-established reputation for their aggressiveness being in conflict with no fewer than seven of the district's fourteen Khunds.
17. Ties bred by marital alliance seem to count for little when set against solidarity with one's clan. For instance, 'If, in the course of a *paukh*, or an unexpected battle, a Khund saw his sister's son fighting a member of the clan, he paid no attention. Khunds did not spare those, like sister's children, who for instance, might be related to them' (related in an interview with a Manai, R.K. Kiri Shak, Chaupal Tahsil, 2 October 1983).
18. Children were also not spared in conflicts, 'Those days, such things

used to happen if the Khunds could not wreak vengeance. Then they would take away their enemy's wife. Such folly. If a daughter were born, they would let her live. If it was a son, he would be killed, even just a baby. They would say vengeance is complete, there is no one left in the enemy's *khandan*' (interview with a Manai, J.R.B.; Khokha, Chaupal Tehsil, 1 October 1983).

19. The combatants from either side would be undressed. Both sides would first seek the blessing of the Goddess and then make their way to a site on the outskirts of the village, where they would exchange volleys of obscene songs and improvised couplets (*lachiya*).
20. The symbolism of such a feast can be analysed at several levels. One may observe, in particular, in this context, the stress placed on the ancient association of food with sacrificial remains. See Malamoud 1989, 'Observations on the concept of "remains" in brahmanism.'
21. 'I believed and said that I would wreak vengeance on behalf of my *khandan*. What was fated to happen would happen. The day was calculated and set. When we returned with the head, a large ceremony was organized, a *havan* was performed, *halva* was passed around, shots were fired into the air, drums rolled, *Devi puja* was performed, and an oriflamme was strung over the Goddess' temple' (related in an interview with a Sajaik, A.S.S.; Devas, Chaupal Tahsil, 8 April 1980).
22 'The Goddess said to me, "Go, my brother, I am with thee." With her own hands, she placed the sacred axe in my hands and tied a string around my right arm. I drank a drop of the blood on the axe. My eyes opened then and I was free of fear, for until then we had felt we were in danger' (interview with a Sajaik, R.R.N.; Narra, Chaupal Tahsil, 8 October 1983). The impossibility of opening one's eyes after a killing unless a drop of the blood remaining on the axe had been placed to the lips, seems to have been customary as evidenced in another interview,'When the victim had been beheaded, the killer was required to drink a bit of blood. If he desisted, he would be forced to do it, for otherwise he could not open his eyes, he could see nothing and his body was paralysed.'
23. Interview with a Manai, J.R.B.; Khoka, Chaupal Tahsil, 1 October 1983.
24. Interview with a Manai, R.K.; Kiri Shak, Chaupal Tahsil, 2 October 1983.
25. When a feud was on, for instance, the pandits would specially train a man for combat (a *thuna*). Spending several days in their exclusive company, he would be subjected to a special regimen and taught special *mantras* designed to lay low members of the rival clan who would be identified by name. The *pandits* would seek advance information on the intended victims, or prepare their horoscopes, so that the *mantras* could prove truly efficacious. When the day of battle was

set, a goat would be sacrificed and the *thuna* covered with the animal's veins. The *thuna* would also bear a pot of burning charcoal on his head.

26. A woman was then required to separate the combatants by crossing the battlefield with a pitcher of water on her head, which she would place before the warriors.
27. Interview with a Sajaik, R.R.N; Narra, Chaupal Tahsil, 8 October 1983.
28. Interview with a Manai, J.R.B; Khokha, Chaupal Tahsil, 1 October 1983
29. *Dakshina* is the ceremonial offering made to Brahmins, which brings a sacrifice to an end. See Malamoud, 1989: 13–35, for an account of the decisive function of such gifts as well as for the distinction between sacrificers and officiants.
30. Interview with a Manai, J.R.B; Khokha, Chaupal Tahsil, 1 October 1983.
31. When a head is brought for immolation in the *havan*, it is called a *mundo ra havan*. 'I beheaded that man for revenge, I brought his head, it is a matter of my honour' (interview with a Sajaik, R.R.N.; Narra, Chaupal Tahsil, 8 October 1983).
32. Interview with a Manai, J.R.B.; Khokha, Chaupal Tahsil, 1 October 1983.
33. Such an identification with the protagonists of the *Mahabharata* by the clans divided into two halves that did not inter-marry is common in the region and draws from local legends recounting the war between the Sathis and the Panshis. It is interesting to note, however, that in areas where the Sathis are in a majority, they, and not the Panshis, are the ones who identify with the Pandavas.
34. It is significant, too, that the emphasis should be on Bhima seeking the Goddess' support atop Mount Kailash, and not on Arjuna turning to Krishna. The reference to Bhima is in fact natural, given the importance of his role during the Pandava brothers' wanderings in the Himalayas. On a more general plane, however, as the work of Madeleine Biardeau shows, Bhima's character as well as the dilemmas he faces are much closer to those that confront the clans involved in feuds. A single example would suffice. Seduced by Hidimba, by whom he even has a son, Bhima does not hesitate to kill her brother, a demon. It may be noted that the worship of Hidimba Devi continues to this day in the Kulu region. Needless to say, in the absence of proof, there is no question of postulating any sort of historic continuity between the world described by the *Mahabharata* and the traditions dealt with in this paper. It is no less important to note however that such a postulate is an integral part of the local traditions.
35. This observation would be valid too in the traditional definition of

'space' as wild space and inhabited space. The characteristic of feuds, from this point of view, is that they blur awareness of this duality which is so important in traditional Hinduism. This duality needs to be reconsidered from the perspective of each conflicting clan. What members of one clan look upon as 'domestic' space could well be considered 'wild' space by their counterparts in the other clan. Their presence, like that of the unavenged dead, represents a permanent threat to the integrity of what each clan looks upon as its domestic space.

36. A significant detail: it was there too that young boys were taken on pilgrimage after their heads were tonsured. On the worship of Bijet-Sri Gul and links with Yama, see Vidal 1987, Chap. XI.
37. Interview with a Manai, J.P.B.; Khokha, Chaupal Tahsil, 1 October 1983.

REFERENCES

Bayly, C.A. 1993. *Rulers, townsmen and Bazaar: North Indian Society in the Age of British Expansion. 1770–1870.* Cambridge: Cambridge University.

Biardeau, M. 1985. 'Introduction et commentaires' in *Le Mahabharata.* translated from Sanskrit by Jean Michael Péterflavi. 2 vols. Paris: Flammarion.

Dumont, L. 1966. *Homo hierarchicus. Essai sur le système des castes.* Paris: Gallimard.

Freitag, S.B. 1991. 'Crime in the Social Order of Colonial North India'. *Modern Asian Studies* 25(2): 227–61.

Haynes, E.S. 1990. 'Rajput Ceremonial Interactions as a Mirror of a Dying Indian State System, 1820–1947'. *Modern Asian Studies* 24(3): 459–92.

Jamous, R. 1993. *La relation frère-soeur. Parenté et rites chez les Meo de l'Inde du Nord.* Paris: Éd. de l'EHESS.

Kolff, D.H.A. 1990. *Naukar, Rajput and Sepoy: The Ethnohistory of the Military Labour Market in Hindustan 1450–1850.* Cambridge: Cambridge University Press.

Larivière, R.W. 1989. 'Justices and Pandits: Some Ironies in Contemporary Readings of the Hindu Legal Past'. *Journal of Asian Studies* 48(4)XI: 757–69.

Malamoud, Ch. 1989. *Cuire le monde.* Paris: La Découverte.

Parek, B. 1989. *Gandhi's Political Philosophy: A Critical Examination.* London: Macmillan.

Parmar, Y.S. 1975. *Polyandry in the Himalayas.* Delhi: Vikas Publishing House.

Vidal, D. 1986. 'Le puits et le sanctuaire: Organisation culturelle et souveraineté dans une ancienne principauté de l'Himalaya occidental'. *Purusartha* 10: *L'espace du temple II*, 31–54. Paris: Éd. de l'EHESS.

———. 1987. *Les culte des divinités locales dans une région de l'Himachal Pradesh.* Paris: ORSTOM.

———. 1989. 'Des dieux face à leurs spécialistes. Conditions de la prêtrise en Himachal Pradesh'. *Purusartha* 12: *Prêtrise, pouvoirs et autorité en Himalaya*, 61–78. Paris: Éd. de l'EHESS.

Wink, A. 1986. *Land and Sovereignty in India: Agrarian Society and Politics under the Eighteenth-Century Maratha Svarajya.* Cambridge: Cambridge University Press.

Yang, A. ed. 1985. *Crime and Criminality in British India.* Tucson: University of Arizona Press.

Community and Violence in Contemporary Punjab

VEENA DAS AND R. SINGH BAJWA

The concept of community was closely tied in the classical sociological literature, to the idea of a spatial, bound, face to face sphere of human relationships based upon an innate moral order. In response to the crisis of modernity represented as the death of God, there was a nostalgic movement in both, classical reflections on loss of community and contemporary commentaries on loss of virtue. For instance, the contrast made by Tönnies (1955) between *Gesellschaft* and *Gemeinschaft* posited community as arising out of a response to the needs of real, organic life whereas society was characterized as a form of social relationship based upon artificial and mechanical relationships of reflective will. Hence his formulation that one goes into *Gessellschaft* (society) as one goes into a strange country. In more recent studies, community has been treated as a resource for remoralizing areas of life denuded of moral meaning by the growth of a bureaucratic, impersonal rationality (see especially Habermas 1986; Unger 1975). We see two major problems in this nostalgic rendering of community. The first is that by ignoring the extent to which violence plays a role in defining community, the nostalgic view gives a rather sanitized view of community. Secondly it overlooks the fact that community in the contemporary context is defined as much by structures of modernity, including bureaucratic law as by a customary, face to face order of social relations.

In the present paper we offer two institutionalized models of violence in contemporary Punjab.[1] In the first model the symbol of martyrdom provides the moral basis for defining the larger Sikh community by establishing a consubstantiation between the violence of sacrifice and the moral community of Sikhs. The second model of violence is based on the negative reciprocity of feud and vendetta[2] through which the specific identity of Jat Sikhs is established within the larger community of Sikhs. For the moment we reserve the question of whether such negative reciprocity can provide the basis for defining a moral community. Finally, in order to avoid the common misunderstanding that community formations occur independently of modern structures of power and governance, we show how the symbols of martyrdom and vengeance are transformed within these structures. Thus martyrdom is used as a symbol to construct Sikh identity in the modern militant movement against the state in India while processes of vengeance become incorporated into the legal discourse on criminality.

Our data consist of three parts. The first is the oral and written discourse of the militant movement in Punjab in which special attention has been paid to the magazines brought out by various militant groups and the oral discourses of the militant leader, Bhindranwale who is revered as a *sant* (saint) by many Sikhs. The second part consists of narrative accounts of on-going feuds within the Jat Sikh community given by participants, eye witnesses of violent encounters and many others who claimed to have special knowledge on several such encounters. The accounts have been collected from the three major areas of Majha, Doab and Malwa regions. Finally we have been fortunate in getting access to lawyer's briefs pertaining to sixty cases of Jat Sikh feuds that have come up in the Sessions Courts of Patiala, Jallandhar, and Amritsar. In some cases, appeals have been made in the High Court of Punjab, and one case is pending in the Supreme Court. The period covered is 1950 to 1987. We are aware of the dangers of using such a heterogeneous set of data, but the nature of the subject rules out the methods of normal anthropological enquiry such as participant observation in either the militant movement or in feuds.

Martyrdom and Feud: The Conceptual Models

We first attempt to construct ideal typical models of martyrdom and feud in terms of a binary opposition which is not sustained in the analysis of the empirical cases, but is 'good to think' with. We present the features of the two discourses in a highly stylized way before showing their modification and mutual contamination in the development of actual cases.

DISCOURSE OF THE MARTYR	DISCOURSE OF FEUD/VENDETTA
(a) creates a unique individual:	(a) splits the community into conflicting formations;
(b) relates the community to the 'other' defined by its oppressive control over the community;	(b) the 'other' is constituted within the community;

(c) violence is turned against the self—the model is self-sacrifice;	(c) violence is ambiguous—lying between the self/other and proclaimed/secret categories;
(d) community is united through the creation of a common narrative of sacrifice;	(d) violence is remembered only through the composition of personal voice;
(e) martyr is commemorated in collective memory.	(e) there are no agreed collective narratives or forms of commemoration.

In the modern militant literature of the Sikhs, martyrdom as a symbol has a special place in the construction of the past. The execution of Guru Teg Bahadur, the defiant 'Epistle of Victory' (*Zafarnama*) addressed to Emperor Aurengzeb by Guru Gobind Singh at the moment when he had lost all including his four sons, the willing submission of Banda Bahadur to torture and his execution, provide root metaphors for Sikh history through which the idea of the self is constructed.[3] The transformation of these root metaphors in contemporary political writing may be seen in the organization of images in which Sikh identity is constructed primarily through the metaphor of martyrdom. The self of the Sikh as it emerges is that of a martyr whose sacrifices have fed the community. Indeed, even when there is a difference of emphasis, an important image in all the texts of modern Sikh militants is that of *charkhi chadna* and *khopdi utarvana*—i.e. being slowly ground to death over a churning wheel or offering one's head at the stake. These are punishments that the defiant Sikhs are said to have received at the hands of several Mughal emperors because of the insistence of the Sikhs to protest against injustice. Consider the following example in which the construction of the self and the construction of the past appear as conjoint themes.

> History has always been repeating itself. Sikh people passed through a critical phase after the death of Banda Bahadur Gurbaksh Singh in 1716, that some historians called it the darkest period of Sikh history [. . .] time again took a new turn with the martyrdom of Bhai Man Singh in 1734 A.D. [. . .] In this way began once again the era of struggle for the Sikhs that subsequently was converted into the golden age of the Sikhs. Which sacrifice is there is the history of the world that Sikhs had not to pay for this conversion? A terribly dark route from the teeth of 'Charhi' to the edge of the sword was traversed. Every inch of the land where we today have assembled was covered by the precious blood of the Khalsa, then and then only could we harness the days when Kashmir, Jamraud, and Ladakh bowed before the Kesri Nisan Sahib and Nanak-Shahi coins could replace the Muslim one's [*sic*].[4]

Thus the image of the community as one created through heroic sacrifice pervades this discourse and threats to the solidarity of the community are also translated into threats to its heroic image as in the following passage.

> . . . the Sikhs have been softened and conditioned during the last fifty years to bear and put up with insults to their religion and all forms of other oppression, patiently and without demur, under the sinister preaching and spell of the narcotic cult of non-violence, much against the clear directive of their gurus their Prophets, not to turn the other cheek before a tyrant, not to take lying down any insult to their religion, their self-respect, and their human dignity.[5]

The defining feature of the discourse of the martyr is that sacrifice is undertaken on behalf of the community. Just as it was said about Banda Bahadur that he was a shy and retiring man, who was compelled into a heroic stance because of the threat to the Sikh community, so it is said about Bhindranwale that he was a religious man who would have liked to have spent his life in quiet meditation if he had not been compelled by the danger to the Sikh identity in modern India to take to political action (*siyasi masle*).

What is the threat to the community that is sought to be averted by the sacrifice offered by the martyr? The first threat is the reduction of life to the sphere of the personal to the exclusion of the political. The paradigmatic text in this context is the *Zafarnama*, the 'Epistle of Victory' addressed to Emperor Aurengzeb by Guru Gobind Singh. According to one interpretation, what Aurengzeb offered to the Guru was a life of peace in return for his silence on the oppression unleashed by the Emperor. As one contributor to the militant discourse told us,

> There was one moment in history when either a revolution could occur or society could continue on the same path. When the Guru addressed the Epistle of Victory at the moment of defeat, he showed the Emperor that the Sikhs were not willing to reduce their life and their faith to tilling their lands and breeding children. At that moment he established a right over the public sphere and the subsequent sacrifices of the Sikhs have been about reclaiming that right.

The sacrifice of the martyr, then, has to be public, spectacular, undertaken on behalf of the community, but also unique because it is undertaken with the specific understanding that the martyr invites violence upon himself. By virtue of this invitation, he forbids a return in the same coin; there is no vengeance because the violence should not be allowed to degenerate into the violence of the feud. It is the stoic acceptance of pain that makes the martyr's blood feed that of the community.

In the narratives woven around the life and death of Bhindranwale, these motifs are repeatedly used. For example, when he was arrested following charges of murder of a prominent journalist against him, his arrest was represented as something that he 'voluntarily gave'. In a speech given just before his imminent arrest, Bhindranwale urged his followers to remain peaceful. 'Every stone thrown at a policeman, every abuse hurled at those who have come to arrest me, will be like a stone thrown at my body, an abuse hurled against me.' In this motif, we can see that the martyr presents his body that can absorb the violence of the oppressor without allowing it become generalized violence in the community. In this sense, the insight provided by the work of Girard (1972) that sacrifice is a means by which violence may be transformed into community is substantiated by the narrative organization of images here. This is not to say that either Bhindranwale or the other writers in the militant magazines are consistent in inviting violence only upon themselves, for as one of us has argued elsewhere, the discourse also directs violence against others. However the exhortations to kill others are always couched in ambiguity, whereas the image of the martyr does not evoke any ambivalence about the morality of the action.

In view of the fact that Sikh history is presented in terms of a series of repetitions in which a community that is at the point of disintegration is recreated through the blood of the martyr, what does one mean when one says that the martyr is unique? This may be understood in two related senses. First, in the case of the feud, violence undertaken by a person may be avenged by the victim or someone acting on behalf of the victim by killing a substitute. In the case of the martyr, the question of substitution does not arise because his sacrifice is unique. Second, martyrdom does not allow the martyr to claim the status of a Guru. In fact every sacrifice is a way of relating to the Guru—the Sikh (lit. 'disciple') 'buys' his Guru by his sacrifice and conversely a martyr undertaking a sacrificial death on behalf of the community is protected by the Guru, which is why he is unaffected by torture and fear of death. It is interesting that the discourse of martyrdom is haunted by the fleeting possibility that it may become converted into the discourse of feud. For example, although Bhindranwale never claimed that he was a *sant*—indeed, such honour can be bestowed only by others on a person—his claims to sainthood were dependent upon the capacity of the community to create a shared narrative about his activities. Such a shared narrative could not be created because there were always doubts whether he was acting on behalf of the community or on the behest of some factional leaders of the Congress party. Further, his manner of dying was not considered by many to be the manner in which a martyr seeks death. Bhindranwale was killed during the Blue Star Operation against militants hidden in the Golden Temple undertaken by the Indian Army in 1984.[6] This operation itself produced contesting claims on the meaning of sacred spaces. For the militants, the Golden Temple was claimed as a sanctuary from which they could legitimately wage a violent conflict against the state. For the state on the other hand, the stockpiling of weapons in the temple was a desecration of the sacred space and a misuse of the *gurdwara*. Whatever the claims and the counterclaims, there is little doubt that the action of the military resulted in death, destruction, and hardship for many innocent pilgrims who were caught between the two opposing forces.

Let us, however, return to the question of the disputes over the manner of dying of Bhindranwale. For some time the militants claimed that he had not been killed but had escaped and would come back to lead the Sikh masses. They claimed that the government of India was engaged in false propaganda when they claimed that Bhindranwale had been killed while hiding in the temple. This is not how a martyr would have courted death, it was claimed. A martyr seeks death with the same passion and ardor as if it were his beautiful bride. A martyr is never 'killed'—he surrenders to death as one would surrender to a lover. However, since no public accounts of such courting of death on the part of Bhindranwale could be sustained, his death could not be put in the genealogy of heroic deaths. For a time it seemed that Bhindranwale would be consecrated as a saint by the evolution of a shared narrative about his heroic life and death—but in the end, the discourse of feud claimed him.

The Feud in the Jat Sikh Community

The anthropological literature has long recognized that the institution of feud is intimately related to conceptions of social order. In the classic monographs of Evans-Pritchard on the Nuer, feud was recognized as an expression of the social order. The typical genealogical map for the stylized representation of feud in his work is one in which men are represented through patrilineal connections. According to the influential segmentary theory developed by him, the genealogical map provides a paradigm of political alliances. The typical feature of this genealogical map is that each man is shown to have *two* sons thus providing the nucleus of two groups of equal size, pitted against each other. The institution of feud provides an opportunity for the dramatic expression of lineage solidarity at every level of the social structure, the typical division of the tribe being the division into maximal, major, minor and minimal lineages.

This mechanical model of segmentation assumes that relations between men can only be conceived through the exercice of paternal authority and filial unity. In a remarkable critique of this model, Meeker (1979) argues that the major failure of such mechanical models of segmentation lies in the fact that they cannot tell us how men's desires are implicated in their genealogies. As an alternate he suggests that, 'The near-Eastern tribal genealogy can be plausibly viewed as the product of men who define themselves as a society of men struggling with one another, a society in which men do not come together to live in peace, but come apart to live by war.'

In the case of the Jat Sikhs, violence and conflict mark the relationships within the *biradari*. The conflicts are mostly over land although as we shall see later, they can also grow out of rivalries over women and can gather in themselves other issues such as betrayals in courts of law, or sharing of spoils in the political arena. However, what is clear is that they do not follow any pattern of genealogical nearness or distance. Of the 75 cases of homicide on which we were able to get detailed data, 38 were cases pertaining to the Jat Sikhs, while the rest of the 37 cases were distributed among other castes such as the Majhabi Sikhs, Adharmis, Ramgariahs, Brahmins, and various service castes. Of the 38 cases 30 involved disputes over land. No clear genealogical pattern emerges in the formation of solidarities and conflicts so that contending parties in the dispute could be patrilateral parallel cousins, one set of brothers against another, a set of brothers against the father, one set of brothers along with the father against another set of brothers. In addition, as disputes unfold over time, new alliances are made so that genealogy alone cannot provide a map of political alliances. *It is our main contention that whereas a genealogical representation of alliances in a feud presumes a degree of descriptive certainty, in fact it is essential that we understand the uncertainty of relationships within the* biradari *and even within the family to understand the nature of vendetta among the Jat Sikhs.*

It may be useful at this point to consider the model of feud and vendetta (as distinct from the model of the martyr) in schematic form to show how differently are these notions structured among the Jat Sikhs.

1. There is no mediation of gods, goddesses, or gurus in the case of vendetta. This mediation is only reserved for the discourse of the martyr. As we showed earlier, several stories about the martyrdom of Sikh heroes dwell upon the torture and slow killing to which they may have been subjected. The narrator, however, always adds a framing sentence to the effect that because of the mediation and protection of the Guru, the pain and suffering were not felt by the martyr. In all the narratives of vendetta that we have collected, any reference to the mediation of exalted beings is absent. This shows that the violence of vendetta cannot be seen as consecrated by the sacred.
2. Genealogy does not provide a map for political alliances. Relations are so uncertain that any combination is possible. This uncertainty attaches itself to the domain of property of which land is the most important signifier, and to the domain of sexuality of which women are the most important signifiers.
3. The possibility of a feud exists when a line, however jagged, can be drawn within the *biradari*.
4. In accordance with the uncertainty of relations to which we alluded earlier, genealogy is never sufficient for political alliances in vendetta. This requires a further contractual relation which has a ritual character. Relations of alliance for purposes of securing vendetta may be secured by taking of vows (e.g. we shall remain friends, *yar*, till our dying breath) or by exchange and mixing of blood.
5. Vendetta is seen as punishment meted to someone who has broken a relatoinship of solidarity by betrayal. This is why vendetta cannot occur between strangers. The symbolic marker that signifies vendetta is a speech form known as *lalkara*. Typically the victim is ambushed or lured into a situation from which he cannot escape. But at the moment of his death, he must know that this death is in the form of an execution. Thus, if he is asleep he must be woken up. If it is dark he must know who his executors are. In addition he must hear the *lalkara* that takes a form such as this: *adalat wich jhuthi gavahi den da maja chakh* ('enjoy the fruit of having given false witness in the court').

We shall demonstrate the above points by one case study. But let us first attempt a definition of community as it is defined through vendetta.

The contrast between the notion of community created through sharing with community created through exchange lies at the heart of many anthropological distinctions, the most prominent of which is the community of descent and the community created through alliance. In his classic study, Lévi-Strauss (1967) shows that it is only through restricted or generalized exchange that a global (in the sense of total) structure of exchange can be built which has at its basis the moral community of men created through exchange of women. However, even in this form of community Lévi-Strauss notices the possibilities of rupture and the ambivalence around exchange as it is expressed through protracted marriage negotiations: female poetry, as well as the tendency to deal with the 'risks' of exchange through curtailing the long cycles of exchange into short cycles. Thus human desire intervenes; it sometimes impels human beings to recognize the limits of their moral communities which are created through laws of exchange by presenting the possibility of evading these laws—at other times '. . . the prohibited marriage appears in spectral form: it gnaws at the social conscience with a kind of nostalgia and remorse' (Lévi-Strauss 1967).

Thus darker passions which underlie all socially approved forms of exchange are recognized by Lévi-Strauss but are banished from his theory of exchange. We suggest that in the case of feud and vendetta we are witnessing this underside of exchange, its shadowy existence to which substance is given through a recognition of the darker passions of man. If rules of marriage exchange give a cultural structure to desire as it is consecrated by society, rules of vendetta give form to desires that are not consecrated by society but are nevertheless recognized. These, then, may be considered as providing rules of disorder. Thus at one level we can compare the creation of community through rules of exchange expressed in marriage and gift-giving (as has been done by Lévi-Strauss and Dumont), with the creation of community through rules of exchange relating to vendetta. Both types of rules split the society by instituting difference and then unite it by exchange. This level is to be opposed to another level at which a different definition of community comes into being through the discourse of the martyr which institutes the *oneness* of community. This non-differentiated unity is expressed in the uniqueness of the martyr, the destruction of resemblance, the intervention of the divine, and through commemoration of the sacrifice of the martyr in public memory.

The violence of vendetta is always viewed with an ambivalence, that is completely absent in the discourse of the martyr. Thus community is not only created through laws and desires that society consecrates but also has a dark side corresponding to the darker passions. This is seen in all narratives that describe the origins of a vendetta. Typically such descriptions make reference to the darker passions. 'His behavior made bitter anger arise within me'; 'The woman saw Amar Singh for the first time and was infatuated. This gave rise to vendetta among the cousins'; 'His neighbor would pass over his fields everyday, knowing he had no right of passage. Smouldering anger arose within him at this slight.'

The recognition that community has a dark underside reflected in rules of vendetta is shown by the fact that such feelings of envy, anger, bitterness and hate are not treated only as individual disorders but as passions, the pursuit of which defines relations between men and values of masculinity among the Jat Sikhs. What then differentiates this form of violence from purely individual instances of violence is the fact that there are well understood rules by which darker passions may be pursued through vendetta which are absent in the case of individual transgressions. For instance, a woman killing another woman in a fit of passion would be treated by the Jat Sikhs as having committed an individual transgression. Her violence could not be made the origin of an ongoing vendetta. In contrast, one may vow to avenge the death of a brother or a friend if they form an alliance against another feuding party.

An Example

This is a case study of a feud which had its origin in 1952 and found its most dramatic expression in 1975 when 22 people were shot dead in the Sessions Court at Jallandhar. We first relate the story as it was told by a friend of one of the principal accused.[7]

It all started in 1952 or 53 over a woman called Joginder Kaur who lived in a moffusil town called Nakodar. She was of incomparable beauty. She was married to Mihan Singh and till then they had lived a happy married life. One day two brothers, Amar Singh and Pyara Singh, who were *biradari* relatives of Mihan Singh came to the village. They happened to meet Joginder Kaur in a relative's house. Joginder Kaur was infatuated by Amar Singh. They met several times and Amar Singh confided his relationship with this woman to his younger brother Pyara Singh. Together they persuaded her to elope with them. They fled to a village away from Punjab, in Pilbhit district, where one of their relatives Umrao Singh had a farm. Mihan Singh, the husband of the woman filed a complaint at the Police Station. After some time, the police were able to trace them to this village in Pilbhit and Umrao Singh, Amar Singh and Pyara Singh were arrested. However, Joginder Kaur made a statement in court that she had gone with Pyara Singh[8] of her own will and that she was married to him.

Mihan Singh had come with many of his relatives to the court ready for a fight. He and his relatives were so humiliated by this public confession of Joginder Kaur that they wanted to kill her along with her lovers right outside the court, but relatives of Amar Singh, Umrao Singh and Joginder Kaur had come prepared for precisely such an encounter. When Mihan Singh saw that they were outnumbered by the other side (*ona da pasa bhari si*), he withdrew swearing vengeance.

That night Amar Singh and Pyara Singh went to have drinks with a friend Charan Singh who was a Nambardar of Nurpur village, and his brother Swaran Singh. A distant cousin of Charan Singh, called Darshan Singh, shot him dead when they were all drunk pretending that he had really wanted to shoot Amar Singh because of an altercation over Joginder Kaur. Darshan Singh was arrested. Pyara Singh was to give witness against Darshan Singh but he took a bribe from Darshan Singh's 'party' and rescinded his earlier statement. Now Swaran Singh swore to take revenge for his brother's death. So the feud now shifted between Amar, Pyara, and Darshan against Swaran Singh and his party.

Swaran Singh had to lie low for several years. In 1960 he came in touch with Udai Singh who had made quite a name for himself as a hired killer. The two men struck a great friendship. Now Swaran Singh, Udai Singh and another cousin Harbhajan Singh disguised themselves as hired labourers and were able to shoot Pyara Singh dead. They were arrested but were acquitted for lack of witnesses.It now fell on Amar Singh to avenge the death of his brother Pyara Singh from his enemies, Swaran Singh, Harbhajan Singh, and Udai Singh.

In 1964 or so, another incident happened.One of the *biradari* called 'Maikian' came to visit people in Amar Singh's village. As they were leaving, their relatives along with Amar Singh and some others came to the borders of the village to see them off. However, one of Amar Singh's enemies had made contact with them and persuaded a member of their clan to take this opportunity and kill him. This man suddenly shot at Amar Singh but even as he was falling, Amar Singh shot him dead. Amar Singh was injured but he recovered. He was also acquitted in the court on the charge of murder as he was supposed to have fired in self-defence.

In 1966, Amar Singh made another attempt to take revenge against Swaran Singh and his party. Amar Singh and his friends went disguised as policemen to Rusulpur village and enacted the whole drama (*pura drama keeta*) of a police raid. They arrested Swaran Singh and his two brothers and as they were bringing them to the outskirts of the village to shoot him, he recognized one Sadhu Singh who was accompanying Amar Singh and cried out that it was an ambush. Amar Singh and his friends shot dead the three brothers. They were arrested but were acquitted again. Meanwhile Harbhajan Singh and a friend called Bau who had been arrested on another murder charge, were also acquitted and they took on the responsibility of avenging the death of Swaran Singh and his brothers.

In 1970 a marriage took place in which Amar Singh was a guest. Harbhajan Singh and Bhaji, along with their friends disguised themselves as military men and positioned themselves in the way in order to ambush and kill Amar Singh. Bhaji threw grenades at their party and Amar Singh and his five supporters were killed. Amar Singh had also made friends with a notorious criminal and smuggler, Mohinder Singh Azad, who in revenge killed a man called Mota Mikka (*motta* meaning 'fat', is the nickname) of Harbhajan's group. Harbhajan made an oath, 'If I survive, I will avenge this killing', Harbhajan was arrested and tried for the five murders and was sentenced to life imprisonment. His other friends were declared absconding. In 1975 he requested the court to be allowed to go and attend the marriage of his brother. His enemies Mohinder Singh Azad and five others came to know that Harbhajan would be present in court for the hearing of his petition. So, disguised as *ragis* (musicians) they took position in a hotel room near the court. When Harbhajan Singh, with his brother, sister's husband and some friends, who had come to see him, was waiting in the courtyard of the *Kachari*, they shot and killed six people and six others were injured.

In the attempt to capture them, the police shot and killed Mohinder Singh Azad and Bissa, one of his associates. Mita, Chindda, and Surinder Singh, the other associates were arrested and given life imprisonment. This was reduced in the High Court and they came out of jail in 1983. Mita and Chindda took shelter into the Golden Temple and joined Bhindranwale's fold. Chindda was butchered by Bhindranwale's men in May 1984, for having killed Surinder Singh Sodhi who was also involved in all this and had become a trusted confidant of Bhindranwale. Mita decided to live a peaceful life and married Joginder Kaur whose elopement with Amar Singh and Pyara Singh gave birth to this whole feud.

As this narrative reveals itself, we are struck by the uncertainty which prevails in all relationships. Mihan Singh loses his wife Joginder Kaur to two of his *biradari* relatives. The woman is mentioned as the first cause of the enmity but we notice that while she may have provided for the solidarity of the two brothers for she is supposed to have been infatuated by both, her husband cannot muster the resources to pursue vendetta against them. Soon the narrative shifts in emphasis and vendetta due to betrayals among men becomes the focus of the story. Cousins betraying each other; friends rescinding in court; and an ever changing composition in which hired assassins, factions against the state level as well as involvement of different sets of relatives make it possible for the story of vendetta to be pursued. In order to appreciate how contingent are the events and relationships through which the story of vendetta is pursued, we simply give below the bare bones of the narrative in sequential terms:

1952/53 A woman's infatuation creates a line of conflict within the *biradari*. An alliance between Amar Singh, Pyara Singh and Umrao Singh defeats the husband and his close relatives through show of force in the court of law.

1953 Pyara Singh gets entangled through pure contingency of having been present in a violent encounter between two cousins—Darshan Singh and Charan Singh. He gives false witness leading to feud between Amar Singh, Pyara Singh, and Darshan Singh—the assassin, on one side—and Swaran Singh—the brother of the slain man, on the other.

1960 Swaran Singh recruits and befriends hired assassin Udai Singh and is also joined by a cousin, Harbhajan Singh, through ties of friendship. Swaran Singh, Udai Singh, and Harbhajan Singh shoot Pyara Singh dead. Amar Singh vows vengeance.

1966 Amar Singh shoots dead Swaran Singh and two of his surviving brothers (the narrative does not mention their active participation in the feud). Harbhajan Singh swears to avenge the death of his friend. He recruits five others. Amar Singh makes friends with a notorious smuggler Mohinder Singh Azad.

1970 In an encounter between the two groups, Harbhajan Singh kills Amar Singh but his associate Mikka Mota is killed by Amar Singh's friend Mohinder Singh Azad.

1975 Harbhajan Singh is arrested but on one occasion when he is out on parole for the day, he is attacked and killed by Mohinder Singh and his associates. In the chase police kill Mohinder Singh and one of his associates, Bissa. Two others—Mita and Chindda—are arrested.

1983 On being released, Chindda and Mita take refuge with Bhindranwale. Chindda is killed in an act of vengeance within the disputing groups of the militants.

Mita decides to live a peaceful life and marries Joginder Kaur who makes an appearance in the narrative only at the beginning and the end.

IN THE COURT OF LAW

We shall now try to see how this narrative is transformed in the context of the court case. We are going to limit ourselves to the judgement in the High Court arising out of the appeal against the judgement of the

Sessions Court in the case of the Jallandhar murders in which Harbhajan was butchered. Although as it is clear from the narrative, that the feud is interspersed with several murders, court cases and criminal trials, we cannot go into all of these here.

The Legal Narrative

In any legal narrative we would find contested versions about the events under legal scrutiny. We give first, the master summary of the case as it appears in the High Court judgement in which appeal was made against the order of Sh. Prithipal Singh Grewal, Addl. Sessions Judge on 24 May 1978 convicting the eight appellants with punishments ranging from seven years to life imprisonment. There was also an appeal made by Surinder Singh who was convicted and awarded death sentence. The summary of the case as pronounced by the judge is as follows.[9]

This appeal arises out of a case in which 6 men lost their lives and 6 men were injured in the courtyard of Sessions Court in Jullundher when they were waiting with the accused Harbhajan Singh who was charged with the murder of Amar Singh 22 men were said to have been responsible for the occurrence. 16 accused persons were prosecuted together. 4 of the accused were acuitted. Mohinder Singh Azad was killed in a police encounter while the case was going on 15 or 16th January. One of the accused Gajjan Singh turned approver and is now being separately prosecuted. 4 of the accused are absconding.

The background of the case is said to be an old enmity extending to 22 years. Murder of 12 persons had already taken place. 2 persons (a father and a son) were killed on May 25, 1978. Five persons concerned in the present case were being prosecuted in earlier cases. They were absconding. Harbhajan Singh was helping the police in pursuing them but was himself placed under arrest for reasons of security.

The Sessions Court had awarded imprisonment from 7 years of life imprisonment on the testimony of Jaswant Singh, brother of Harbhajan Singh who was himself injured and who was supported by Charan Singh. The court examined the testimony of Preetam Singh who was in charge of Police Post No. 4 and who is supposed to have found Jaswant Singh as he was going in an injured state to the police post. The court found this testimony to be suspect because although the incident occurred at 11 in the morning, the FIR was only filed at 7 in the evening. Thus the testimony regarding time of recording of FIR is considered unreliable and it seems likely that the FIR was dictated by the police. The car plate No. in which the assailants were escaping was identified by Jaswant Singh. It is improbable that in an injured state Jaswant Singh would have been able to read and remember precisely the car plate No. The suspicion is therefore strengthened that the FIR was recorded later and information about the car was supplied to the police after they had found the abandoned car in which the assailants had escaped.

About the major assailants, Malkiat Singh and Surinder Singh who were supposed to have first fired and killed Harbhajan Singh, and who were absconding, the court felt that their behavior strengthened the case against them. The case against the other appellants was that they fired from outside the court walls in order to help the five major assailants to escape. This firing resulted in injuries and death of a constable and a hawker. These appellants were supposed to have helped the two major accused because of the old enmity over women and because of their involvement in smuggling. The court rejected these motives and stated that if the motives were ascribed collectively then the *guilt of each particular appellant became difficult to establish.*

This reasoning of the court was further strengthened because the corroborative evidence of Charan Singh could not be trusted as he had been convicted of several excise offenses and therefore it would be easy for the police to influence him in giving collaborative evidence. Gajjan Singh who had turned approver was not brought as witness because he was not willing to support the prosecution. Finally the police had been unable to supply the various pertinent documents including the *roznamchah*.

The court's conclusion was that 'Taking advantage of a heinous occurrence which had taken place, the police wanted to collect together as many dangerous persons as possible for being prosecuted in this case.' Thus while the court acquitted the 8 persons who had appealed, it reduced the death sentence against Surinder Singh on the ground that the FIR as well as the evidence of the police personnel was perjured and it was not possible to prove as to whose act was responsible for which murder.

Discussion

In the modern legal system, vendetta becomes transformed into crime. However, the nature of this transformation is not very clear for one could also say that from another perspective it is the procedures of the court and the investigative procedures which become part of the uncertainty of relations which are the mark of the culture of vendetta.

First of all, courts introduce a new arena of uncertainty simply because the normal assumption that the court proceedings take place in the natural language of the people is not valid here. Two kinds of transformations at the level of language take place in the court and even before that in the investigative proceedings. The first transformation relates to the oral discourse being converted into a written one. The judge in the High Court was certain that the FIR had been dictated because of the timing and the manner in which details had been specified. But in fact it is common practice in the police station that the FIR must follow a format dictated by the presiding police officer. In almost very FIR that we have examined that reports a murder, there is a formulaic beginning: 'We were coming to you to report this murder when we saw a police patrol quite near the place of murder and we reported it.' Thus the FIR filed by Harbhajan's brother that said that the police man had found him injured and bandaged and willing to give a statement as eye witness of the murder was contrived; but this formulaic rendering is simply part of the linguistic culture of police conventions at the local level of the *thana*.

Secondly, in the transformation of their narrative, the people filing FIRs, have to rely upon the recording of someone in the police station. This fact can be used by the police to record things which the witness may not have stated or it may be a tool in the hands of the person appearing in court to deny earlier statements. In the Sessions Court, Jaspal Singh who was the eye witness and had initially given the whole history of the feud, completely denied his statements. For instance, he stated, 'I did not say in my statement that Tejpal Singh, Mohan Singh, Monni and others were part of the gang of Amar Singh and Pyara Singh.' When confronted with his earlier statement, he said that it is so recorded but 'I did not say it.'

Thirdly, the relation between a person and his speech in a court of law becomes a mediated relationship because of nature of language as well as canons of evidence. In the legal process it is often assumed that the canonic level of the law (here rules of evidence) assume the referential level. However, I would submit that the referential level is itself created by the canon of the law. Thus in describing events, people would often assume both in the *thana* and in the court that the validity of the statements would be judged by some judicial canons and then tailor their description accordingly. Thus one person describing a murder may say that a particular person inflicted a wound about six inches below the neck. Even if such a description is true, it is not often the language of everyday life. Now what has happened in this description is that the eye witness who has probably been involved in several such cases, imagines what the post-mortem report would say and produces evidence in accordance with that canon. Again a court may find, as the High Court did, that the very precision is suspect since a person witnessing a gruesome murder may not be able to remember the precise location of a wound in terms of inches. Thus nature of memory in the judicial process is quite different from the social context.

In establishing the legal person in criminal proceedings then, the person is not only a cognitive and a moral person, but also one who is constructed by the court as a manipulator of the legal process. This is most evident in the strictures that are often passed at the High Court level upon the investigative agencies. For instance, perjuring the FIR or violating police procedure by not keeping the *roznamchah* is often grounds for reducing the sentence of someone facing trial or acquitting him. In fact, from our evidence those who take part in the culture of vendetta have assimilated court procedure into their own culture. This is why acquittal of people known to be involved in murders are frequent even when there have been eye witnesses. And as we saw, giving false evidence in court has become a major part of the vendetta culture.

For those cases which come up to the High Court, the interest of the trial is that it often shows the agencies of the case themselves involved at some level in this culture of vendetta. In the case of Gajjan Singh, the police had taken the case as convenient for implicating all those who were involved either in the feud or were otherwise eluding the police net. Hence although only six people were named in the first information report, the inspector had persuaded other witnesses to name other people. One witness, the court found, had acted as police witness in 200 excise cases. Similarly evidence was procured from one person by turning him into approver.

It is also interesting to note that while the Sessions Judge was willing to accept enmity as motive for the murders, the High Court found it insufficient motive to fix individual guilt.

From the perspective of the participants in vendetta—men whose lives seem to be defined by the singular search for avenging the murders and betrayals through which the uncertainty of relationships reveals itself—the court becomes a further arena in which the vendetta may be pursued. It is a symbol both of an institution run by rules but one whose 'enunciative powers' can be used by the forces of the community in accordance with its own rules of disorder. In the transformation from *vouloir* to *savoir* to *pouvoir* that Greimas (1976) saw as essential to the legal discourse as a semiotic discourse, the court and the police reveal a series of rules through which illegalities must be pursued. Here, ironically, is an instance in which community integrates the legal culture in its own culture of uncertainty and disorder.

Concluding Comments

We have described two opposing ways of constructing the community through violence. The discourse of the martyr by attracting violence upon itself, provides a means of transforming violence into community. In the modern extremist discourse, we have shown how such a discourse provides a way of organizing memory and thus using the concept of the community as a resource to challenge the ideological hegemony of the state. The simultaneous existence of the discourse of vendetta, on the other hand, constructs community through the dark underside of exchange—recognizing and giving form to the darker passions of man which are also implicated in the creation of community. These forms of community also touch the institutions of the state and give it a character as in the case of legal institutions. Thus rather than opposing community and society as two different modes of constructing experience, we have tried to show the plurality in the definition of community itself and located the different points in which it shapes and is, in turn, shaped by the institutions of the state in contemporary Punjabi society.

NOTES

1. We take this opportunity to express our deep gratitude to all those people who were willing to share their knowledge and experience with us. We are deeply conscious of the risks that many people have taken in making this work possible. We especially remember the stimulating discussions with our friend, Sheetal Das, a policeman of fierce integrity who was tragically shot dead. In the course of this work we encountered world views that were far removed from our rather banal lives and we never ceased to be amazed by the humour with which such differences were negotiated. A fellowship at the Center for the Study of Developing Societies, Delhi, enabled the author, Dr. R.S. Bajwa, to take study leave for six months for which we are both grateful.

2. Some authors have suggested that the term feud should be used when violence is organized according to some structural patterns and vendetta when the motives for revenge are purely personal. We find it difficult to make such a neat distinction since structure and personal choice seem to be woven together in defining these forms of violence among the Jat Sikhs in Punjab.
3. For an account of these sacrifices and the discrepancies between Muslim and Sikh sources on the nature of these accounts, see Singh (1963).
4. 'Message to the Delegates of the 1st annual Dal Khalsa Conference', held at Gurdaspur on 8–9 December 1979, by S. Gajinder Singh, Panch Dal Khalsa.
5. See *They Massacre Sikhs*, A white Paper by Sikh Religious Parliament (Shiromani Gurudwara Prabandhak Committee), Amritsar, date not given.
6. The absence of an agreed narrative on the Blue Star Operation makes it very difficult to find a way of writing about it. The Indian state claimed that the operation against terrorists became necessary because they were using the Golden Temple as a sanctuary to escape from due processes of law and for perpetrating violence against innocent citizens. It is claimed in the militant literature that this operation was undertaken to humiliate the Sikhs by attacking and desecrating their most sacred spaces. Most Sikhs construed this as an attack on their community. While it was true that the Golden Temple was used as a sanctuary by the terrorists and even ordinary criminals, it was also true that many innocent pilgrims were injured, killed, or arrested during this operation.
7. There are other versions of the feud that we have collected, but we will not consider them in this paper in order to avoid unbearable complexities. However, we would like to note that in our interview with Joginder Kaur, she emphasized the 'honourable' ways of pursuing violence and contrasted it with the unprincipled violence of the terrorists. There was also greater place for her own active role in luring enemies to places where they could be killed by men, but like the men she also defined herself as people 'whose lives were lived in violence (*maran kattan vale log*)'.
8. In the narrative a clear distinction is never made between the brothers as both of them were assumed to be her lovers. We should not therefore look for an individualized relation here.
9. Names of persons as they appear in the narrative of the informants and as they appear in the summary by the judge do not always correspond, because the police tried to implicate many other notorious characters in the case.

REFERENCES

Dumont, L. (1966), *Homo Hierarchicus. Essai sur le système des castes.* Paris: Gallimard.

Evans-Pritchard, E.E. (1968), *Les Nuer. Description des modes de vie et des institutions politiques d'un peuple nilote.* Paris: Gallimard (1st edn. 1937).

Girard, R. (1972), *La violence et le sacré*. Paris: Grasset ('Pluriel').

Greimas, A.J. and E. Landowski (1976), 'Analyse scientifique d'un discours juridique', in A.J. Greimas, ed., *Sémiotique et sciences sociales.* Paris: Seuil.

Habermas, J. (1986), 'Civil disobedience: Litmus Test for the Democratic Constitutional State', *Journal of Sociology*, XXVI.

Lévi-Strauss, C. (1967), *Les structures élémentaires de la parenté*, Paris-La Haye: Mouton.

Meeker, M.J. (1979), *Literature and Violence in North Arabia.* Cambridge, Cambridge University Press ('Cambridge Studies in Cultural System' 3).

Singh, K. (1963), *History of the Sikhs.* Princeton, NJ: Princeton University Press, 2 vols.

Tönnies, F. (1955), *Community and Association.* Transl. by Ch. P. Loomis, London: Routledge and Kegan Paul.

Unger, R.M. (1975), *Knowledge and Politics.* New York: The Free Press.

Opposing Gandhi: Hindu Nationalism and Political Violence

CHRISTOPHE JAFFRELOT

In his remarkable article on the killing of Gandhi, Ashis Nandy explains the act of Nathuram Godse by resorting to a rich assortment of factors. He first lays stress on the animosity that the Mahatma aroused amongst the conservative and declining elite by bringing the masses into the political arena, and then goes on to underscore the incompatibility between the Gandhian emphasis on feminine values and the martial ethos of Godse's social milieu in Maharashtra: 'To the extent Gandhi rejected the Kshatriya identity by his constant emphasis on pacifism and self-control, he posed a threat to the warrior-cultures of India.'[1] Amongst these 'warrior-cultures', Nandy points out, were the Chitpavans, i.e. Godse's caste. This factor however, needs to be qualified. Interpreting Godse's crime as related to the Chitpavan culture may reflect an essentialist, ahistorical perspective.

The Chitpavan culture, as any group-culture, is not a given but an ever evolving framework. This 'warrior-culture' is more aptly analysed as a 'discursive genre', in the sense of Bakhtin,[2] that is the basic, structuring element on which a *political* culture is elaborated through numerous mediations and re-interpretations. These tribulations must be reconstituted if one wants to avoid the trap of culturalism.[3] The Chitpavan ethos was re-worked and combined with other elements, sometimes specific to local traditions, sometimes imported and indigenized to construct a new political culture that I would call violent Hindu nationalism and with which Godse got imbued. On the one hand, the proponents of this ideology claimed that they found justification for their ideas in the *Bhagavad Gita*, as Gandhi did with his notion of *ahimsa* but they naturally interpreted this text in a radically different way. On the other hand, they made no secret of their fascination with the technical refinements of modern violence and European militarism. The Maharashtrian version of Hindu nationalism was thus an ideology constructed from heterogeneous elements, of which the Chitpavan ethos was not necessarily the most decisive.

The Building of a Maharashtrian Ideological Tradition

The Chitpavans are particularly 'conscious of a common link'.[4] In Maharashtra, the full-blood Kshatriyas were very few and the Chitpavans were prompt to fill up the social space left vacant by the former. They served in large numbers in the armies of Shivaji and the Maratha empire in the eighteenth century. As a result, they imbibed aspects of the Kshatriya ethos and evolved a special moral synthesis. Ram Das, Shivaji's Brahmin counsellor, exemplified this mixture of asceticism appropriate to brahminism and martial valour. The Chitpavans came to occupy every rung of the administration in the Maratha Confederation after one of them, Balaji Vishvanath Rao, became the Peshwa (prime minister). He began to distribute offices and land to his 'caste-fellows'.[5] This practice was institutionalized during the reign of Bajirao Balaji and Balaji II, who usurped the throne after the death of King Sahu, a scion of Shivaji's dynasty. Poona, the capital of the Peshwas, became associated with the Chitpavans although many of them continued to live in the coastal Konkan districts (Ratnagiri, Thana, Kolaba, etc.).

The fall of the Maratha empire spelt the decline of the Chitpavans, who became mere *shastris* and *pandits*. However, they were quick to exploit the opportunities that the British administration offered to the literati. They soon overran schools and colleges as well as the administrative and political space, first through socio-religious reform movements such as the Sarvajanik Sabha and then through the Congress. Their awareness of constituting a distinct group was reinforced by such modern developments. In 1914, one G.V. Apte began to write a history of Chitpavan families on the basis of the replies he got to a questionnaire published in the press. The high rate of response he received, for an operation that was publicized as eminently useful in establishing the highlights of the caste's ancestry, bears witness to a veritable 'Chitpavan revival'.[6]

The memory of bygone glory must certainly have bred amongst the Chitpavans a penchant for violent nationalism. Terrorist acts in the Bombay Presidency were more often than not their handiwork. In 1897, the Chapekar brothers killed two British officials who had fought the plague epidemic without respecting the intimacy of Hindu homes. For Ashis Nandy, 'The Maharashtrian Brahmins saw themselves as the previously powerful, now weakened, competitors of the British. So terrorism directed against the Raj came naturally to them. Their aim was the redemption of their "lost glory".'[7] However, at the end of the nineteenth century, a significant number of Chitpavans, such as M.G. Ranade and G.K. Gokhale, were ranked amongst the 'Moderates' in the Congress and disapproved of these radical methods. Besides, the ideology of nationalist violence, which crystallized in the late nineteenth century Maharashtra, was founded less on the Chitpavan ethos than on a reinterpretation of the *Bhagavad Gita*. The Chitpavan culture was only one of the building blocks of a much more complex political culture.

TILAK, THE *GITA* AND GANDHI

Bal Gangadhar Tilak, a Chitpavan from Poona, began to reinterpret the *Gita* as a sacred text legitimizing the use of violence in the anti-British freedom struggle by the late nineteenth century.[8] His study of the 'secret of the [*Bhagavad*] *Gita*', sought to refute Shankara's and Ramanuja's commentaries. In Tilak's view, by excessively emphasizing the acquisition of Knowledge, in the case of Shankara, and Devotion, in the case of Ramanuja, these two philosophers had neglected *Karma Yoga* (the Yoga of action) which, to his mind, was the core teaching of Krishna to Arjuna.[9] According to him, every act, even a violent act, is legitimate if it is executed for the well-being of the world and without attachment to its fruits. This is a (partial) re-interpretation, for Krishna refers to the duty of the Kshatriyas. For him violent action is a part of the *dharma* of this *varna*; Tilak, for his part, applies his message extensively to all men and with the 'salvation'of the nation in view.[10] Tilak also justified political violence independently from the rules of combat. For instance, he justified Shivaji's killing of General Afzulkhan, an emissary of the emperor Aurangzeb, although it was Shivaji himself who had invited the general for negotiations. It was on these very grounds that the major controversy between Tilak and Gandhi broke out in 1920.[11]

Gandhi's *ahimsa* was a response to the loss of self-esteem in the Hindu psyche, that was brought about by the colonial stereotypes. Europeans tended to look at Hindus as a puny and effeminate 'race'. By refusing to resort to physical resistance, but adopting a feminine attitude which made him appear as a victim of the British, Gandhi sought to give India a prestigious identity based on the acceptance of suffering. This technique was not tantamount to submission, but aimed instead to defend one's rights by creating quiet feelings in the other, the oppressor. Through a sense of sacrifice Gandhi thus restored the dignity to the nation.[12] Gandhi held that 'the *Mahabharata* had demonstrated the futility of violence',[13] and justified it by laying claim to the spirit, and not the letter, of the *Gita*. In the introduction to his Gujarati translation of the *Gita*, he wrote, 'Let it be granted that according to the letter of the *Gita* it is possible that warfare is consistent with the renunciation of fruit [of action]. But after 40 years' unremitting endeavour fully to enforce the teaching of the *Gita* in my own life, I have in all humility felt that perfect renunciation is impossible without perfect observance of *ahimsa* in every shape and form.'[14]

This strategy was poles apart from the one advocated by the 'Extremists' and Hindu nationalists who sought to regain their self-esteem by laying claim to a glorious past in which their ancestors displayed a remarkable virility, and resorted to violence. The need to revive this physical strength was emphasized in Bengal since the advent of Vivekananda and the Anushilan Samiti,[15] but it developped also in Maharashtra, with Tilak and his followers. Not only Tilak's revivalism and defence of Hindu traditions contrasted with Gandhi's ecumenism and syncretism, but he strongly opposed the notion of *ahimsa*. In doing so, he repeatedly referred to the *Bhagavad Gita*, denouncing Gandhi's quietist reading of this text. Tilak's culture of violence had crystallized before Gandhi became a key figure of Indian nationalism, however, he further elaborated this political idiom in reaction to the Mahatma's discourse.[16]

Gandhi portrayed Tilak as a leader for whom the end justified the means in an article in *Young India*. The latter riposted immediately, in the following terms,

> Politics is a game of worldly people and not of sadhus and instead of the maxim *Akkodhena jine kodham* (conquer anger by non-anger) as preached by Buddha, I prefer to rely on the maxim of Shri Krishna, *Ye yatha maam prapadyante taannstathaira bhajamyahang* (I give to them reward in the same manner and to the same extent that they worship me). That explains the whole difference and also the meaning of my phrase, 'responsive co-operation'. Both methods are equally honest and righteous. But, one is more suited to this world than the other.[17]

Tilak thus countered Gandhi by resorting to arguments based on *realpolitik* and his own reinterpretation of the *Gita*. Savarkar would proceed in a similar fashion, further elaborating the repertoire of violent Hindu nationalism.

SAVARKAR AND THE INDIGENIZATION OF EUROPEAN TERRORISM

Vinayak Damodar Savarkar too was a Chitpavan Brahmin, a member of the same clan as Nana Sahib (heir to the Peshwa title, who was one of the heroes of the Revolt of 1857) and Tilak,[18] whose nationalism he admired.[19] He learned the history of the Maratha confederation from the *bhakars* (ballads narrating the exploits of the chiefs of the defunct empire) read to him by his father. In 1900, while he was student of Ferguson College, he founded the Mitra Mela, a secret society whose proclaimed activity was to organize the Ganesh and Shivaji festivals initiated by Tilak in Poona. Savarkar established very strict rules for those who wanted to join the Mitra Mela, exacting a vow from the 'initiates' that they would be willing to sacrifice themselves for the cause of the nation's freedom. In 1905, he transformed the Mitra Mela into the Abhinav Bharat Society (the Young India Society), which was explicitly inspired by a passionate reading of Mazzini's writings on the 'new' Italy, as well as clandestine works such as Frost's *Secret Societies of the European Revolution—1776–1876*, especially with regard to the organization of the Russian nihilists.[20] These European influences were to be decisive in the manner in which Savarkar laid down the tenets of a violent nationalism. A recommendation letter from Tilak brought him a scholarship to pursue his studies in London, which he had sought only so that contact with European revolutionary groups would better instruct him in the 'art' of terrorism.[21] Although his nationalism has been largely moulded by European influences, Savarkar attempted to vernacuralize this foreign ideology. When the execution of the Chapekar brothers was announced in 1898, Savarkar vowed before the goddess Ashtabuja (a form of Durga) that he would avenge their death by giving his body and soul to the cause of his country's liberation.[22] His political *imaginaire* repeatedly harks back to the Hindu idiom of sacrifice. An entire chapter of his work on the Revolt of 1857 portrays the insurrection as 'The Great Sacrifice', wherein history is overwhelmed by imagination:

> While the date of this National Vengeance is approaching nearer and yet nearer, it is lent proper that the requisite sacrifice should be offered to the sacred and terrible God of Fire, the Lord of us all, so that the presiding deity of this grand work may be propitiated. This presiding Goddess of National Anger is rising from the Yajna Kunda with all her limbs! What a terrible fierceness! Be propitious, O Goddess, be propitious! We offer the perfect offering of our presiding deity herself in order that thou mayest be propitious. Accept this offering, which we are going to offer! All the cartridges that can be found in the Dum-Dum factory, dip them, cook them, in cows' and pigs' blood, bring them as a complete offering for the presiding Goddess of the Sacrifice.[23]

This highly emotional piece of nationalist rhetoric is revealing of Savarkar's attempt at translating his violent ideology in Hindu terms.

Doubtless, this ability to vernacularize bits and pieces of European nationalism would explain the success that his books, including his biography of Mazzini,[24] enjoyed amongst the Maharashtrian intelligentsia which partly rallied behind his terrorist methods. A.L. Kanhere, a Chitpavan student of seventeen, who killed Judge Jackson, was one of them. Jackson was the judge who had dispatched V.D. Savarkar's brother, Ganesh, to the penal colony in the Andamans, on a charge of seditious writing. It was to avenge his brother that V.D. Savarkar himself took part in the 1911 conspiracy to eliminate Curzon-Wyllie, an adviser to the Secretary of State for India in London. The method used—attack with a firearm or a bomb—drew inspiration from European techniques of terrorism, but V.D. Savarkar's discourse was replete with Hindu references, to sacrifice in particular. After the murder of Curzon-Wyllie, Savarkar took refuge for a while in Paris. Remorse seized him upon learning that his younger brother had been arrested. He returned to London to take part in the 'national sacrifice'. Arrested immediately thereafter, he justified his act by invoking the motif of Hindu religious sacrifice in a letter to his sister-in-law, whom he assimilates to the Goddess and the Mother-Country, 'and now here am I, O Mother, bound to Thy Sacrificial Pillar! What of These! Had we been seven instead of only three [brothers], I would have Sacrificed them all—in thy cause. Thy Cause is Holy! Thy Cause I believed to be the Cause of God and in serving it I knew I served the Lord!'[25]

Savarkar was publicizing a political culture that combined nationalism with violence in the same vein as Tilak. Both were Chitpavan Brahmins, but this 'background' alone did not explain their ideology. Their discourse, in fact, relied on reinterpretations of Hinduism, whether they came from the *Gita* or from the notion of sacrifice. Savarkar largely drew his violent nationalism from European revolutionary or terrorist groups but vernacularized these sources of inspiration. Such a process of indigenization was even more evident from the political culture of Tilak's other followers from the Hindu Mahasabha.

THE HINDU MAHASABHA AND THE MARTIAL ETHOS

THE 'TILAKITES' AGAINST *AHIMSA*

In Maharashtra, Tilak's former lieutenants started as early as the 1920s to dominate the Hindu Mahasabha which, at that time, was a kind of lobby within the Indian National Congress. Like their former mentor, they raised their voice in protest against Gandhi's attempts to make *ahimsa* the central value of the nationalist combat. N.C. Kelkar, a Chitpavan brahmin who played a key role in both the Congress and the Hindu Mahasabha in Maharashtra in the 1920s (before becoming president of the latter at an all India level in 1927), promoted anti-Gandhi propaganda in the two newspapers of which he was editor-in-chief, the *Kesari* and the *Maratha*.[26] The *Maratha* inveighed against Gandhi's effort, 'to define even political ideals in terms of spirituality. . . We can hardly refrain from raising our voices in protest at this attack on the political sphere based upon erroneous, half-baked and half-digested spiritual ideas.'[27] In 1924, the paper reacted even more vehemently when Gandhi visited Poona: 'there is a radical, fundamental difference between his shadowy, flimsy philosophy and [the] hard-headed political knowledge which Maharashtrians have inherited from their illustrious predecessors'.[28]

Of all Tilak's lieutenants, it was Moonje who most consistently insisted that a martial ethos should be inducted among Hindus. A Deshastha Brahmin from Nagpur, which was a milieu that retained some nostalgia for the Maratha empire and continued to profess loyalty to the Bhonsle kingdom.[29] B.S. Moonje was an eye surgeon who rose to the very apex of the Congress party in the Central Provinces after World War I, and founded the Nagpur unit of the Hindu Mahasabha in the 1920s. Although he was a Maharashtrian Brahmin, he was not a vegetarian and, to the great displeasure of the *Sanatanists*,[30] he even proclaimed the virtues of eating meat.[31] He liked to refer to himself as a 'Maratha Brahmin'[32] and to introduce himself as, 'a Brahmin by caste and by temperament perhaps a Kshatriya',[33] particularly because he used to hunt. In 1920, in fact, he started shooting clubs which were meant to be contemporary versions of the traditional *akharas*. Moonje's forebears had served in the Bhonsle armies,[34] and he nursed ardent memories of them: 'Our family has a tradition of loyal service to the Royal Bhonsla House of Nagpur, which we regard as our proud heritage. The Maratha States are Historic relics of the Maratha Empire of India, of not very long ago and as such it is our sacred duty to aspire for the return of those proud days of our grandfathers and work selflessly for the same.'[35]

Moonje, more than any other among Tilak's followers, was resolutely opposed to *ahimsa*. 'In our religion,' he claimed, 'violence in the defence of one's rights is not condemned.'[36] This drove him to add that he 'like[d] the Muslims for the virile vigilance with which they protect their racial interests . . . , which, alas, is visibly lacking in the present-day Hindu race'. Moonje would never relent. In 1945, he sent a letter to Gandhi proclaiming that his party, the Hindu Mahasabha, was in favour of 'violence organized and disciplined on modern scientific lines'.[37] Like Savarkar, Moonje drew inspiration from European militarism and integrated it with the martial traditions of Hinduism.

VIOLENCE AND MILITARISM

Military training, in Moonje's view, was a priority for strengthening the Hindu community.[38] As a result of his persistent efforts in the Central Provinces Legislative Council, the British appointed an inquiry commission (the Skein Committee) whose terms of reference reflected Moonje's concern for India's military weakness. The Committee's report underlined the need to Indianize half of the armed forces over a fifteen-year period. To that end, the Committee created a board to supervise recruitment of officers for training at Sandhurst. Recognized as a specialist on military affairs by the British, who referred to him as 'Colonel', Moonje was appointed to this board in 1925. This enabled him to realize how under-prepared the Indian candidates were and led him to found a non-official Military School. His project became a reality only a decade later, in 1935, but the intervening period of slow ripening was extremely instructive.

In 1930, Moonje seized the occasion of his trip to Europe as a member of the first Round Table Conference to visit military schools in France, Germany and Italy, where he 'saw the work of the Ballila movement.'[39] He then met Mussolini who was delighted that an Indian should want 'to see his army and institutions dispensing military education'.[40] On his return, as he travelled around India to raise funds for his school, Moonje's project became increasingly popular as much because of his international expertise as because of his incessant references to India's martial traditions. Certainly, Moonje was eager to borrow military techniques from the West. However, he was equally keen to equate these modern techniques with the Indian martial traditions. During a 1935 visit to Andhra, he declared:

> *Chhandogya Upanishad* says, 'One strong man with a rifle in hand can bring round a hundred men of education to tremble in fear before him.' This very sentiment is expressed in an equally picturesque and inspiring manner by an eminent German professor, Ewald Banace, who says 'Certainly, the pen is good, but the sword is good too, and often far better, and we want both to be equally honoured among German people. . . . But the sword is the older weapon and it is the final—the ultimate one. Therefore, it should take the first place'.[41]

Moonje laid claim to rediscovering Indian concepts in Western practices. For instance, he presented 'guerrilla' as a technique of war recommended by Kautilya, updated by the Marathas in their conflicts with the Mughals, and recognized by European strategists in the 1940s as a superior means of waging war. From this arises his comment on a quote from 'Dr. Goebbels', whose writings and speeches Moonje seems to have read assiduously. He wrote, 'The Russians have found a new way of making war contrary to recognized rules. At night, they attack the German line with a team of polar dogs drawing sledges on which machine guns are mounted. . . . This is a typical guerrilla raid, the like of which was done by Santaji Ghorpade [a general of the Maratha empire] more than 200 years ago. . . .'[42] In his view, not only did Indian guerrilla techniques enjoyed the advantage of anteriority, they were also underpinned by an ontology, the *Dharma Yudha* (or, war for *dharma*), forbidding treacherousness towards a diminished enemy. For instance,

> so long as the Modern European implements of warfare hold the place of honour on battle fields, we Hindus have to imitate and assimilate them; so that when we shall have come into our own and shall be ourselves master of our war machine, we may then take advantage of our position in the world to demonstrate to the people the superiority, moral and spiritual, of the principles on which our Rules of Righteous Warfare have been formulated.[43]

Moonje explicitly recognized the need for emulating Western warfare techniques but this was merely a detour in his view, a device aiming at restoring the Hindu superiority from both a moral and physical point of view.[44]

The Princes were amongst the first to support Moonje's project, which finally saw the light of day in 1935 at Nasik, as the Bhonsle Military School. There were Maratha chieftains amongst them: the Bhonsles, after whom the school was named, were amongst the first to contribute funds, as were the Holkars of Indore,[45] the Gaekwads of Baroda and the Scindias of Gwalior, with the last named inaugurating the institution in March 1938.[46] Maratha Maharajas of smaller states such Dewas and Dhar[47] were part of an outer ring of supporters, like the Maharajas of Bikaner and Patiala.[48] The growth of the Nasik school remained limited, partly because of the high cost of boarding and tuition (Rs. 35 a month) and partly because of its Maharashtrian tropism (the medium of instruction was Marathi). Moonje had, however, initiated a process of militarization which involved the import of European notions, with a view to vernacularize them, but also the collaboration with the British, in view of imbuing the Hindus with modern warfare techniques. This strategy was subsequently adopted by the Hindu Mahasabha and gained momentum during World War II.

'HINDUIZE ALL POLITICS AND MILITARIZE HINDUDOM'

This slogan was propagated by Savarkar in the 1940s, while he was the President of the Hindu Mahasabha. After being condemned in 1911 to a life sentence in the Andaman Islands' penal colony for the murder of Curzon-Wyllie, Savarkar had been granted conditional release in 1924 and a suspension of his sentence in 1937. Almost immediately thereafter, he became the President of the Hindu Mahasabha,[49] which in Maharashtra was headed at that time by other followers of Tilak. When he came back from the Andamans, he was greeted at an official ceremony by N.C. Kelkar and Moonje who presented to him a copy of the *Bhagavadgita*.[50]

In 1940, the Working Committee of the Hindu Mahasabha announced that it would be willing to cooperate with Britain if the War became the occasion to 'militarize the Hindus', to abrogate the Arms Act, to abolish the distinction between 'martial races' and 'non-martial races', to indianize the army in entirety and to intensify the military training of Indian cadet-officers.[51] Savarkar looked upon the War Committees as the crucible for a Hindu army that would eventually take on the real enemies, the Muslims.[52] As early as July, Moonje was part of the War Committee of the Central Provinces. He justified this collaboration with the British by arguing that the Hindu Mahasabha 'should take the fullest advantage of whatever occasions arise for militarising the Hindus'.[53] Hindu Sabhaites became members of the War Committees in Bengal, the United Provinces[54] and the Bombay Presidency.[55] Such enlistment in the regular army developed in parallel with the growth of militias.

MILITIAS AND PARA-MILITARY GROUPS

In the late 1930s, the Secretary General of the Hindu Mahasabha, Ganpat Rai considered that, 'What the Hindus require at this juncture is a regular army [for] when communal riots break out in the cities of India, Hindus cry out for rescue force to relieve them from the clutches of the aggression.'[56] The Rashtriya Swayamsevak Sangh (RSS) was first perceived by the Hindu Sabhaites as the embryo of such an 'Hindu army'. However, this was not acceptable to its leaders, who were not inclined to play any role in the political arena, lest such a move may attract reprisals from the British. Ground work at the grassroot level, through the *shakhas*, remained the RSS' leadership priority.[57] In the early 1940s, many Hindu Sabhaites were deeply disappointed by the RSS which seemed to be acting against their interests, as evident from an internal report entitled, 'What should be the attitude of the Hindu Mahasabha towards the RSS?'[58]

At its Calcutta session in December 1939, therefore, the Hindu Mahasabha founded a Hindu Militia, following a resolution proposed by Moonje. Moonje justified such a move by pointing out that in the event of a British defeat in the War, 'Muslim nations beyond the North-West Frontier [Province] could invade India and the Muslims here may help them.'[59] Those were times in which para-military groups flourished,[60] especially in north India. The Mahabir Dal of the Arya Samaj developed in Punjab, which was one of the areas most prone to Hindu-Muslim riots. The Arya Vir Dal had eight hundred members throughout the North-West Frontier Province, Bombay and Delhi; while the Arya Yuwak Sangh had eight hundred members in Ajmer-Merwara; and the Agni Dal, another Arya Samaji offshoot, had six hundred members in Punjab, etc.

In its organization, the Hindu Militia, better known as the Ram Sena (the Army of Ram), resembled the fascist paramilitary groups which had emerged in Europe during the inter-War period. For instance, the Bal Sena (Children's Army) called to mind the Ballila movement which Moonje had observed in Italy; the militia's uniform included *khaki* short and shirt, an ochre coloured scarf and a staff bearing the party's standard. As for its activities, Moonje's ideas even in a telegraphic form speak for themselves, '1. All must assemble daily at some place. 2. Military drill. 3. Lathi, kathi, sword. 4. Physical Training. 5. Ideology 6. Pamphlets and booklets with particular reference to past History. 7. Sunday and holidays: touring villages in batches of ten or twenty for mass organisation. 8. Rifling, shooting, riding, cycling, motoring, etc. 9. Camp in Puja, Diwali or summer vacation.'[61]

On 17 March 1940, the Ram Sena was inaugurated by Moonje, who was appointed President for five years. However, operations were directed by the Secretary General, J.P. Verma who was a member of 'an aristocratic Kayasth family',[62] and a very dynamic leader. His untimely death in July 1940 could not be adequately compensated by the nomination of V.G. Deshpande in his place. Soon after, the Hindu Militia was eclipsed by the Hindu Rashtra Dal (HRD). Established in 1942 by Savarkar, the HRD received the support of the 'Tilakites' whom the British referred to as 'the Kesari group'. It drew its recruits from those who were disenchanted with the RSS's reluctance to get involved in politics. Foremost amongst these was one more Chitpavan, Nathuram Godse, who scoffed at the RSS strategy as 'organization for the sake of organization'.[63]

The Killing of Gandhi

Nathuram Godse was the son of a junior-level postal employee from a village lying between Bombay and Poona. Although his great interest in history and religion had led him to read voraciously when he was young (he knew the *Bhagavad Gita* by heart), he showed no real inclination towards studies and therefore failed in the Matriculation examination. He was left with little recourse other than to take to tailoring, which of course was a degrading task for a Chitpavan. Chance, by way of his father's transfer, took him to Ratnagiri, where his innate nationalism led him towards Savarkar, who was easily accessible, though he was still in detention. Both men kept in touch after Savarkar became president of the Hindu Mahasabha. So much so that Godse joined the Hindu Rashtra Dal and became the editor-in-chief of the Savarkarite newspaper, *Agrani*.

Godse's hostility to Gandhi intensified as the Partition was approaching. When the Mahatma floated the idea, in April 1947, of offering Jinnah the post of President of the nation so that a 'partition' may be averted, *Agrani* denounced, 'the slavish pro-Islamic mentality of this "Quisling" of the Hindu nation';[64] after the unleashing of communal riots, on 12 April 1947, the newspaper launched a violent campaign against Gandhi,

> We clearly tell Mr. Gandhi that if the rivers of Hindu blood that he has made to flow or the encouragement that he has indirectly given to such outrages, by the advocacy of his cowardly philosophy, is at least to be partially undone, then Gandhi should accept the defeat of his cowardly and worthless non-violence and should, for the defence of his self-respect (if any is left to it), commit suicide: if not, he should bid good bye for ever to Indian politics.[65]

Agrani's successor, the *Dainik Hindu Rashtra*, founded just before the Partition, also focused on this issue, 'The Motherland was vivisected, the vultures tore pieces of flesh [from her], the chastity of Hindu women was violated on the open streets, everything was lost and the big guns of the Congress eunuchs watching the rape committed on their own wives have begun to growl at you. How long can one bear this?'[66]

In the eyes of the Hindu nationalists, Gandhi had questioned the very tradition of virility by sacrificing India's territorial integrity. At his trial, Godse justified his killing of the Mahatma in a lengthy plea in which he made his ideological opposition to Gandhi very clear and related it to this questioning of the Indian manliness:

> I had never made a secret about the fact that I supported the ideology of the school which was opposed to that of Gandhiji. I firmly believed that the teaching of absolute Ahimsa, as advocated by Gandhiji, would ultimately result in the emasculation of the Hindu community and thus make the community incapable of resisting the aggression or inroads of other communities, especially the Muslims. To counter this evil, I resolved to enter public life and formed a group of persons who held like views.[67]

By his own admission, Godse belonged to an ideological stream fed by Hindu nationalism and political violence against Gandhi, a school of thought that began with Tilak and was perpetuated by 'Tilakites' such as Savarkar and Moonje. He, too, was a Chitpavan Brahmin, but this social background could hardly account for his political orientations alone. The fact that he adhered to a Hindu nationalist and violent ideology played a more significant role.[68] The fact that Godse belonged to this 'school of thought' is evident from the *realpolitik* he displayed, which is reminiscent of Tilak's attitude. He sought to rid India of Gandhi because he was an idealist whose good intentions could only produce disaster,[69] since, in his view, the Mahatma was guided by selfish whims: 'I declare here before man and God that in putting an end to Gandhi's life, I have removed one who was a curse to India, a force for evil and who had, during 30 years of an egoistic pursuit of hare-brained policy, brought nothing but misery and unhappiness.' Such *realpolitik* was but one component of a political culture that had been initially shaped by Tilak.

Another important element of Godse's political repertoire laid in his reinterpretation of the *Gita*. By the end of his trial, he said,

> In fact, honour, duty and love of one's own kith and kin and country might often compel us to disregard non-violence. I could never conceive that an armed resistance to the aggressor is unjust. I will consider it a religious and moral duty to resist and if possible to overpower such an enemy by the use of force. Shree Ramchandra killed Ravan in a tumultuous fight and relieved Sita. Shree Krishna killed Kansa to end his wickedness. In the *Mahabharat*, Arjun had to fight and slay quite a number of his friends and relations, including the revered Bhishma, because the latter was on the side of the aggressor. It is my firm belief that in dubbing Rama, Krishna and Arjuna as guilty of violence is to betray a total ignorance of the springs of human action. It was the heroic fight put up by the Chhatrapati Shivaji Maharaj that first checked and eventually destroyed Muslim tyranny in India. It was absolutely correct tactics for Shivaji to kill Afzul Khan as the latter would otherwise have surely killed him. In condemning Shivaji, Rana Pratap and Guru Govind as misguided patriots, Gandhiji has merely exposed his self-conceit'.[70]

Godse's views echo the old Tilakite interpretation of the *Gita*, but Godse went further in the sense that he pretended to be Arjuna and litterally put the *Mahabharata* on stage.

> My respect for the Mahatma's character was deep and deathless. It therefore gave me no pleasure to kill him. Indeed my feelings were like those of Arjuna when he killed 'Dronacharya', his Guru, at whose feet he had learnt the art of war. But the Guru had taken the side of the wicked Kauravas and for that reason he felt no compunction in finishing his revered Guru. Before doing so, however, he first threw an arrow at the feet of Dronacharya as a mark of respect for the Guru: the second arrow he aimed at the chest of the Guru and finished him. My feelings towards

Gandhi were similar. I hold him first in the highest respect and therefore on January 30, I bowed to him first, then at point blank range, fired three successive shots and killed him. My provocation was his constant and consistent pandering to the Muslims. I had no private grudge, no self-interest, no sordid motive in killing him. It was his provocation over a period of 20 years, which finally exhausted my patience; and my inner voice [a distinctively Gandhian phrase] urged me to kill him, which I did. I am not asking for any mercy.[71]

It was as if Godse had taken the *Mahabharata* as a guide for reading the situation of post-Partition India, a grammar in which the Muslims were assimilated to the Kauravas, Gandhi to the traitorous Drona and he himself to Arjuna. This is evidenced by another passage of his speech before the court: '[Gandhism] will mean not only Muslim rule over the entire country but the extinction of Hinduism itself. I believe in Lord Krishna's promise that whenever religion is in danger and contrary forces raise their head, I shall assume incarnation for the re-establishment of religion. I believe with the poet prophet Jayadev that in the tenth Incarnation, the Lord Almighty will act through human beings.'[72]

One of the Mahatma's son, Ramdas Gandhi, sought an encounter (which never took place) with Godse in a letter where he cited a *shloka* from the *Gita*, 'O Achyuta [Lord Krishna], because of your kind favour my ignorance has disappeared and I have regained my sense of duty. Here I stand with all my doubts resolved and shall do your bidding.' Ramdas Gandhi pleaded with Godse to 'introspect a little so that at the end of our proposed meeting you will be able to recite this couplet from the *Gita* along with us'.[73] Godse was delighted with the proposal, for he knew the *Gita* by heart and would constantly recite entire chapters in prison, like his brother Gopal, one of his accomplices, who saw it as a means to appease his anxieties.[74] In reply, he wrote, 'I thank you for having reminded me of the verses, "My ignorance has disappeared, I have regained normalcy" from the *Bhagavad Gita*. In my opinion, not only these verses in the *Gita* but the whole of the *Gita* is an invaluable poem replete with meaning and beauty. After Arjuna has said, "I will do as you say", he had directly translated into practice the words of Lord Krishna, "Remember me and fight.".'[75] Obviously, Ramdas Gandhi's conception of the *Gita* was very different from his own. Deriving from Tilak, Godse's reading of the *Gita* continued until the very end to determine his vision of his own crime. A little before his execution, he wrote to his parents:

You are the students of the *Geeta* and have also learnt the Puranas. Lord Krishna had recited this *Geeta* to enlighten Arjun and the very same Lord Krishna had with his Sudarshan Wheel chopped off the head of an Aryan king, Shisupal, not on a battlefield but on a sacrificial ground, the Rajsooya Yagnyabhoomi! Who will say that Lord Krishna committed sin in doing so? For the welfare of the world at large, Lord Krishna destroyed several other conceited, insolent and haughty high-placed people in war and by other means; and in the advice given to Arjun in his *Geeta*, he has repeatedly urged Arjun on to kill his sinful relatives, and in the end made him take up foresken [*sic*] Gandeeva's bow and fight.

Sin and moral rectitude are to be sought not in a man's act but in his motive behind that act. Here in our very country, hundreds and thousands of Hindu women were being molested, raped and carried away forcibly to be converted to Islam and the perpetrators of these atrocious deeds were being helped in all possible ways. In such circumstances, I could not sit silent and watch helplessly all this through fear of losing my life or of incurring public censure and wrath.

My mind is pure and my feelings are absolutely righteous; millions of people might speak in million different ways, but my mind has not become uneasy or shaken with repentance even for the moment. If there is any Heaven, I shall certainly have my place reserved there for me.[76]

Godse was sentenced to death like one of his accomplices, Apte, who had been the manager of *Agrani* and *Dainik Hindu Rashtra*. They went to the scaffold proclaiming, 'Long live Undivided India!', with a copy of the *Bhagavad Gita* in hand. The previous evening, they had read the second, the eleventh and the eighteenth chapter along with their accomplices.[77] A ritual similar to that of the early twentieth century terrorists, of whom the Savarkarites regarded themselves the direct descendants, was thus re-enacted.

Interestingly, while Ramdas Gandhi stuck to the interpretation of the *Gita* that his father spelled out in the 1920s, the Mahatma himself had tended to understand the Hindu nationalist interpretation of it by the end of his life. The violence unleashed by the Partition, in his view, epitomized the inefficacy of his methods. He explicitly questioned his reading of the *Gita* after the first, aborted assassination attempt by Godse and his acolytes, when one of Godse's accomplices, Madanlal, was arrested. Gandhi asked for his pardon, 'No one should look down upon the misguided young man who had thrown the bomb. He probably looked upon me as an enemy of Hinduism. After all, had not the *Gita* said that, whenever there was an evil-minded person damaging religion, God sent someone to end his life?'[78]

Gandhi's eldest son, Harilal remained all his life fascinated by this un-gandhian interpretation of the *Gita*. One of his brothers, Devadas, pointed out that, 'One book he always spoke of with reverence and great satisfaction was Lokamanya Tilak's famous treatise on the *Bhagavad Gita*. He carried a copy with him everywhere and even when he did not have even a shirt to wear, he would still have with him a copy of the *Gita Rahasya*.'[79]

Such an attitude was symptomatic of his restless rebellion against his father. Both things—the Mahatma's questioning of his initial interpretation of the *Gita* and his son's selection of this text as the symbol of his revolt—are reconfirmations of the key role of the *Gita* in structuring India's political culture. Godse is not so much the representative of a Chitpavan culture than a by-product of one of the most profound ideological cleavages in India during the Gandhian era, between those who look at Hinduism as the religion of *ahimsa* and those who consider that violence is legitimized by this very creed. Interpreting the *Gita* is naturally a key exercise in this ideology-building process.

Conclusion

Thus, Godse embodied the opposition to Gandhi, as part of a school of thought which is more than a hundred years old and had begun to take shape even before the Mahatma entered the stage. By the late nineteenth century, Tilak had already laid the foundations for an ideology that cut away radically from the Gandhian message in that it recognized the validity of recourse to violence in the freedom struggle. Ashis Nandy largely attributes this dimension to the 'warrior-culture' of the Chitpavans. Certainly, there were elective affinities between this tradition and violent nationalism. Similar conclusions could probably be derived from the case of Bengal, which was another area relatively hostile to Gandhi. In Bengal, the *shakta* culture, the cult of Kali-Durga, had also elective affinities with violent forms of political action, as evident from the development of the terrorist groups in the nineteenth century[80] and Subhas Chandra Bose, whom Godse claimed as his own, is probably one of the most obvious heirs. However, these regional traditions do not tell the whole story. They need to be seen in relation to other, pan-Indian cultural dimensions, such as the message of the *Gita* and they need to be seen as part of an ideology-building process which was borrowing different elements from diverse sources. Certainly, every political culture emanates from a 'discursive genre' that predates it and the Chitpavans' martial ethos induced a predisposition towards violent Hindu nationalism. However, the reasoning must not be articulated in terms of inheritance and legacy alone. This ideology resulted from an historical process of construction in which 'alien' elements were also incorporated. Christian writings, which Gandhi encountered in England and elsewhere, were no less decisive than his Gujarati background in turning the Mahatma towards non-violence. Similarly, Savarkar was fascinated by Mazzini (among other European radical nationalists) and Moonje was attracted by European fascism. Their ideology resulted from a strategic synthesis between the culture in which they had been born and that to which they had been exposed. They shaped it with the objective of resisting domination, whatever be its nature (ideological, socio-economic or political) and the effectivity of this domination. They also changed the enemies. They targeted first the British, and then the Muslims and Gandhi. By contrast, their method remained the same: they favoured violent means. They claimed that this posture was rooted in the Hindu culture but it was largely an imagination or a construction of their tradition.[81] For Rajni Kothari, the 'construction of tradition' consists in legitimizing the introduction of practices and ideas originating in the West and presenting them as analogous to indigenous tradition or as virtually contained in them.[82] In the present case, the Hindu nationalists claimed to have discovered in their own tradition, particularly efficacious military techniques discovered in Europe, with the objective of flattering their nationalist pride and importing them more effectively to fight against the Muslims. I have referred to this elsewhere as a strategy of stigmatization and emulation of so called 'threatening' others.[83] This alchemy is clearly evident in Moonje's efforts to transplant in India what he learned in fascist Europe, taking great care to establish an equivalence between the Mussolini-Goebbels kind of violence and that of Shivaji. However, this imagination of a tradition of violent nationalism has indigenous roots since one of the most popular text of Hinduism, the *Gita*, laid itself to such an approach of politics.

Indeed in this ideology-building process, one of the mainstays was the quest for some religious sanction to the legitimacy of violent nationalism. From Tilak to Godse, Hindu nationalist leaders have referred to the *Gita* as *the* text which justified their resorting to violence and even endowed it with some sacred flavour.

Interestingly, this is also the main source from which Gandhi drew his notion of *ahimsa*. These contradictory exegesis suggest that the *Gita* played a key role in the construction of these political repertoires. On the one hand there are those who conclude from their interpretation of the text that Hinduism is basically inclined towards non-violence, and, on the other hand, those who read the *Gita* as an indictment of *ahimsa* politics. This pillar of the Hindu high tradition, therefore, is more important than regional cultures—such as, the Chitpavan ethos— in the making of violent or non-violent nationalisms. In fact, violent Hindu nationalism also found expression in regions other than Maharashtra and Bengal, for instance in Punjab, where 'Extremists' like Lajpat Rai made the same reading of the *Gita* as Tilak. In 1908, he wrote that, 'Once Dharma cannot be anything but righteous, hence anything which is necessary to be done in the performance of Dharma cannot be sinful. A Raja commits no sin in punishing thieves, robbers, dacoits and murderers. A patriot warrior commits no sin in killing the enemies of his country in fair fight.'[84]

What needs to be scrutinized, therefore, is first the relationship between the high tradition and the local or caste cultures and more especially the way the latter mediate the former; and secondly, the manner in which this material is used in the ideology-building process, a process that also consists in assimilating foreign elements.

NOTES

1. A. Nandy, 'Final Encounter—The Politics of the Assassination of Gandhi', in A. Nandy, *At the Edge of Psychology*, Delhi: Oxford University Press, 1980, p. 78.
2. For an analysis of this notion, see J.F. Bayart, *L'illusion identitaire*, Paris: Fayard, 1996.
3. On the historicization of political cultures as an antidote to culturalism, see J.F. Bayart, op. cit. Ashis Nandy does indeed pay attention to historical processes in that he explains Chitpavan Brahmin hostility to the entry of the masses into the political arena (brought about by Gandhi) in terms of their loss of social status. However, he hardly deals with another historical process, that is the making, during the pre-Independence years of the twentieth century, of the ideology of a violent, Hindu nationalism from which Godse drew his inspiration.
4. G. Johnson, 'Chitpavan. Brahmins and Politics in Western India in the Late Nineteenth and Early Twentieth Centuries', in E. Leach and S.N. Mukherjee (eds.), *Elites in South Asia*, Cambridge: Cambridge Uni-

versity Press, 1970, p. 100. They ignore the authority of their own caste *panchayat* but recognize the authority of the Shankaracharya of Shankeshwar (whose agents are vested with the power to settle their internal conflicts).

5. Ibid.
6. M. Patterson, 'Chitpavan Brahman Family Histories; sources for a study of social structures and social change in Maharashtra', in M. Singer and B. Cohn (eds.), *Structure and Change in Indian Society*, Jaipur: Rawat, 1996 [1968], p. 403.
7. A. Nandy, *At the Edge of Psychology*, op. cit., p. 78.
8. The first Marathi edition of this book on '*the secret of Gita*' compiles texts and speeches going back to the year 1902. It appeared in 1915, whilst the first Gujarati edition, which Gandhi may have read, came out in 1917. For a list of editions in various regional languages, see page 5 of the first English edition, B.G. Tilak, *Srimad Bhagavadgita Rahasya*, Poona: Tilak Bros., 1935.
9. The passages in which this thesis is most clearly set out are: B.G. Tilak, *Srimad Bhagavadgita Rahasya or Karma Yoga Shastra*, Poona, 1935, pp. 424, 478 and 645.
10. See M. Adenwalla, 'Hindu concepts and the Gita in early Indian thought', in R.A. Sakai (ed.), *Studies on Asia*, Lincoln: University of Nebraska Press, 1961.
11. There are enough indications that the two men advocated positions that were radically divergent. Certain passages from *Hind Swaraj* are a term by term contrast to Tilak's book. Thus, for example, Tilak writes 'assuming for the sake of argument that some villain has come with a weapon in his hands to kill you, or to commit rape on your wife or daughter, or to set fire to your house, or to steal all your wealth, or to deprive you of your immovable property . . . , then should you close your eyes and treat with unconcern such a villain (*atatayin*) saying, "*Ahimsa paramo dharmah*"? Or should you as much as possible punish him, if he does not listen to reason?' (Tilak, *Srimad Bhagavadgita Rahasya*, op.cit., p. 43). Gandhi, naturally, perceives things quite differently. If a robber were to enter your home, he writes, 'Instead of being angry with him, you take pity on him. You think that this stealing habit must be a disease with him. Henceforth you, therefore, keep your doors and windows open; you change your sleeping-place, and you keep your things in a manner most accessible to him. The robber comes again, and is confused, as all this is new to him; nevertheless, he takes away your things. But his mind is agitated. He inquires about you in the village, he comes to learn about your broad and loving heart, he repents, he begs your pardon, returns you your things, and leaves off the stealing habit. He becomes your servant, and you find for him

honourable employment' (M.K. Gandhi, *Hind Swaraj: Indian Home Rule*, Madras: Ganesh & Co., 1922, p. 81).

12. L.I. Rudolph and S.H. Rudolph, *The Modernity of Tradition: Political Development in India*, Chicago: The University of Chicago Press, 1967, p. 161 and A. Nandy, *At the Edge of Psychology*, op. cit., pp. 73–5.
13. B.R. Nanda, *Gandhi and religion*, New Delhi: Oxford University Press, 1990, p. 5.
14. Cited in M.N. Srinivas, 'Gandhi's religion', *Economic & Political Weekly*, 24 June 1995, p. 1490. Such a reading of the *Gita* is difficult to understand and has inspired critical comments, even from people who cannot be accused of being hostile to the Mahatma. To Srinivas, the fact that Gandhi can discover non-violence in the Gita 'seems puzzling to say the least' (ibid., p. 1489).
15. J. Roselli, 'The self-image of effeteness: physical education and nationalism in nineteenth century Bengal', *Past and Present*, 86, 1980.
16. In the *Gita*, Krishna exhorts Arjuna to go to war against his own kinsmen by arguing that violence is a duty when it is exercised in view of preserving the *dharma*. Violence carried out in this spirit of renunciation, with no heed to the fruit of such acts, is legitimate and even enables the sovereign to attain *moksha* (M. Biardeau, Introduction. Le Mahabharata, vol. 1, Paris: Garnier Flammarion, 1985, p. 37).
17. Cited in N.G. Jog, *Lokamanya Bal Gangadhar Tilak*, New Delhi: Ministry of Information and Broadcasting, 1979, p. 199. Jayakar also reports the following revealing words of Tilak, 'I was under the impression that Gandhi was a Jain, because all his opinions and teaching savour of the Jain religion—non-violence, *satyagraha*, etc. All these are more in keeping with Jain teaching than the Hindu religion. But these means are of no use in politics, which is required to change its attitude from time to time. Exalted religious principles or abstracted doctrines about truth are not of much value in the present political game' (cited in M.R. Jayakar, *The Story of My Life*, vol. 1, Bombay: Asia Publishing House, 1958, p. 387).
18. V.S. Anand, Savarkar, *A Study in the Evolution of Indian Nationalism*, London: Woolf, 1967, p. 19.
19. Chitragupta, *Life of Barrister Savarkar*, Bombay: Acharya Balarao Savarkar, 1987 (1st edn. 1926), p. 11.
20. Home Department (Political), Proceedings for the year 1911, p. 8713, April 1910, Pro. No. 47, India Office Library and Record (London).
21. I. Yajnik, *Shyamaji Krishnavarma*, Bombay: Lakshmi Publications, 1950. Savarkar was quick to establish his leadership over India House, an institution which had been founded by S.K. Varma, a follower of Tilak and one of the first Arya Samajists of Bombay, with a view to receive students and train them in 'extremist' nationalism.

22. H. Srivastava, *Five Stormy Years: Savarkar in London*, New Delhi: Allied Publishers, 1983, p. 3.
23. An Indian Nationalist, (V.D. Savarkar), *The Indian War of Independence of 1857* (no publisher, no place), 1909, pp. 56–8.
24. In his biography of Savarkar, Keer writes, 'Savarkar's *Mazzini* was the first book to enjoy an uncommon popularity in Maharashtra. It was so dearly loved that leading papers and leading men in Maharashtra extolled it to the skies and it was taken out in procession by young and old devotees' (D. Keer, *Veer Savarkar*, Bombay: Popular Prakashan, 1988 [1950], p. 34).
25. Cited in H. Srivastava, op. cit., p. 226.
26. During this period, the *Kesari* was the largest circulated weekly in the Bombay Presidency: 13,000 copies in 1901, 23,000 in 1927. (Prem Narain, *Press and Politics in India*, 1885–1905, Delhi: Munshilal Manoharlal, 1968, p. 305, and 'Annual Report on Indian and Anglo-vernacular newspapers published in the Bombay Presidency for 1927', Confidential Proceedings in the Home Department for the year 1928, Government of Bombay P/Conf./74 IOLR.)
27. *The Maratha*, 10 September 1922, p. 430.
28. Ibid., 7 September 1924, p. 437.
29. D.E.U. Baker, *Changing Political Leadership in an Indian Province—The Central Provinces and Berar, 1919–39*, Delhi: Oxford University Press, 1979, p. 16.
30. *Tribune*, 9 November 1927 in Jayakar Papers, National Archives of India, File no. 741.
31. *Dharmaveer Dr. B.S. Moonje Commemoration Volume*, Nagpur: Birth Centenary Celebration Committee, 1972, p. 5.
32. Letter dated 23 April 1932 to Maharajah Scindia, Moonje Papers, NMML (Microfilm Section), reel no. 7.
33. Moonje's letter to Raja Ichalkarang, dated 18 May 1936, ibid., reel no. 11.
34. His father, in fact, would often tell him 'I should never forget that my bones belong to the . . . Bhonsle. I feel I must honour the tradition of military service which I had inherited from my grand-father' (Moonje's letter dated 6 January 1935, Moonje Papers, NMML, Microfilm Section, reel no. 10).
35. Extract from Moonje's letter to Maharajah Scindia, dated 4 July 1938, cited in V. Hardas, 'A Brief life sketch', in *Dharmaveer Dr. B.S. Moonje Commemoration Volume*, op. cit., p. 7.
36. *The Maratha*, 18 June 1922.
37. Moonje Papers, NMML (Mss. Section), Letter of 10 September 1945.
38. The militarization of the Hindus had been a long-standing obsession with Moonje. As early as 1910, he wrote to exhort Madan Mohan Malaviya to add a Department of 'Military Science' to the proposed

Banaras Hindu University. When Malaviya replied, 'Knowledge itself is power', Moonje responded, 'Then "mananusmara yudhyacha" of the *Gita* would be futile!' (Cited in M.B. Niyogy, 'Dharmaveer Dr. Balakrishna Shivram Moonje', in *Dharmaveer Dr. B.S. Moonje Commemoration Volume*, op. cit., pp. 59–60.)

39. M.N. Ghatate, 'Dr. B.S. Moonje—Tour of European Countries', in ibid., pp. 68–9.
40. V.G. Deshpande, in ibid., p. 25.
41. Cited in G.V. Subbarao, 'A Sterling Patriot', ibid., p. 53.
42. B.S. Moonje, 'Speech on guerrilla warfare', *Dharmaveer Dr. B.S. Moonje*, op. cit., p. 127.
43. Ibid., p. 129.
44. Such an instrumentalization process exemplifies once more what I have analysed as a strategy of stigmatization and emulation of 'threatening others' (see C. Jaffrelot, *The Hindu nationalist movement*, Delhi: Penguin, 1999, Chap. 1).
45. Ibid., reel no. 11, Moonje's letter to N.C. Kelkar, dated 10 April 1936.
46. *Hindu Outlook*, 30 March 1938, p. 1.
47. Moonje Papers, NMML (Microfilm Section), reel no. 10, Moonje's letter to Appasahib Kelkar, dated 25 February 1936.
48 Ibid., reel no. 11, Moonje's letter dated 16 June 1936.
49. It was not unusual to transit thus from terrorist action to the Hindu Mahasabha. That was the course followed by Bhai Parmanand in Punjab (see Bhai Parmanand, *The Story of My Life*, Delhi: S. Chand, 1982) and by many who opposed Gandhi in Bengal. Foremost among the Hindu Mahasabhaites of Bengal was B.C. Chatterjee who explained in 1940 that the difference between the Congress and the Hindu Mahasabha was that the latter believed in violence and spurned the Communal Award (Andersen W., 'The Rashtriya Swayamsevak Sangh—III. Participation in Politics', *Economic and Political Weekly*, p. 679). The trajectory of Ashutosh Lahiry is even more revealing. He was the scion of a *bhadralok* family of the 'rural aristocracy' (Ashutosh Lahiry Papers, NMML (Mss. Section), 'A Short Life Sketch', p. 1397), and his father owned an entire village in Patna district. Lahiry interrupted his Post Graduate studies in 1912 to follow, as a number of other *bhadralok* students in Calcutta did at that time, Jatindra Nath Mookerjee, one of the leaders of the revolutionary movement. Sent to the Andaman Islands for the looting of a village, allegedly in order to finance the purchase of explosives (Home Department (Political) Proceedings for the year 1920, Pro. No. 314, IOLR), he emerged from there in 1921 and joined the non-cooperation movement soon after. This cost him another year in prison, during which he realized that he had misinterpreted the Gandhian movement in which so many Bengali revolutionaries had wrongly believed that they had found a framework for their

violent militancy. On being released in 1924, he applied himself to the task of developing the Hindu Mahasabha in Bengal, and was in fact its principal architect from 1930 onwards (Moonje Papers, NMML [Microfilm Section], reel no. 9, Letter from Moonje to A. Lahiry, dated 27 September 1930). The fact of being alongside Savarkar in the Andaman Islands penal colony had probably reinforced his Hindu nationalist convictions.

50. The *Maratha*, 31 August 1924, p. 428.
51. Resolution of the Hindu Mahasabha Working Committee, 21–2 September 1940, L/P&J/8/683, vol. 2, p. 344. The Hindu Mahasabha wished to seize the War as an opportunity to offer its services to the Government, because at that very moment, the Muslim League sought to stake its claim to the creation of Pakistan. Savarkar clearly presented matters in this perspective to the Viceroy, Lord Linlithgow, in September 1940: 'no help the Moslems have given or can ever give to the Government can ever outweigh the help which the Government has already received and is sure to receive in future from Hindudom as a whole in India' (Savarkar Papers, reel no. 6, file no. 13; letter from Savarkar to the Viceroy, dated 12 September 1940).
52. Savarkar Papers, reel no. 6. Savarkar's letter, dated 28 September 1940 to Moonje.
53. Ibid., Moonje's letter to the Viceroy, dated 1 July 1940.
54. Ibid., anonymous letter in July 1940.
55. Ibid., Savarkar's letter to the Viceroy, dated 15 July 1940.
56. Ganpat Rai's letter to Moonje, dated 3 April 1939, Savarkar Papers, reel no. 4, file no. 8.
57. See C. Jaffrelot, *The Hindu Nationalist Movement*, op. cit., Chap. 1.
58. M.G. Chitnavis Papers, NMML, report dated 7 February 1940.
59. *Indian Annual Register*, Calcutta, 1939, vol. 2, p. 340.
60. A British report of 1940 pointed out that, 'Since the beginning of the . . . year, there has been an unparalleled intensification of the volunteer movement throughout the country. Primarily the panic caused by the unfavourable developments in the war situation in Europe [the French debacle] has been responsible for the feverish anxiety on the part of the great communities and political parties to establish strong and disciplined volunteer forces for use in an emergency. Increasing communal mistrust combined with a general apprehension on internal disorder or external aggression, has given a strong impetus to volunteer activity in several provinces' (note on the volunteer movement in India, 23 August 1940, L/P&J/ Coll. 17—C 81, IOLR).
61. 'Hindu Militia (Ram Sena)', M.G. Chitnavis Papers, file no. 91, NMML.
62. V.G. Deshpande, 'Brief life sketch of late Mr. J.P. Verma', M.G. Chitnavis papers, file no. 91.

63. Hindu Mahasabha Papers, p. 51, 'The Provincial Hindu Sabha—January 1945', p. 45, NMML.
64. *Report of the Commission of Inquiry into Conspiracy to murder Mahatma Gandhi*, Part II, Delhi: Government of India, 1970, pp. 68–9.
65. Ibid., p. 69.
66. Ibid., p. 71.
67. N. Godse, *May it please Your Honour*, Delhi: Surya Prakashan, 1989, p. 42.
68. Gopal Godse, Nathuram's younger brother, described his caste as a 'school of thought' of which the Hindu Mahasabha was the spokesman (interview with G. Godse at New Delhi, on 10 November 1990), but this political culture was a *construction* which implied a profound interpretation of the Chitpavan ethos. Incidentally, many Chitpavans, including N.V. Gadgil were on the Congress side and admired Gandhi in the 1940s.
69. *The World Quarterly*, vol. 1, no. 1, Spring, 1950, special issue 'Gandhi murder trial', p. 46.
70. N. Godse, *May it please your Honour*, op. cit., p. 46.
71. *The World Quarterly*, op. cit., p. 61.
72. Ibid.
73. Cited in G. Godse, *Gandhiji's Murder and After*, Delhi: Surya Prakashan, 1989, p. 65.
74. Ibid., p. 362. Gopal Godse specified that Chapters 2, 11 and 18 were the ones he preferred (ibid., p. 135).
75. Cited in ibid., p. 123.
76. Cited in ibid., pp. 352–3.
77. Manohar Malgaonkar, *The Men Who Killed Gandhi*, Delhi: Orient Paperbacks, 1981, pp. 187–8.
78. Cited in ibid., p. 123.
79. Devadas Gandhi, 'My Brother', 1948, reprinted in *Hindustan Times*, 19 July 1998.
80. These organizations often practised martial exercises with a religious overtone which found particular expression in their initiation ceremony: the members of the Anushilan Samiti took an oath of allegiance to the organization before the image of Kali, with the *Bhagavad Gita* in one hand and a revolver in the other (U. Mukherjee, *Two great revolutionaries: R.B. Bose* and *J.N. Mukherjee*, Calcutta: Firma K.L. Mukhopadhyay, 1966, p. 17), the presence of the goddess serving as a reminder that the movement drew its ethic of violence partly from the ritual of the *Shakta* sect, something *Ananda Math*, Bankim Chandra Chatterjee's famous novel, abundantly testifies.
81. For Eric Hobsbawm, the invention of tradition entails establishing an artificial continuity between two historical periods with a view

to legitimize an innovation. The 'novelty' is then made out to be a link with forgotten forms (E. Hobsbawm, 'Introduction: Inventing Traditions', in E. Hobsbawm and T. Ranger (eds.), *The Invention of Tradition*, Cambridge: Cambridge University Press, 1983). In the case under review, it was not only a matter of legitimizing novel elements but also those that were imported. This is an aspect of the invention of tradition that Eric Hobsbawm does not directly take into account, perhaps because transfers from one culture to another were less important in his area of study, Europe, than in a nation on the 'periphery', such as India. Terence Ranger, the other editor of *The Invention of Tradition*, who is concerned mainly with how colonizers and missionaries reified African identities and imposed new traditions, acknowledges that such an approach leads to neglect in the study of how these inventions were re-appropriated by the 'natives' and integrated in their imagination. With a view to cover this lacuna, he seeks to substitute the word 'imagination' for 'invention'. Ranger thus emphasizes that, 'traditions imagined by whites were reimagined by blacks; traditions imagined by certain black interest groupes were reimagined by others' (T. Ranger, 'The invention of tradition revisited; the case of colonial Africa', in T. Ranger and O. Vanghan (eds.), *Legitimacy and the State in Twentieth Century Africa*, Houndmills: Macmillan, 1993, p. 81). Such a formulation highlights a notion that is not clear in the previous expression, i.e. the tactical motivation underlying the re-appropriation by the natives of an existing invention of Western origin. Ranger's 'imagination of tradition' calls to mind Rajni Kothari's approach wherein he employs another word, the 'construction' of tradition.

82. R. Kothari, 'Tradition and Modernity Revisited', *Government and Opposition*, Summer 1968, pp. 273-93.
83. C. Jaffrelot, *The Hindu Nationalist Movement*, op. cit., Chap. 1.
84. Lajpat Rai, *The Message of the Bhagavad Gita*, Published by the author, Allahabad, 1908, pp. 23–4. In an article which appeared in 1916 in the famous *Modern Review*, Lajpat Rai criticized Gandhi's *ahimsa* by arguing that this notion 'overdone and misapplied is a gangrene that poisons the system'. In 1922 he declared in the same vein, 'I do not believe in non-violence as an absolute article of faith to be respected and practised under all circumstances and in all conditions.' (Cited in V.P. Bhatia, 'The violence-non-violence' debate. Where Subhas agreed with Lajpat Rai, *Organiser*, 16 February 1997, p. 13.)

Index